Page

INTRODUCTION

THE BPP STUDY TEXT

Aims of this Study Text

To provide you with the knowledge and understanding, skills and application techniques that you need if you are to be successful in your exams

This Study Text has been written around the **Audit and Internal Review** syllabus.

- It is **comprehensive**. It covers the syllabus content. No more, no less.
- It is written at the **right level**. Each chapter is written with the ACCA's **study guide** in mind.
- It is targeted to the **exam**. We have taken account of the **pilot paper and all sittings so far**, questions put to the examiners at ACCA conferences and the assessment methodology.

To allow you to study in the way that best suits your learning style and the time you have available, by following your personal Study Plan (see page (vii))

You may be studying at home on your own until the date of the exam, or you may be attending a full-time course. You may like to (and have time to) read every word, or you may prefer to (or only have time to) skim-read and devote the remainder of your time to question practice. Wherever you fall in the spectrum, you will find the BPP Study Text meets your needs in designing and following your personal Study Plan.

To tie in with the other components of the BPP Effective Study Package to ensure you have the best possible chance of passing the exam (see page (v))

Recommended period of use	Elements of the BPP Effective Study Package
From the outset and throughout	**Learning to Learn Accountancy** Read this invaluable book as you begin your studies and refer to it as you work through the various elements of the BPP Effective Study Package. It will help you to acquire knowledge, practise and revise, efficiently and effectively.
Three to twelve months before the exam	**Study Text and i-Learn** Use the Study Text to acquire knowledge, understanding, skills and the ability to apply techniques. Use BPP's **i-Learn** product to reinforce your learning.
Throughout	**Big Picture Posters** Display these where you're studying and give yourself a feel for the overall shape of the paper and the connections between syllabus areas. Examiners have stressed that you will need to be able to link up different areas when you take the exam. The visual stimulation the posters provide will help you remember the key areas of the syllabus.
Throughout	**Virtual Campus** Study, practise, revise and take advantage of other useful resources with BPP's fully interactive e-learning site with comprehensive tutor support.
Throughout	**i-Pass** **i-Pass**, our computer-based testing package, provides objective test questions in a variety of formats and is ideal for self-assessment.
One to six months before the exam	**Practice & Revision Kit** Try the numerous examination-format questions, for which there are realistic suggested solutions prepared by BPP's own authors. Then attempt the two mock exams.
From three months before the exam until the last minute	**Passcards** Work through these short, memorable notes which are focused on what is most likely to come up in the exam you will be sitting.
One to six months before the exam	**Success Tapes and CDs** The tapes and CDs cover the vital elements of your syllabus in less than 90 minutes per subject. They also contains exam hints to help you fine tune your strategy.

HELP YOURSELF STUDY FOR YOUR ACCA EXAMS

Exams for professional bodies such as ACCA are very different from those you have taken at college or university. You will be under **greater time pressure before** the exam – as you may be combining your study with work as well as in the exam room. There are many different ways of learning and so the BPP Study Text offers you a number of different tools to help you through. Here are some hints and tips: they are not plucked out of the air, but **based on research and experience.** (You don't need to know that long-term memory is in the same part of the brain as emotions and feelings – but it's a fact anyway.)

The right approach

1 **The right attitude**

Believe in yourself	Yes, there is a lot to learn. Yes, it is a challenge. But thousands have succeeded before and you can too.
Remember why you're doing it	Studying might seem a grind at times, but you are doing it for a reason: to advance your career.

2 **The right focus**

Read through the Syllabus and Study guide	These tell you what you are expected to know and are supplemented by exam focus points in the text.
Study the Exam Paper section	Past papers are likely to be a reasonable guide of what you should expect in the exam.

3 **The right method**

The whole picture	You need to grasp the detail – but keeping in mind how everything fits into the big picture will help you understand better. • The **Introduction** of each chapter puts the material in context. • The **Syllabus content, Study guide** and **Exam focus points** show you what you need to **grasp.** • BPP's Big Picture Posters will help you see the links here.
In your own words	To absorb the information (and to practise your written communication skills), it helps **put it into your own words.** • **Take notes.** • Answer the **questions** in each chapter. As well as helping you absorb the information you will practise your written communication skills, which become increasingly important as you progress through your ACCA exams. • Draw **mind maps**. We have an example for the whole syllabus. • Try 'teaching' to a colleague or friend.

Give yourself cues to jog your memory	The BPP Study Text uses **bold text** to **highlight key points** and **icons** to identify key features, such as **Exam focus points** and **Key terms.** • Try **colour coding** with a highlighter pen. • Write **key points** on cards.

4 **The right review**

Review, review, review	It is a **fact** that regularly reviewing a topic in summary form can **fix it in your memory**. Because **review** is so important, the BPP Study Text helps you to do so in many ways. • **Chapter roundups** summarise the key points in each chapter. Use them to recap each study session. • The **Quick quiz** is another review technique to ensure that you have grasped the essentials. • Use the **Key term** index as a quiz. • Go through the **Examples** in each chapter a second or third time.

Developing your personal Study Plan

One thing that the BPP Learning to Learn Accountancy book emphasises (see page (iv)) is the need to prepare (and use) a study plan. Planning and sticking to the plan are key elements of learning success.

There are four steps you should work through.

Step 1. How do you learn?

First you need to be aware of your style of learning. The BPP Learning to Learn Accountancy book commits a chapter to this **self-discovery**. What types of intelligence do you display when learning? You might be advised to brush up on certain study skills before launching into this Study Text.

> BPP's **Learning to Learn Accountancy** book helps you to identify what intelligences you show more strongly and then details how you can tailor your study process to your preferences. It also includes handy hints on how to develop intelligences you exhibit less strongly, but which might be needed as you study accountancy.

Are you a **theorist** or are you more **practical**? If you would rather get to grips with a theory before trying to apply it in practice, you should follow the study sequence on page (x). If the reverse is true (you need to know why you are learning theory before you do so), you might be advised to flick through Study Text chapters and look at questions, case studies and examples (Steps 7, 8 and 9 in the **suggested study sequence**) before reading through the detailed theory.

Step 2. How much time do you have?

Work out the time you have available per week, given the following.

- The standard you have set yourself
- The time you need to set aside later for work on the Practice & Revision Kit and Passcards
- The other exam(s) you are sitting
- Very importantly, practical matters such as work, travel, exercise, sleep and social life

		Hours
Note your time available in box A.	A	

Step 3. Allocate your time

• Take the time you have available per week for this Study Text shown in box A, multiply it by the number of weeks available and insert the result in box B.	B	
• Divide the figure in Box B by the number of chapters in this text and insert the result in box C.	C	

Remember that this is only a rough guide. Some of the chapters in this book are longer and more complicated than others, and you will find some subjects easier to understand than others.

Step 4. Implement

Set about studying each chapter in the time shown in box C, following the key study steps in the order suggested by your particular learning style.

This is your personal **Study Plan**. You should try and combine it with the study sequence outlined below. You may want to modify the sequence a little (as has been suggested above) to adapt it to your **personal style**.

BPP's *Learning to Learn Accountancy* gives further guidance in developing a study plan and deciding when and where to study.

ACCA
STUDY TEXT

Paper 2.6

Audit and Internal Review

IN THIS JUNE 2004 EDITION

- Targeted to the syllabus and study guide
- Quizzes and questions to check your understanding
- Clear layout and style designed to save you time
- Plenty of exam-style questions with detailed guidance from BPP
- Chapter roundups and summaries to help revision

FOR EXAMS IN DECEMBER 2004

BPP Professional Education
June 2004

First edition 2001
Fourth edition June 2004

ISBN 0 7517 1667 7 (Previous edition 0 7517 1156 X)

British Library Cataloguing-in-Publication Data
A catalogue record for this book is available from the British Library

Published by

BPP Professional Education
Aldine House, Aldine Place
London W12 8AW

www.bpp.com

Printed in Great Britain by W M Print
45-47 Frederick Street
Walsall, West Midlands
WS2 9NE

We are grateful to the Association of Chartered Certified Accountants for permission to reproduce past examination questions and the pilot paper. The answers have been prepared by BPP Professional Education.

Suggested study sequence

Tackle the chapters in the order you find them in the Study Text. Taking into account your individual learning style, you could follow this sequence.

Key study steps	Activity
Step 1 **Topic list**	Each numbered topic is a numbered section in the chapter.
Step 2 **Introduction**	This gives you the **big picture** in terms of the **context** of the chapter. The content is referenced to the **Study Guide**, and **Exam Guidance** shows how the topic is likely to be examined. In other words, it sets your **objectives for study.**
Step 3 **Knowledge brought forward boxes**	In these we highlight information and techniques that it is assumed you have 'brought forward' with you from your earlier studies. If there are topics which have changed recently due to legislation for example, these topics are explained in more detail.
Step 4 **Explanations**	Proceed methodically through the chapter, reading each section thoroughly and making sure you understand.
Step 5 **Key terms and Exam focus points**	• **Key terms** can often earn you *easy marks* if you state them clearly and correctly in an appropriate exam answer (and they are indexed at the back of the text). • **Exam focus points** give you a good idea of how we think the examiner intends to examine certain topics.
Step 6 **Note taking**	Take brief notes if you wish, avoiding the temptation to copy out too much.
Step 7 **Examples**	Follow each through to its solution very carefully.
Step 8 **Case examples**	Study each one, and try to add flesh to them from your own experience – they are designed to show how the topics you are studying come alive (and often come unstuck) in the real world.
Step 9 **Questions**	Make a very good attempt at each one.
Step 10 **Answers**	Check yours against ours, and make sure you understand any discrepancies.
Step 11 **Chapter roundup**	Work through it very carefully, to make sure you have grasped the major points it is highlighting.
Step 12 **Quick quiz**	When you are happy that you have covered the chapter, use the **Quick quiz** to check how much you have remembered of the topics covered.
Step 13 **Question(s) in the Question bank**	Either at this point, or later when you are thinking about revising, make a full attempt at the **Question(s)** suggested at the very end of the chapter. You can find these at the end of the Study Text, along with the **Answers** so you can see how you did. We highlight those that are introductory, and those which are of the standard you would expect to find in an exam.

Short of time: *Skim study technique*?

You may find you simply do not have the time available to follow all the key study steps for each chapter, however you adapt them for your particular learning style. If this is the case, follow the **skim study** technique below (the icons in the Study Text will help you to do this).

- Study the chapters in the order you find them in the Study Text.
- For each chapter:
  - Follow the key study steps 1-3, and then skim-read through step 4. Jump to step 11, and then go back to step 5.
  - Follow through steps 7 and 8, and prepare outline answers to questions (steps 9/10).
  - Try the Quick Quiz (step 12), following up any items you can't answer, then do a plan for the Question (step 13), comparing it against our answers.
  - You should probably still follow step 6 (note-taking), although you may decide simply to rely on the BPP Passcards for this.

Moving on...

However you study, when you are ready to embark on the practice and revision phase of the BPP Effective Study Package, you should still refer back to this Study Text, both as a source of **reference** (you should find the list of key terms and the index particularly helpful for this) and as a **refresher** (the Chapter Roundups and Quick Quizzes help you here).

And remember to keep careful hold of this Study Text – you will find it invaluable in your work.

More advice on Study Skills can be found in the BPP **Learning to Learn Accountancy** book

SYLLABUS

Aim

To develop knowledge and understanding of the audit process and its application in the context of the external regulatory framework and for business control and development.

Objectives

On completion of this paper, candidates should be able to:

- understand the nature, purpose and scope of auditing and internal review, including the role of external audit and its regulatory framework, and the role of internal audit in providing assurance on risk management and on the control framework of an organisation
- identify risks, describe the procedures undertaken in the planning process, plan work to meet the objectives of the audit or review assignment and draft the content of plans
- describe and evaluate accounting and internal control systems and identify and communicate control risks, potential consequences and recommendations
- explain and evaluate sources of evidence, describe the nature, timing and extent of tests on transactions and account balances (including sampling and analytical procedures) and design programs for audit and review assignments
- evaluate findings, investigate inconsistencies, modify the work program as necessary, review subsequent events, and justify and prepare appropriate reports for users within and external to the organisation, including recommendations to enhance business performance
- discuss and apply the requirements of relevant Statements of Auditing Standards
- demonstrate the skills expected in Part 2.

Position of the paper in the overall syllabus

Paper 2.6 builds on the knowledge and understanding by Paper 1.1 Preparing Financial Statements and to a lesser extent Paper 1.2 Financial Information for Management.

Candidates will be expected to be familiar with Paper 2.5 Financial Reporting, including the requirements of the accounting standards examined within it. They will also be expected to be familiar with Paper 2.1 Information Systems.

Paper 2.6 provides the knowledge and understanding of the audit process which is then developed in Paper 3.1 Audit and Assurance Services.

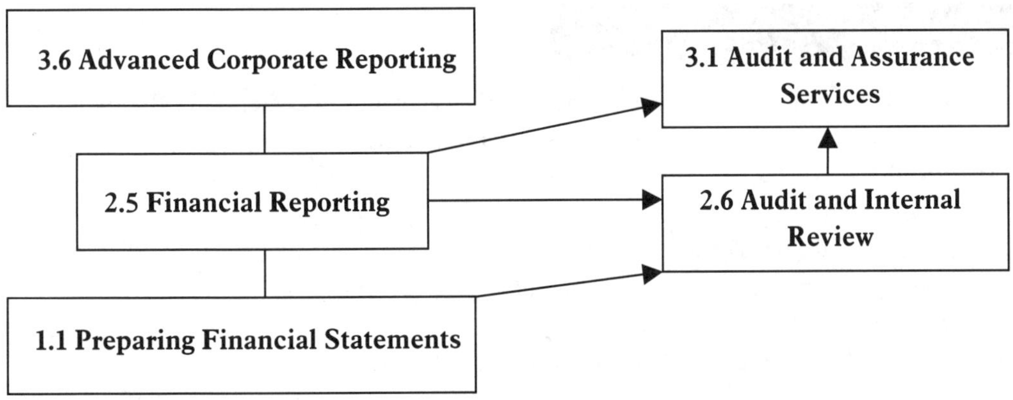

SYLLABUS

1 Audit framework

(a) The development and changing nature of audit, the social role of audit.

(b) Statutory audits, accountability, stewardship and agency.

(c) Professional ethics and codes of conduct, their application to external audit and internal audit, responsibility for fraud and error.

2 Internal audit and internal review

(a) The role of internal audit and internal review and their relationship with:

(i) Corporate governance
(ii) Risk management
(iii) Organisational control
(iv) Corporate objectives

(b) Scope and functions of internal audit, the nature and extent of internal audit assignments.

(c) Outsourced internal audit functions.

(d) The nature and extent of internal review assignments including operational, systems, value for money and financial reviews.

3 Regulation

(a) Statements of Auditing Standards:

(i) Their development and role
(ii) Their relationship with International Standards of Auditing.

(b) Auditors:

(i) Regulation and supervision
(ii) Their relationship with Government
(iii) The role of the Auditing Practices Board and other UK standard-setting bodies.

4 Planning and risk

(a) Objectives of audit and review assignments, the relevance of stakeholder dialogue.
(b) Communicating the objectives of audit and review assignments.
(c) Analytical procedures.
(d) Risk assessment.
(e) Materiality, tolerable error, and sample sizes.
(f) Design and documentation of the plan and work program.
(g) Co-ordination of the work of others.
(h) Information Technology in planning and risk assessment.

5 Internal control

(a) Objectives of internal control systems.

(b) Inherent weaknesses in internal control systems.

(c) The use of internal control systems by auditors.

(d) Transaction cycles (revenue, purchases, payroll, inventory, capital expenditure).

(e) The evaluation of internal control systems by auditors including internal control checklists and tests of control.

(f) Communication with management.

6 Other audit and internal review of evidence

(a) Financial statement assertions: assets, liabilities, income and expenditure, including accounting estimates.

(b) Assertions reported on and opinions provided in review assignments.

(c) Analytical procedures as substantive evidence.

(d) Balance and transaction testing.

(e) Computer-assisted audit techniques, their uses and limitations.

(f) Management representations.

(g) Audit sampling and other selective testing procedures.

(h) Subsequent events review.

(i) Going concern reviews.

(j) The overall review of evidence obtained.

(k) Modifications to the plan and work program in the light of findings.

7 Reporting

(a) Format and content of unqualified and qualified external audit reports on financial statements.

(b) Format and content of review reports and other reports on assignment objectives.

(c) Recommendations for the enhancement of business performance

Excluded topics

Audit of groups is not examinable at this level. Candidates should be aware of the content, wording and meaning of audit reports and they may be asked to prepare the explanatory paragraphs for inclusion in a qualified audit report. However, candidates are not expected to draft full audit rcports.

Exposure drafts (EDs) are not examinable for Paper 2.6

KEY AREAS OF THE SYLLABUS

The key topic areas are as follows:

- Professional ethics as they apply to accountants working in public practice and in business
- Risk assessment and the response to assessed risks for external auditors
- The role of internal audit in risk management and corporate governance
- Internal controls
- Substantive audit evidence

Paper 2.6

Audit and Internal Review
(United Kingdom)

Study Guide

1 THE NATURE, PURPOSE AND SCOPE OF AUDIT AND REVIEW

Explain the:

- Nature and development of audit and review
- Concepts of accountability, stewardship and agency
- Concepts of materiality, true and fair presentation and reasonable assurance
- Reporting as a means of communication to different stakeholders
- Need for auditors to communicate with those charged with governance
- High level of assurance provided by audit assignments and risk-based approaches; the moderate level of assurance provided by review assignments and procedural approaches; assignments in which no assurance is provided

NB: Students are expected to be aware of the nature and purpose of non-financial audit and review services as described in Session 6. Internal review questions will focus on financial and systems reviews in the context of companies and small not-for-profit organisations.

2 STATUTORY AUDITS

Describe the:

- UK regulatory framework in which statutory audits take place
- Development and status of the Auditing Practices Board Statements of Auditing Standards and their relationship with International Standards on Auditing
- Reasons for, and mechanisms for, the regulation of auditors by Government and other regulatory agencies including other UK standard-setters
- Types of opinion provided in statutory audit assignments
- Limitations of statutory audits

3 INTERNAL AUDIT AND INTERNAL REVIEW I

Explain the:

- Meaning of corporate governance and describe corporate governance objectives and the major elements of good corporate governance practice
- Development and role of internal audit in achieving corporate objectives and as part of good corporate governance practice
- Relative merits of out-sourcing internal audit and internal review services to external auditors and others, and the associated problems
- Difference between the role of external audit and internal audit

(Note: candidates are expected to be aware of the major areas covered by the codes of corporate governance appliance in the UK (such as the Combined Code) and, in particular, the recommendations made in relation to internal audit.)

4 INTERNAL AUDIT AND REVIEW II

Explain and illustrate the:

- Function of internal audit in the context of corporate risk management and organisational control
- Elements and use of the commonly recognised control frameworks and control components such as those issued in common with the Combined Code

5 INTERNAL AUDIT AND REVIEW III

Describe the:

- Elements of best

practice in the structure and operations of an internal audit function
- Scope of internal audit work and the limitations of the internal audit function
- Types of report provided in internal audit and internal review assignment

6 INTERNAL AUDIT AND INTERNAL REVIEW II

Describe and illustrate the:

- Nature and purpose of internal review assignments including:
  - value for money
  - best value
  - IT
  - financial
- Nature and purpose of operational internal audit and review assignments including:
  - procurement
  - marketing
  - treasury
  - HR

7 PROFESSIONAL ETHICS AND PROFESSIONAL CODES OF CONDUCT I

- Describe the sources of, and enforcement mechanisms associated with, professional ethics and professional codes of conduct
- Define the fundamental concepts of professional ethics
- Define the detailed requirements of, and illustrate and analyse the application of, professional ethics in the context of independence objectivity and integrity
- Distinguish between the elements of professional ethics applicable to internal auditors and those applicable to external authors
- Describe the responsibilities of internal and external auditors for the prevention and detection of fraud and error

8 PROFESSIONAL ETHICS AND PROFESSIONAL CODES OF CONDUCT II

- Describe the requirements of professional ethics and other requirements in relation to the acceptance of audit and review assignments, including situations in which there is an imposed limitation in audit scope
- Define the detailed requirements of, and illustrate and analyse the application of, professional ethics in the context of confidentiality and conflicts of interest
- Describe the importance of engagement letters and describe their contents

9 PRELIMINARY PLANNING PROCEDURES

- Distinguish between risk-based, procedural and other approaches to audit and review work
- Describe the sources and nature of information gathered in planning audit and review assignments
- Describe the knowledge of the business required by auditors
- Describe the purpose of analytical procedures in planning and illustrate the application of such procedures
- Describe the components of risk and use of information technology in risk analysis
- Illustrate and explain the importance of the application of risk analysis
- Define and illustrate the concepts of materiality and tolerable error
- Evaluate misstatements

10 THE WORK PLAN, THE WORK PROGRAM AND DOCUMENTATION

- Describe and illustrate the contents of work plans, work programs and working papers
- Describe the nature of documentation required for different types of assignment
- Explain the importance of documentation
- Illustrate the use of information technology in the audit

11 THE WORK OF OTHERS

Describe the:

- Extent to which external auditors are able to rely on the work of:
  - internal audit
  - experts
  - service organisations

  and recognise where reliance is needed
- Extent to which internal auditors are able to rely on the work of:
  - experts
  - service organisations
- Conditions that must be met before reliance can be placed on the work of others and the planning considerations in co-ordinating the work of others
- Division of responsibilities between auditors and others
- Extent to which reference to the work of others can be made in the audit and review reports

12 INTERNAL CONTROL I

- Describe the objectives of internal control systems and the responsibility for internal control systems in the context of organisational objectives
- Describe the importance of internal control to auditors
- Describe and illustrate the limitations of internal control systems in the context of fraud and error
- Explain the need to modify the audit plan in the light of the results of tests of control
- Distinguish between tests of control and substantive tests

13 INTERNAL CONTROL II – SALES, PURCHASES AND STOCK

- Describe, illustrate and analyse how internal control systems over sales, purchases and stock cycles operate in both large and small entities
- Describe and illustrate the use by auditors of internal control checklists for sales, purchases and stock cycles
- Describe and tabulate tests of control of sales, purchases and stock for inclusion in a work program
- Explain and illustrate how structural and operational weaknesses in sales, purchases and stock systems should be reported to management and how recommendations should be made

14 INTERNAL CONTROL III – REVENUE EXPENDITURE AND CAPITAL EXPENDITURE

- Describe, illustrate and analyse how internal control systems over revenue and capital expenditure transaction cycles operate in both large and small entities
- Describe and illustrate the use by auditors of internal control checklists for revenue and capital expenditure transaction cycles
- Describe and tabulate tests of control of revenue and capital expenditure for inclusion in a work program
- Explain and illustrate how structural and operational weaknesses in revenue and capital expenditure systems should be reported to management and how recommendations should be made

15 INTERNAL CONTROL IV – PAYROLL

- Describe, illustrate and analyse how internal control systems over the payroll transaction cycle operate in both large and small entities
- Describe and illustrate the use by auditors of internal control checklists for the payroll transaction cycle
- Describe and tabulate tests of control of payroll for inclusion in a work program
- Explain and illustrate how structural and operational weaknesses in payroll systems should be reported to management and how recommendations should be made

16 INTERNAL CONTROL V – BANK AND CASH

- Describe, illustrate and analyse how internal control systems over the bank and cash transaction cycle operate in both large and small entities
- Describe and illustrate the use by auditors of internal control checklists for the bank and cash transaction cycle
- Describe and tabulate tests of control of bank and cash for inclusion in a work program
- Explain and illustrate how structural and operational weaknesses in bank and cash systems should be reported to management and how recommendations should be made

17 OTHER AUDIT AND REVIEW EVIDENCE I

- Describe the sources and relative merits of the different types of evidence available
- Describe the financial statement assertions commonly reported on and the principles and objectives of balance and transaction testing
- Distinguish between the interim and the final audit
- Describe and illustrate how analytical procedures are used as substantive procedures
- Explain the problems associated with the audit and review of accounting estimates
- Describe the types of evidence available in smaller entities
- Evaluate the quality of evidence collected

18 OTHER AUDIT AND REVIEW EVIDENCE II – DEBTORS AND PREPAYMENTS

- Describe and tabulate for inclusion in a work program the substantive procedures, including debtors circularisations, used in obtaining evidence in relation to debtors and prepayments, and the related income statement entries
- Explain the purpose of substantive procedures in relation to financial statement assertions concerning debtors and prepayments

19 OTHER AUDIT AND REVIEW EVIDENCE III – STOCK

- Explain the importance of stock
- Describe stock counting procedures
- Explain cut off
- Describe and tabulate for inclusion in a work program the substantive procedures used in obtaining evidence in relation to stock, including the auditors' attendance at stocktaking
- Explain the purpose of substantive procedures including direct confirmation of stock held by third parties in relation to financial statement assertions concerning stock

20 OTHER AUDIT AND REVIEW EVIDENCE IV – CURRENT LIABILITIES AND ACCRUALS

- Describe and tabulate for inclusion in a work program the substantive procedures including supplies statement reconciliations and creditor circularisations used in obtaining evidence in relation to current liabilities and accruals, and the related income statement entries
- Explain the purpose of substantive procedures in relation to financial statement assertions concerning current liabilities and accruals

21 OTHER AUDIT AND REVIEW EVIDENCE V – BANK AND CASH

- Describe and tabulate for inclusion in a work program the substantive procedures including bank confirmation reports used in obtaining evidence in relation to bank and cash, and the related income statement entries
- Explain the purpose of

substantive procedures in relation to financial statement assertions concerning bank and cash

22 OTHER AUDIT AND REVIEW EVIDENCE VI – FIXED ASSETS AND LONG-TERM LIABILITIES

Syllabus reference 6a

- Describe and tabulate for inclusion in a work program the substantive procedures used in obtaining evidence in relation to fixed assets and long-term liabilities and the related income statement entries
- Explain the purpose of substantive procedures in relation to financial statement assertions concerning fixed assets and long-term liabilities

23 OTHER AUDIT AND REVIEW EVIDENCE VII

- Explain the need for sampling
- Distinguish between statistical and non-statistical sampling
- Describe and illustrate the application of the basic principles of statistical sampling and other selective testing procedures
- Describe and illustrate the use of computer assisted techniques in obtaining evidence

(Note: candidates will not be required to perform detailed sampling calculations)

24 GOING CONCERN REVIEWS

- Explain the importance of going concern reviews
- Describe the procedures to be applied in performing going concern reviews
- Describe the disclosure requirements relating to going concern issues
- Describe the reporting implications of the findings of going concern reviews

25 AUDIT FINALISATION AND THE FINAL REVIEW

Describe the:

- Quality of management representations as audit evidence
- Circumstances in which obtaining management representations is necessary and the matters on which representations are commonly obtained
- Purpose of the subsequent events review
- Procedures to be undertaken in performing a subsequent events review
- Importance of the overall review of evidence obtained
- Problems associated with the application of accounting treatments
- Significance of unadjusted differences

26 REPORTING I

Syllabus reference 7a

- Describe, illustrate and analyse the format and content of unqualified and qualified statutory audit reports

27 REPORTING II

Describe, illustrate and analyse the format and content of:

- Internal review reports and other reports dealing with recommendations for the enhancement of business performance

28 NOT-FOR-PROFIT ORGANISATIONS

- Apply audit and review techniques to small not-for-profit organisations
- Explain how the audit and review for small not-for-profit organisations differs from the audit and review of for-profit organisations

THE EXAM PAPER

The examination is a three hour paper constructed in two sections. The bulk of the questions will be discursive but some questions involving computational elements will be set from time to time.

Section A is compulsory. The questions will cover the key elements of the syllabus relevant to both internal and external audit assignments. Section B requires candidates to answer two out of three questions. The questions will cover all areas of the syllabus.

		Number of Marks
Section A:	3 compulsory scenario-based questions (no single question will exceed 25 marks)	60
Section B:	Choice of 2 from 3 questions (20 marks each)	40
		100

ADDITIONAL INFORMATION

This paper encompasses:

1 Internal review, which may be provided either by internal auditors or may be outsourced to external auditors.

2 External audit.

References to audit and auditors mean both internal and external audit and auditors, except where otherwise indicated.

Candidates need to be aware that questions involving knowledge of new examinable regulations will not be set until at least six months after the last day of the month in which the regulation was issued.

The Study Guide provides more detailed guidance on the syllabus. Examinable documents are listed in the 'Exam Notes' section of *Student Accountant*.

Analysis of past papers

The analysis below shows the topics which have been examined in all sittings of the current syllabus so far and in the Pilot Paper.

December 2003

Section A

1 Internal audit risk assessment, controls and control procedures
2 Payroll, controls and tests
3 Group concern

Section B

4 Overall review and subsequent events
5 Risks in NFP, tests on income and expenditure
6 Confidentiality

June 2003

Section A

1 Audit risk assessment
2 Stock count procedures
3 Conflict of interest, audit evidence (FRS 12), impact on audit report

Section B

4 Using the work of internal audit
5 Reporting to management (internal and external auditors)
6 Internal controls (fixed assets) and sampling

December 2002

Section A

1 Objectivity
2 Internal control systems
3 Audit of creditors and provisions

Section B

4 Audit evidence
5 Audit of stock
6 Internal audit, risk management

June 2002

Section A

1 Accepting internal audit engagement, business risk
2 Audit of cash and bank
3 Professional and reporting issues

Section B

4 Analytical procedures, materiality
5 Letters of representation
6 Independence, other services

December 2001

Section A

1 Role of internal/external auditors, outsourcing
2 Risk, audit work
3 Purchase controls, report to management

Section B

4 Debtors' audit, circularisation
5 Analysis of audit and review report
6 Auditing standards, audit regulations

Pilot Paper

Section A

1 Professional ethics
2 Audit risk and going concern
3 Role of internal audit

Section B

4 Fixed assets, depreciation
5 Internal controls, sales and debtors
6 Stock, management letter

CURRENT ISSUES

The framework of auditing in the UK is in a time of great change, hence this Study Text only attempts to cover documents examinable in December 2004.

Candidates at Paper 2.6 do not need to know the detail of exposure drafts as they will not be examined on them. However, it is important that candidates have an up to date awareness of current issues, so, although the following matters should not be examinable in detail in the December 2004 exam, they are summarised here to make you aware of them.

1 UK adoption of International Auditing Standards from 2005

2 Draft ethical standards issued by the APB

1 UK adoption of ISAs

The Auditing Practices Board (APB), whose work shall be looked at in detail in Chapter 2 of this Study Text, is the body that issues statements of auditing standards (SASs) in the UK for auditors to follow. It has announced that it shall be adopting International Standards of Auditing (ISAs), which are issued by the International Audit and Assurance Standards Board (the international equivalent of the APB), from the end of this year. The standards are being exposed in the UK prior to their adoption, to ensure that all UK matters are considered.

In recent years, new UK auditing standards have been formulated in conjunction with international auditing standards, so that the majority of existing ISAs are similar to existing SASs. There are several new standards which are a departure from existing UK standards, as they are more far-reaching and prescriptive than the existing UK standards.

2 Draft ethical standards issued by the APB

The UK government has determined that, in the future, ethical guidance for auditors in the UK will be set by an independent standard setter rather than the professional bodies to which auditors belong. The APB, the independent standard setter, has issued draft ethical guidance (outlined in the January 2004 edition of the Practice and Revision Kit) which should become authoritative in the UK from September 2004, at which time it will supersede the guidance of the professional bodies.

The ACCA's professional code will be examinable in December 2004, and hence has been included in this Study Text in Chapter 4. The spirit of the guidance from the APB is very similar to the ACCA's guidance, although it includes some more prescriptive requirements which you should be aware of going forward. Should you go on to attempt Paper 3.1 Audit and Assurance Services, the relevant ethical guidance will be included in that Study Text.

OXFORD BROOKES BSc (Hons) IN APPLIED ACCOUNTING

The standard required of candidates completing Part 2 is that required in the final year of a UK degree. Students completing Parts 1 and 2 will have satisfied the examination requirement for an honours degree in Applied Accounting, awarded by Oxford Brookes University.

To achieve the degree, you must also submit two pieces of work based on a **Research and Analysis Project.**

- A 5,000 word **Report** on your chosen topic, which demonstrates that you have acquired the necessary research, analytical and IT skills.
- A 1,500 word **Key Skills Statement**, indicating how you have developed your interpersonal and communication skills.

BPP was selected by the ACCA and Oxford Brookes University to produce the official text *Success in your Research and Analysis Project* to support students in this task. The book pays particular attention to key skills not covered in the professional examinations.

BPP also offers courses and mentoring services.

THE OXFORD BROOKES PROJECT TEXT CAN BE ORDERED USING THE FORM AT THE END OF THIS STUDY TEXT.

OXFORD INSTITUTE OF INTERNATIONAL FINANCE MBA

The Oxford Institute of International Finance (OXIIF), a joint venture between the ACCA and Oxford Brookes University, offers an MBA for finance professionals.

For this MBA, credits are awarded for your ACCA studies, and entry to the MBA course is available to those who have completed their ACCA professional stage studies. The MBA was launched in 2002 and has attracted participants from all over the world.

The qualification features an introductory module (*Foundations of Management*). Other modules include *Global Business Strategy*, *Managing Self Development,* and *Organisational Change & Transformation.*

Research Methods are also taught, as they underpin the **research dissertation**.

The MBA programme is delivered through the use of targeted paper study materials, developed by BPP, and taught over the Internet by OXIIF personnel using BPP's virtual campus software.

For further information, please see the Oxford Institute's website: www.oxfordinstitute.org.

CONTINUING PROFESSIONAL DEVELOPMENT

ACCA is introducing a new continuing professional development requirement for members from 1 January 2005. Members will be required to complete and record 40 units of CPD annually, of which 21 units must be verifiable learning or training activity.

BPP has an established professional development department which offers a range of relevant, professional courses to reflect the needs of professionals working in both industry and practice. To find out more, visit the website: www.bpp.com/pd or call the client care team on 0845 226 2422.

SYLLABUS MINDMAP

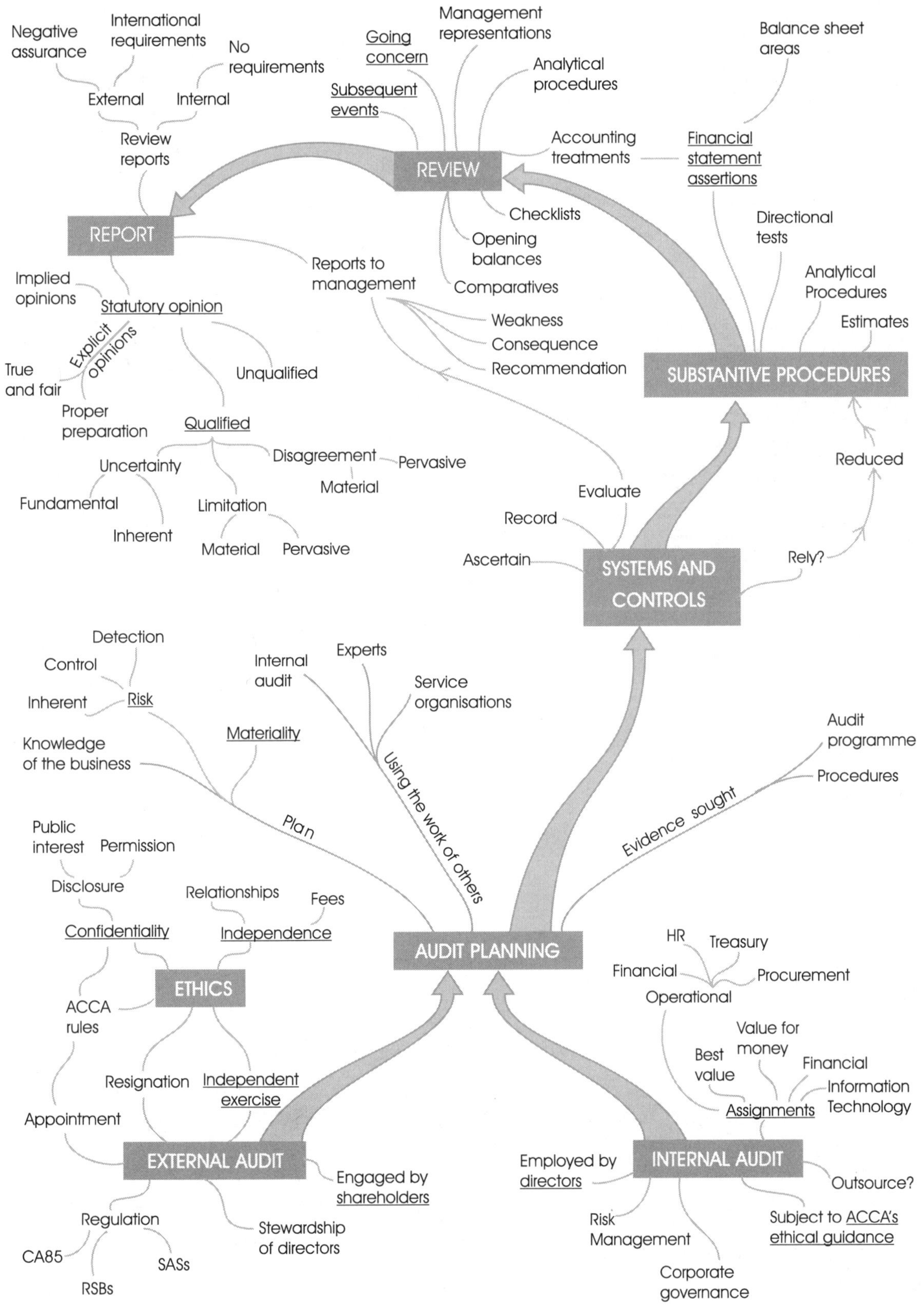

Part A
Framework

Chapter 1

THE NATURE AND PURPOSE OF ASSURANCE

Topic list		Syllabus reference	Study guide
1	The purpose of assurance	1	1,3
2	The nature of assurance services	1	1
3	Assurance and reports	1	1,2
4	The chronology of an audit	1	1

Introduction

First we need to consider **why there is a need for assurance in relation to financial and non-financial information**. You learnt about the nature of a company in Paper 2.2. The main reason assurance is required is the fact that the ownership and management of a company are not necessarily the same. We will introduce concepts of **agency, accountability** and **stewardship.**

Secondly, it is important to understand **what assurance services exist**. The key assurance services which your syllabus concentrates on are the audit (statutory and non-statutory), reviews, and internal reviews. Although it is strictly defined, many people do not understand what an audit is and what it is designed to achieve. This results in an **expectations gap**, which is discussed more in Chapter 19.

The effect of audits and reviews is that people interested in the accounts of an entity are given a level of **assurance** as to the quality of the contents of the accounts. The audit report focuses on the truth and fairness of the accounts. It gives reasonable assurance, rather than an absolute assurance. The degrees of assurance given by audits and reviews are discussed in section 3.

While audits will vary according to the nature of the clients' businesses, most will follow standard stages overall. The **chronology of a typical statutory audit** is set out in section 4.

The rest of the Study Text builds on themes identified in this chapter. This is shown in the table below.

Part A	The regulations and codes of practice surrounding auditors
Part B	Planning audit and other assurance work
Parts C+D	Carrying out audit work
Part E	Reporting

This chapter explains the basis of auditing and explains the distinction between audit and review. The mechanics of these issues are explained throughout the Study Text. Questions in the exam could draw on matters in this chapter, **in conjunction** with the knowledge you will obtain later in the Study Text.

1 THE PURPOSE OF ASSURANCE

1.1 The key reason for having an audit or review can be seen by working through the following scenario.

> **Purpose of assurance scenario**
>
> Laine decides to set up a business selling flowers. She gets up early in the morning, visits the market, and sets up a stall by the side of the road. For the first year, all goes well. She sells all the flowers she is able to buy and she derives some income from the business.
>
> However, Laine feels that she could sell more flowers if she was able to transport more to the place where she sells them, and also knows that there are several other roads nearby that she could sell flowers, if she could be in two places at once. She could achieve these two things by buying a van, and by employing other people to sell flowers on the other roads.
>
> Laine needs more money to achieve this expansion of her business. She decides to ask her rich friend Glyn to invest in the business.
>
> Glyn can see the potential of Laine's business and wants to invest, but he doesn't want to be involved in the management of the business. He also does not want to have liability for the debts of the business if the business fails. He therefore suggest that they set up a limited company. He will own the majority of the shares and be entitled to dividends. Laine will be managing director and be paid a salary for her work.
>
> At the end of the first year of trading as a limited company, Glyn receives a copy of the financial statements. Profits are lower than expected, so his dividend will not be a large as he had hoped. He knows that Laine is paid a salary so does not care as much as him that profits are low.
>
> Glyn is concerned by the level of profits and feels that he wants further assurance on the accounts. He doesn't know whether they give a true reflection on the last year's trading, particularly as the profits do not seen as high as those Laine had predicted when he agreed to invest.

1.2 The solution is that the **assurance** Glyn is seeking can be given by an independent **audit or review** of the financial statements. An auditor can provide the two things that Glyn requires:

- A **knowledgeable review** of the company's business and of the accounts
- An **impartial view**, since Laine's view might be biased.

1.3 Other people will also view the company's accounts with interest, for example:

- Creditors of the company
- The Inland Revenue

1.4 The various people interested in the accounts of a company are sometimes referred to as **stakeholders**. Although they will all judge the accounts by different criteria, **they will all gain assurance** from learning that the accounts they are reading have been subject to an independent report.

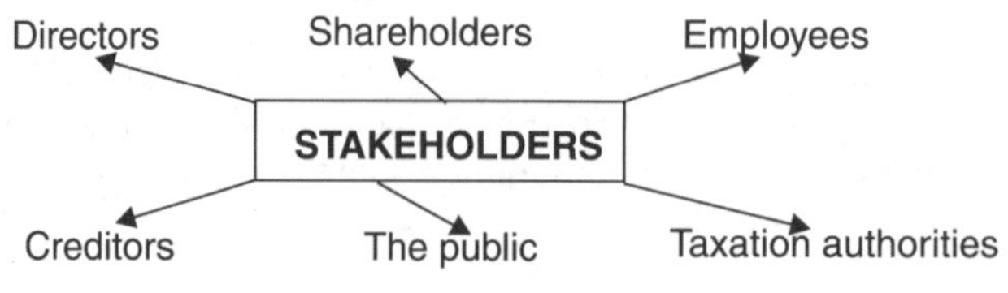

1.5 The example of Glyn and Laine is a simple one. In practice companies may have thousands of shareholders and may not know the management personally. It is therefore important that directors are **accountable** to shareholders. Directors act as **stewards** of the shareholders' investments. They are **agents** of the shareholders.

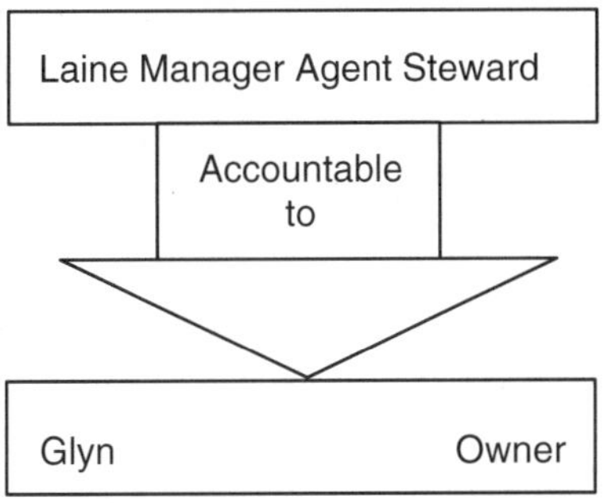

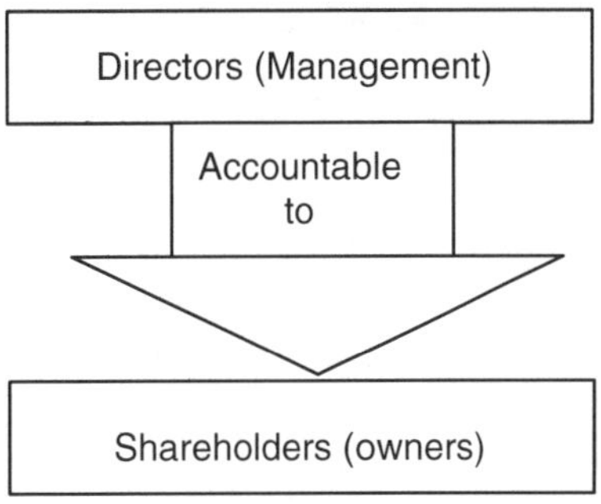

KEY TERMS

Accountability is the quality or state of being accountable, that is, being required or expected to justify actions and decisions. It suggests an obligation or willingness to accept responsibility for one's actions.

Stewardship is the practice of being a steward, that is, someone employed to manage another person's property.

Agents were introduced in paper 2.2 *Corporate and Business Law*. Agents are people employed or used to provide a particular service. In the case of a company, the people being used to provide the service of managing the business also have the second role of being people in their own right trying to maximise their personal wealth (through salary or profit/share schemes).

1.6 You may ask, 'what are the directors accountable for?' It is important to understand the answer to this question. The directors are accountable for the **shareholders' investment**. The shareholders have bought shares in that company (they have invested). They **expect a return** from their investment. As the **directors** manage the company, they are **in a position to affect that return.**

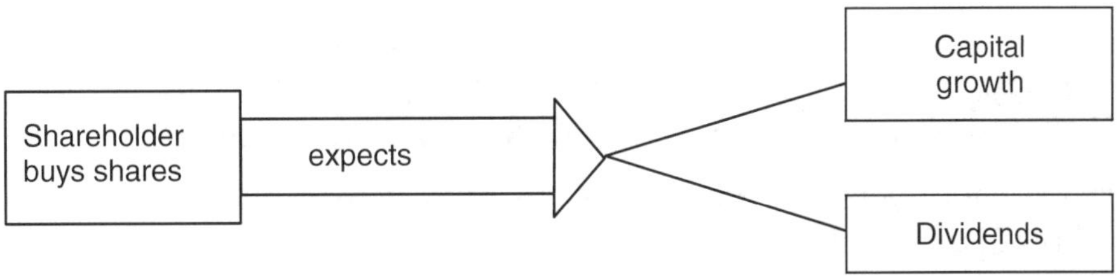

1.7 The exact nature of the return expected by the shareholder will depend on the type of company he has chosen to invest in: that is part of his investment risk analysis. Certain issues are true of any such investment, however. For example, if the directors **mismanage** the company, and it goes **bankrupt**, it will neither provide a source of future dividends, not will it create capital growth in the investment – indeed, the opposite is true, and even the original investment is likely to be lost.

1.8 **Accountability** therefore covers a range of issues. These are shown in the diagram on the next page.

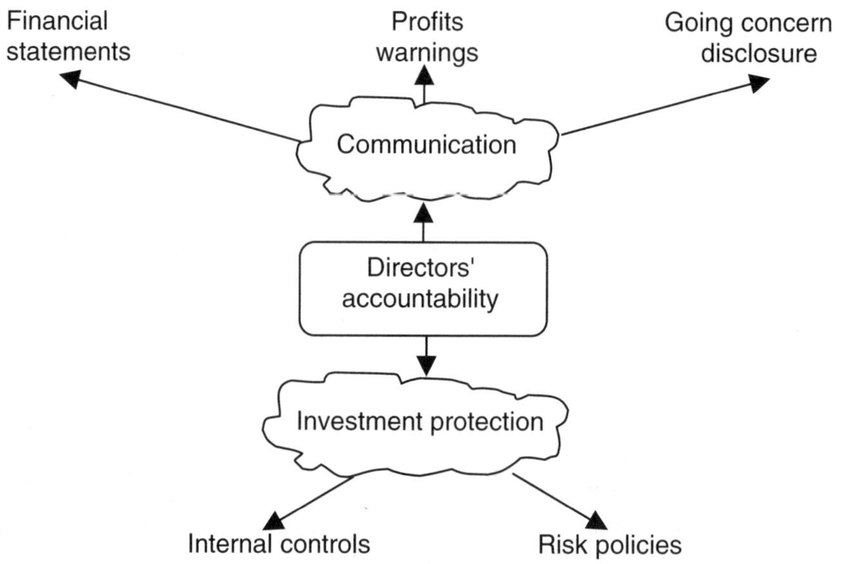

1.9 These issues are often discussed under the umbrella title '**corporate governance**', where 'governance' indicates the management (governing) role of the directors, and 'corporate' indicates that the issue relates to companies (bodies corporate).

1.10 This can be illustrated by our scenario, where we saw Laine taking up a corporate governance position in relation to Glyn.

Corporate governance

KEY TERM

'**Corporate governance** is the system by which companies are directed and controlled.'

Cadbury Committee report

'Good governance ensures that constituencies (stakeholders) with a relevant interest in the company's business are fully taken into account.' *Hampel Committee report*

1.11 The issue of corporate governance has existed since companies began to be used commonly as part of business. However, in the late twentieth century, some high profile frauds and questionable business practices led to **public and government attention** being firmly fixed on **business management**. In the late 1990s, a series of committees were set up to consider the matter.

1.12 The key committees were:

- Cadbury Committee 1992 (corporate governance)
- Greenbury Committee 1995 (directors' remuneration)
- Hampel Committee 1995 (corporate governance)
- Turnbull Committee 1999 (corporate governance)

1.13 These committees made various **recommendations** about how companies should be run and monitored to provide **safeguards** to shareholders.

Question: Corporate governance

Based on your knowledge of company law, which type of company do you think is most likely to be affected by the need for good corporate governance measures?

Answer

Clearly, it is in the interest of all shareholders that all companies are well-managed so as to maximise returns from their investment. However, in the UK, only public limited companies are entitled to sell shares to the general public. This means that in **many** cases (although not all), shareholders in private (Ltd) companies will be more closely connected to the directors than in public limited company (plcs). In fact, many Ltd companies in the UK are 'owner-managed', in other words, their shareholders and directors are one and the same. This is not always the case, and some Ltd companies are large affairs where owners and managers are very clearly distinct from one another.

While all public limited companies are entitled to sell shares to the public, in practice, the public are most likely to invest in shares that are **listed** on an exchange, for example, the Stock Exchange. This makes them key candidates for the need of good corporate governance

1.14 Although the issues raised in the answer to the question above are generalisations, corporate governance issues have **historically** tended to be **directed** at **listed, public limited companies.**

1.15 In 1998, the Stock Exchange issued a **Combined Code** of corporate governance requirements drawn from the recommendations of the Cadbury, Greenbury and Hampel Committees. Following this Code is **mandatory** for **companies listed on the Stock Exchange** (who have to disclose their reasoning for any non-compliance) but can be seen as **good practice** for **any UK company.**

Combined Code

Principles of the Combined Code	
The board	Every company should be headed by an effective board, which is collectively responsible for the success of the company. There should be a clear division of responsibilities at the head of the company between the running of the board and the executive responsibility for the running of the company's business. No one individual should have unfettered powers of decision. The board should include a balance of executive and non-executive directors (and in particular independent non-executive directors) such that no individual or small group of individuals can dominate the board's decision taking. There should be a formal, rigorous and transparent procedure for the appointment of new directors to the board. The board should be supplied in a timely manner with information in a form and of a quality appropriate to enable it to discharge its duties. All directors should receive induction on joining the board and should regularly update and refresh their skills and knowledge. The board should undertake a formal and rigorous annual evaluation of its own performance and that of its committees and individual directors.

Principles of the Combined Code	
	All directors should be submitted for re-election at regular intervals, subject to continued satisfactory performance. The board should ensure planned and progressive refreshing of the board.
Remuneration	Levels of remuneration should be sufficient to attract, retain and motivate directors of the quality required to run the company successfully, but a company should avoid paying more than is necessary for this purpose. A significant proportion of executive directors' remuneration should be structured so as to link rewards to corporate and individual performance.
	There should be formal and transparent procedure for developing policy on executive remuneration and for fixing the remuneration packages of individual directors. No director should be involved in deciding his or her own remuneration.
Accountability and audit	The board should present a balanced and understandable assessment of the company's position and prospects.
	The board should maintain a sound system of internal control to safeguard shareholders' investment and the company's assets.
	The board should establish formal and transparent arrangements for considering how they should apply the financial reporting and internal control principles and for maintaining an appropriate relationship with the company's auditors.
Relations with institutional shareholders	There should be a dialogue with shareholders based on the mutual understanding of objectives. The board as a whole has responsibility for ensuring that a satisfactory dialogue with shareholders takes place.
	The board should use the AGM to communicate with investors and to encourage their participation.

Depending on the size of the company, this may involve setting up an internal audit department.

Turnbull recommendations

1.16 The Turnbull Report adds some additional guidelines in relation to internal control systems.

KEY TERM

An **internal control system** comprises the control environment and control procedures. It includes all the policies and procedures (internal controls) adopted by the directors and management of an entity to ensure, as far as practicable, the orderly and efficient conduct of its business, including adherence to internal policies, the safeguarding of assets, the prevention and detection of fraud and error, the accuracy and completeness of the accounting records, and the timely preparation of reliable financial information. Internal controls may be incorporated within computerised accounting systems. However the internal control system extends beyond those matters which relate directly to the accounting system.

TURNBULL GUIDELINES
Have a **defined process** for the **review** of effectiveness of **internal control.**
Review **regular** reports on **internal control.**
Consider **key risks** and how they have been **managed.**
Check the **adequacy** of **action taken** to remedy weaknesses and incidents.
Consider the **adequacy** of **monitoring.**
Conduct an **annual assessment** of risks and the effectiveness of internal control.
Make a **statement** on this process in the **annual report.**

POINT TO NOTE

We will investigate **internal control systems, control environment** and **control procedures** in more detail in Chapter 9.

Assurance provision

1.17 As you can see from the above tables, many of the requirements in relation to corporate governance necessitate **communication** between the directors and the shareholders.

1.18 By law, **directors** of all companies are **required to produce financial statements** annually which give a **true and fair view** of the affairs of the company and its profit or loss for the period. They are also **encouraged** to **communicate with shareholders** on matters relating to **directors' pay** and benefits (this is required by law in the case of public limited companies), **going concern** and **management of risks.**

1.19 But how are the shareholders to know whether the directors' communications are **accurate**, or present a **fair picture**? We are back to the problem that Glyn had in the scenario we presented at the beginning of this section. He knew that Laine's view might be **biased** in a different way to his own, and he sought **assurance** on the information he was presented with.

KEY TERM

An **assurance engagement** is one where a professional accountant evaluates or measures a subject matter that is the responsibility of another party against suitable criteria, and expresses an opinion which provides the intended user with a level of assurance about that subject matter.

2 THE NATURE OF ASSURANCE SERVICES

2.1 A definition of an assurance service was given above. It is an engagement **to express an opinion giving assurance** to a set of people **on information which is the responsibility of others**.

2.2 That definition sums up two of the major features of the audit and internal review syllabus, audits and reviews.

Statutory and non-statutory audits

KEY TERM

An **audit** is an exercise whose objective is **to enable auditors to express an opinion** whether the financial statements

- Give a **true and fair view** (or equivalent) of
  - The entity's affairs at the period end, and of
  - Its profit and loss (or income and expenditure) for the period then ended
- And have been **properly prepared** in accordance with the applicable reporting framework (for example relevant legislation and applicable accounting standards) or, where the specific requirements prescribe the term, whether the financial statements 'present fairly'.

2.3 In an audit, the auditor **gives an opinion** to the **members** (shareholders in a company) of an organisation on the financial statements which are the responsibility of the directors. It is important to remember that the auditors only have a **duty** to report to the **shareholders**.

2.4 The Cadbury Report in 1992 described the audit as 'one of the **cornerstones of corporate governance**'. Registered companies have been required or encouraged to appoint auditors since the first Companies Act was passed in 1844. The legal requirements have developed in that time. From 1900, all registered companies were required to have an audit in relation to the balance sheet, from 1929 this was extended to the profit and loss account. From 1948, law required more detailed profit and loss disclosures to be audited. The Companies Acts in 1985 and 1989 implemented EC directives which contained auditor related requirements.

2.5 Audits are required under statute in the case of a large number of undertakings. As noted, under companies legislation (currently Companies Act 1985), most companies are required to have an audit. There are also requirements for:

- Building Societies (Building Societies Act 1965)
- Trade Unions/employer associations (Trade Union and Labour Relations Act 1974)
- House Associations (various pieces of related legislation)
- Certain charities (various pieces of legislation, depending on status)

2.6 The statutory audit can bring various advantages to the company and shareholders. The key benefit to shareholders is the impartial view provided by the auditors. However, the company benefits from professional accountants reviewing the accounts and system as part of the audit. Benefits might include recommendations being made in relation to accounting and control systems and the possibility that auditors might detect fraud and error.

POINTS TO NOTE

Statutory audits will be discussed in more detail in Chapter 2. A chronology of a typical audit showing the auditors' work on accounts and systems is given in Section 4 of this Chapter. The techniques auditors use will be discussed in Parts B-E of this Study Text.

2.7 **Non-statutory audits** are performed by independent auditors because the owners, proprietors, members, trustees, professional and governing bodies or other interested parties want them, rather than because the law requires them. In consequence, **auditing may extend** to every type of undertaking which produces accounts, including:

- Clubs
- Charities (some of these will require statutory audits as well)
- Sole traders
- Partnerships

POINT TO NOTE

Some of these organisations do not operate for profit, and this has a specific impact on the nature of their audit. The audit of not for profit organisations will be considered in Chapter 21.

2.8 Auditors may also give an **opinion** on **statements other than annual accounts**, for example,

- Summaries of sales in support of a statement of royalties
- Statements of expenditure in support of applications for regional development grants
- The circulation figures of a newspaper or magazine

2.9 In all such audits the auditors must take into account any **regulations** contained in the internal rules or constitution of the undertaking. Examples of the regulations which the auditors would need to refer to in such assignments would include:

- Any rules of the clubs, societies and charities
- Partnership agreements

Advantages of the non-statutory audit

2.10 In addition to the advantages common to all forms of audit a non-statutory audit can bring other advantages. For example, the audit of the accounts of a **partnership** may be seen to have the following advantages.

(a) It can provide a means of **settling accounts** between the partners.

(b) Where audited accounts are available this may make the **accounts more acceptable** to the **Inland Revenue** when it comes to agreeing an individual partner's liability to tax.

(c) The **sale of** the business or the **negotiation of loan** or overdraft facilities may be made easier if the firm is able to produce audited accounts, as the bank will take assurance from the audit.

(d) An audit on behalf of a **'sleeping partner'** (one not involved with management) is useful since generally such a person will have little other means of checking the accounts of the business, or confirming the share of profits due to him or her.

Question: Non-statutory audit

Some of the advantages above will also apply in the audit of the accounts of a sole trader, club or charity. Which ones? And can you think of others?

Reviews

2.11 An audit can be used to give assurance to a variety of stakeholders on a variety of issues. However, an audit is an exercise designed to give a high level of assurance (as we shall see later) and involves a high degree of testing and therefore cost. In some cases, stakeholders may find that they receive **sufficient assurance** about an issue from a less detailed engagement, for example, a review. A review can provide a cost-efficient alternative to an audit where an audit is not required by law.

KEY TERM

The objective of a **review engagement** is to enable an auditor to state whether, on the basis of procedures which do not provide all the evidence that would be required in an audit, anything has come to the auditor's attention that causes the auditor to believe that the financial statements are not prepared, in all material respects, in accordance with an identified financial reporting framework.

2.12 The major result for recipients of a review engagement is that the **level of assurance** they gain from a review engagement is not as high as from an audit. This is discussed in Section 3.

2.13 The procedures carried out in a review engagement are similar to an audit, but they are not as detailed. There is a higher reliance on the use of analytical procedures. However, the approach is similar.

POINTS TO NOTE

As the techniques used in audits and reviews are similar, the methods and procedures you will encounter in Parts B-E of this Study Text are relevant to both audits and reviews. Bear in mind that for a review, less detailed procedures will be carried out and sample sizes are likely to be smaller. Analytical procedures, which are used heavily in review engagements, are discussed in Chapter 12.

2.14 In the UK, guidance on how to audit is produced by the Auditing Practices Board. This is discussed further in Chapter 2. There is currently **no UK guidance** from the APB **on undertaking a review**. Auditors need to use their **professional judgement** to ascertain the **level of work required** to give the **appropriate level of assurance on a review assignment**.

Internal audit

KEY TERM

Internal audit is an appraisal or monitoring activity established by management and directors, for the review of the accounting and internal control systems as a service to the entity. It functions by, amongst other things, examining, evaluating and reporting to management and the directors on the adequacy and effectiveness of components of the accounting and internal control systems.

2.15 Up to now in this Chapter we have discussed assurance services where an independent outsider provides an opinion on financial information. However, the syllabus is also concerned with the assurance that can be provided to management (and by implication, to other parties) by **internal auditors**.

2.16 As we saw previously as part of their corporate governance duties, listed company directors are required, and all directors are advised, to review the effectiveness of the company's risk management and internal control systems. They should also consider the need for an **internal audit function to help them carry out their duties.**

2.17 Larger organisations may therefore appoint full-time staff whose **function is to monitor and report on the running of the company's operations**. Internal audit staff members are in themselves a type of control. Although some of the work carried out by internal auditors is similar to that performed by external auditors, there are **important distinctions** between the **nature** of the two functions, in terms of their responsibilities, scope and relationship with the company.

POINT TO NOTE

Internal audit will be discussed in more detail in Chapter 3.

3 ASSURANCE AND REPORTS 12/01

3.1 External auditors give an opinion on the **truth and fairness** of financial statements. This is **not an opinion of absolute correctness**. 'True' and 'fair' are terms used in legislation, but they are not defined in law. The following definitions are generally accepted definitions.

KEY TERMS

True. Information is factual and conforms with reality, not false. In addition the information conforms with required standards and law. The accounts have been correctly extracted from the books and records.

Fair. Information is free from discrimination and bias and in compliance with expected standards and rules. The accounts should reflect the commercial substance of the company's underlying transactions.

3.2 The audit report refers to the fact that an auditor obtains evidence 'on a test basis', he does not check everything. He is therefore giving 'reasonable' not 'absolute' assurance.

KEY TERM

An audit gives the reader **reasonable assurance** on the truth and fairness of the financial statements. The audit report does not guarantee that the financial statements are correct, but that they are true and fair within a reasonable margin of error.

3.3 One of the reasons that an auditor does not give absolute assurance is the **inherent limitations** of audit.

Limitations of audit **6/02**

3.4 The assurance auditors give is governed by the fact that auditors use **judgement** in deciding what audit procedures to use and what conclusions to draw, and also by the limitations of every audit.

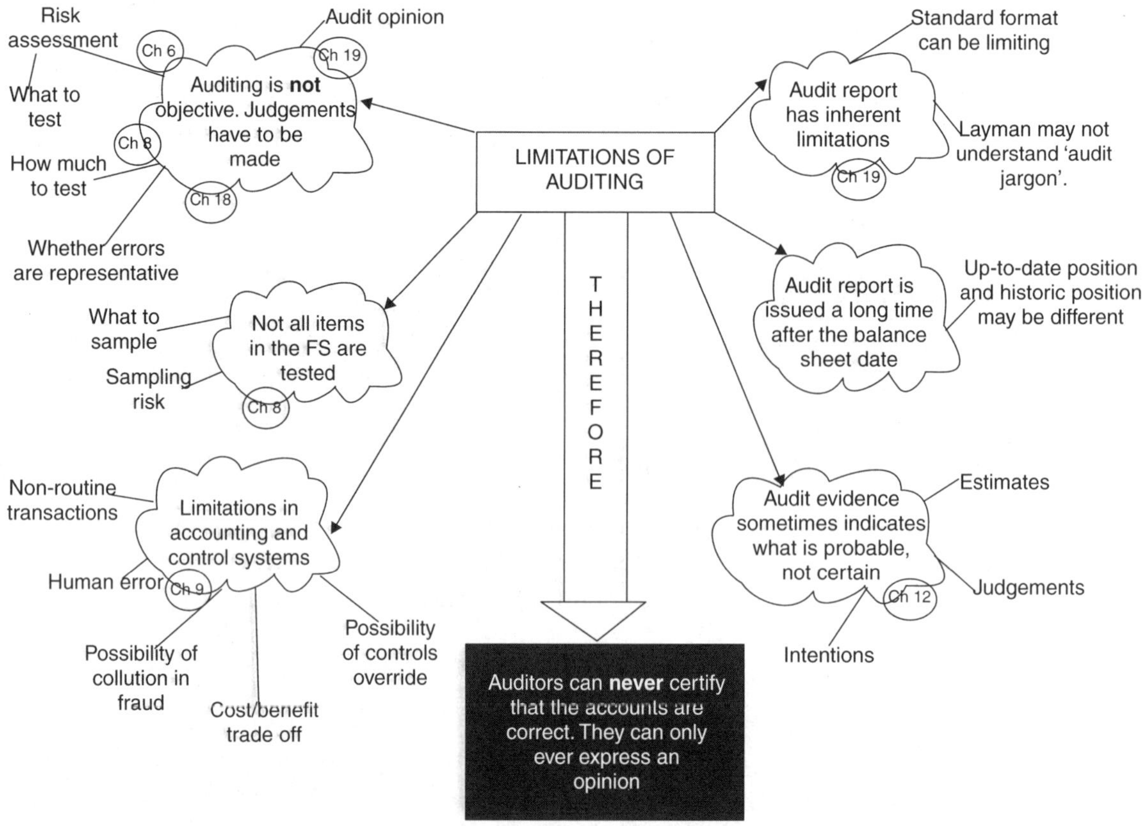

3.5 Errors, known as misstatements may exist in financial statements and may be significant to readers. Auditors will plan their work on this basis, that is, with **professional scepticism**. The concept of 'significance to readers' is the concept of **materiality**.

KEY TERM

Materiality is an expression of the relative significance or importance of a particular matter in the context of financial statements as a whole.

A matter is material if its omission or misstatement would reasonably influence the decisions of an addressee of the auditors' report.

Materiality may also be considered in the context of any individual primary statement within the financial statements or of individual items included in them.

POINT TO NOTE

Materiality will be discussed in Chapter 6.

3.6 The auditors' task is to decide whether accounts show a **true and fair view**. The auditors are not responsible for establishing whether the accounts are correct in every particular.

- It can take a great deal of time and trouble to check the correctness of even a very small transaction and the resulting benefit may not justify the effort.
- Financial accounting inevitably involves a degree of estimation which means that financial statements can never be completely precise.

3.7 Although the definition of materiality refers to the decision of the addressees of the audit report (the company's members), their decisions may well be influenced by other entities who use the accounts.

3.8 EXAMPLE

If the accounts are to be used to secure a bank loan, what is significant to the bank will influence the way members act.

3.9 Therefore the views of other users of the accounts must be taken into account if they influence the members of the company.

Question: Materiality

Define the term 'not material' and state in which context it might be used.

Answer

Generally speaking, transactions or other events will be seen as material in the context of an enterprise's financial statements, if their omission or misstatement would reasonably influence the decisions of an addressee of the auditors' report. The report lends some credibility to those statements which will have been prepared by the management of the enterprise.

In order to form an opinion on truth and fairness, the auditors will need to exercise their professional judgement and experience in relation to the question of materiality. It will be important for the auditors to assess materiality not merely in monetary terms but also in the overall context of the company's financial statements, statutory requirements and recognised best accounting and auditing practice.

Levels of assurance

3.10 'Assurance' here means the auditors' **satisfaction** as to the **reliability** of the **assertion** made by one party for use by another party.

3.11 Directors prepare financial statements for the benefit of members. They **assert** that the financial statements give a true and fair view. The auditors provide **assurance** on that assertion. To provide such assurance, the auditors must:

- Assess risk
- Plan procedures
- Conduct procedures
- Assess results
- Express an opinion

3.12 The degree of satisfaction achieved and, therefore, **the level of assurance which may be provided,** is **determined by** the nature of **procedures performed** and their results.

3.13 An **audit** can be distinguished from other assurance engagements in the following ways.

(a) **Audit engagement:** the auditor provides a high, but not absolute, level of assurance that the information audited is free of material misstatement. This is expressed positively in the audit report as **reasonable assurance.**

(b) **Review engagement:** the auditor provides a moderate level of assurance that the information subject to review is free of material misstatement. This is expressed in the form of **negative assurance.**

KEY TERM

Negative assurance is when an auditor gives an assurance that nothing has come to his attention which indicates that the financial statements have not been prepared according to the framework. In other words, he gives his assurance in the absence of any evidence to the contrary.

(c) **Agreed-upon procedures:** the auditor simply provides a report of the actual findings, so **no assurance** is expressed. Users of the report must instead judge for themselves the auditor's procedures and findings, and draw their own conclusions from the auditor's work.

(d) **Compilation engagement:** (for example, the preparation of accounts) users of the compiled information gain some benefit from the accountant's (as opposed to auditor's) involvement, but **no assurance** is expressed in the report.

4 THE CHRONOLOGY OF AN AUDIT

4.1 Certain common elements form a major part of the auditors' or reviewers' work on any client.

(a) **Making such tests** and enquiries as they consider necessary to form an opinion as to the reliability of the accounting records as a basis for the preparation of accounts

(b) **Checking the accounts** against the underlying records

(c) **Reviewing the accounts** for compliance with relevant standards, for example, the Companies Act and accounting standards

Determine audit approach

Stage 1 Determine the **scope** of the audit and the auditors' approach. For statutory audits the scope is laid down by the Companies Act 1985 and expanded by Auditing Standards.

The auditors should prepare an **audit plan,** which should be placed on file. The contents of the plan will be considered at Chapter 6.

Ascertain the system and controls

Stage 2 Determine the **flow of documents** and **extent of controls** in existence in the client's system.

This is a fact finding exercise which is achieved by discussing the accounting system and document flow with all the relevant departments (for example, sales, purchases, cash, stock and accounts personnel).

It is good practice to make a rough record of the system during this fact finding stage which will be converted to a formal record at Stage 3.

Stage 3 Prepare a **comprehensive record** of the **system to facilitate evaluation** of the systems. The records may be in various formats (for example, charts, narrative notes, internal control questionnaires and flowcharts).

Stage 4 Confirm that the **system recorded** is the same as that **in operation.**

This is achieved by performing walk-through tests. These involve tracing a handful of transactions through the system and observing the operation of controls over them.

This check is useful because sometimes client staff will tell the auditors what they **should be doing** rather than **what is actually done.**

Assess the system and internal controls

Stage 5 **Evaluate the systems** to gauge their reliability and formulate a basis for testing their effectiveness in practice.

Auditors will be able to recommend any improvements and also determine the extent of further tests at Stages 6 and 8 below.

Test the system and internal controls

Stage 6 *(This should only be carried out if the controls are evaluated as effective at Stage 5. If not, Steps 6 and 7 should be omitted.)*

If controls are effective, tests should are designed to establish compliance with the system should be selected and performed.

Tests of controls, which cover a larger number of items than walkthrough tests and cover a more representative sample of transactions through the period, should be carried out.

If **controls are strong,** the records should be reliable and the amount of detailed testing can be reduced. If **controls are ineffective** in practice, more extensive substantive procedures will be required.

Stage 7 After evaluating the systems and testing controls, auditors normally send an interim **report to management** identifying weaknesses and recommending improvements.

Test the financial statements

Stages 8 and 9 These tests are concerned with **substantiating the figures** given **in the final financial statements.**

Substantive tests also serve to assess the effect of errors, should errors exist.

Before designing a substantive procedure it is essential to consider whether any errors produced could be significant. If the answer is no, there is no point in performing a test.

Review the financial statements

Stage 10 The financial statements should be reviewed to determine the overall reliability of the account by making a **critical analysis of content and presentation.**

Express an opinion

Stage 11 The auditors evaluate the evidence that they have obtained and they **express their opinion** to members in the form of an **audit report.**

Stage 12 The **final report to management** is an important **non-statutory end product** of the audit. The purpose of it is to make further **suggestions for improvements** in the systems and to **place on record specific points** in connection with the audit and the accounts.

Chapter roundup

- An assurance engagement is essentially an **impartial**, **knowledgeable** scrutiny and review.
- This syllabus is particularly concerned with **audit** (both statutory and non statutory), **review** and the assurance provided to management by **internal audit**.
- The auditors' report on company accounts is in terms of **truth** and **fairness**. This is generally taken to mean accounts are:
  - Factual
  - Free from bias
  - Reflect the commercial substance of the business's transactions
- The APB also points out that audits at best give **reasonable assurance** that the accounts are free from material misstatement.
- As well as audits of accounts, there are various other types of audits and reviews, statutory and non-statutory. The level of assurance given in such an exercise may be lower than for a statutory audit.
- **Internal auditors** are employed as part of an organisation's system of controls. Their responsibilities are determined by management and may be wide-ranging.
- The **key** stages of the audit process are:
  - Determine audit approach
  - Ascertain the accounting system and internal controls
  - Assess the accounting system and internal controls
  - Test the accounting system and internal controls
  - Test the financial statements (substantive testing)
  - Review the financial statements
  - Express an opinion

Quick quiz

1 Complete the APB's **definition** of an audit:

An audit is an exercise whose objective is to enable auditors to .... whether the financial statements give .... (or equivalent) of the entity's affairs at .... and of .... for the period then ended and have been .... in accordance with .... (for example relevant legislation and applicable accounting standards) or, where other specific requirements prescribed their terms, whether the financial statements 'present fairly'.

2 Link the correct definition to each term.

(i)	Accountable	(iv)	True
(ii)	Steward	(v)	Fair
(iii)	Agent	(vi)	Materiality

(a) An expression of the relative significance or importance of a particular matter in the context of the financial statements as a whole.

(b) A person employed to provide a particular service.

(c) Factual and conforming with reality. In conformity with relevant standards and law and correctly extracted from accounting records.

(d) A person employed to manage other people's property.

(e) Free from discrimination and bias and in compliance with expected standards and rules. Reflecting the commercial substance of underlying transactions.

(f) Being required or expected to justify actions and decisions

3 For which of the following is an audit a statutory obligation? (There is more than one correct answer.)

Limited companies

Clubs

Partnerships

Building societies

Charities

Trade Unions

Housing associations

Sole traders

4 Put the following stages of an audit in the correct order.

- Assess the system and internal controls
- Test the financial statements
- Determine audit approach
- Express an opinion
- Ascertain the system and controls
- Review the financial statements
- Test the system and internal controls

5 Tests of control cover a large number of transactions while walkthrough tests will be limited to one or two.

True ☐

False ☐

6 A partnership might benefit from having an audit even though it is not required to do so by law. Tick the correct advantages below.

(a) Means of settling accounts between partners ☐

(b) Ensures that partners' remuneration will be made public ☐

(c) May make the accounts more acceptable to the Inland Revenue ☐

(d) The individual partners will not have to prepare tax returns ☐

(e) May facilitate the negotiation of a loan ☐

(f) May benefit a 'sleeping partner' who otherwise has little knowledge of partnership affairs ☐

Answers to quick quiz

1 Express an opinion, a true and fair view, the period end, the profit or loss (or income and expenditure), properly prepared, the applicable reporting framework.

2 (i) (f) (iv) (c)
(ii) (d) (v) (e)
(iii) (b) (vi) (a)

3 Limited companies, building societies, trade unions, housing associations, **some** charities.

4
- Determine audit approach
- Ascertain the system and controls
- Assess the system and internal controls
- Test the system and internal controls
- Test the financial statements
- Review the financial statements
- Express an opinion

5 True

6 (a), (c), (e) and (f). (b) would not necessarily be a result of an audit and would not be an advantage anyway. (d) is simply untrue.

Now try the question below from the Exam Question Bank

Number	Level	Marks	Time
1	Introductory	n/a	15 mins

78154

Chapter 2

STATUTORY AUDIT AND REGULATION

Topic list		Syllabus reference	Study guide
1	The statutory audit requirement	1	2
2	Audit regulation	3	2
3	Rights and duties of auditors	3	2
4	Auditing standards	3	2
5	International auditing standards	3	2

Introduction

This chapter describes the **statutory requirement** for certain companies to have an audit, and the discussion which exists over exemption from that requirement.

It also examines the main bodies and the major factors which govern auditing. You should particularly note how the **audit monitoring regime** works and what inspectors are looking for.

The legal **requirements, rights and duties** of auditors are outlined in section 3.

The chapter then goes on to discuss the role of the Auditing Practices Board and the scope of the guidance it issues. You should understand the authority of **SASs, Practice Notes** and **Bulletins**. The detailed requirements of the SASs you are required to know (most of them) are discussed throughout the rest of this Study Text.

The regulatory framework for auditors discussed in this chapter and the ethical framework discussed in Chapter 4 are very important. They could be examined together as part of a scenario question on planning or accepting appointment.

The examiner has stated that an understanding of the overall regulatory regime is essential to an understanding of external audit and could be examined in the compulsory section of the exam in the future. It was examined as an optional question in December 2001.

1 THE STATUTORY AUDIT REQUIREMENT

1.1 As noted in Chapter 1, the majority of companies are required to have an audit under the Companies Act 1985. Members of companies which are **dormant** have the right to dispense with an audit. There are some exceptions to this requirement, notably the exception for small, limited companies.

1.2 **Small company audit exemption**

(a) A company is **totally exempt** if it qualifies as a small company under s 246 of the Companies Act 1985, its **turnover is not more than £5.6m** and its **balance sheet total is not more than £2.8m.**

(b) These **exemptions do not apply to public companies, banks, insurers, insurance brokers, those authorised under the Financial Services Act, trade unions, employers' associations, parent companies or subsidiaries.**

(c) Members of **groups** can claim exemption from audit.

(d) A company is not exempt if **members holding 10%** or more of its shares **demand an audit** at least a month before the end of the financial year.

(e) Where a company takes advantage of an exemption its directors must make a **statement on the balance sheet**. Among other things, this statement must acknowledge the directors' responsibility for ensuring that proper accounting records are kept, and for preparing accounts that give a true and fair view and comply with the Companies Act.

1.3 This exemption was extended to companies with a turnover of £5.6m in 2004. Prior to that, the turnover limit had been £1m. Some accountancy bodies have expressed concerns at the number of companies that will now be exempt from the statutory audit requirement.

1.4 There has long been a **debate over the benefits of an audit to small companies.** As discussed in Chapter 1, many small companies are owned by the same people that manage them, and the benefit of an independent review of the stewardship of those managers has significantly less value than in a company where owners and management are different sets of people.

Who?	**Benefit of audit**	**Drawbacks of audit**
Shareholders	Shareholders not involved in management need the reassurance given by audited accounts. Furthermore, the existence of the audit deters the directors from treating the company's assets as their own to the detriment of minority shareholders. Audited financial statements are invaluable in arriving at a fair valuation of the shares in an unquoted company either for taxation or other purposes.	Where all the shareholders are also executive directors or closely related to them, the benefit gained from an audit may not be worth its cost.

Who?	Benefit of audit	Drawbacks of audit
Banks and other institutional creditors	Banks rely on accounts for the purposes of making loans and reviewing the value of security.	There is doubt whether banks rely on the audited accounts of companies to a greater extent than those of unincorporated associations of a similar size which have not been audited. A review of the way in which the bank accounts of the company have been conducted and of forecasts and management accounts are at least as important to the banks as the appraisal of the audited accounts. There is no reason why a bank should not make an audit a precondition of granting a loan.
Trade creditors	Creditors and potential creditors should have the opportunity to assess the strength of their customers by examining audited financial statements either themselves or through a credit company.	In practice, only limited reliance is placed on the accounts available from the Registrar of Companies as they are usually filed so late as to be of little significance in granting short term credit.
Tax authorities	The Inland Revenue and Customs & Excise rely on accounts for computing corporation tax and checking VAT returns.	There is little evidence to suggest that the tax authorities rely on audited accounts to a significantly greater extent than those, which, whilst being unaudited have been prepared by an independent accountant.
Employees	Employees are entitled to be able to assess audited accounts when entering wage negotiations and considering the future viability of their employer.	There is little evidence to suggest that, in the case of small companies, such assessments are made.
Management	The audit provides management with a useful independent check on the accuracy of the accounting systems and the auditor is frequently able to recommend improvements in those systems.	If the law were changed, the management of a company could, if they so desired, still elect to have an independent audit. It is likely, however, that a systems **review** accompanied by a management consultancy report would represent a greater benefit for a similar cost.

The statutory audit opinion

1.5 The Companies Act requires the auditors to state **explicitly** (s 235) whether in their opinion the annual accounts have been properly prepared in accordance with the Act and in particular whether a **true and fair view** is given.

EXPLICIT OPINIONS
In the balance sheet, of the **state of the company's affairs** at the end of the financial year
In the profit and loss account, of the **company's profit or loss** for the financial year

1.6 In addition certain requirements are reported on **by exception**. The auditor only has to report if they have not been met. The following are matters with which the auditors **imply** satisfaction in an unqualified report under s 237 of the Companies Act 1985.

IMPLIED OPINIONS
Proper accounting records have been kept and proper returns adequate for the audit received from branches not visited.
The **accounts** are in **agreement** with the **accounting records** and returns.
All information and **explanations** have been **received** as the auditors think necessary and they have had access at all times to the company's books, accounts and vouchers.
Details of **directors' emoluments** and other benefits have been correctly **disclosed** in the financial statements.
Particulars of loans and other **transactions** in favour of **directors** and others have been correctly **disclosed** in the financial statements.
The **information** given in the **directors' report** is **consistent** with the **accounts.**

The standard report

1.7 A standardised report is required by Statement of Auditing Standards 600 *Auditors' report on financial statements*.

POINTS TO NOTE

This report will be looked at in detail in Chapter 19. A list of the Statement of Auditing Standards relevant to this syllabus is given in section 4.

2 AUDIT REGULATION

2.1 In the UK there are a large number of different accountancy, or accountancy-related, institutes and associations, such as the Association of Chartered Certified Accountants (ACCA) or the Chartered Institute of Management Accountants (CIMA).

2.2 All these bodies vary from each other, depending on the nature of their aims and the specialisms their members wish to attain. They are all, however, characterised by various attributes, stringent entrance requirements (examinations and practical experience), strict codes of ethics and technical updating of members.

2.3 The membership of all these bodies is scattered through practice, industry, government and public bodies.

Recognised Supervisory Bodies

2.4 The EC 8th Directive on company law requires that persons carrying out statutory audits must be approved by the authorities of EU member states. The authority to give this approval in the UK is delegated to Recognised Supervisory Bodies (RSBs). An auditor must be a member of an RSB and be eligible under its own rules. The ACCA is a RSB as are some of the institutes and associations mentioned above.

2.5 The RSBs are required to have rules to ensure that persons eligible for appointment as a company auditor are either (4(1), Sch 11, CA 1989):

- Individuals holding an appropriate qualification
- Firms controlled by qualified persons

2.6 A number of other requirements concern the procedures which RSBs must follow to **maintain** the **competence** of **members**.

2.7 Professional qualifications, which will be prerequisites for membership of an RSB, will be offered by Recognised Qualifying Bodies ('RQBs') approved by the Secretary of State.

Eligibility as auditor

2.8 Membership of a Recognised Supervisory Body is the main prerequisite for eligibility as an auditor. An audit firm may be either a body corporate, a partnership or a sole practitioner.

2.9 The Companies Act 1985 also requires an auditor to hold an '**appropriate qualification**'. A person holds an 'appropriate qualification' if he or she has gained one of the following.

- Acknowledgement that he or she has met **existing criteria** for appointment as an auditor under CA 1985
- A **recognised qualification** obtained in the UK
- An **approved overseas qualification**

Ineligibility as auditor

2.10 The Companies Act sets out the following reasons that a person would be **ineligible** for appointment as company auditor.

Being an **officer** or **employee** of the company
Being a **partner** or **employee** of such a person
Being a **partnership** in which such a person is a partner
Ineligible by any of the above three reasons for appointment as auditor of any parent or subsidiary undertaking or a subsidiary undertaking of any parent undertaking of the company
There exists between him or her or any associate (of his or hers) and the company (or any company) a **connection** of any description as may be specified in regulations laid down by the Secretary of State

2.11 The legislation does **not** disqualify the following from being an auditor of a limited company:

- A shareholder of the company
- A debtor or creditor of the company
- A close relative of an officer or employee of the company

2.12 However, the regulations of the accountancy bodies applying to their own members are stricter than statute in this respect.

2.13 Under the Companies Act 1985, a person may also be ineligible on the grounds of '**lack of independence**'. The definition of lack of independence is to be determined by statutory instrument following consultation with the professional bodies.

2.14 Under s 389 CA 1985, if during their term of office a company auditor becomes ineligible for appointment to the office, he must vacate office and give notice in writing to the company.

Question: Audit regulation

Outline the role of the Recognised Supervisory Bodies (RSBs).

Answer

See Paragraphs 2.4 - 2.7.

Legal requirements on appointment to and removal from a company audit

Knowledge brought forward from 2.2

You will have studied the legal requirements relating to the appointment and removal of auditors from office in your studies for *2.2 Corporate and Business Law*. Here is a brief summary:

Appointment

Per the Companies Act 1985, auditors are appointed by and are answerable to the shareholders primarily. They are appointed (or reappointed) annually at the general meeting and they hold office until the next general meeting at which accounts are laid. In exceptional circumstances, the directors (to fill a casual vacancy or before the first ever general meeting) and the secretary of state (if none are appointed at the general meeting) may appoint auditors.

The law currently provides that private (Ltd) companies may disapply the requirements to re-appoint auditors annually, by passing an elective resolution.

The auditors' fees will be fixed by whoever made the appointment, or in such a manner as the general meeting determine.

Removal

If the auditors resign, they are required to submit a written notice and a statement of circumstances and can require the directors to call a general meeting for the auditors to discuss the reasons they have resigned.

> If the auditors are removed from office (other than by not being re-elected at the general meeting) they are entitled to be sent special notice of the resolution. They can make representations on why they ought to stay in office, which they can require the directors to state in the notice of the meeting given to shareholders that such representations have been made. If the resolution is passed, the auditors must submit a statement of circumstances.

Independent regulation

2.15 The professional bodies (RSBs) which carry out audit work in the UK have long been self-regulating. Currently, the role of regulator is devolved to the Financial Reporting Council (FRC), which is partly funded by the profession. The FRC is a unified, independent regulator. It has three key roles:

- To set accounting and auditing standards
- To proactively enforce and monitor them
- To oversee the self-regulatory professional bodies

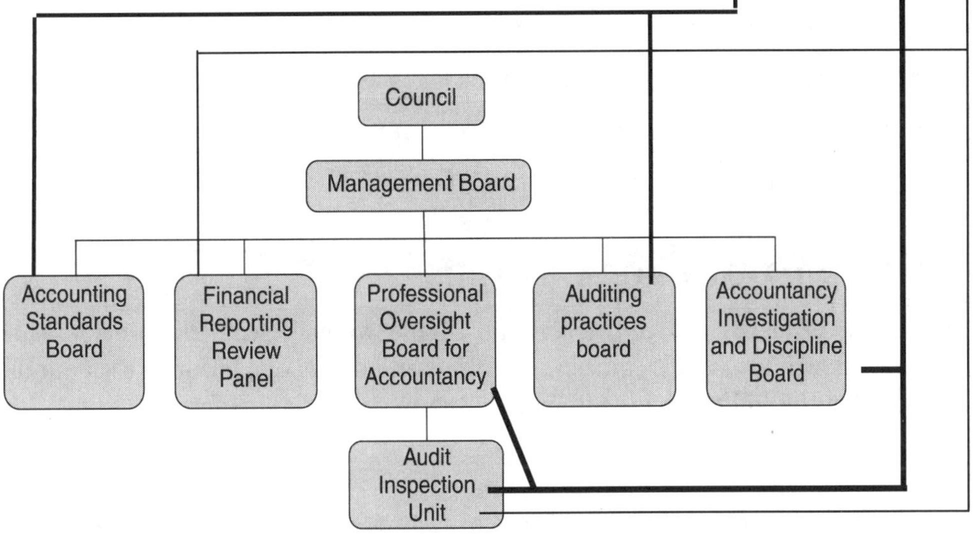

2.16 The above diagram shows the various arms of the FRC, and how it carries out its main aims. We shall look in detail at the Auditing Practices Board in section 4.

2.17 The FRC contains the **Professional Oversight Board**. This has a wide remit in overseeing the conduct of accountants generally. It will also set up a new inspection unit to monitor the audits of listed companies, major charities and pension funds. The Professional Oversight Board will also oversee the ethical agenda of accountants. A new **Investigation and Discipline Board** will be created as part of the FRC to provide an independent forum for hearing significant public interest disciplinary cases.

2.18 The new regulator has not currently been given **statutory backing**. The Government believes that there is a strong case that statutory regulation will be necessary to ensure that the regulator operates effectively, but is currently considering the matter further.

2.19 The FRC is **funded** jointly by the **accountancy profession** (through the Consultative Committee of Accountancy Bodies – CCAB), the **City** (the London Stock Exchange together with the banking and investment community) and the **Government**.

Other supervision and monitoring

2.20 RSBs must also implement procedures for inspecting their registered auditors on a regular basis. ACCA has a **monitoring unit**.

2.21 The frequency of inspection depends on the number of partners, number of offices and number of listed company audits (these factors are also reflected in the size of annual registration fees payable).

2.22 The following features should be apparent in each practice visited by the monitoring unit.

- A **properly structured audit approach**, suitable for the range of clients served and work undertaken by the practice
- Carefully instituted **quality control procedures**, revised and updated constantly, to which the practice as a whole is committed. This will include:
  - Staff recruitment
  - Staff training
  - Continuing professional development
  - Frequent quality control review
- **Commitment to ethical guidelines**, with an emphasis on independence issues
- An emphasis on **technical excellence**
- Adherence to the '**fit and proper**' criteria by checking personnel records and references
- Use of internal and, if necessary, external **peer reviews** or consultations
- **Appropriate fee** charging per audit assignment

3 RIGHTS AND DUTIES OF AUDITORS

3.1 The audit is primarily a statutory concept, and, as we have seen, eligibility to conduct an audit is set down in statute. Similarly, the rights and duties of auditors are set out in statute, to ensure that the auditors have sufficient power to carry out an effective audit.

Duties

3.2 The principal statutory duties of auditors in respect of the audit of a limited company are set out in ss 235 and 237 CA 1985. The auditors are required to report on every balance sheet and profit and loss account laid before the company in general meeting.

3.3 As we have seen in section 1, only compliance with legislation and **truth** and **fairness** of accounts need to be explicitly referred to in the audit report; the other matters can be reported **by exception only**.

Rights

3.4 The Companies Act provides statutory rights for auditors to enable them to carry out their duties.

3.5 The principal rights are set out in the table below.

Access to records	A right of access at all times to the books, accounts and vouchers of the company
Information and explanations	A right to require from the company's officers such information and explanations as they think necessary for the performance of their duties as auditors
Attendance at/notices of general meetings	A right to attend any general meetings of the company and to receive all notices of and communications relating to such meetings which any member of the company is entitled to receive
Right to speak at general meetings	A right to be heard at general meetings which they attend on any part of the business that concerns them as auditors
Rights in relation to written resolutions	A right to receive a copy of any written resolution proposed
Right to require laying of accounts	A right to give notice in writing requiring that a general meeting be held for the purpose of laying the accounts and reports before the company (if elective resolution dispensing with laying of accounts in force)
On resignation	A right to required directors to call a general meeting to discuss circumstances of resignation. A right to require directors to circularise members with an auditor statement about resignation. A right to receive notice of general meetings (1) where their tenure would have expired (2) where casual vacancy caused by the resignation is to be filled. A right to speak at the above meetings on matters which concern them.
On removal	A right to make representations on why they should stay in office and have them sent to members. A right to receive notice of and speak at general meeting (1) at which their tenure would have expired (2) where casual vacancy caused by their removal is being filled.

Rights to information

3.6 If auditors have not received all the information and explanations they consider necessary, they should state this fact in their audit report.

3.7 The Act makes it an offence for a company's officer knowingly or recklessly to make a statement in any form to an auditor which:

- Purports to convey any information or explanation required by the auditor
- Is materially misleading, false or deceptive

The penalty is a maximum of two years' imprisonment, a fine or both (s 389A(2)).

POINT TO NOTE

The government are considering new companies legislation in which officers of a company would be required to disclose any information they felt was relevant to the auditors.

4 AUDITING STANDARDS 12/01

Rules governing audits

4.1 We discussed in Chapter 1 the various stakeholders in a company, and the number of people who might read a company's accounts. Consider also that a number of these readers will not just be reading a single company's accounts, but will also be reading the accounts of a large number of companies, and making comparisons between them.

4.2 Readers **want assurance** when making comparisons **that the reliability of the accounts does not vary from company to company**. This assurance will be obtained not just from knowing each set of accounts has been audited, but knowing that each set of accounts has been audited to **common standards**.

4.3 Hence there is a need for audits to be **regulated** so that auditors follow the same standards. As we see in this chapter, auditors have to follow rules issued by a variety of bodies. As we saw above, some obligations are imposed by **Parliament,** for company auditors by the Companies Act 1985. Some obligations are imposed by the professional bodies to which auditors are required to belong (such as the **ACCA**). Some obligations may, in future, be imposed by the independent regulator, the FRC.

4.4 The detailed requirements that auditors are obliged to follow are set by the **Auditing Practices Board** (APB) which is a part of the FRC.

The APB and Statements of Auditing Standards (SASs)

4.5 Auditing standards are set by the Auditing Practices Board (APB) which is a part of the Financial Reporting Council. The APB:

- Can issue auditing standards in its own right without having to obtain the approval of all the professional accounting bodies
- Has strong representation from outside the accounting profession
- Has a commitment to openness, with agenda papers being circulated to interested parties, and an annual report being published

4.6 The APB has changed in nature as a body since it has been in operation, but the information the APB issued in a document in May 1993 entitled *The scope and authority of APB pronouncements* is still valid. The APB makes three categories of pronouncement.

- Statements of Auditing Standards (SASs)
- Practice Notes
- Bulletins

4.7 The scope of **SASs** is as follows.

> 'SASs contain basic principles and essential procedures ('Auditing Standards') which are indicated by bold type and with which auditors are required to comply, except where otherwise stated in the SAS concerned, in the conduct of any audit of financial statements.'

4.8 The APB also publishes SASs which apply to:

- Audits and related services provided by auditors other than audits of financial statements
- Specific types of audits, for example audits of specialised industries

4.9 Apart from statements in bold type, SASs also contain other material which is not prescriptive but which is designed to help auditors interpret and apply auditing standards. The APB document also states that auditing standards need not be applied to immaterial items (items which are not significant to the accounts).

POINT TO NOTE

We introduced the concept of materiality in Chapter 1. It will be looked at in more detail in Chapter 6.

4.10 The FRC, assisted by the Financial Services Authority, will monitor compliance with Auditing Standards and can take disciplinary action, including the removal of eligibility to perform audits from individuals and firms. The professional bodies such as ACCA will also monitor their member's compliance with auditing standards.

4.11 **Practice Notes** are issued 'to assist auditors in applying Auditing Standards of general application to particular circumstances and industries'.

4.12 **Bulletins** are issued 'to provide auditors with timely guidance on new or emerging issues'.

4.13 Practice Notes and Bulletins are persuasive rather than prescriptive, but they indicate good practice and have a similar status to the explanatory material in SASs. Both Practice Notes and Bulletins may be included in later SASs.

Exam focus point

The following documents are examinable at 2.6. This list is not a comprehensive list of existing auditing standards.

No	Title	Issue date
	Glossary of terms	
010	The scope and authority of APB pronouncements	April 2003
100	Objective and general principles governing an audit of financial statements	Mar 1995
110	Fraud and error	Jan 1995
120	Consideration of law and regulations	Jan 1995
130	The going concern basis in financial statements	Nov 1994
140	Engagement letters	Mar 1995
150	Subsequent events	Mar 1995
160	Other information in documents containing audited financial statements (Revised)	Oct 1999
200	Planning	Mar 1995
210	Knowledge of the business	Mar 1995
220	Materiality and the audit	Mar 1995
230	Working papers	Mar 1995
300	Accounting and internal control systems and audit risk assessments	Mar 1995
400	Audit evidence	Mar 1995
410	Analytical procedures	Mar 1995
420	Audit of accounting estimates	Mar 1995
430	Audit sampling	Mar 1995
440	Management representations	Mar 1995
450	Opening balances and comparatives	Mar 1995
470	Overall review of financial statements	Mar 1995
480	Service organisations	Jan 1999
500	Considering the work of internal audit	Mar 1995
520	Using the work of an expert	Mar 1995
600	Auditors' reports on financial statements	May 1993
601	Imposed limitation of audit scope	Mar 1999
610	Communication of audit matters to those charged with governance	June 2001

Auditing Guidelines

No	Title	Issue date
405	Attendance at stocktaking	Oct 1983

Other Documents

No	Title	Issue date
PN 13	The audit of small businesses	July 1997
PN 16	Bank reports for audit purposes	Aug 1998
	Bulletin 2001/02 Revisions to the wording of auditors' reports on financial statements and the interim review report	*Jan 2001
	Briefing Paper: Providing assurance on the effectiveness of internal control	July 2001
	Briefing Paper: Effective communication between audit committees and external auditors	Sept 2002
	ACCA's rules of Professional Conduct	

* Students will not be examined on those sections of this document that deal with the review report, or Stock Exchange requirements.

Note
Students are advised that questions will be based on the principles and good practice set out in the Auditing Standards and Guidelines.

SAS 100 Objectives and general principles governing an audit

4.14 The APB give general guidance about an audit of financial statements in this SAS. This covers matters we have considered in Chapter 1. SAS 100 states, 'in undertaking an audit of financial statements auditors should:

(a) Carry out procedures designed to obtain sufficient appropriate audit evidence, in accordance with Auditing Standards contained in SASs, to determine with reasonable confidence whether the financial statements are free of material misstatement

(b) Evaluate the overall presentation of the financial statements, in order to ascertain whether they have been prepared in accordance with relevant legislation and accounting standards and

(c) Issue a report containing a clear expression of their opinion on the financial statements'.

4.15 Most importantly, the standard makes clear that the auditors do not bear any responsibility for the preparation and presentation of the financial statements.

The responsibility for the preparation and presentation of the financial statements is that of the directors of the entity. Auditors are responsible for forming and expressing an opinion on the financial statements. The audit of the financial statements does not relieve the directors of any of their responsibilities.

Application of SASs to small businesses

4.16 The Auditing Practices Board published in July 1997 Practice Note 13 *The Audit of Small Businesses*. The Practice Note states that the audit of small businesses is influenced by a number of factors. These include:

(a) The **characteristics of small businesses**. The most important characteristics are **concentration of ownership** and **management** in a few/single individual(s), the business having few sources of income and uncomplicated activities and limited internal controls and the potential for management override.

(b) The **professional relationship** between the business and its auditors. Auditors will often provide a range of **other services** as well as auditing, particularly accounting services. The Practice Note stresses the importance of the auditors maintaining objectivity despite providing other services, and not taking over the role of management.

(c) Audits of small businesses may also be affected by the fact that **small teams of auditors** may be **involved** and the rules governing the content of small businesses' financial statements.

4.17 The Practice Note then goes on to give a detailed commentary on how specific SASs impact upon the audit of small businesses.

SAS 110 Fraud and error

4.18 Amongst the signs of fraud that may be particularly relevant to small businesses are the owner-manager making no distinction between business and personal transactions and the owner-manager's lifestyle being materially inconsistent with remuneration levels.

SAS 130 Going concern

4.19 The Practice Note points out that a small business's continuation as a going concern may depend on a single factor, for example funds not being withdrawn.

SAS 230 Working papers

4.20 If accountancy work is being used as audit evidence, the work performed, the evidence obtained and the conclusions drawn are recorded as for normal audit work.

SAS 400 Audit evidence

4.21 The Practice Note emphasises that accountancy work can provide audit evidence for certain objectives, but is unlikely to provide sufficient evidence of completeness and valuation.

5 INTERNATIONAL AUDITING STANDARDS

5.1 There is increasingly a call for accounting and auditing practice to be comparable on a global scale. The International Federation of Accountants (IFAC) and the International Accounting Standards Board (IASB) both work towards creating international standards. International Auditing Standards are issued by the International Audit and Assurance Standards Board (IAASB), a sub-committee of IFAC.

5.2 Currently these accounting and auditing standards can be used as best practice, but only have force of law where countries have adopted them as such. As UK companies are required to follow UK accounting standards and auditing standards, using international standards for statutory accounts would be inappropriate.

5.3 However, the EC has issued a directive that from 2005, all companies listed in the EC should report their group accounts according to International Accounting Standards (IASs). This gives weight to an argument that UK auditors should use International Standards on Auditing (ISAs).

5.4 International and UK standards are similar, as the UK's APB pays great attention to International Standards when issuing SASs. The APB and the IAASB are working on a convergence project with regard to auditing standards. There are some matters in which the UK hopes ISAs can be improved to bring them up to UK standard.

JUNE 2005 CANDIDATES

The APB has announced its intention to adopt international standards in the UK from 2005. These are being exposed in the UK first to ensure that all UK matters are considered. The ISAs **will not be examinable in December 2004.** However, the adopted standards could well be **examinable in June 2005**. June 2005 candidates should use a later edition of the Study Text, to be published in September 2004, if required.

Chapter roundup

- The Companies Act requires the majority of companies to have an audit. Some small companies and dormant companies are exempt from the requirement.
- Auditors must hold an **appropriate qualification** and to be a member of a **recognised supervisory body.**
- A person is **ineligible** to act as auditor if he is an **employee** or officer or has various other close connections with the company.
- Recognised supervisory bodies must follow a number of procedures to ensure their members are **fit** and **proper** and **competent** and that audit work is conducted **properly.**
- Legislation affecting auditors is introduced by the government on its own initiative or in response to European Commission **directives.**
- Details concerning the appointment and removal of auditors, and their rights and duties, can be found in the Companies Acts.
- Auditors in the UK are regulated by the Financial Reporting Council.
- The Auditing Practices Board issues:
    - SASs
    - Practice Notes
    - Bulletins
- SASs contain **basic principles** and **procedures** with which auditors must comply as well as other material designed to help auditors.
- **Accounting standards** are set by the **Accounting Standards Board** and have a direct impact on the accounts on which auditors are reporting.
- The Auditing Practices Board takes account of standards set by the **International Audit and Assurance Standards Board** when setting auditing standards and contributes to the production of new ISAs.

Quick quiz

1 People can be ineligible to be company auditors under

- The Companies Act 1985
- The requirements of their RSB

Using the reasons given, fill in the table below.

Reasons

(a) Officer or employee of the company
(b) Creditor of the company
(c) Not a member of an RSB
(d) A partner of someone in (a)
(e) A close relative of an officer of the company
(f) Does not hold a recognised qualification

Ineligible under law	**Ineligible under RSB rules**

2 Match the APB document to its status.

Statements of Auditing Standards - bold script	PERSUASIVE
Statement of Auditing Standards - other materials	PERSUASIVE
Practice notes	EXPLANATORY
Bulletins	PRESCRIPTIVE

3 (a) A person does not have to satisfy membership criteria to become a member of a Recognised Supervisory Body

True ☐

False ☐

(b) Auditing is regulated by the government in the UK.

True ☐

False ☐

(c) The Auditing Practices Board issues auditing standards which auditors are require to follow.

True ☐

False ☐

4 Which of the following features should the Joint Monitoring Unit not expect to find when visiting audit firms?

(a) Properly structured audit approach
(b) Quality control procedures
(c) Peer reviews
(d) Charging of unsubstantiated fees

Answers to quick quiz

1

Ineligible under law	Ineligible under RSB rules
(a) Officer/employee	(a) Officer/employee
(c) Not a member of an RSB	(b) Creditor
(d) A partner of someone in (a)	(d) A partner of someone in (a)
(f) No appropriate qualification	(e) Close relative of officer

2

Statement of Accounting Standards - bold script	PRESCRIPTIVE
Statement of Auditing Standards - other materials	EXPLANATORY
Practice notes	PERSUASIVE
Bulletins	PERSUASIVE

3 (a) False. All RSBs have stringent membership requirements.
(b) False. It is regulated by RSBs and the FRC.
(c) True. Auditors face discipline by their RSB if they do not.

4 (d)

Now try the question below from the Exam Question Bank

Number	Level	Marks	Time
2	Introductory	n/a	30 mins

Chapter 3

INTERNAL AUDIT AND REGULATION

Topic list		Syllabus reference	Study guide
1	Internal audit	2	3
2	Risk management and organisational control	2	4
3	Internal audit assignments	2	5
4	Operational internal audit assignments	2	6
5	Regulation	1	3
6	Outsourcing the internal audit function	2	3

Introduction

Internal auditing is **different from external auditing**, although the **techniques used** for many of the assignments internal audit will are carry out are very **similar** to those which will be outlined in detail in Parts B, C and D of this Study Text.

Internal audit is **established by management** to **assist in corporate governance** by assessing internal controls and helping in risk management. It can be a department of employees, or, as discussed in Section 6, can be **outsourced** to expert service providers.

The **ethical requirements** of internal auditors are different from those of external auditors due to the nature of the function. This will be discussed in Chapter 4.

Various **assurance assignments** which may be undertaken by internal auditors, and their role with regard to **fraud**, are outlined in Sections 3 and 4. While the techniques used may be similar to external auditors, the **focus and reasons** behind the audit may **differ**.

There are no statutory requirements in relation to internal audit. Reporting will be discussed in detail in Part E of this Study Text.

Internal review is an important part of the syllabus, and there was a complete question on internal audit in the pilot paper (in the exam question bank) and the ethics question had a section on internal auditors. The role of internal audit was explored in the December 2001 paper, particularly with regard to fraud. In the 2002 papers, risk management was focused on.

1 INTERNAL AUDIT 12/01, 6/02, 12/02

1.1 The following definition of internal audit was given in Chapter 1, for comparison with other forms of assurance service and providers.

KEY TERM

Internal audit is an appraisal or monitoring activity established by management and directors, for the review of the accounting and internal control systems as a service to the entity. It functions by, amongst other things, examining, evaluating and reporting to management and the directors on the adequacy and effectiveness of components of the accounting and internal control systems.

1.2 Internal audit is generally a feature of large companies. It is a function, provided either by employees of the entity or sourced from an external organisation, which assists management in **achieving corporate objectives.**

1.3 If internal audit exists to assist management in achieving corporate objectives, it is important to ask '**what are corporate objectives**?' Obviously, these will vary from company to company, and will be found, for example, in companies' mission statements and strategic plans.

1.4 However, some corporate objectives will not vary so much between companies, and are linked to a key corporate issue we have already discussed at length, the issue being **good corporate governance**.

1.5 The codes of corporate governance that we have already looked at highlight the need for businesses to maintain **good systems of internal control** to manage the risks the company faces. **Internal audit** can play a **key role in assessing and monitoring** internal control policies and procedures.

1.6 The Combined Code highlights the importance of internal audit by stipulating that directors of companies that do not have an internal audit department should re-consider the need for one annually.

Distinction between internal and external audit

1.7 The best way to see the difference between internal and external audit is to revise a key term.

KEY TERM

An **external audit** is an exercise whose objective is to enable auditors to express an opinion whether the financial statements give a true and fair view (or equivalent) of the entity's affairs are the period end and of its profit and loss for the period then ended and have been properly prepared in accordance with the applicable reporting framework.

1.8 Contrast the definition of external audit with the definition of internal audit above. The **external audit** is **focused on** a very small item, the **financial statements**, whereas the **internal audit is focused on the operations of the entire business**.

1.9 The following table **highlights the differences** between internal and external audit.

	Internal audit	External audit
Reason	Internal audit is an activity designed to **add value** and improve an **organisation's operations**.	An exercise to enable auditors to **express an opinion on the financial statements**.
Reporting to	Internal audit report to the **board of directors**, or other people charged with governance, such as the audit committee.	The external auditors report to the **shareholders**, or members, of a company on the stewardship of the directors.
Relating to	As demonstrated in the reason for their existence, internal audit's work relates to the **operations of the organisation**.	External audit's work relates to the **financial statements**. They are concerned with the financial records that underlie these.
Relationship with the company	Internal auditors are very often **employees of the organisation**, although sometimes the internal audit function is outsourced.	External auditors are **independent of the company and its management**. They are appointed by the shareholders.

1.10 The table shows that although some of the procedures that internal audit undertake are very similar to those undertaken by the external auditors, **the whole basis and reasoning of their work is fundamentally different.**

2 RISK MANAGEMENT AND ORGANISATIONAL CONTROL

2.1 The Turnbull guidelines refer to risk. All companies face risks arising from their activities. This risk is known as business risk.

KEY TERM

Business risk is the risk inherent to the company in its operations. It is risks at all levels of the business.

2.2 Business risk is described as consisting of three types of risk:

- **Operational risk** (for example, the risk that suppliers won't supply products when needed, or that the workforce will strike)
- **Financial risk** (for example, that exchange rate fluctuations will cause a substantial cost on imported stock or that interest rates will rise and make the company's loans too expensive to maintain)
- **Compliance risk** (for example, that the company might unwittingly break the law and be fined, or a listed company not comply with the Combined Code and be boycotted by institutional investors)

2.3 Business risk cannot be eliminated, but it must be **managed** by the company.

2.4 Risks to the business can exist on an individual department and individual level and also on a higher, strategic level. Employees at all levels should be involved in identifying risks.

2.5 Depending on the risk identified, company policy may be set at a department or at Board level. Broadly speaking, there are four potential responses a company can take to any given risk:

- Accept risk (ie, live with it – only acceptable if it is a low risk)
- Reduce risk (by instituting a system of internal control as protection)
- Avoid risk (by not engaging in that activity or not accepting a contract)
- Transfer risk (by taking out insurance)

Question: Risk management

For the following two departments, think of (a) a risk that the company might face and (b) what policy they might adopt in respect of it.

(i) Purchasing department
(ii) Human resources department

Answer

Purchasing department

A key risk is the risk that suppliers will not deliver goods when the company needs them in order to be able to produce goods on time for its customers.

The company can reduce this risk by setting up a system of internal control in respect of contracting with suppliers and ensuring that it does not contract with suppliers unless they have certain quality standards in place.

Human resources department

A key risk is the risk that the HR will recruit staff who are not capable of carrying out their roles in the organisation.

The company can reduce this risk by setting up a system of internal control so that no one is employed until they have provided evidence of their qualifications and references from previous employers.

2.6 Designing and operating internal control systems is a key part of a company's risk management. This will often be done by employees in their various departments, although sometimes (particularly in the case of specialised computer systems) the company will hire external expertise to design systems.

The role of internal audit

2.7 The internal audit department has a two-fold role in relation to risk management.

- Monitoring the company's overall risk management policy and ensuring it operates effectively.
- Monitoring the strategies implemented to ensure that they continue to operate effectively.

2.8 Going back to the diagram in Paragraph 2.3, this can be shown as:

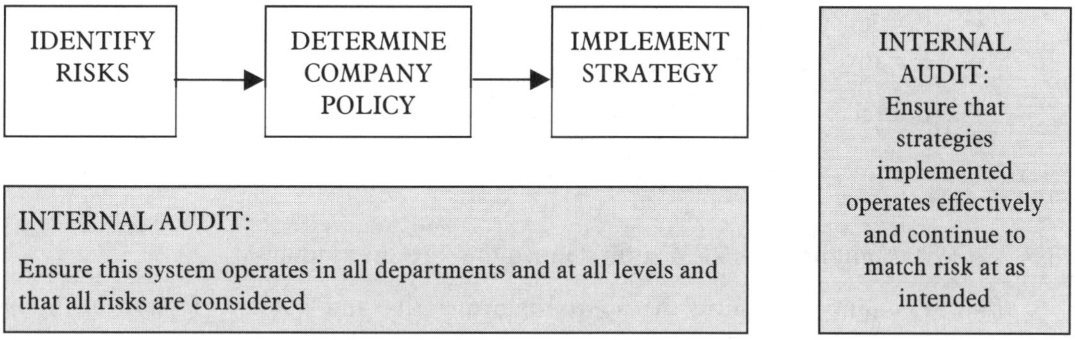

2.9 As a significant risk management policy in companies is to implement internal controls to reduce them, internal audit have a key role in assessing systems and testing controls.

POINT TO NOTE

Internal audit's work on operational systems and controls will be looked at in more detail later in this chapter and also in Chapter 11.

2.10 Internal audit may assist in the development of systems. However, their key role will be in **monitoring the overall process** and in **providing assurance** that the **systems** which the departments have designed **meet objectives** and **operate effectively**.

2.11 It is important that the internal audit department retain their **objectivity** towards these aspects of their role, which is another reason why internal audit would generally not be involved in the assessment of risks and the design of the system.

3 INTERNAL AUDIT ASSIGNMENTS

3.1 In the next two sections we will consider a number of the detailed assignments which an internal auditor could get involved in.

Exam focus point

You should read through these two sections now to learn **what an internal auditor does** and to **reinforce the difference between an internal audit and the statutory (external) audit** introduced in Chapter 2. However, don't worry too much about the mechanics of **how** they test the following things – you are going to be introduced to the techniques of auditing in the next few parts of this Text.

Value for money

3.2 EXAMPLE

A good example of value for money is a bottle of Fairy Liquid. If we believe the advertising, Fairy is good 'valuc for moncy' bccausc it washes half as many plates again as any other washing up liquid. Bottle for bottle it may be more expensive, but plate for plate it is cheaper. Not only this but Fairy gets plates 'squeaky' clean. To summarise, Fairy gives us VFM because it exhibits the following characteristics.

- Economy (more clean plates per pound)
- Efficiency (more clean plates per squirt)
- Effectiveness (plates as clean as they should be)

These are the three Es of VFM.

The three Es

3.3 A 1990 Audit brief on VFM audit defined the three Es as follows.

(a) **Economy**: attaining the appropriate quantity and quality of physical, human and financial resources (**inputs**) at lowest cost. An activity would not be economic, if, for example, there was over-staffing or failure to purchase materials of requisite quality at the lowest available price.

(b) **Efficiency**: this is the relationship between goods or services produced (**outputs**) and the resources used to produce them. An efficient operation produces the maximum output for any given set of resource inputs; or it has minimum inputs for any given quantity and quality of product or service provided.

(c) **Effectiveness**: this is concerned with how well an activity is achieving its policy objectives or other intended effects.

3.4 The internal auditors will **evaluate these three factors** for any given business system or operation in the company. Value for money can often only be judged by **comparison**. In searching for value for money, present methods of operation and uses of resources must be **compared with alternatives.**

3.5 Economy, efficiency and effectiveness can be studied and measured with reference to the following.

Inputs	Economy
Inputs means money or resources - the labour, materials, time and so on consumed, and their cost. For example, a VFM audit into state secondary education would look at the efficiency and economy of the use of resources for education (the use of schoolteachers, school buildings, equipment, cash) and whether the resources are being used for their purpose: what is the pupil/teacher ratio and are trained teachers being fully used to teach the subjects they have been trained for?	Economy is concerned with the cost of inputs, and it is achieved by obtaining those inputs at the lowest acceptable cost. Economy does not mean straightforward cost-cutting, because resources must be acquired which are of a suitable **quality** to provide the service to the desired standard. Cost-cutting should not sacrifice quality to the extent that service standards fall to an unacceptable level. Economising by buying poor quality materials, labour or equipment is a 'false economy'.

Outputs	Efficiency
Outputs mean the results of an activity, measurable as the services actually produced, and the quality of the services. In the case of a VFM audit of secondary education, outputs would be measured as the number of pupils taught and the number of subjects taught per pupil; how many examination papers are taken and what is the pass rate.	Efficiency means the following. (a) Maximising output for a given input, for example maximising the number of transactions handled per employee or per £1 spent (b) Achieving the minimum input for a given output
Impacts	**Effectiveness**
Impacts are the effect that the outputs of an activity or programme have in terms of achieving policy objectives. Policy objectives might be to provide a minimum level of education to all children up to the age of 16, and to make education relevant for the children's future jobs and careers. This might be measured by the ratio of jobs vacant to unemployed school leavers.	Effectiveness means ensuring that the outputs of a service or programme have the desired impacts; in other words, finding out whether they succeed in achieving objectives, and if so, to what extent. In a profit-making organisation, objectives can be expressed financially in terms of target profit or return. In NFP (not for profit) organisations, effectiveness cannot be measured this way, because the organisation has non-financial objectives. The effectiveness of performance in NFP organisations could be measured in terms of whether targeted non-financial objectives have been achieved.

Selecting areas for investigation

3.6 Value for money checklists can be used. The following list identifies areas of an organisation, process or activity where there might be scope for significant value for money improvements. Each of these should be reviewed within individual organisations, with a view to assessing its economy, efficiency and effectiveness.

- Service delivery (the actual provision of a public service)
- Management process
- Environment

3.7 An alternative approach is to look at areas of spending. A value for money assessment of economy, efficiency, and effectiveness would look at whether:

- Too much money is being spent on certain items or activities, to achieve the targets or objectives of the overall operation.
- Money is being spent to no purpose, because the spending is not helping to achieve objectives.
- Changes could be made to improve performance.

3.8 An illustrative list is shown below of the sort of spending areas that might be looked at, and the aspects of spending where value for money might be improved.

- Employee expenses
- Premises expenses
- Supplies and services
- Establishment expenses
- Capital expenditure

Problems with VFM auditing	
Measuring outputs	For example, the outputs of a fire brigade can be measured by the number of call-outs, but it is not satisfactory to compare a call-out to individuals stuck in a lift with a call-out to a small house fire or a major industrial fire or a road accident etc.
Defining objectives	In not for profit organisations the quality of the service provided will be a significant feature of their service. For example, a local authority has, amongst its various different objectives, the objective of providing a rubbish collection service. The effectiveness of this service can only be judged by establishing what standard or quality of service is required.
Sacrifice of quality	Economy and efficiency can be achieved by sacrificing quality. Neither outputs nor impacts are necessarily measured in terms of quality. For example, the cost of teaching can be reduced by increasing the pupil:teacher ratio in schools, but it is difficult to judge the consequences of such a change on teaching standards and quality.
Measuring effectiveness	For example, the effectiveness of the health service could be said to have improved if hospitals have greater success in treating various illnesses and other conditions, or if the life expectancy of the population has increased, but a consequence of these changes will be overcrowded hospitals and longer medical waiting lists.
Overemphasis in cost control	There can be an **emphasis** with VFM audits on **costs and cost control** rather than on achieving more benefits and value, so that management might be pressurised into 'short term' decisions, such as abandoning capital expenditure plans which would create future benefits in order to keep current spending levels within limits.
Measuring efficiency	In profit-making organisations, the efficiency of the organisation as a whole can be measured in terms of return on capital employed. Individual profit centres or operating units within the organisation can also have efficiency measured by relating the quantity of output produced, which has a **market value** and therefore a quantifiable financial value, to the inputs (and their cost) required to make the output. In NFP organisations, output does not usually have a market value, and it is therefore more difficult to measure efficiency. This difficulty is compounded by the fact that, since NFP organisations often have many different activities or operations, it is difficult to compare the efficiency of one operation with the efficiency of another. For example, with the police force, it might be difficult to compare the efficiency of a serious crimes squad with the efficiency of the traffic police.

Best value

3.9 'Best value' is a new performance framework introduced into local authorities by the government. They are required to publish annual best value performance plans and review all of their functions over a five year period.

3.10 As part of 'Best value' authorities are required to strive for continuous improvement by implementing the '4 Cs':

- **Challenge.** How and why is a service provided?
- **Compare.** Make comparisons with other local authorities and the private sector.
- **Consult.** Talk to local taxpayers and services users and the wider business community in setting performance targets.
- **Compete.** Embrace fair competition as a means of securing efficient and effective services.

3.11 The **external auditors** will report on the annual best value performance plan.

Internal auditors and best value

3.12 One of internal audit's **standard roles** in a company is to **provide assurance that internal control systems are adequate to promote the effective use of resources and that risks are being managed properly**.

3.13 In relation to best value, **this role can be extended** to ensure that the authority has arrangements in place to achieve best value, that the risks and impacts of best value are incorporated into normal audit testing and that the authority keeps abreast of best value developments.

3.14 As best value depends on assessing current services and setting strategies for development, **internal audit can take part in the 'position audit'**, as they should have a good understanding of how services are currently organised and relate to each other.

3.15 As assurance providers, they key part internal audit will play is in **giving management assurance that their objectives and strategies in relation to best value are being met.**

Information technology

3.16 An information technology audit is a **test of control in a specific area of the business**, the computer systems.

3.17 Increasingly in modern business, computers are vital to the functioning of the business, and therefore the controls over them are some of the most important in the business.

3.18 It is **likely to be necessary to have an IT specialist in the internal audit team** to undertake an audit of the controls, as some of them will be programmed into the computer system.

3.19 The diagram below shows the various areas of IT in the business which might be subject to a test of controls by the auditors.

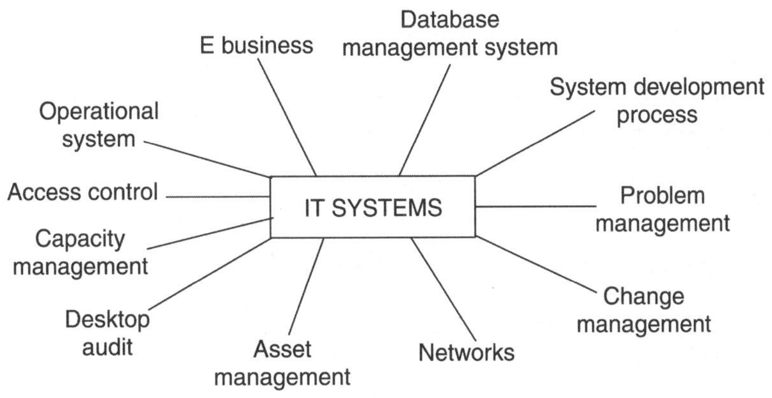

Financial

3.20 The financial audit is internal audit's **traditional role,** which involved reviewing all the available evidence (usually the company's records) to substantiate information in management and financial reporting.

3.21 This role in many ways echoed the role of the external auditor, and was not a role in which the internal auditors could add any particular value to the business. **Increasingly, it is a minor part of the function of internal audit.**

Fraud 12/01

3.22 Fraud is a **key business risk**. It is the responsibility of the directors to prevent and detect fraud. As the **internal auditor has a role in risk management** he is involved in the process of managing the risk of fraud.

3.23 The internal auditor can help to **prevent** fraud by their work **assessing the adequacy and effectiveness of control systems** and **detect** fraud by **being mindful** when carrying out their work and **reporting any suspicions.**

3.24 The very **existence of an internal audit** department may act as a **deterrent** to fraud. The internal auditors might also be called upon to undertake special projects to investigate a suspected fraud.

4 OPERATIONAL INTERNAL AUDIT ASSIGNMENTS 12/03

KEY TERM

Operational audits are audits of the operational processes of the organisation. They are also known as management or efficiency audits. Their prime objective is the monitoring of management's performance, ensuring company policy is adhered to.

Approaching operational internal audit assignments

4.1 There are two aspects of an operational assignment:

- Ensure policies are adequate
- Ensure policies work effectively

Adequacy

4.2 The internal auditor will have to review the policies of a particular department by:

- Reading them
- Discussion with members of the department

4.3 Then the auditor will have to assess whether the policies are adequate, and possibly advise the board of improvements which could be made.

Effectiveness

4.4 The auditor will then have to examine the effectiveness of the controls by:

- Observing them in operation
- Testing them

4.5 This will be done on similar lines to the testing of controls to be discussed in Section C, where the control objectives for these areas will be set out.

POINT TO NOTE

The review of a company's risk management system discussed in Section 2 of this Chapter is an example of an operational audit. Some others are discussed below.

Procurement

KEY TERM

Procurement is the process of **purchasing** for the business.

4.6 A procurement audit will therefore concentrate on the **systems of the purchasing department**(s).

4.7 The internal auditor will be checking that the system achieves key objectives and that it operates according to company guidelines.

POINT TO NOTE

The control objectives and systems will be similar to those to be discussed in Chapter 10, where we look at the purchases and expenses system. However, internal audit will also be concerned with considerations beyond the scope of the external auditor, which we shall consider in Chapter 11.

Marketing

KEY TERM

Marketing is the **process of assessing and enhancing demand for the company's products.**

4.8 Marketing and its link with sales is very important for the business, and therefore, the internal auditor but as the **associated systems do not directly impact on the financial statements**, they do not usually concern the external auditor.

4.9 It is important for the internal auditor to review the marketing processes to ensure:

- The process is **managed efficiently**
- **Information is freely available** to manager demand
- **Risks** are being **managed** correctly.

4.10 An audit may be especially critical for a marketing department which may be complex with several different teams, for example:

- Research
- Advertising
- Promotions
- After sales

4.11 It is vital to ensure that information is passed properly within the department, and activities are streamlined.

Treasury

KEY TERM

Treasury is a function within the finance department of a business. It **manages the funds of a business.**

4.12 It is vital to a business that funds are managed so that cash is available when required.

4.13 There are risks associated with treasury, in terms of interest rate risk and foreign currency risk, and the auditor must ensure that the **risk is managed in accordance with company procedures**.

4.14 As with marketing audits, it is vital to ensure that **information is available** to the treasury department, so that they can **ensure funds are available when required.**

Human resources

KEY TERM

The **human resources** department on one hand **procures a human resource** (employee) for the operation of the business and on the other **supports those employees in developing the organisation.**

4.15 It is important to ensure that the processes ensure that people are available to work as the business requires them and that the overall development of the business is planned and controlled.

4.16 Again, **ensuring company policies are maintained and information is freely available are key factors for internal audit to assess.**

POINT TO NOTE

All these cycles are looked at in more detail in Chapter 11.

Question: Internal control procedures

The growing recognition by management of the benefits of good internal control, and the complexities of an adequate system of internal control have led to the development of internal auditing as a form of control over all other internal controls. The emergence of the internal auditors as experts in internal control is the result of an evolutionary process similar in many ways to the evolution of independent auditing.

Required

(a) Explain why the internal and independent auditors' review of internal control procedures differ in purpose.

(b) Explain the reasons why internal auditors should or should not report their findings on internal control to the following selection of company officials:

(i) The board of directors
(ii) The chief accountant

Answer

(a) The internal auditors review and test the system of internal control and report to management in order to improve the information received by managers and to help in their task of running the company. The internal auditors will recommend changes to the system to make sure that the management receives objective information which is efficiently produced. The internal auditors will also have a duty to search for and discover fraud.

The external auditors review the system of internal control in order to determine the extent of the substantive work required on the year end accounts. The external auditors report to the shareholders rather than the managers or directors.

External auditors usually however issue a letter of weakness to the managers, laying out any areas of weakness and recommendations for improvement in the system of internal control. The external auditors report on the truth and fairness of the financial statements, not directly on the system of internal control. The auditors do not have a specific duty to detect fraud, although they should plan their audit procedures so as to detect any material misstatement in the accounts on which they give an opinion.

(b) (i) *Board of directors*

A high level of independence is achieved by the internal auditors if they report directly to the Board. There may be problems with this approach.

(1) The members of the Board may not understand all the implications of the internal audit reports when accounting or technical information is required.

(2) The Board may not have enough time to spend considering the reports in sufficient depth. Important recommendations might therefore remain unimplemented.

A way around these problems might be to delegate the review of internal audit reports to an audit committee, which would act as a kind of sub-committee to the main board. The audit committee might be made up largely of non-executive directors who have more time and more independence from the day-to-day running of the company.

(ii) *Chief accountant*

It would be inappropriate for internal audit to report to the chief accountant, who is largely in charge of running the system of internal control. It may be feasible for him or her to receive the report as well as the Board. Otherwise, the internal audit function cannot be effectively independent as the chief accountant could suppress unfavourable reports or could just not act on the recommendations of such reports.

5 REGULATION

5.1 Internal auditing is not regulated in the same ways that statutory auditing is. There are **no legal requirements** associated with becoming an internal auditor.

5.2 The **scope** and **nature** of **internal audit's work** is more likely to be set by **company policy** than by any external guidelines.

5.3 The Auditing Practices Board does no issue detailed auditing standards in relation to internal audit work. **Where** they are **applicable,** the standards set out in Auditing Standards are likely to be **good practice,** but they are not prescriptive in the same ways that they are for external auditors.

Institute of Internal Auditors

5.4 In contrast to external auditors, **internal auditors are not required to be members of a professional body** such as ACCA. However, this does not mean they cannot be, and many are. There is also a global Institute of Internal Auditors (the IIA) which internal auditors **may** also become members of. Some people are members of both ACCA and IIA.

5.5 The IIA has over 6,000 members in the UK and Ireland and it is dedicated to representing and promoting the interests of internal auditors.

5.6 It issued 'Standards for the Professional Practice of Internal Auditing'. These are not examinable, so are not detailed in this Study Text, but you should be aware of the them as being another Code of Good Practice that internal auditors can follow, providing a framework for providing a wide range of internal audit services.

6 OUTSOURCING THE INTERNAL AUDIT FUNCTION 12/01

6.1 While, as we have just discussed, the scope of the internal auditor's work is different to that of the external auditor, there are many features that can link them.

6.2 The key linking factor is that the **techniques** which are used to carry out audits are the same for internal and external auditors.

6.3 It can be expensive to maintain an internal audit function consisting of employees. The Turnbull guidelines state that the directors should consider the need for them annually. However, the directors may conclude that the cost is prohibitive.

6.4 It is possible that the monitoring and review required by a certain company could be done in a small amount of time and full-time employees cannot be justified.

6.5 It is possible that a number of internal audit staff are required, but the cost of recruitment is prohibitive, or the directors are aware that the need for internal audit is only short-term.

6.6 In such circumstances, it is possible to **outsource the internal audit function**, that is, purchase the service from outside.

6.7 Therefore, many of the **larger accountancy firms offer internal audit services**. It is possible that the same firm might offer one client both internal and external audit services. In such circumstances the firm would have to be aware of the independence issues this would raise for the external audit team.

Question: Independence

Paragraph 6.7 refers to the independence issues which would arise through the audit firm offering both internal and external audit services to the same client.

(a) What do you think are the independence issues?
(b) Why should the issues affect the external audit team rather than the internal audit team?

Answer

(a) External auditors are employed to give an assurance to the members of a company about the stewardship of the directors and the management of that entity. They are **independent verifiers**. If the firm provides internal audit services to the entity, two issues arise:

(i) Internal auditors report to the director so there is a **link between the firm and the directors** which is a block to independence.

(ii) The firm provides 'other services' to an external audit client, and the partners must consider whether this affects their objectivity in relation to the audit, and renders them no longer impartial

The specific guidance about auditor independence will be considered in more detail in Chapter 4.

(b) The issues arise for the external audit team as independence is a key ethical issue for external auditors. **As internal auditors provide a service to the directors,** by whom they are employed, the issue of independence is a more tricky issue. It relates more to 'independence in the mind'. Internal auditors are not required to be 'seen to be independent' in the same way that external auditors are.

Ethical issues for internal auditors are also discussed in Chapter 4.

Advantages of outsourcing

6.8 The advantage of outsourcing internal audits is that outsourcing can overcome all the problems mentioned above.

- Staff need to be recruited, as the **service provider has good quality staff.**
- The service provider has specialist skill and can assess what management require them to do. As they are external to the operation, this will not cause operational problems.
- Outsourcing can provide an **immediate** internal audit department.
- The service contract can be for the **appropriate time scale** (a two week project, a month, etc)
- Because the **time scale is flexible**, a **team of staff** can be provided if required.
- The service provider could also provide less than at team, but, for example, could provide one member of staff on a full-time basis for a short period, as a **secondment.**

6.9 Outsourced internal audit services are provided by many audit firms, particularly the big five. This can range from a team of staff for a short term project, or a single staff member on a long term project.

6.10 However, the fact that internal audit services are typically provided by external auditors can raise problems as well:

- The company might wish to **use the same firm** for internal and external audit services, but this may lead to **complications for the external auditors.**
- The **cost** of sourcing the internal audit function might be high enough to make the directors choose not to have an internal audit function at all.

6.11 A key advantage of outsourcing internal audit is that **outsourcing can be used on a short term basis**, to:

- Provide immediate services
- Lay the basis of a permanent function, by setting policies and functions
- Prepare the directors for the implications of having an internal audit function
- Assist the directors in recruiting the permanent function.

Chapter roundup

- Internal audit is an appraisal or monitoring activity established by management and directors, for the review of the accounting and internal control systems as a service to the entity.
- It assists management in achieving corporate objectives, particularly, in achieving good corporate governance.
- Why many of the techniques internal and external auditors use are similar, the basis and reasoning of their work is different.
- Internal audit have two key roles to pay in relation to organisational risk management:
  - Ensuring the company's risk management system operates effectively
  - Ensuring that strategies implemented in respect of business risks operate effectively
- Internal audit can be involved in many different assignments as directed by management. Examples include:
  - Value for money
  - Best value
  - IT
  - Financial
- As part of their function, internal auditors have a role in preventing and detecting fraud.
- Internal audit traditionally undertake operational audits, examples of which include:
  - Procurement
  - Marketing
  - Treasury
  - HR
- When carrying out operational audits, internal auditors will
  - Assess adequacy of company policies
  - Assess their effectiveness in practice
- Internal audit is not regulated in the same ways as external auditing in the UK.
- Internal auditors may be members of bodies such as ACCA or IIA, or both. The IIA issue guidance for members to follow (this is not examinable).
- The APC (as it was then) issued guidance in the form of auditing guideline 308 '*Guidance for Internal Auditors*'
- Internal audit departments may consist of employees, or may be sourced from external service providers.
- Advantages of sourcing in internal audit include speed, cost, and a tailored answer to internal audit requirements.

Quick quiz

1 What is internal audit?

2 Complete the Turnbull Guidelines (which were given in Chapter 1)

TURNBULL GUIDELINES
Have a .... for the ....of effectiveness of ....
Review .... reports on ....
Consider .... and how they have been ....
Check the .... of .... to remedy weaknesses and incidents.
Consider the .... of ....
Conduct an .... of risks and the effectiveness of internal control.
Make a .... on this process in the ....

3 Name three key differences between internal and external audit.

1 ....

2 ....

3 ....

4 Link the value for money 'E' with its definition.

(a) Economy
(b) Efficiency
(c) Effectiveness

(i) The relationships between the goods and services produced (outputs) and the resources used to produce them.

(ii) The concern with how well an activity is achieving its policy objectives or other intended effects.

(iii) Attaining the appropriate quantity and quality of physical, human and financial resources (inputs) at lowest cost.

5 Name five areas of the computer system which might benefit from an IT audit.

1 ....

2 ....

3 ....

4 ....

5 ....

6 Internal auditors are not required to consider fraud.

True ☐

False ☐

7 Define the following areas of a business, which an internal auditor might conduct a review of:

(a) Procurement
(b) Marketing
(c) Treasury
(d) Human resources

8 It is possible to buy in an internal audit service from an external organisation.

True ☐

False ☐

Answers to quick quiz

1 **Internal audit** is an appraisal or monitoring activity established by management and directors, for the review of the accounting and internal control systems as a service to the entity.

2 defined process, review, internal control
regular, internal control
key risks, managed
adequacy actions taken
adequacy, monitoring
annual assessment
statement, annual report

3 1 External report to members, internal to directors
2 External report on financial statements, internal on systems, controls and risks
3 External are independent of the company, internal often employed by it

4 (a) (iii), (b) (i), (c) (ii)

5 See para 4.11

6 False

7 (a) The purchasing department

(b) The process which assesses and enhances demand for a product.

(c) Function (often within finance department) which manages funds.

(d) Department which procures a human resource and manages development of the organisation.

8 True

Now try the question below from the Exam Question Bank

Number	Level	Marks	Time
3	Exam	20	36 mins

Chapter 4

PROFESSIONAL CODES OF ETHICS AND BEHAVIOUR

Introduction

In Chapter 2 we looked at some of the regulation surrounding the auditor. Here we look at the (sometimes more stringent) **requirements of the RSBs**, **specifically the ethical guidance from ACCA**, the association you are studying to join. **Internal auditors** are subject to the requirements of any professional body to which they belong. The only professional body specifically for internal auditors is the Institute of Internal Auditors. We will look briefly at their guidance.

The ethical matters covered in this chapter are **very important**. Ethical matters could arise in almost every type of exam question. You must be able to apply the ACCA's guidance on ethical matters to any given situation, but remember that **common sense** is usually a good guide.

We firstly examine what a client has the legal **right to demand** from their auditors under the terms of their **contract** with them. The most important qualities are that the auditors carry out their work with due **professional care**.

Auditors are also subject to **ethical requirements imposed by their professional bodies**. The principle of **independence**- that auditors must not only be independent but must be seen to be independent- is very important. In a number of cases whether a particular situation is a threat to independence is not clear-cut; is auditor independence compromised by providing services other than audit to an audit client, for example.

One area where client requirements may conflict with the requirement for auditors to act ethically is whether the auditor should keep the affairs of clients secret, or disclose them to others without obtaining the client's consent. We shall see that professional guidance tries to strike a balance between stressing the importance of keeping the affairs of clients **confidential**, and stating that in certain instances auditors should consider disclosing (or have to) client details to third parties.

Lastly we shall consider the position of the **internal auditor** with regard to professional ethics.

Questions about independence often involve discussion of topical, controversial issues, for example provision of services other than audit to audit clients. You should keep an eye open for articles in *Student Accountant* and financial press in these areas. Exam questions will generally require you to consider both sides of a controversial topic. The ethics question on the pilot paper examined independence and the practical issue of other services.

1 DUE CARE, SKILL AND COMPETENCE

ACCA's *Fundamental principles*

'Members should carry out their professional work with due skill, care, diligence and expedition and with proper regard for the technical and professional standards expected of them as members.'

1.1 All accountants (not just auditors) in public practice are obliged by law to provide services of appropriate quality. Unless an accountant and client have agreed otherwise, there is an implied duty of care that an accountant owes to a client under s 13 Supply of Goods and Services Act 1982. This relates to **all services** provided by an accountancy firm: external audit, internal audit, accounts, preparation work, tax work etc.

1.2 The professional guidance statement *Professional Liability* published in 1994 makes the following further points.

(a) The degree of skill and care will depend on the work: a higher degree will be required for work:

- Of a **specialised nature**
- Where negligence is likely to **cause substantial loss**

These particularly apply where the accountant represented himself as being experienced.

(b) The duty will not be absolute; opinions or advice will not give rise to claims just because they are proved wrong in the light of later events.

The auditors' duty of care

1.3 Thus auditors must employ **reasonable care** in all they do, in particular:

(a) Auditors must use **generally accepted auditing techniques** when seeking to satisfy themselves that the matters upon which they reports accurately reflect the true financial state of his client's business.

(b) If auditors come across any matter which puts them **upon enquiry** then they have a duty to investigate such a matter until they are able to resolve it to their own reasonable satisfaction. Auditors should not accept any explanation unless they have first carried out such investigations as will enable them properly to assess whether the explanation offered a reasonable one.

2 RULES OF PROFESSIONAL CONDUCT **Pilot paper**

2.1 There are a number of ethical issues which are of great importance in the client-auditor relationship. Why? Because, as we saw in Chapter 1 in the case of Glyn and Laine, it is important that the auditor is **impartial**, and independent of management, so that he can give an **objective** view. SAS 100 requires auditors to comply with the professional guidance of their RSB when carrying out audits.

2.2 The onus is always on the auditor not only to be ethical but also to be **seen** to be ethical. To this end, the Association publishes *Rules of Professional Conduct.* **All** members **and** students of the ACCA must adhere to these rules. Guidance is in the form of:

- Fundamental principles
- Specific guidance
- Explanatory notes

The Fundamental Principles	
Integrity	Members should behave with integrity in all professional, business and personal financial relationships. Integrity implies **not merely honesty but fair dealing and truthfulness.**
Objectivity	Members should strive for **objectivity** in all professional and business judgements. (Objectivity is the **state of mind** which has **regard to all considerations relevant** to the task in hand **but no other**, it presupposes **intellectual honesty.**)
Competence	Members should not accept or perform work which they are not **competent** to undertake **unless** they obtain such **advice and assistance** as will enable them competently to carry out the work.
Due skill and care	Members should carry out their professional work with **due skill, care, diligence** and **expedition** and with **proper regard** for the **technical** and **professional standards** expected of them as members.
Courtesy	Members should behave with **courtesy** and **consideration towards all** with whom they come into contact during the course of performing their work.

3 STATEMENT 1: INTEGRITY, OBJECTIVITY AND INDEPENDENCE

ACCA Statement

'A member's objectivity must be beyond question if he (or she) is to report as an auditor. That objectivity can only be assured if the member is, and is seen to be, independent.'

'The threat to independence may be reduced by the nature and extent of the precautions taken by the practice to guard against loss of objectivity.'

3.1 The statement points out that, although the rules refer specifically to company audits under the Companies Acts, 'the spirit of the guidance applies equally to other audit situations'. The rules are given as 'guidance' so that they are matters of judgement for the auditors rather than being hard and fast rules.

Exam focus point

You should note that legal independence is a set of relationships which are prohibited (see Chapter 2). Professional independence is however an **attitude of mind**; the detailed guidelines listed below are just guidelines and audit firms may feel justified in taking stricter measures than the guidelines suggest.

Why do independence and objectivity matter so much? 12/02

3.2 Independence and objectivity matter because of:

(a) The **expectations** of those directly affected, particularly the members of the company. The audit should be able to provide **objective** assurance that the directors can never provide on the accounts.

(b) The **public interest**. Companies are public entities, governed by rules requiring the disclosure of information.

3.3 Threats to independence and objectivity could arise for the following reasons.

The auditors' own **personal interest**. The auditors may fear, for example, the loss of fees.
When carrying out the audit, the auditors **review work** that their **own firm** has **done previously**, for example, preparing accounts or making a valuation.
If the auditors get involved in **disputes** concerning the client. They may end up **acting for or against** the **client**, which undermines the appearance of objectivity.
If the auditors are involved with the client for a long time, they may become **unduly sympathetic** towards directors and management, and thus too inclined to trust their unsupported word.
The auditors may be **intimidated** by a **dominant** or **aggressive atmosphere** at the clients.

3.4 What can the auditor do to preserve objectivity? The simple answer is to **withdraw from any engagement** where there is the **slightest threat** to objectivity. However there are disadvantages in this strict approach.

- Clients may lose an auditor who knows their business
- It denies clients the freedom to be advised by the accountant of their choice.

3.5 A better approach would be as follows

Step 1. **Consider** whether the **auditors' own objectivity** and the **general safeguards** operated in the professional environment are **sufficient** to offset the threat

Step 2. Consider whether **safeguards over and above** the general safeguards are required, for example specified partners or staff not working on an assignment.

However the ultimate option must always be **withdrawing** from an **engagement** or refusing to act.

4 THREATS TO INTEGRITY, OBJECTIVITY AND INDEPENDENCE

4.1 Section A of Statement 1 deals with **independence and the audit**. Most of the section is taken up by discussions of possible risk areas (that is, threats to independence) and **recommendations** about safeguards in respect of them.

Threats to independence

Undue dependence on an audit client

> **ACCA Statement**
>
> 'Objectivity may be threatened or appear to be threatened by undue dependence on any audit client or group of connected clients.'

4.2 The statement recommends that, in general, the recurring work paid by one client or group of connected clients should not exceed **15%** of the gross practice income. In the case of

listed and other **public interest** companies, the figure should be **10%** of the gross practice income.

Question: Undue dependence

You are the practice manager of the Liverpool office of a large, national firm of Chartered Certified Accountants. Revenue in the Liverpool office represents 18% of the national firm's income. The Liverpool office has two major clients, whose recurring fees constitute 30% and 41% of the office's annual income. This year, undertaking a special project for the latter client will take the total income from the client to the Liverpool office to 60% of the year's income.

Comment on any issues this raises with regard to the independence of the firm.

Answer

Tutor's note. There is **no model answer** to a question like this, as the matter is one of judgement. If you are faced with an issue such as this in the exam, the examiner will be interested in what matters you have considered, not just what answer you have come to. Of course, if you are asked to draw a conclusion you should do, based on the matters you have considered.

Matters to consider in relation to this situation include:

(1) ACCA's guidance: objectivity may be threatened or appear to be, by undue independence on any audit client. Recurring fees paid by one client should not exceed 15% of gross practice income. (10% for listed companies.)

(2) Despite high percentages for Liverpool office, percentages are less than 10% of the income of the whole practice.

(3) Does the practice operate nationally? (ie do partners share in a national 'pot' of profit?) Or, does each office run independently to its network? (If so, Liverpool's independence appears to be affected.)

(4) Do other offices undertake work for any branches of the clients, or any connected companies of the client? (If so, the fee percentages will be higher.)

(5) Do the Liverpool partners ensure that partners from other offices periodically review audit files and opinions in relation to these clients?

(6) Does the Liverpool office review the risk to its independence by these clients on a regular basis?

4.3 New practices may not be able to satisfy such criteria and extra care will be necessary in such circumstances to safeguard independence.

4.4 A review of the risk to independence should be instituted for all large fees, certainly 10% (public interest 5%) and greater of gross practice income.

4.5 The statement also suggests that **non-recurring fees might affect independence** if they are large enough.

Overdue fees

ACCA Statement

'The existence of significant overdue fees from an audit client or group of associated clients can be a threat or appear to be a threat to objectivity akin to that of a loan.'

4.6 Financial self-interest is obviously involved here. Firms must therefore ensure that overdue fees, along with fees from current work, could not be construed as a loan.

Actual or threatened litigation

ACCA Statement

'A firm's objectivity may be threatened or appear to be threatened when it is involved in, or even threatened with litigation in relation to a client.'

4.7 Litigation of certain sorts will represent a 'breakdown of the relationship of trust' between auditor and client. This would impair the independence of the auditor or cause the directors of the client to become unwilling to disclose information to the auditor. A dispute which is only in relation to audit fees may not cause such problems.

4.8 The point at which the firm should cease to act as auditors will vary from case to case. Auditors should be wary whenever it appears that litigation might occur.

Associated firms/influences outside the practice

ACCA Statement

'A firm's objectivity may be threatened or appear to be threatened as a result of pressures arising from associated practices or organisations, or from other external sources, such as bankers, solicitors, government or those introducing business.'

4.9 The problems of independence in relation to large and prestigious clients may arise in connection with the activities of an associated practice or organisation of the client. Factors to be considered by the firm include the closeness of the association and the strength of the associate's interest in the firm's retaining the client.

Family and other personal relationships

ACCA Statement

'A member's objectivity may be threatened or appear to be threatened as a consequence of a family or other close personal or business relationship.'

4.10 Problems arise if an officer or senior employee of an audit client is **closely connected** with the partner or senior staff member responsible for the conduct of the audit.

KEY TERM

The following people will normally be regarded as **closely connected** with a person.

(a) His (or her) spouse or cohabitee other than a spouse from whom the person is separated, or, in the case of a shareholding, a spouse or cohabitee of whose financial affairs the person has been denied knowledge

(b) His (or her) minor children, including stepchildren

(c) A company in which he or she has a 20 per cent interest or more

The following persons will normally be regarded as being closely connected with a

- A partner or, in the case of a corporate practice, a director or shareholder
- A person closely connected with the above
- An employee of the practice

Note. The categories in these paragraphs are not exhaustive of the relationships which might threaten independence.

4.11 It also includes any relative to whom regular financial assistance is given or who is indebted to the staff member or partner.

4.12 Proximity needs to be taken into account, including whether the partner or staff member is involved in the audit and the position of the person in the client's office (the more junior, the less risk).

4.13 Problems can also arise if partners or staff have been involved on the audit for too long, as illustrated by the Robert Maxwell affair.

Case example

The Joint Disciplinary Scheme report on the case suggested that the senior partner, who had been involved with Maxwell for many years, placed excessive trust in Maxwell and influenced the attitude of other Coopers and Lybrand personnel.

4.14 S 27 CA 1989 prevents an officer or employee of a company (or their partner) from becoming an auditor of that company. ACCA rules extend this prohibition for its members to **two years** after ceasing to be an officer or employee of the company.

Beneficial interests in shares and other investments and trusts

ACCA Statements

'A member's objectivity may be threatened or appear to be threatened where he (or she) holds a beneficial interest in the shares or other forms of investment in a company upon which the practice reports.'

'The objectivity of a practice may be threatened or appear to be threatened where a partner or a person closely connected with the partner has a beneficial interest in a trust having a shareholding in an audit client company.'

'A member's objectivity may be threatened or appear to be threatened by trustee shareholdings and other trustee investments.'

'Where a partner or staff member holds shares in any capacity in a company which is an audit client of the practice they should not be voted at any general meeting of the company in relation to the appointment, removal or remuneration of auditors.'

4.15 Staff and partners should not have shareholdings in client businesses. (This includes beneficial shareholdings held by a spouse or minor child.)

(a) If shares are acquired involuntarily (by marriage or inheritance) then they should be disposed of at the earliest opportunity.

(b) Where an Act of Parliament or the articles of the client company require the auditor to be a shareholder, then the auditor should hold only the minimum number of shares and the holding should be disclosed in the accounts of the client company.

4.16 Beneficial holdings in unit trusts and so on are not precluded, nor are modest personal savings in a client building society or other similar institution.

4.17 Where a trust, in which a partner or a person closely connected with a partner is a beneficiary, holds or acquires shares in a company audited by the practice where:

(a) The partner is and wishes to remain a trustee; the shareholding should be regarded as equivalent to a beneficial shareholding, and the practice should cease to report.

(b) The partner is not a trustee; he should cease personally to report as soon as he becomes aware of the shareholding.

4.18 Where an employee has an interest in a trust having a shareholding in an audit client, that employee should not be employed on the audit of that client.

4.19 The practice should not have a public company as an audit client if a partner (or the spouse of a partner) is a trustee of a trust holding shares in that company and the holding is in excess of **10% of**:

- The **issued share capital** of the company, or
- The **total assets comprised** in the trust

4.20 A trust holding of 10% or more (as described above) of **any** company will indicate problems with independence.

Loans

ACCA Statement

'Objectivity may be threatened or appear to be threatened by a loan to or from an audit client.'

4.21 No loans or guarantees should be undertaken unless they are with client financial institutions in the normal course of business (but the loan cannot be applied for partnership capital and the partner concerned must not be the engagement partner).

Goods and services/hospitality

ACCA Statement

'Objectivity may be threatened or appear to be threatened by acceptance of goods, services or hospitality from an audit client.'

Acceptance on normal commercial terms, or with only a modest benefit, is acceptable.

Safeguards against loss of integrity and objectivity

4.22 There are a number of factors in the professional environment which should help maintain members' independence. **Training** is important, as is the support given by the ACCA in the form of the Code of Ethics and advice in specific instances.

4.23 Independence is also very carefully considered by the **Joint Monitoring Unit**, and sanctions may be imposed against firms or individuals who breach guidance.

4.24 The situation within firms is also important. Firms should regard their **reputation** for independence as crucial, and there should be strong internal pressures towards independence.

4.25 Specific measures should also be introduced by firms. Ethical issues should be considered as part of **training** and **quality control procedures**. Firms should carefully consider whether **clients** should be **accepted** (this is discussed further in Chapter 5), and before each audit starts, whether there are any **threats to independence**. **Review** and **consultation** procedures are also important.

ACCA Statement

'Every audit firm should establish adequate review machinery, including an annual review, in order to satisfy itself that each engagement may properly be accepted or be continued having regard to the guidance given in this statement, and to identify situations where independence may be at risk and where the appropriate safeguards should be applied.'

4.26 Many proposals have been put forward to help safeguard the independence of auditors and these are discussed in the following paragraphs.

Rotation of auditor appointments

4.27 It has been argued that the long-term nature of the company audit engagement tends to create a loss of auditor independence, due to an increasing familiarity with the company's management and staff, which works against the shareholders' and the public's interest.

4.28 For this reason, it has been argued that there should be a rotation of the audit appointment every few years, preventing any unnecessary loss of independence which the present situation is thought to cause. This issue has been high on the international agenda in recent times.

4.29 However, rotation of auditors is not be very popular in practice, owing to:

(a) The disadvantages of **upsetting** the **client company** with continual changes of audit staff

(b) The **high costs** of **recurring first audits**

(c) The ability of auditors to retain a fresh approach to the audit by **rotating members** of the **audit staff** internally so that no member is permanently assigned to it, including the reporting partner

(d) The loss of **trust** and **experience** built up over time and the risk to audit effectiveness it would entail

4.30 As part of its recent review of the accountancy profession, the government has asked firms to ensure that lead partners for audit clients are rotated every five years, not returning to lead the audit again for five years.

Audit committees

4.31 One American innovation which has had a significant impact in this country is the audit committee.

4.32 One of the main reasons for audit committees arises from the difficulty auditors have in combating instances where the executive directors of a company are determined to mislead them. As a result it is felt that an audit committee, preferably drawn from '**non-executive**' **directors** of a client company, provides an **invaluable independent liaison** between the board and the auditors, thus strengthening the auditors' position and improving communication.

4.33 Other advantages that arise from the existence of an audit committee include:

(a) **Increased confidence** in the credibility and objectivity of financial reports.

(b) **Allows** the **executive directors to devote their attention to management.**

(c) The audit committee might provide an **impartial body** for the auditors to consult

(d) The audit committee can monitor the independence of the audit firm by reviewing personal relationships, the other services the firm provides and the duration of the contract between them

4.34 **Opponents** of audit committees **argue** that:

(a) **Selecting sufficient non-executive directors** with the necessary competence in auditing matters for the committee to be really effective can be too difficult.

(b) Such **formalised reporting procedure** may dissuade the auditors from raising matters of judgement and limit them to reporting only on matters of fact.

4.35 Under the Combined Code, it is mandatory for listed companies to form audit committees.

5 STATEMENT 2: THE PROFESSIONAL DUTY OF CONFIDENCE 12/03

5.1 Information acquired in the course of professional work should not be disclosed except where

- **Consent has been obtained** from the client, employer or other proper source, or
- There is a **public duty** to disclose, or
- There is a **legal** or **professional right or duty** to disclose.

5.2 A member acquiring information in the course of professional work should neither use nor appear to use that information for his **personal advantage** or for the **advantage of a third party**.

5.3 In general, where there is a right (as opposed to a duty) to disclose information, a member should only make disclosure in pursuit of a public duty or professional obligation.

5.4 A member must make clear to a client that he **may only act** for him **if the client agrees to disclose in full** to the member **all information relevant** to the engagement.

5.5 Where a member agrees to serve a client in a professional capacity both the member and the client should be aware that it is an **implied term** of that agreement that the **member will not disclose** the client's affairs to any other person save with the client's consent or within the terms of certain recognised exceptions.

RECOGNISED EXCEPTIONS
Obligatory disclosure
If a member knows or suspects his client to have committed **treason**, **drug-trafficking** or **terrorist** offences, he is obliged to disclose all the information at his disposal to a competent authority.
Under SAS 120 *Consideration of law and regulations* auditors should consider whether **non-compliance with laws and regulations** affects the accounts. Auditors may have to include in their audit report a statement that non-compliance has led to significant uncertainties, or non-compliance means that the auditors disagree with the way certain items have been treated in the accounts.
Voluntary disclosure
Disclosure is reasonably necessary to **protect** the **member's interests**, for example to enable him to sue for fees or defend an action for, say, negligence.
Disclosure is **compelled** by **process of law**, for example where in an action a member is required to give evidence or discovery of documents.
There is a **public duty** to disclose, say where an offence has been committed which is contrary to the public interest.
Disclosure is to **non-governmental bodies** which have statutory powers to compel disclosure.

5.6 If an ACCA member is requested to assist the police, the Inland Revenue or other authority by providing information about a client's affairs in connection with enquiries being made, he should first enquire under what **statutory authority** the information is demanded.

5.7 Unless he is satisfied that such statutory authority exists he should **decline** to give any information until he has obtained his client's authority. If the client's authority is not forthcoming and the demand for information is pressed the member should not accede unless so **advised by his solicitor**.

5.8 If a member knows or suspects that a client has committed a wrongful act he must give careful thought to his own position. He must ensure that he has not prejudiced himself by, for example, relying on information given by the client which subsequently proves to be incorrect.

5.9 However, it would be a **criminal offence** for a **member to act positively**, without lawful authority or reasonable excuse, in such a manner as **to impede with intent the arrest** or prosecution **of a client whom he knows or believes to have committed an 'arrestable offence'**.

6 INTERNAL AUDIT ETHICS

6.1 It is important to remember that if the internal auditor is a member of ACCA, he is subject to the ACCA's ethical guidance, just as if he was an external auditor.

ACCA's ethical guidance

6.2 An essential feature of the ACCA's ethical guidance is that it applies to members and students of ACCA, regardless of their employment and the nature of the job they do.

6.3 Clearly, as can be seen from the analysis in the rest of this Chapter, much of the detail of the guidance relates to external auditors. However, all members of ACCA are bound by the general ethical principles and are **expected to adhere to the spirit of the guidance**.

6.4 Therefore an internal auditor who is a member of ACCA must abide by ACCA's ethical guidelines. In particular, the issue of **objectivity** is as important for internal auditors as for external auditors. In order to ensure a professional standard, internal auditors should have care for the task in hand and no other.

Exam focus point

Remember in exam question that an internal auditor who is a member of ACCA is bound by the guidelines of ACCA. You might also want to refer to ethical guidelines that are more directly applicable to internal audit.

Objectivity and independence

6.5 We have discussed various matters which affect the independence of the external auditor from the company, for example, guidance over the level of fees charged, litigation and personal relationships. It is harder to see how an internal auditor can gain 'independence' in his relationship with the company, when it employs him, pays his wages and the people he audits are his colleagues.

6.6 The first key issue is organisational status. The internal audit department must have the support of management to enable it to function. The head of internal audit must have direct reporting access to senior management and the audit committee, if relevant.

6.7 In terms of personal objectivity, this is a matter for each internal auditor to consider personally. He must seek objectivity in mind. The following matters must be considered.

- Avoiding conflicts of interest
- Freedom from undue influences in the organisation
- No undertaking non-audit duties where possible
- Objectivity when auditing matters he has had responsibility for

Specific ethical guidance for internal auditors

6.8 The Institute of Internal Auditors (IIA) was introduced in Chapter 3. It has a number of joining requirements, as there are for people seeking to join ACCA. It also issues a code of professional ethics for its members.

6.9 However, it is important to your to understand that an internal auditor is only bound by the following code of ethics if he is a member or student of the IIA. They are useful for other internal auditors as a **reference point only**.

Ethical guidance of the Institute of Internal Auditors

1	Members shall exercise honesty, objectivity and diligence in the performance of their duties and responsibilities.
2	Members shall exhibit loyalty in all matters pertaining to the affairs of their organisation or to whomever they may be rendering a service. However, members shall not knowingly be a party to any illegal or improper activity.
3	Members shall not knowingly engage in acts or activities which are discreditable to the profession of internal auditing or to their organisation.
4	Members shall refrain from entering any activity which may be in conflict with the interests of their organisation or which would prejudice their ability to carry out objectively their duties and responsibilities.
5	Members shall not accept anything of value from an employee, client, customer, supplier or business associate of their organisation which would impair or be presumed to impair their professional judgement.
6	Members shall undertake only those services which they can reasonably expect to complete with professional competence.
7	Members shall adopt suitable means to comply with the standards for the professional practice of internal auditing.
8	Members shall be prudent in the use of information acquired in the course of their duties. They shall not use confidential information for any personal gain nor in any manner which would be contrary to law or detrimental to the welfare of their organisation.
9	Members, when reporting on the results of their work, shall reveal all material facts known to them which, if not revealed, could either distort reports of operations under review or conceal unlawful practices.
10	Members shall continually strive for improvement in the proficiency, effectiveness and quality of their service.
11	Members, in the practice of their profession, shall be ever mindful of their obligation to maintain the high standards of competence, morality and dignity promulgated by the Institute. Members shall abide by the Articles and uphold the objectives of the Institute.

Exam focus point

You are studying for a qualification from ACCA, not IIA. You do not have to learn this code of ethics. It is reproduced here to help you to think about the ethics of auditing from the point of view of the internal auditor.

7 AREAS OF CONTROVERSY

Multiple services — Pilot paper

ACCA Statement

'There are occasions where objectivity may be threatened or appear to be threatened by the provision to an audit client of services other than the audit.'

7.1 In Chapter 3 we discussed the possibility that the same firm of accountants could provide both internal and external audit services to the same client.

7.2 The issue is not restricted to offering internal audit services to external audit clients. Accountancy firms, even small ones, often offer a **wide range of business services**. An audit firm's services portfolio could also include:

- Payroll services
- Asset management/custody
- Preparing financial statements
- Preparing taxation returns
- Valuation services
- Information technology services
- Recruitment assistance
- Tax planning
- Corporate finance services
- Management consultancy

7.3 The provision of other services to audit clients is a **highly controversial** issue. As you can see from ACCA's statement above, it recognises that it can cause an auditor's **objectivity** to be **impaired** but issues no hard and fast rules about when providing other services is or is not allowed.

7.4 The following problems exist:

- The perception that a company gave its auditors some lucrative consultancy work **in exchange** for a clean audit report.
- The auditors may end up making **management decisions** for the company which would harm their independence
- The auditor undertaking **self-review**, that is auditing his own work.

7.5 However the provision of other services may have **advantages** to the audit firm.

- Auditors would have more confidence in work prepared by their firm.
- Carrying out accounting and tax work enhances audit staff's expertise.
- Non-audit services may smooth out seasonal audit work.

7.6 Clients may find the following benefits associated with having one firm provide all their accountancy-related services:

- They use a single adviser whom they **trust**
- The **overall** cost of all the services is likely to be lower.

7.7 The problem with small or sole practitioners auditing very small companies for whom they prepare accounts is probably insurmountable. The DTI has now removed the requirement for some small companies to have an audit, and so for such companies who have dispensed with an audit this problem has been solved. Where accountants still undertake the audit, they must ensure that the **audit** work (as opposed to any accountancy or tax work) is **planned** and **executed**, and perhaps most importantly, properly **recorded**. Also if possible, they might use different staff for the accounts preparation from those carrying out the audit.

7.8 Larger audit firms have countered the problem by the use of **separate departments** for each service within the firm (consultancy, audit, taxation and so on).

7.9 **Another important safeguard** is the **engagement letter**, which should separately identify the non-audit services provided and make clear the extent of directors' responsibilities (responsibility for accounting records, ensuring accounts give a true and fair view, taxation matters are disclosed and so on).

POINT TO NOTE

The engagement letter is discussed further in Chapter 5.

7.10 The response of the profession to the criticisms about the provision of other services to audit clients has been limited. The issue has been firmly placed in the spotlight again in the 21st century, in light of some major corporate failures in the US. The US Stock Exchange regulator has forbidden listed companies to purchase other services from their auditor. It is unlikely that the UK would pursue such a measure, preferring a guidelines approach.

Exam focus point

Questions on independence often focus on provision of other services, as this has continued to be a controversial area. This was the case on the pilot paper, and in December 2002.

Opinion shopping

7.11 If a company is unhappy with the audit opinion which it receives (or may receive) from its current auditors, then it might approach other audit firms for a **second opinion**.

7.12 There are two potential problems inherent in this situation.

- The other firm of auditors may form a negligent opinion because they are not necessarily in possession of all the facts.
- The original auditor may be put under pressure to accept the second opinion, which compromises his independence.

7.13 To avoid such a situation there should be constant communication between both sets of auditors. The second firm of auditors has a **professional duty to seek permission** for an approach to the current auditors from the client.

POINT TO NOTE

Professional duties on acceptance are discussed in Chapter 5.

Conflicts of interest 6/03

7.14 In some ways conflict of interest problems are similar to the difficulties firms have in maintaining independence. Conflicts of interest can arise in a variety of circumstances and each problem has to be dealt with on its own merits. There are no rules to deal with most of the situations, outside the Association's rules about independence and integrity, and the solution will usually be based on common sense as much as ethical behaviour.

7.15 We have already dealt with conflict of interest in terms of auditor independence, particularly in situations where there is a financial or personal interest in a client company.

7.16 Conflicts of interest can also arise when a firm has two (or more) audit clients, both of whom have reason to be unhappy that their auditors are also auditors to the other company.

This situation frequently arises when the companies are in **direct competition** with each other, and particularly when the **auditors have access to** particularly **sensitive information**.

7.17 These situations are difficult for the auditors: it may involve the loss of a substantial client, even though the staff and engagement partners on each of the audits are different.

7.18 Companies may have this attitude because of the highly competitive nature of their industry. Others may be sensitive because of the work they do for governments in defence or other controversial areas.

Avoidance of conflicts of interest

7.19 In general, where conflicts of interest arise, there should be **full** and **frank explanation** to those involved by the audit firm, coupled with any action necessary to disengage from one or both positions.

7.20 Conflicts should, so far as possible, be avoided by **not accepting** any appointment or assignment in which conflict seems likely to occur.

7.21 This avoidance of clients causing a conflict of interest is more important for smaller audit firms. The larger firms can overcome a conflict by building a 'Chinese wall' within the firm. This would mean that the respective audits are undertaken by different audit 'groups', the engagement partners are different and all the other audit staff are allowed to work on one of the clients only.

e.g.

Case example

An example of very competitive companies which appeared to agree with this type of arrangement was that of **British Airways** and **British Caledonian** (before they merged). Both companies were audited by the same large accountancy firm and yet the airline business is one of the most competitive in the world and confidential information is held at a premium.

7.22 It is possible, of course, that some clients might not agree to such an arrangement. The increasing number of mergers which have taken place within the accountancy profession recently have caused conflict of interest problems.

e.g.

Case example

British Telecom was not happy when its auditors merged with the firm which audited Cable and Wireless. The new firm was forced to drop one of the audits.

7.23 Legal cases, such as Prince Jefri of Brunei and KPMG, and in connection with the merger of Robson Rhodes and Pannell Kerr Foster, have also cast doubt on the ability of accountants to rely on Chinese walls.

Safeguards

7.24 Whenever accountants are acting for two clients who are in a **directly adversarial** situation, both should be informed and asked to **give consent** for the accountant to continue to act for both.

7.25 Other situations, for example clients in competition, might be covered by a paragraph in the **engagement letter.**

7.26 If consent has not been given in an adversarial situation, a Chinese wall may be effective providing the departments concerned are **physically separated** and there are **strict procedures** and **monitoring** in place. The Chinese wall needs to be part of the organisational culture of the organisation.

7.27 Another situation which can arise is where two audit clients fall into dispute with each other. The auditors might be asked to arbitrate, but this would leave the auditors open to accusations of conflict of interest.

7.28 It would be better to advise the companies to obtain arbitration from an independent accountant. The auditors should not investigate one client on behalf of another, nor pass on any knowledge of either client in such a situation. This is not always easy, particularly when the auditors can see the whole picture, but the companies cannot. The auditors must be extremely tactful and firm.

Question: Other services (I)

Southern Engineering Ltd has undergone a period of substantial growth following its establishment five years ago by two engineers. Because of a lack of accounting expertise within the company it has traditionally looked to its auditors, Smith and Jones, for accounting services in the preparation of annual financial statements as well as for the statutory audit function. Smith and Jones have also provided advice in connection with the company's accounting and internal control systems.

Smith and Jones is a two partner firm of certified accountants whose clients are mainly sole traders, partnerships and small limited companies. Although Southern Engineering Ltd was originally a typical small company client, its growth over the last five years has meant that it now accounts for approximately 20% of Smith and Jones' gross fee income and the company has indicated that it may wish to issue shares on the Alternative Investment Market in the near future.

Required

(a) Discuss the extent to which it is acceptable and desirable that Smith and Jones have in the past provided the three services of statutory audit, advice in connection with systems, and accountancy services in the preparation of annual financial statements to Southern Engineering Ltd.

(b) Discuss the acceptability and desirability of Smith and Jones continuing to act in the future as auditors to Southern Engineering Ltd while continuing to provide the other services.

Answer

(a) Auditors, especially of small companies, often provide other, non-audit services. The risk arises that, in such cases, the auditor's objectivity may be impaired. This is particularly possible where the auditor is involved in advising the client on systems, as it becomes difficult for the auditor to remain sufficiently detached to comment critically on any weaknesses or shortcomings which appear when systems are implemented. A clear distinction must be drawn between the auditor's advisory capacity - in systems or accountancy work - and the executive responsibility, which is still that of the company's management. Undue involvement with non-audit services must be avoided, lest it detracts from the auditor's essential independence and objectivity.

(b) The ethical guidance of the accounting bodies recommends that fee income from a single client should not exceed 15% of a practice's total gross fees. As Southern Engineering's fees now represent 20% of fee income (and would, presumably, increase when the company makes an issue on the AIM) it seems Smith and Jones have to consider ways of reducing their dependence on this one client. This might well be done by continuing as auditors but ceasing to provide accounting services and systems advice. (In any case, the ethical guidelines suggest that the auditors of a public company should not assist with accountancy save in exceptional circumstances.)

Smith and Jones should keep the situation under review, even after they have moved to a pure audit role, to ensure that they are not again becoming unduly dependent on Southern Engineering as it expands.

Question: Other services (II)

An auditor must ensure that his independence is not being compromised by providing other services to audit clients, and by other actions.

The additional services an auditor may provide include:

(a) Taxation, preparing the company's corporation tax computation and negotiating with the Inland Revenue; dealing with the tax affairs of the company's directors

(b) Preparing periodic management accounts of the company, quarterly and annual accounts

(c) Advising the directors on legal and accounting matters in relation to the company, for example, preparing submissions to the bank to obtain additional finance, advising on changes in share ownership and capital structure of the company and valuation of the company's shares

(d) Attending meetings of the board of directors

Required

In relation to a private company, of which you are auditor, consider:

(i) The benefits which may arise to the auditor and client in providing *each* of the above services

(ii) The extent to which providing *each* of these services may compromise your independence, and the action you would take to minimise the risk to your independence of providing these services

Answer

In all cases, the auditor will of course enjoy income additional to the audit fee. The client will probably benefit from a saving in using the same professional for all these types of work, because information gained on one assignment can be used on others, and the client will not be paying for the learning time of a new advisor. The client's staff and management should also save time, as they should not need to explain the business repeatedly to different people. (It has to be admitted, however, that changes in audit and other staff do often result in the client's needing to explain the same point in successive years.) The following individual comments may be made.

(a) *Taxation.* It is customary for the company's taxation liability to be at least checked, and often computed, as part of routine audit work. It is unlikely that independence would be impaired by this, or by routine correspondence with the Inland Revenue. Similarly, it is normal for an auditor to deal with directors' tax affairs. A problem would, however, arise here if there were any dispute between the company and its directors, as the auditor would suffer a conflict of interests and would probably be best advised to relinquish either the audit or the tax advisory role.

(b) *Accounts preparation.* This clearly gives the auditor a very good opportunity to keep in touch with the company's performance during the year and to take note of any possible audit problems as soon as they arise. There is, however, a risk that the auditor will not be as detached in carrying out the audit of accounts he or she has prepared as would be the case if the client had produced the accounts.

(c) *Advice to directors.* Clearly, the auditor will be able to draw on knowledge of the company in giving advice. There is a significant risk, however, that independence will be compromised, particularly if the advice turns out to have been mistaken. If the auditor has prepared a profit forecast for submission to the bank which subsequently proves over-optimistic, he or she may find it difficult to require the client to reflect the actual result in the year end accounts.

(d) *Board meetings.* There is a risk here that the auditor may completely forfeit independence by becoming too closely involved in the running of the company. The Companies Act regards as a director anyone who carries out the functions of a director, and an auditor would be exposed to this presumption if he or she attended meetings regularly. It would therefore be advisable for the auditor to attend only the board meetings at which the annual accounts are approved by the board.

Whistleblowing

7.29 The Public Interest Disclosure Act 1998 gives protection to 'workers' who make qualifying disclosures (they whistleblow).

KEY TERM

A **qualifying disclosure** is 'any disclosure of information which, in the reasonable belief of the worker making the disclosure, tends to show one or more of the following:

(a) That a criminal offence has been committed, is being committed or is likely to be committed

(b) That a person has failed, is failing or is likely to fail to comply with any legal obligation to which he is subject

(c) That a miscarriage of justice has occurred, is occurring or is likely to occur

(d) That the health or safety of any individual has been, is being or is likely to be endangered

(e) That the environment has been, is being or is likely to be damaged

(f) That information tending to show any matter falling within any one of the preceding paragraphs has been, is being or is likely to be deliberately concealed.'

7.30 Whistleblowing is potentially a tricky ethical area for internal auditors for the following reasons.

- They are in a position to access knowledge they might feel necessitated a public disclosure themselves
- They may be given information by a whistleblower, or be in a position to be a point of contact for concerned employees

7.31 The internal auditor must be prepared to deal with any case individually, but should, as general policy, facilitate lines of communication within the company so as to restrict the need to whistleblow externally.

Exam focus point

Ethics is a key topic area. It is likely to be examined regularly.

Chapter roundup

- The auditors' **duty of care** has been defined by case law over time. Auditors must employ reasonable care
- **Independence** and objectivity are the most important characteristics of auditors. Guidance is given in the *Rules of Professional Conduct.*
- Potential **threats** to objectivity include:
  - Undue dependence on an audit client
  - Family and other personal relationships
  - Beneficial interests in shares
  - Acceptance of hospitality
  - Provision of other services
- Auditors have a professional duty of **confidentiality**. However they may be compelled by law or consider it desirable in the **public interest** to disclose details of client's affairs to third parties.
- Internal auditors who are members of a professional body (say ACCA) are bound by that body's professional guidance. **Objectivity** in each situation is a key issue for internal auditors, both on a department and an individual level.
- Current discussion is focused on auditor independence including the **other services** auditors sell to audit clients, **opinion shopping,** conflicts of interest and audit rotation. A key issue for internal auditors might be whistleblowing.

Quick quiz

1 Match each ethical principle.

(a) Integrity
(b) Objectivity
(c) Competence
(d) Due skill and care
(e) Courtesy

(i) Strive for .... in all professional and business judgements. .... is the state of mind which has regard to all considerations relevant to the task in hand but no other, it presupposes intellectual honesty.

(ii) Carry out their professional work with ...., ..., diligence and expedition and with proper regard for the technical and professional standards expected of them as members.

(iii) Behave with .... in all professional, business and personal financial relationships, (.......................... implies not merely honesty but fair dealing and truthfulness).

(iv) Behave with .... and consideration towards all with whom they come into contact during the course of performing their work.

(v) Not accept or perform work which they are not .... to undertake unless they obtain such advice and assistance as will enable them to competently carry out the work.

2 Statement 1: *Integrity, objectivity and independence* applies only to statutory audits.

True ☐

False ☐

3 Fill in the blanks.

In general, the recurring work paid by the client or group of connected clients should not exceed ....% of the gross practice income.

In the case of .... or other .... companies, the figure should be ....% of gross practice income.

4 Of the following list of people who would not normally be considered a closely connected person for audit independence purposes.

(a) Spouse
(b) Personal doctor
(c) Company in which person holds 59% of shares
(d) Company in which person holds 22% of shares
(e) Company in which person holds 8% of shares
(f) Minor stepchild
(g) Estranged spouse
(h) Sister
(i) Adopted minor child

5 Using the factors given, complete the table.

(a) Forms an independent liaison between board and auditors
(b) Leads to increased confidence in creditability and objectivity of reporting
(c) Formalised reporting procedure may dissuade auditors from raising matters of judgement
(d) Impartial body for auditors to consult in the event of conflicts of interest
(e) Difficulty in selecting sufficient non-executive directors with the necessary competence

Advantages of an audit committee	Disadvantages of an audit committee

6 (a) Which of the following are legitimate reasons for breach of client confidentiality?

(i) Auditor **suspects** client has committed treason
(ii) Disclosure **needed** to protect auditor's own interests
(iii) Information is **required** for the audit of another client
(iv) Auditor **knows** client has committed terrorist offence
(v) There is a **public duty** to disclose
(vi) Auditor **considers** there to be non-compliance with law and regulations
(vii) Auditor **suspects** client has committed fraud

(b) Of the above reasons, which are voluntary disclosures and which are obligatory disclosures.

Answers to quick quiz

1 (a) (iii)
(b) (i)
(c) (v)
(d) (ii)
(e) (iv)

2 False. 'The spirit of the guidance applies equally to other audit situations.'

3 15, listed, pubic interest, 10

4 (b)

(e) The percentage guide is 20%

(g)

(h) Sister is not mentioned in the generally accepted definition but auditor judgement would have to be exercised; depending on the closeness of the relationships etc.

5

Advantages	Disadvantages
(a), (b), (d)	(c), (e)

6 (i) O
(ii) V
(iv) O
(v) V
(vi) O

(*NB*. In the case of (vii), the auditor should not take action outside the company until he is certain. When he is certain, he should seek legal advice.)

Now try the question below from the Exam Question Bank

Number	Level	Marks	Time
4	Exam	20	36 mins

Chapter 5

AUDIT ACCEPTANCE

Introduction

In Chapter 2, we looked at some of the legal requirements in relation to statutory audits. In this Chapter, following on from the overview of professional ethics in Chapter 4, we look at some of the **practical and ethical matters an external auditor has to consider when accepting professional work**.

ACCA have issued guidance on **advertising** and **obtaining professional** work. Setting fees for new clients can be controversial. **Lowballing** is a particular area where problems can arise.

The **procedures** to be carried out both **before** and **after** the **acceptance** of a new client are straightforward and easy to learn. These are outlined in section 2.

In the current climate, the **acceptance of a new client can entail** the undertaking of a **significant amount of risk**. Audit firms, particularly larger firms, now tend towards fairly stringent **client acceptance procedures**. This client screening helps to establish good 'high level' controls in a (potential) client. We look at this in section 3.

Accepting an audit engagement includes an element of risk. In sections 4 and 5 we look at two **specific areas of auditing guidance** which look at the **risky areas** of fraud and error, and compliance with law and regulations. The issues raised in these SASs are matters which should be **considered at an initial stage** as well as during the course of audits.

The **engagement letter** is an audit document of fundamental importance as it lays out the **scope** of the auditor's work and it **highlights the respective responsibilities of directors and auditors**.

Risk and ethics are both important topics on this syllabus. Client acceptance is likely to be examined in the context of professional ethics, as it was on the pilot paper.

1 TENDERING AND OBTAINING WORK

Statement 3: Advertising, Publicity and Obtaining Professional Work

1.1 Guidance is given as follows.

(a) Members should not obtain or seek work in an **unprofessional manner**.

(b) Members can advertise but should have regard to **relevant advertising codes** and standards.

(c) Members should **not make disparaging references** to or comparisons with the services of others.

(d) Members should **not quote fees** without great care to not mislead as to the precise range of services and time commitment that fees are intended to cover, but they can offer free consultations to discuss level of fees.

(e) **No fees, commission** or reward should be given to third parties in return for the introduction of clients.

Fee negotiation and lowballing

1.2 The audit fee is a sensitive subject for most companies. It represents a cost for something the company often does not really want and the fees may be perceived as too high just for this reason. The auditors must ensure that they can provide a quality audit for the price.

Tendering

1.3 Many large companies invite **tenders** for their audit work. The directors then have the opportunity to compare directly a range of offers.

1.4 Generally, a tender will take the form of detailed written proposals and a presentation. Factors include:

- The **level** of **expertise** each firm has in the industry
- **Similar companies** audited by each firm (good for expertise, bad for confidentiality?)
- **National** and **international presence**
- The proposed fee

Audit firms which tender for such audits will usually give at least an indication of the level of fees in the next few years, including likely overall rate rises. Fee levels are very important to most companies, and are often the determining factor.

1.5 In all situations, the auditors should quote a fee based on the estimated hours worked by each member of staff required on the audit, multiplied by their hourly rate plus any travel or other expenses to be incurred during the audit. They may also charge a premium for more complex audits.

Lowballing

1.6 Sometimes it appears that firms are charging less than 'market rate' for an audit, especially when tendering for new clients. This practice is known as **lowballing.**

1.7 It is not considered ethically wrong to charge a low price for an audit in itself. However, the auditors must ensure that they carry out an audit of the quality demanded by auditing standards and must ensure that the 'cut-price' audit fee does not call their independence into question.

1.8 This is always going to be a topical debate, but in terms of negotiating the audit fee the following factors need to be taken into account.

(a) The audit is perceived to have a **fluctuating** '**market price**' as any other commodity or service.

(b) Companies can reduce external audit costs through various **legitimate measures:**

- Extending the size and function of internal audit
- Reducing the number of different audit firms used world-wide
- Selling off subsidiary companies leaving a simplified group structure to audit
- The tender process itself simply makes auditors more competitive
- Exchange rate fluctuations in audit fees

(c) Auditing firms have **increased productivity**, partly through the use of more sophisticated information technology techniques in auditing.

1.9 In any case, an auditing firm lays itself open to accusations of loss of independence if it reduces its fees to below a certain level, particularly if it is difficult to see how such fees will cover direct labour costs, for example, where firms use the audit as a 'loss leader' to obtain profitable consultancy work from audit clients.

1.10 When such non-audit services are offered to a client by the auditors there can, of course, be an apparent loss of independence. The allegation may arise that the price of an 'acceptable' audit opinion is lucrative taxation or consulting work.

2 APPOINTMENT ETHICS

2.1 This section covers the procedures that the **auditors must** undertake to **ensure that their appointment is valid** and that they are clear to act. These matters are also covered in Statement 5: *Changes in Professional Appointment* in the ACCA's *Rules of Professional Conduct.*

Before accepting nomination

2.2 Before a new audit client is accepted, the auditors must ensure that there are no **independence** or **other ethical problems** likely to cause conflict with the ethical code. Furthermore, new auditors should ensure that they have been appointed in a proper and legal manner.

2.3 The nominee auditors must carry out the following procedures:

ACCEPTANCE PROCEDURES	
Ensure **professionally qualified** to act	Consider whether disqualified on legal or ethical grounds
Ensure **existing resources adequate**	Consider available time, staff and technical expertise
Obtain references	Make independent enquiries if directors not personally known. See Section 4 of this chapter
Communicate with present auditors	Enquire whether there are reasons/circumstances behind the change which the new auditors ought to know, also courtesy See flowchart on page 81 for process

Example letters

2.4 This is an example of a initial communication.

> To: Retiring & Co
> Certified Accountants
>
> Dear Sirs
>
> Re: New Client Co Ltd
>
> We have been asked to allow our name to go forward for nomination as auditors of the above company, and we should therefore be grateful if you would please let us know whether there are any professional reasons why we should not accept nomination...... .
>
> Acquiring & Co
>
> Certified Accountants

2.5 Having negotiated these steps the auditors will be in a position to accept the nomination, or not, as the case may be. These procedures can be demonstrated most easily in a decision chart, as shown on the next page.

Procedures after accepting nomination

2.6 The following procedures should be carried out after accepting nomination.

(a) **Ensure** that the **outgoing auditors' removal** or **resignation** has been **properly conducted** in accordance with the Companies Act 1985.

(b) **Ensure** that the **new auditors' appointment is valid**. The new auditors should obtain a copy of the resolution passed at the general meeting appointing them as the company's auditors.

(c) Set up and **submit a letter of engagement** to the directors of the company.

> **POINT TO NOTE**
>
> Letters of engagement are discussed in Section 5 of this chapter.

Other matters

2.7 Where the previous auditors have fees still owing by the client, the new auditors need not decline appointment solely for this reason. They should decide how far they may go in aiding the former auditors to obtain their fees, as well as whether they should accept the appointment.

2.8 Once a new appointment has taken place, the **new auditors should obtain all books and papers which belong to the client from the old auditors**. The former accountants should ensure that all such documents are transferred, **unless** they have a lien (a legal right to hold on to them) over the books because of unpaid fees. The old auditors should also pass any useful information to the new auditors if it will be of help, without charge, unless a lot of work is involved.

Appointment decision chart

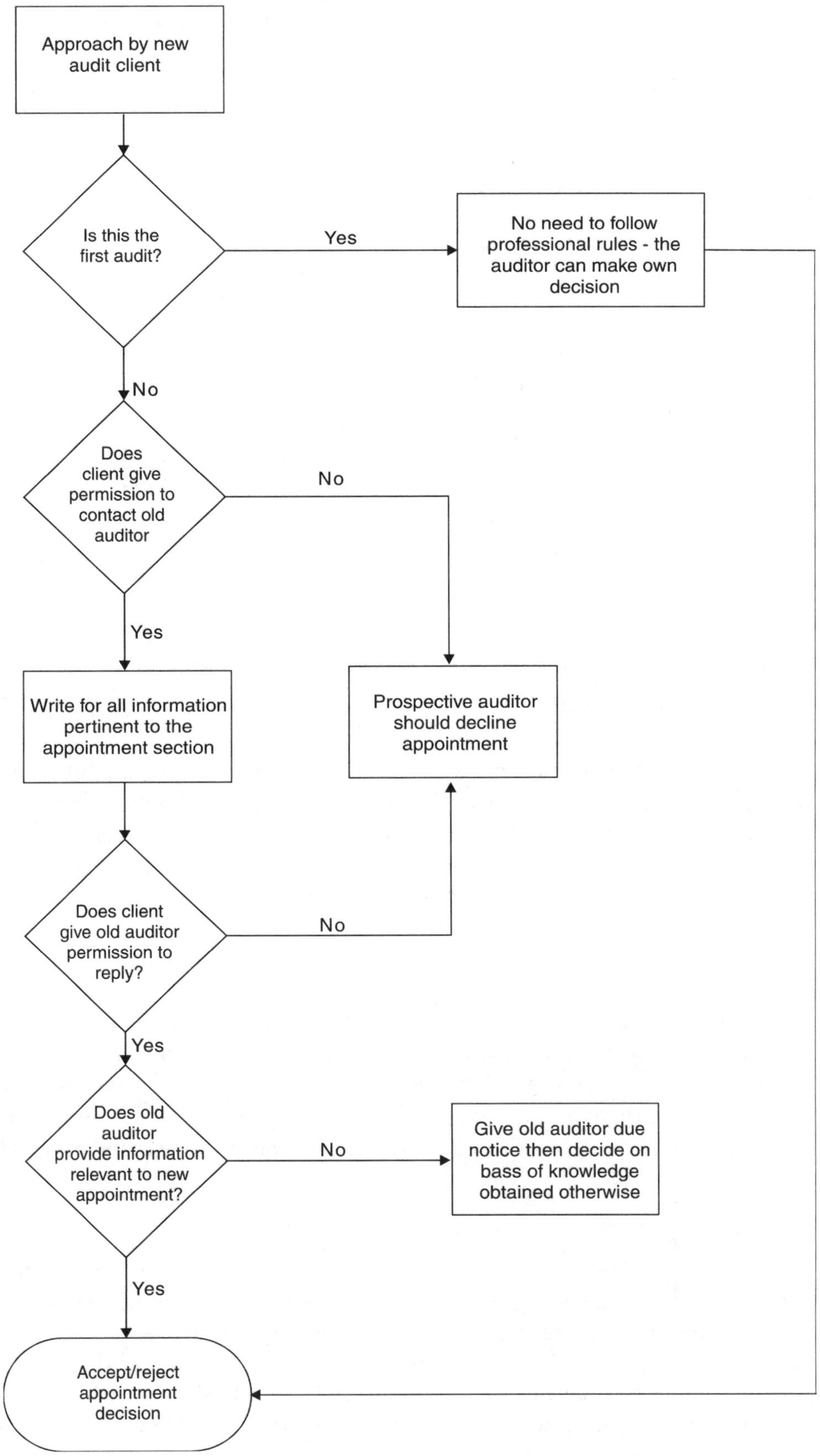

3 CLIENT SCREENING

3.1 As well as contacting previous auditors many firms, particularly larger firms, carry out **stringent checks** on potential client companies and their management. There are a number of reasons for this, as we will see shortly.

Basic factors for consideration

Management integrity

3.2 The integrity of those managing a company will be of great importance, particularly if the company is controlled by one or a few dominant personalities.

Risk

3.3 The following table contrasts low and high risk clients.

LOW RISK	HIGH RISK
Good long-term prospects	Poor recent or forecast performance
Well-financed	Likely lack of finance
Strong internal controls	Significant control weaknesses
Conservative, prudent accounting policies	Evidence of questionable integrity, doubtful accounting policies
Competent, honest management	Lack of finance director
Few unusual transactions	Significant related party or unexplained transactions

3.4 Where the risk level of a company's audit is determined as anything other than low, then the specific risks should be identified and documented. It might be necessary to assign specialists in response to these risks, particularly industry specialists, as independent reviewers. Some audit firms have procedures for closely monitoring audits which have been accepted, but which are considered high risk.

Engagement economics

3.5 Generally, the expected fees from a new client should reflect the **level of risk** expected. They should also offer the same sort of return expected of clients of this nature and reflect the overall financial strategy of the audit firm. Occasionally, the audit firm will want the work to gain entry into the client's particular industry, or to establish better contacts within that industry. These factors will all contribute to a total expected economic return.

Relationship

3.6 The audit firm will generally want the relationship with a client to be **long term**. This is not only to enjoy receiving fees year after year; it is also to allow the audit work to be enhanced by better knowledge of the client and thereby offer a better service.

3.7 Conflict of interest problems are significant here; the firm should establish that no existing clients will cause difficulties as competitors of the new client. Other services to other clients may have an impact here, not just audit.

Ability to perform the work

3.8 The audit firm must have the **resources** to perform the work properly, as well as any **specialist knowledge or skills**. The impact on existing engagements must be estimated, in terms of staff time and the timing of the audit.

SOURCES OF INFORMATION ABOUT NEW CLIENTS	
Enquiries of other sources	Bankers, solicitors
Review of **documents**	Most recent annual accounts, listing particulars, credit rating
Previous accountants/auditors	Previous auditors should disclose fully all relevant information
Review of **rules and standards**	Consider specific laws/standards that relate to industry

Approval

3.9 Once all the relevant procedures and information gathering has taken place, the company can be put forward for approval. The engagement partner will have completed a client acceptance form and this, along with any other relevant documentations, will be submitted to the managing partner, or whichever partner is in overall charge of accepting clients.

> **Exam focus point**
>
> In the exam you may be given a 'real-life' client situation and asked what factors you would consider in deciding whether to accept appointment. The ethical considerations covered in Chapter 4 and in this chapter are likely be relevant.

4 FRAUD AND ERROR 12/01

4.1 Look back at the table of risk factors on page 82 and remind yourself of some of the high risk factors which are listed there.

4.2 Many of the high risk factors listed are issues which could potentially result in a high risk of fraud and error arising.

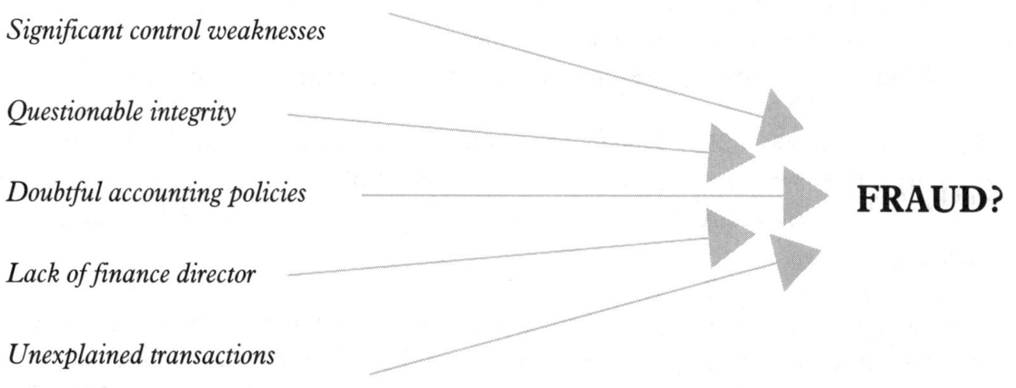

4.3 Fraud is an emotive issue. If news of a major fraud on a company hits the headlines, the question that is often asked is 'how did this happen?' Invariably when questions like that are asked, people raise **questions about the audit** that has taken place on that company's financial statements.

4.4 A major problem for the auditor can be that the public does not understand the auditors' role with regard to fraud. This forms part of an '**expectations gap**' which exists between what auditors actually do and what people think that they do.

4.5 We are going to briefly consider here what the auditors' role is in relation to fraud and error, and consider when the **risk** of fraud and error arising is **too great** for the auditor even **to accept** the engagement.

SAS 110 *Fraud and error*

4.6 SAS 110 requires auditors to plan and perform their work, they must evaluate it, and then report to members **recognising** that fraud and error **may exist** and **materially affect** the financial statements.

4.7 The most important thing to understand with regard to fraud is that **the auditor has no duty** (specifically no statutory duty) **to prevent or detect fraud**.

4.8 With regard to the statutory audit, the auditor must be aware that two potential causes of the financial statements being misstated are fraud or error existing.

KEY TERMS

Fraud comprises both the use of deception to obtain an unjust or illegal financial advantage, and intentional misrepresentation by management, employees or third parties.

Error is an unintentional mistake.

4.9 EXAMPLES

The SAS gives the following list of examples of what fraud may involve:

- Falsification or alteration of accounting records or other documents
- Misappropriation of assets or theft
- Suppression or omission of the effects of transactions from records or documents
- Recording of transactions without substance
- Intentional misapplication of accounting policies, or
- Wilful misrepresentations of transactions or of the entity's state of affairs

4.10 What this list of 'fraudulent behaviour' might help you to see is that the detection of fraud committed by management is going to be extremely difficult because it is designed not to be found. Particularly where the fraud is fraud by omission, the auditor is unlikely to detect fraud as part of an audit.

4.11 The standard does not expect the auditors to detect fraud as a matter of course. Rather, it requires auditors to be **aware**, when planning and performing their audit, that fraud may exist, and more particularly, it highlights a number of **factors which the auditor should be alert to**, which could point to fraud being perpetrated.

Planning

4.12 The auditors must assess the risk of fraud and error and then design audit procedures to have a reasonable expectation of detecting material misstatements caused by fraud and errors. The factors which may indicate fraud or error are given in an appendix to the SAS, which is reproduced here:

Fraud and error	
Previous experience or incidents which **call into question** the **integrity** or **competence** of **management**	Management dominated by one person (or a small group) and no effective oversight board or committee
	Complex corporate structure where complexity does not seem to be warranted
	High turnover rate of key accounting and financial personnel
	Personnel (key or otherwise) not taking holidays
	Significant and prolonged under-staffing of the accounting department
	Frequent changes of legal advisers or auditors
Particular financial reporting pressures within an entity	Industry volatility
	Inadequate working capital due to declining profits or too rapid expansion
	Deteriorating quality of earnings, for example increased risk taking with respect to credit sales, changes in business practice or selection of accounting policy alternatives that improve income
	The entity needs a rising profit trend to support the market price of its shares due to a contemplated public offering, a takeover or other reason
	Significant investment in an industry or product line noted for rapid change
	Pressure on accounting personnel to complete financial statements in an unreasonably short period of time
	Dominant owner-management
	Performance-based remuneration
Weaknesses in the **design** and **operation** of the **accounting and internal controls system**	A weak control environment within the entity
	Systems that, in their design, are inadequate to give reasonable assurance of preventing or detecting error or fraud
	Inadequate segregation of responsibilities in relation to functions involving the handling, recording or controlling of the entity's assets
	Indications that internal financial information is unreliable
	Evidence that internal controls have been overridden by management
	Ineffective monitoring of the operation of system which allows control overrides, breakdown or weakness to continue without proper corrective action
	Continuing failure to correct major weakness in internal control where such corrections are practicable and cost effective

Fraud and error	
Unusual transactions	Unusual transactions, especially near the year end, that have a significant effect on earnings Complex transactions or accounting treatments Unusual transactions with related parties Payments for services (for example to lawyers, consultants or agents) that appear excessive in relation to the services provided
Problems in **obtaining sufficient appropriate audit evidence**	Inadequate records, for example incomplete files, excessive adjustments to accounting records, transactions not recorded in accordance with normal procedures and out-of-balance control accounts Inadequate documentation of transactions, such as lack of proper authorisation, supporting documents not available and alternation to documents (any of these documentation problems assume greater significance when they relate to large or unusual transactions) An excessive number of differences between accounting records and third party confirmations, conflicting audit evidence and unexplainable changes in operating ratios Evasive, delayed or unreasonable responses by management to audit inquires Inappropriate attitude of management to the conduct of the audit, eg time pressure, scope limitation and other constraints
Some factors unique to an **information systems environment** which relate to the conditions and events described above	Inability to extract information from computer files due to lack of, or non-current, documentation of record contents or programs Large numbers of program changes that are not documented, approved or tested Inadequate overall balancing of computer transactions and data bases to the financial accounts

4.13 Auditors are therefore 'put on enquiry' when such factors exist – in other words, they have a **professional duty to satisfy themselves** that **any concerns raised** have been **answered** to their satisfaction.

When fraud or error are indicated

4.14 The SAS then goes on to outline what the auditors should do if their suspicions are raised.

4.15 The SAS states:

'When planning the audit the auditors should assess the risk that fraud or error may cause the financial statements to contain When auditors become aware of information which indicates that fraud or error may exist, they should obtain an understanding of the nature of the event and the circumstances in which it has occurred, and sufficient other information to evaluate the possible effect on the financial statements. If the auditors believe that the indicated fraud or error could have a material effect on the financial statements, they should perform appropriate modified or additional procedures. (SAS 110.4)

When the auditors become aware of, or suspect that there may be, instances of error or fraudulent conduct, they should document their findings and, subject to any requirement to report them direct to a third party, discuss them with the appropriate level of management.

(SAS 110.5)

The auditors should consider the implications of suspected or actual error or fraudulent conduct in relation to other aspects of the audit, particularly the reliability of management representations.' (SAS 110.6)

Reporting

4.16 Lastly the SAS goes on to consider what the auditors should do, or rather, to whom they should report, in the event of them uncovering a fraud. Remember that, as you learnt in Chapter 4, the auditors have a professional duty of confidentiality. The SAS says 'the auditors should as soon as practicable communicate their findings to the appropriate level of management, the board of directors or the audit committee if

(a) They suspect or discover fraud, even if the potential effect on the financial statements is immaterial, or

(b) Material error is found to exist'.

4.17 Such a discovery might also have an impact on the audit report.

POINT TO NOTE

We shall consider the audit report in Chapter 19.

4.18 If auditors do detect a management fraud, they may consider it to be so serious that it is necessary to report it to the relevant authority in the public interest. Such a decision would not be taken lightly, and should only be taken once **legal advice** had been sought. The auditors have a duty of confidentiality, but in **exceptional circumstances**, where the matter is one of **public interest**, they may have to make such a disclosure.

4.19 The SAS says, 'where the auditors become aware of a suspected or actual instance of fraud they should

(a) Consider whether the matter may be one that ought to be reported to a proper authority in the public interest: and where this is the case

(b) Except in the circumstances covered in SAS 100.12, discuss the matter with the board of directors, including any audit committee (SAS 110.10)

Where, having considered any views expressed on behalf of the entity and in the light of any legal advice obtained, the auditors conclude that the matter ought to be reported to an appropriate authority in the public interest, they should notify the directors in writing of their view and, if the entity does not voluntarily do so itself or is unable to provide evidence that the matter has been reported, they should report it themselves. (SAS 110.11)

When a suspected or actual instance of fraud casts doubt on the integrity of the directors auditors should make a report direct to a proper authority in the public interest without delay and without informing the directors in advance. (SAS 110.12)'

Fraud and audit acceptance

4.20 Several issues have been raised here from the point of view of the audit firm:

- Auditors should plan and perform procedures whilst being **aware** that fraud may exist
- Fraud, however, may be extremely **difficult to discover**
- Auditors must **satisfy themselves** if put on enquiry

- If the auditors detect or suspect fraud, they must consider whether it is in the public interest to **report** it, having sought **legal advice**.
- Fraud is an emotive issue, which may bring bad **publicity** to the firm, deserved or not

4.21 Cast your mind back to the high risk factors which were identified on page 82. **It might be that an audit firm would choose not accept a client** which was identified as **high risk** at the outset, because the chances of conducting a cost effective audit which fulfils professional requirements might be too low, even if the indicators were false, and there was no fraud being perpetrated at the company.

5 LAW AND REGULATIONS

5.1 Another issue raised by the risk factors on page 82 is the issue of the auditors' consideration of law and regulation. This issue has two aspects:

- Areas of non-compliance where the matter may **materially affect the financial statements**
- Areas where the **auditors could unwittingly become liable** for failing to report matters arising, for example, money laundering

5.2 The auditing standard approaches this issue in a similar way to the standard on fraud and error.

SAS 120 *Consideration of law and regulations*

5.3 The standard sets out the respective duties of directors and auditors in relation to compliance with law and regulations. The directors have a duty to ensure that the company complies with any relevant legislation and regulation.

5.4 The auditors do not have a duty to prevent non-compliance. However, similarly to their duty in relation to fraud and error, they have a **duty to plan, perform and evaluate** their audit work in order to have a **reasonable expectation** of **detecting material misstatements** which may arise through non-compliance.

Planning

5.5 The SAS states: 'auditors should plan and perform their audit procedures, and evaluate and report on the results thereof, recognising that non-compliance by the entity with law or regulations may materially affect the financial statements. (SAS 120.1)

The auditors should obtain sufficient appropriate audit evidence about compliance with those laws and regulations which relate directly to the preparation of, or the inclusion or disclosure of specific items in, the financial statements. (SAS 120.2)

The auditors should perform procedures to help identify possible or actual instances of non-compliance with those laws and regulations which provide a legal framework within which the entity conducts its business and which are central to the entity's ability to conduct its business and hence to its financial statements by

(a) Obtaining a general understanding of the legal and regulatory framework applicable to the entity and the industry and of the procedures followed to ensure compliance with that framework

(b) Inspecting correspondence with relevant licensing or regulatory authorities

(c) Enquiring of the directors as to whether they are on notice of any such possible instances of non-compliance with law or regulations, and

(d) Obtaining written confirmation from the directors that they have disclosed to the auditors all those events of which they are aware which involve possible non-compliance, together with the actual or contingent consequences which may arise therefrom. (SAS 120.3)

When carrying out their procedures for the purpose of forming an opinion on the financial statements, the auditors should in addition be alert for instances or possible or actual non-compliance with law or regulations which might affect the financial statements. (SAS 120.4)'

When non-compliance is indicated

5.6 If the auditors' suspicions are raised, the SAS goes on to say that they should **gain an understanding** of what has happened so that they can evaluate the effect on the financial statements. They should also **document their findings** and **discuss them with management**, unless they are required to report them directly to a third party.

5.7 They should also consider the implications of this non-compliance on representations made to them by management during the course of the audit.

Reporting

5.8 The reporting requirements of SAS 120 are very similar to SAS 110:

Auditors suspect or detect non-compliance with law and regulations	1. Discuss with management or the audit committee, or ensure that they are aware of the issue.	(SAS 120.8)
	2. If the non-compliance appears to be material or intentional, they should discuss it with management without delay.	(SAS 120.9)
There is a statutory duty to report.	Make the report to the relevant authority without delay.	(SAS 120.12)
There is no statutory duty to report.	1. Consider whether it is in the public interest to report and discuss it with the directors.	(SAS 120.13)
	2. Take legal advice, and report it to the relevant authority if it is in the public interest	(SAS 120.14)
	3. If the suspicion causes them to no longer have confidence in the integrity of the directors, report it to the relevant authority without delay or discussion with the entity.	(SAS 120.15)

Compliance with law/regulations and audit acceptance

5.9 Similarly to the issue of fraud, this is an area which can bring **complexity** to the audit and a severe risk of **bad publicity**. If high **risk factors** such as the entity operating in a highly regulated environment, or a complex corporate structure exist, an **audit firm may decline appointment** feeling that a cost effective audit will be difficult to achieve.

5.10 Another risk arising to the audit firm is the risk of personal liability arising if the entity is a mask for illegal activities such as money laundering. SAS 120 mentions money laundering in paragraph 19.

5.11 Auditors are **required by law** to **disclose suspicions** of the laundering of money deriving from drug trafficking or relating to terrorist offences. It is also a criminal offence to disclose such reporting. Auditors have a **statutory duty not to let their client know if they have made such a report.**

5.12 While risk factors such as **complex corporate structures** and doubts over the **integrity of management** may not be (and often are not) based in the fact that the company is operating for illegal purposes, an **audit firm may decline appointment** to entities with such factors, as the risk to the audit firm of the reverse being true is too great to take on.

6 THE ENGAGEMENT LETTER

6.1 An engagement letter should:

- Define clearly the **extent** of the **auditors' responsibilities** and so minimise the possibility of any misunderstanding between the client and the auditors
- Provide **written confirmation** of the **auditors' acceptance** of the appointment, the scope of the audit, the form of their report and the scope of any non-audit services

6.2 If an engagement letter is not sent to clients, both new and existing, there is scope for argument about the precise extent of the respective obligations of the client and its directors and the auditors. The contents of an engagement letter should be discussed and agreed with management before it is sent.

6.3 Guidance is available in the form of the SAS 140 *Engagement letters*, which applies to **audit** engagements. It states that the terms of the engagement should be agreed with the client and recorded in writing. It should be reviewed regularly and updates mode in writing too.

Timing

6.4 The auditors should send an engagement letter to all new clients soon after their appointment as auditors and, in any event, **before the commencement of the first audit** assignment.

Content of letter

6.5 This is shown in the example given in an Appendix to the SAS, which is reproduced below. The main emphasis is on the 'principal relevant responsibilities of the directors and the auditors and the scope of the audit'.

Form of reports

6.6 The letter should identify any reports which the auditors will submit **in addition to** the statutory audit report, such as reports to the directors/managers on material internal control weaknesses. Confidentiality aspects of such reports should be mentioned.

Other matters

6.7 The other matters which the SAS highlights for possible inclusion in the engagement letter are as follows.

- Fees and billing arrangements
- Procedures where the client has a complaint about the service
- Where appropriate, arrangements concerning the involvement of:
  - Other auditors and experts in some aspect of the audit
  - Internal auditors and other staff of the entity
- Arrangements, if any, to be made with the predecessor auditors, in the case of an initial audit
- Any restriction of the auditors' liabilities to the client (when such possibility exists; not possible with limited companies)
- Where appropriate, the country by whose laws the engagement to be governed
- A reference to any further agreements between the auditors and the client
- A proposed timetable for the engagement

6.8 The following example of an engagement letter for a UK limited company client. Remember that it is not necessarily comprehensive or appropriate to every audit as each client is different; it must be tailored to meet the specific requirements of the engagement.

AN EXAMPLE OF AN ENGAGEMENT LETTER

To the directors of..

The purpose of this letter is to set out the basis on which we (are to) act as auditors of the company (and its subsidiaries) and the respective areas of responsibility of the directors and of ourselves.

Responsibility of directors and auditors

1 As directors of the above company, you are responsible for ensuring that the company maintains proper accounting records and for preparing financial statements which give a true and fair view and have been prepared in accordance with the Companies Act 1985. You are also responsible for making available to us, as and when required, all the company's accounting records and all other relevant records and related information, including minutes of all management and shareholders' meetings.

2 We have a statutory responsibility to report to the members whether in our opinion the financial statements give a true and fair view of the state of the company's affairs and of the profit or loss for the year and whether they have been properly prepared in accordance with the Companies Act 1985 (or other relevant legislation). In arriving at our opinion, we are required to consider the following matters, and to report on any in respect of which we are not satisfied:

(a) whether proper accounting records have been kept by the company and proper returns adequate for our audit have been received from branches not visited by us;

(b) whether the company's balance sheet and profit and loss account are in agreement with the accounting records and returns;

(c) whether we have obtained all the information and explanations which we think necessary for the purposes of our audit; and

(d) whether the information in the directors' report is consistent with the financial statements.

In addition, there are certain other matters which, according to the circumstances, may need to be dealt with in our report. For example, where the financial statements do not give full details of directors' remuneration or of their transactions with the company, the Companies Act requires us to disclose such matters in our report.

3 We have a professional responsibility to report if the financial statements do not comply in any material respect with applicable accounting standards, unless in our opinion the non-compliance is justified in the circumstances. In determining whether the departure is justified we consider:

(a) whether the departure is required in order for the financial statements to give a true and fair view; and

(b) whether adequate disclosure has been made concerning the departure

Our professional responsibilities also include:

(a) including in our report a description of the directors' responsibilities for the financial statements where the financial statements or accompanying information do not include such a description; and

(b) considering whether other information in documents containing audited financial statements is consistent with those financial statements.

4 Our audit will be conducted in accordance with the Auditing Standards issued by the Auditing Practices Board, and will include such tests of transactions and of the existence, ownership and valuation of assets and liabilities as we consider necessary. We shall obtain an understanding of the accounting and internal control systems in order to assess their adequacy as a basis for the preparation of the financial statements and to establish whether proper accounting records have been maintained by the company. We shall expect to obtain such appropriate evidence as we consider sufficient to enable us to draw reasonable conclusions therefrom

5 The nature and extent of our procedures will vary according to our assessment of the company's accounting system and, where we wish to place reliance on it, the internal control system, and may cover any aspect of the business's operations. Our audit is not designed to identify all significant weaknesses in the company's systems but, if such weaknesses come to our notice during the course of our audit which we think should be brought to your attention, we shall report them to you. Any such report may not be provided to third parties without our prior written consent. Such consent will be granted only on the basis that such reports are not prepared with the interests of anyone other than the company in mind and that we accept no duty or responsibility to any other party as concerns the reports.

6 As part of our normal audit procedures, we may request you to provide written confirmation of oral representations which we have received from you during the course of the audit on matters having a material effect on the financial statements. In connection with representations and the supply of information to us generally, we draw your attention to section 389A of the Companies Act 1985 under which it is an offence for an officer of the company to mislead the auditors.

7 In order to assist us with the examination of your financial statements, we shall request sight of all documents or statements, including the chairman's statement, operating and financial review and the directors' report, which are due to be issued with the financial statements. We are also entitled to attend all general meetings of the company and to receive notice of all such meetings.

8 The responsibility for safeguarding the assets of the company and for the prevention and detection of fraud, error and non-compliance with law or regulations rests with yourselves. However, we shall endeavour to plan our audit so that we have a reasonable expectation of detecting material misstatements in the financial statements or accounting records (including those resulting from fraud, error or non-compliance with law or regulations), but our examination should not be relied upon to disclose all such material misstatements or frauds, errors or instances of non-compliance as may exist.

9 (Where appropriate). We shall not be treated as having notice, for the purposes of our audit responsibilities, of information provided to members of our firm other than those engaged on the audit (for example information provided in connection with accounting, taxation and other services).

10 Once we have issued our report we have no further direct responsibility in relation to the financial statements for that financial year. However, we expect that you will inform us of any material event occurring between the date of our report and that of the Annual General Meeting which may affect the financial statements.

Other services

11 You have requested that we provide other services in respect of .... The terms under which we provide these other services are dealt with in a separate letter. We will also agree in a separate letter of engagement the provision of any services relating to investment business advice as defined by the Financial Services Act 1986.

Fees

12 Our fees are computed on the basis of the time spent on your affairs by the partners and our staff and on the levels of skill and responsibility involved. Unless otherwise agreed, our fees will be billed at appropriate intervals during the course of the year and will be due on presentation.

Applicable law

13 This (engagement letter) shall be governed by, and construed in accordance with, (English) law. The Courts of (England) shall have exclusive jurisdiction in relation to any claim, dispute or difference concerning the (engagement letter) and any matter arising from it. Each party irrevocably waives any right it may have to object to an action being brought in those Courts, to claim that the action has been brought in an inconvenient forum, or to claim that those Courts do not have jurisdiction.

14 Once it has been agreed, this letter will remain effective, from one audit appointment to another, until it is replaced. We shall be grateful if you could confirm in writing your agreement to these terms by signing and returning the enclosed copy of this letter, or let us know if they are not in accordance with your understanding of our terms of engagement.

Yours faithfully

Certified Accountants

Recipient of letter

6.9 The letter should be addressed to the board of directors or audit committee of the organisation to be audited. The terms of the letter should be evidenced as accepted by the organisation by the signature of an appropriate senior person.

Changes in terms or nature of an engagement

6.10 Once it has been agreed by the client, an engagement letter will, if it so provides, remain effective from one audit appointment to another until it is replaced.

6.11 However, the engagement letter should be reviewed annually to ensure that it continues to reflect the client's circumstances. The SAS suggests that the following factors may make the agreement of a new letter appropriate.

- Any indication that the client **misunderstands** the objective and scope of the audit
- A **recent change of management**, board of directors or audit committee
- A **significant change in ownership**, such as a new holding company
- A **significant change in the nature or size** of the client's business
- Any **relevant change in legal or professional requirements**

6.12 It may be appropriate to remind the client of the original letter when the auditors decide a new engagement letter is unnecessary for any period.

6.13 In the case of a change in the terms of engagement prior to completion, this may result from:

- A **change in circumstances** affecting the need for the service
- A **misunderstanding** as to the nature of an audit or of the related service originally requested
- A **restriction** on the **scope** of the **engagement**, whether imposed by management or caused by circumstances

6.14 The auditors should consider such a request for change, and the reason for it, very seriously, particularly in terms of any restriction in the scope of the engagement. Auditors may have to withdraw from the engagement.

Question: New auditors

You are a partner in Messrs Borg Connors & Co, Certified Accountants. You are approached by Mr Nastase, the managing director of Navratilova Enterprises Ltd, who asks your firm to become auditors of his company. In return for giving you this appointment Mr Nastase says that he will expect your firm to waive fifty per cent of your normal fee for the first year's audit. The existing auditors, Messrs Wade Austin & Co have not resigned but Mr Nastase informs you that they will not be re-appointed in the future.

Required

(a) What action should Messrs Borg Connors & Co take in response to the request from Mr Nastase to reduce their first year's fee by fifty per cent?

(b) Explain the procedure a company must go through to remove its auditors and appoint another firm of auditors in their place.

(c) Are Messrs Wade Austin & Co within their rights in not resigning when they know Mr Nastase wishes to replace them? Give reasons for your answer.

Answer

(a) The request by Mr Nastase that half of the first year's audit fee should be waived is quite improper. If this proposal were to be accepted it could be held that Borg Connors & Co had sought to procure work through the quoting of lower fees. This would be unethical and would result in disciplinary proceedings being taken against the firm.

It should be pointed out to Mr Nastase that the audit fee will be determined, in accordance with normal practice, by reference to the work involved in completion of a satisfactory audit taking into consideration the nature of the audit tasks involved and the level of staff required to carry out those tasks in an efficient manner. Mr Nastase should further be informed that if he is not prepared to accept an audit fee arrived at in this way and insists on there being a reduction then regrettably the nomination to act as auditor will have to be declined.

(b) Under the provisions of ss 391 to 393 Companies Act 1985 there are certain statutory procedures which must be followed by a company if it wishes to remove its existing auditors and appoint another firm of auditors in their place. The main rules relevant to this situation are summarised below.

(i) The general rule is that every company shall at each annual general meeting (AGM) appoint an auditor to hold office from the conclusion of that meeting until the conclusion of the next AGM.

(ii) Removal of the auditors requires the passing of an ordinary resolution of which special notice (28 days) has been given, the auditors being entitled to receive a copy of this resolution. If the resolution is passed then the company must notify the Registrar within 14 days of the date of the meeting.

(iii) Where an attempt has been made to remove the auditors during their term of office, or where notice of a resolution to appoint other persons in their place has been received by the company, the auditors may make representations as to why they think they ought to stay in office.

Provided they are not received too late and are of reasonable length they may require the company to:

(1) State in any notice of the resolution given to the members that representations have been made, and

(2) Send a copy of the representations to the members

(iv) If the representations are not sent out, either because they were received too late or because of the company's default, the auditors may require that they are read at the meeting. This will not prejudice their normal right to speak at the meeting.

(v) The auditors' representations need neither be sent out nor read at the meeting if, on the application of the company or any other person who claims to be aggrieved, the court is satisfied that the auditors' right is being abused to obtain needless publicity for defamatory matter.

(vi) The removed auditors have two further rights which are:

(1) They are entitled to receive all notices relating to the general meeting at which their term of office would have expired and of any general meeting at which it is proposed to fill the casual vacancy caused by their removal.

(2) They are entitled to attend such meetings and to speak at them on any part of the business which concerns them as former auditors.

Finally it should be emphasised that the power to remove an auditor rests with the members and not with the directors.

(c) Wade Austin & Co have every right not to resign even though they may be aware that Mr Nastase, the managing director of the company, wishes to replace them. The auditors of a company are appointed by, and report to, the members of a company and the directors are not empowered, as directors, to remove the auditors.

If the reason for the proposed change arises out of a dispute between management and the auditors then the auditors have a right to put forward their views as seen above and to insist that any decision should be made by the members, but only once they have been made aware of all pertinent facts concerning the directors' wishes to have them removed from office as auditors.

Chapter roundup

- Auditors have guidance from ACCA on advertising and obtaining professional work. They most controversial area is often fee-setting, with such problems as **lowballing.**
- The **present** and **proposed auditors** must **communicate** about the client prior to the audit being accepted.
- The client must be asked to give permission for this communication to occur. If the client **refuses** to give **permission,** the proposed auditors must **decline nomination.**
- The proposed auditors must also ensure they:
  - Are **professionally qualified** to act
  - Have **sufficient resources**
  - Seek **references**
- Most firms have **client acceptance procedures** reviewing the **management integrity** and **risk** of the prospective client, as well as the **likely profitability** of the engagement.
- **Investigations** may be carried out for high-risk clients
- Two issues which may be highlighted by risk factors are **fraud and error** and **the auditors' consideration of law and regulation**.
- These issues can bring such **complexity** to the audit that the audit firm may choose to decline the audit if it appears particularly high risk
- Auditing guidance in these areas requires auditors to **plan and perform** their audits so as to have a **reasonable chance of detecting problems which cause material misstatements**. It also sets out the **reporting requirements** in the event of fraud or non-compliance being uncovered.
- An engagement letter should be sent to all new clients. The letter should:
  - **Specify** the **respective responsibilities** of directors and the auditors
  - Lay down the **scope** of the **auditors' work**

Quick quiz

1 Complete the following definition of **lowballing.**

The practice of ...., usually at ...., for the audit of large companies.

2 Complete the questions that should be in the diagram.

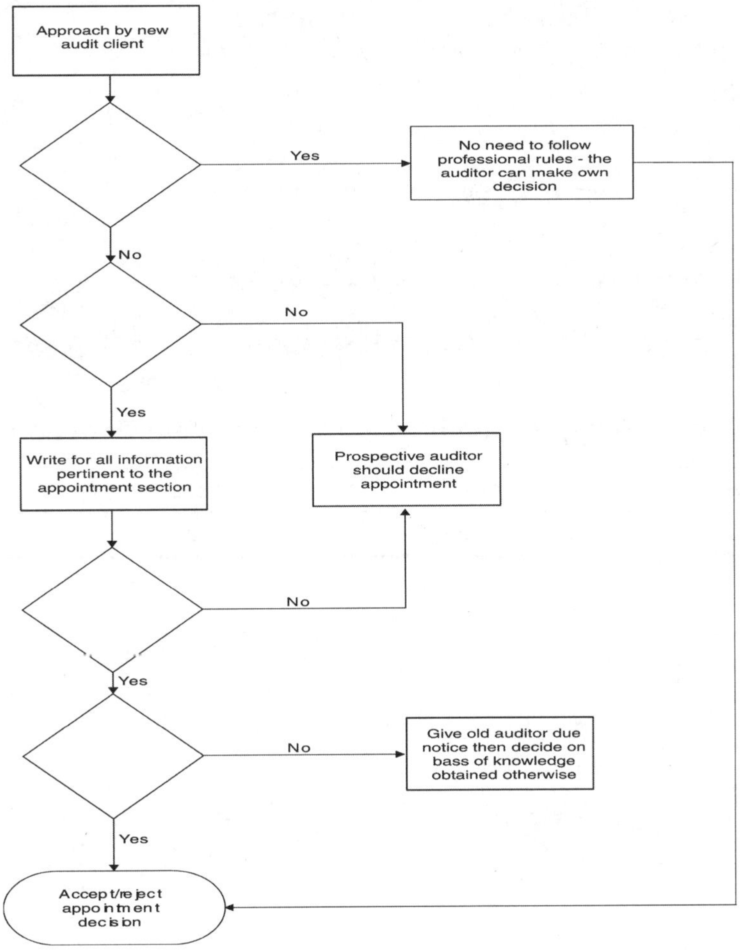

3 Auditors have a duty to detect fraud

True ☐

False ☐

4 Auditors should always report non-compliance with law and regulations to the statutory authority.

True ☐

False ☐

5 An engagement letter is only ever sent to a client before the first audit.

True ☐

False ☐

6 Ring the items that are unlikely to be found in an engagement letter.

(a) Responsibilities of directors and auditors
(b) Detailed audit procedures
(c) Other services
(d) Agreed fee
(e) Reference to applicable law

Answers to quick quiz

1 undercutting, tender

2
- Is this the first audit?
- Does the client give permission to contact the old auditor?
- Does client give old auditor permission to reply?
- Does old auditor provide information relevant to new appointment?

3 False

4 False

5 False. It should be re-issued if there is a change in circumstances.

6 (b)

(d) Reference will be made to how the fee is set, but no mention of the actual fee will be made as it will fluctuate over time.

Now try the question below from the Exam Question Bank

Number	Level	Marks	Time
5	Introductory	n/a	30 mins

Part B
Planning

Chapter 6

PLANNING

Topic list		Syllabus reference	Study guide
1	Planning	4	9
2	Knowledge of the business	4	9
3	Audit risk	4	9
4	Materiality	4	9
5	Planning a review	4	9
6	Planning an internal audit	4	9

Introduction

The **initial stage** of any audit or review work is planning. Auditing standards require that auditors plan their work. This involves two elements, a **general strategy** for the audit, (called the audit plan) and a **detailed approach** to the work (called the audit programme). In order to be able to develop such plans, auditors must have a **good knowledge of the business** they are planning to audit.

Usually, auditors will adopt a **risk-based approach** to an audit, to ensure that their attention is **focused** on the **important matters** relating to the financial statements, and the **potential problems**. The syllabus states that **risk assessment** is a key area in the syllabus. You must therefore ensure that you understand the principles set out in Section 3 of this chapter. **Analytical procedures** are a useful tool for assessing risks.

Materiality, or the importance of matters to financial statement users, is connected with audit risk. It is important for auditors to consider at the planning stage what level of **error** is **acceptable** in the financial statements they are auditing. Remember, we learnt in Chapter 1 that an audit is not a guarantee of 100% accuracy. We look at materiality and **tolerable error** in Section 4.

Lastly, we look at some specific point relating to planning review assignments and internal audit work.

As risk assessment and the response to assessed risks is a key area in the syllabus, you should anticipate that there may be a question in this area. Work through the questions in the chapter and ensure, when you come on to revision, that you attempt the relevant risk questions in the Practice & Revision Kit as well. Risks have been examined in the Pilot Paper, December 2001 and June 2003. Candidates were required to explain the concept of materiality in June 2002.

1 PLANNING

1.1 An effective and efficient audit relies on proper planning procedures. SAS 200 *Planning* states that '**auditors should plan the audit work so as to perform the audit in an effective manner**' and they should '**develop and document an overall audit plan describing the expected scope and conduct of the audit**'.

1.2 **Objectives of planning**

- Ensure that **appropriate attention** is devoted to the different areas of the audit
- Ensure that **potential problems** are **identified**
- **Facilitate review**
- **Assign** the proper **tasks** to members of the audit team

1.3 The SAS distinguishes between general audit strategy and detailed audit approach.

KEY TERMS

An **audit plan** is the formulation of the general strategy for the audit, which sets the direction for the audit, describes the expected scope and conduct of the audit and provides guidance for the development of the audit programme.

An **audit programme** is a set of instructions to the audit team that sets out the audit procedures the auditors intend to adopt and may include references to other matters such as the audit objectives, timing, sample size and basis of selection for each area. It also serves as a means to control and record the proper execution of the work.

Audit approach

1.4 In the past auditors took a **procedural approach**, where they would have attempted to vouch each transaction in financial statements. How, auditors usually take a **risk-based approach** which is believed to be more efficient and cost-effective.

1.5 In the risk-based approach, auditors analyse the risks associated with the client's business, transactions and systems, and direct their testing to risky areas. They are therefore not concerned with individual routine transactions, although they will still be concerned with material, non-routine transactions.

1.6 The process usually followed is:

- Assess and evaluate the accounting system and controls and carry out tests of controls if applicable
- Carry out substantive tests, focused on risky and material balances

Audit plan

1.7 The following is an example of an audit plan.

Client: N Jones (Newspapers) Ltd Accounts to 30 June 2004	Prepared by: ARM Date: 28/5/04 Reviewed by: Date:

Terms of the engagement

Standard audit assignment for normal Companies Act report.
Refer to engagement letter for contractual commitments.

The company and its business

Established confectioners, tobacconists and newsagents with main shop in high street and a branch in Kings Road Estate. New branch opened in the year, see Schedule X and permanent audit file for detailed updating work. Turnover £6 million.

Special audit problems

Review gross margins and directors' salaries to ensure that both appear reasonable in the light of other evidence, the nature and location of the business and the proprietor's standard of living. Reported earnings can be a problem in a cash business like this one.

Results of analytical review

Analytical review should be carried out as soon as the results are available. In the past, gross margins have been in the region of 30% (newspapers), 10% (tobacco), 20% (confectionery).

Materiality

Should be based on 5% of profits when the results are available. Currently set at £20,000 based on figures for the 10 months to 30 April 2004.

Risk evaluation and audit approach

Do not place reliance on internal controls – so audit control risk is rendered high. Adopt a substantive approach. In relation to potential understatement of sales, check till rolls to cash book, estimate the sales mix and purchase mix and predict a gross margin.

Other matters

Liaison with internal audit	- NONE
Stocktake	- HW attended 30 June, notes filed
Experts	- NONE REQUIRED

Budget and fee

Fee £25,000
For detailed time budget see 10.2

Staffing

Audit senior	2 weeks
Audit junior	10 days

Timetable

Audit report to be signed by 30 September 2004.

> **POINT TO NOTE**
>
> These issues will be discussed in more detail in the rest of this chapter.

1.8 **A structured approach to planning**

- **Updating knowledge** of the client
- Preparing the **detailed audit approach**
- Making **administrative decisions** re staffing/budgets

Audit programme

1.9 SAS 200 states that '**auditors should develop and document the nature, timing and extent of planned audit procedures required to implement the overall audit plan**' and '**the audit work planned should be reviewed, and if necessary, revised during the course of the audit**'.

> **POINT TO NOTE**
>
> We shall look at examples of audit programmes in Part D of this Study Text.

2 KNOWLEDGE OF THE BUSINESS

2.1 SAS 210 *Knowledge of the business* states that '**auditors should have or obtain a knowledge of the business of the entity to be audited which is sufficient to enable them to identify and understand the events, transactions and practices that may have a significant effect on the financial statements or the audit thereof**'.

2.2 The appendix to the SAS gives a list of matters which an auditor should consider, which are shown in the mindmap on the following page. However, the SAS states that this list is 'not exhaustive, nor is it intended that all the matters listed will be relevant to every engagement'.

2.3 **Obtaining the knowledge**

- Prior to acceptance of an engagement (as part of the tender process)
- Following acceptance
- Updating knowledge for succeeding periods
- Continuously throughout the audit

2.4 **Sources of knowledge**

- **Previous experience** of the client and its industry
- **Visits** to the client's premises and plant facilities
- **Discussion with** the client's **staff** and **directors**
- **Discussion with other auditors** and legal advisors within the industry
- **Discussion with knowledgeable people outside the client** (economists/regulators)
- **Publications** related to the industry
- **Legislation and regulations** that significantly affect the client
- **Documents produced** by the client
- **Professional literature** giving industry-specific guidance

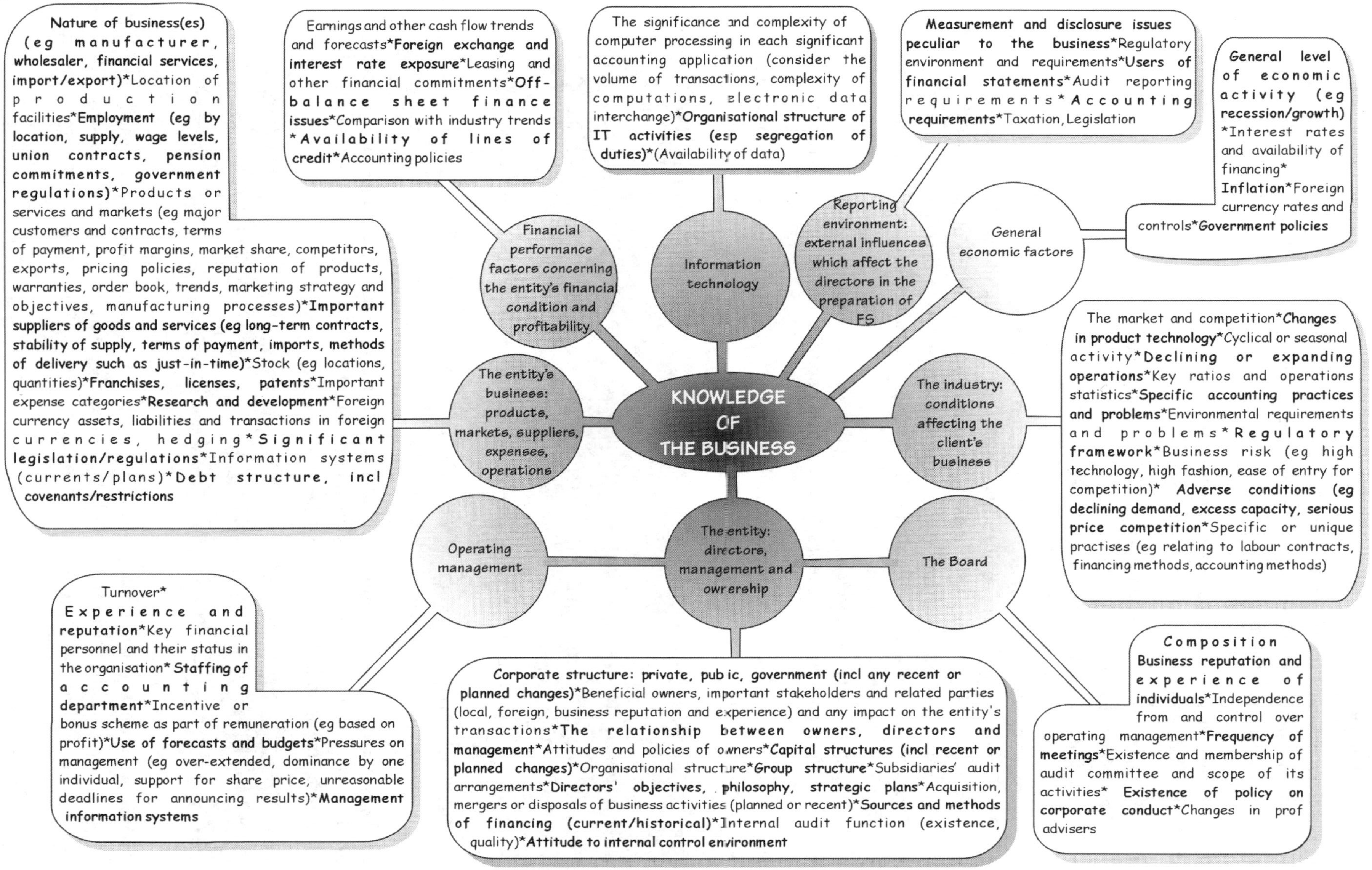
KNOWLEDGE OF THE BUSINESS
Financial performance factors concerning the entity's financial condition and profitability
Information technology
Reporting environment: external influences which affect the directors in the preparation of FS
General economic factors
The entity's business: products, markets, suppliers, expenses, operations
The industry: conditions affecting the client's business
Operating management
The entity: directors, management and ownership
The Board
Nature of business(es) (eg manufacturer, wholesaler, financial services, import/export)*Location of production facilities*Employment (eg by location, supply, wage levels, union contracts, pension commitments, government regulations)*Products or services and markets (eg major customers and contracts, terms of payment, profit margins, market share, competitors, exports, pricing policies, reputation of products, warranties, order book, trends, marketing strategy and objectives, manufacturing processes)*Important suppliers of goods and services (eg long-term contracts, stability of supply, terms of payment, imports, methods of delivery such as just-in-time)*Stock (eg locations, quantities)*Franchises, licenses, patents*Important expense categories*Research and development*Foreign currency assets, liabilities and transactions in foreign currencies, hedging*Significant legislation/regulations*Information systems (currents/plans)*Debt structure, incl covenants/restrictions
Earnings and other cash flow trends and forecasts*Foreign exchange and interest rate exposure*Leasing and other financial commitments*Off-balance sheet finance issues*Comparison with industry trends *Availability of lines of credit*Accounting policies
The significance and complexity of computer processing in each significant accounting application (consider the volume of transactions, complexity of computations, electronic data interchange)*Organisational structure of IT activities (esp segregation of duties)*(Availability of data)
Measurement and disclosure issues peculiar to the business*Regulatory environment and requirements*Users of financial statements*Audit reporting requirements*Accounting requirements*Taxation, Legislation
General level of economic activity (eg recession/growth) *Interest rates and availability of financing* Inflation*Foreign currency rates and controls*Government policies
The market and competition*Changes in product technology*Cyclical or seasonal activity*Declining or expanding operations*Key ratios and operations statistics*Specific accounting practices and problems*Environmental requirements and problems*Regulatory framework*Business risk (eg high technology, high fashion, ease of entry for competition)* Adverse conditions (eg declining demand, excess capacity, serious price competition*Specific or unique practises (eg relating to labour contracts, financing methods, accounting methods)
Turnover* Experience and reputation*Key financial personnel and their status in the organisation* Staffing of accounting department*Incentive or bonus scheme as part of remuneration (eg based on profit)*Use of forecasts and budgets*Pressures on management (eg over-extended, dominance by one individual, support for share price, unreasonable deadlines for announcing results)*Management information systems
Corporate structure: private, public, government (incl any recent or planned changes)*Beneficial owners, important stakeholders and related parties (local, foreign, business reputation and experience) and any impact on the entity's transactions*The relationship between owners, directors and management*Attitudes and policies of owners*Capital structures (incl recent or planned changes)*Organisational structure*Group structure*Subsidiaries' audit arrangements*Directors' objectives, philosophy, strategic plans*Acquisition, mergers or disposals of business activities (planned or recent)*Sources and methods of financing (current/historical)*Internal audit function (existence, quality)*Attitude to internal control environment
Composition Business reputation and experience of individuals*Independence from and control over operating management*Frequency of meetings*Existence and membership of audit committee and scope of its activities* Existence of policy on corporate conduct*Changes in prof advisers

2.5 **Using the knowledge**

- **Assess risks** and **identify problems**
- **Plan and perform** the audit **effectively** and **efficiently**
- **Evaluate audit evidence**

2.6 The following audit areas are subject to judgement which may be affected by knowledge of the business are given by the SAS as follows.

- **Developing the overall audit plan** and the **audit programme**
- **Considering risks**
- Assessing **inherent risk** and **control risk**
- Determining a **materiality** level remains appropriate
- Considering the complexity of the entity's **information systems**
- Identifying areas where **special audit considerations and skills** may be necessary
- Assessing **audit evidence** to establish appropriateness/the validity of assertions
- Evaluating **accounting estimates** and **representations** by the directors
- **Recognising conflicting information** (for example, contradictory representations)
- **Recognising unusual circumstances**
- **Making informed enquiries** and assessing the reasonableness of answers
- **Considering the appropriateness of accounting policies** and accounts disclosures

2.7 In some of the areas discussed above, particularly **risk identification, analytical procedures** will be a useful tool.

KEY TERM

Analytical procedures are the analysis of relationships:

(a) Between items of financial data, or between items of financial and non-financial data, deriving from the same period, or

(b) Between comparable financial information deriving from different periods to identify consistencies and predicted patterns or significant fluctuations and unexpected relationships, and the results of investigation thereof

2.8 Auditors are required by auditing standards to carry out analytical procedures at the planning stage of an audit to identify areas of potential audit risks and to help in planning the nature, timing and extent of audit procedures.

POINT TO NOTE

We will look at analytical procedures in more detail in Chapter 12.

2.9 Knowledge of the entity can only be used effectively if it is **communicated** to members of the audit team, so will usually be provided in the audit planning documentation. SAS 210 requires that the audit engagement partner communicates the knowledge to the team.

3 AUDIT RISK

Pilot paper, 12/01, 6/03

KEY TERM

Audit risk is the risk that auditors may give an inappropriate opinion on the financial statements.

Exam focus point

It is **vital** that you understand and learn this definition and the component parts of audit risk discussed below.

3.1 Audit risk is the risk that the auditors give an unqualified opinion on the accounts when they should have given a qualified opinion (or *vice versa*) **or** they give an opinion qualified for a particular reason where that reason was not justified.

3.2 Auditors apply judgement to determine **what level of risk** pertains to different areas of a client's system and **devise appropriate audit tests** so that the greatest audit effort is directed at the riskiest areas, so that the chance of detecting errors is improved and excessive time is not spent on 'safe' areas.

3.3 SAS 300 *Accounting and internal control and audit risk assessments* states that '**auditors should:**

(a) **Obtain an understanding of the accounting and internal control system sufficient to plan the audit and develop an effective audit approach; and**

(b) **Use professional judgement to assess the components of audit risk and to design audit procedures to ensure it is reduced to an acceptably low level**'.

3.4 **Audit risk can never be completely eliminated.** The auditors are called upon to make subjective judgements in the course of forming an opinion and so fraud or error may possibly go undetected.

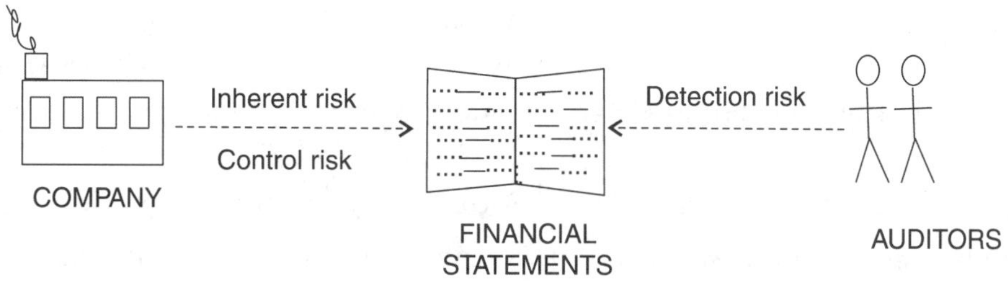

3.5 Audit risk is made up of three components: inherent risk, control risk and detection risk. These are illustrated in the above diagram, and will be explained in more detail below.

Inherent risk

KEY TERM

Inherent risk is the susceptibility of an account balance or class of transactions to material misstatement, either individually or when aggregated with misstatements in other balances or classes, irrespective of related internal controls.

3.6 Inherent risk is the risk that items will be misstated due to characteristics of those items, such as the fact they are **estimates** or that they are **important** items in the accounts. The auditors must use their professional judgement and all available knowledge to assess inherent risk.

3.7 SAS 300 states '**in developing their audit approach and detailed procedures, auditors should assess inherent risk in relation to financial statement assertions about material account balances and classes of transactions, taking account of factors relevant both to the entity as a whole and to the specific assertions**'.

FACTORS AFFECTING CLIENT AS A WHOLE	
Integrity and **attitude to risk** of directors and management	Domination by a single individual can cause problems
Management experience and **knowledge**	Changes in management and quality of financial management
Unusual pressures on management	Examples include tight reporting deadlines, or market or financing expectations
Nature of business	Potential problems include technological obsolescence or over-dependence on single product
Industry factors	Competitive conditions, regulatory requirements, technology developments, changes in customer demand
Information technology	Problems include lack of supporting documentation, concentration of expertise in a few people, potential for unauthorised access

FACTORS AFFECTING INDIVIDUAL ACCOUNT BALANCES OR TRANSACTIONS	
Financial statement **accounts prone to misstatement**	Accounts which require adjustment in previous period, require high degree of estimation or judgement, or which may significantly affect profitability or liquidity
Complex accounts	Accounts which require expert valuations or are subjects of current professional discussion
Assets at risk of being **lost or stolen**	Cash, (consider opportunities for unauthorised payments), stock, portable fixed assets (computers)
High volume of **transactions**	Accounting system may have problems coping
Quality of **accounting systems**	Strength of individual departments (sales, purchases, cash etc)
Unusual transactions	Transactions for large amounts, with unusual names, not settled promptly (particularly important if they occur at period-end)
	Transactions that do not go through the system, that relate to specific clients or processed by certain individuals
Staff	Staff changes or areas of low morale

Exam focus point

You should remember these lists when we consider substantive testing of individual audit areas in later chapters. The factors listed affect the choice of audit tests and also the extent of testing.

Control risk

KEY TERM

Control risk is the risk that a material misstatement would not be prevented, or detected and corrected on a timely basis, by the accounting and internal control systems.

3.8 If controls operate effectively, there is a strong chance that there are fewer errors in the financial statements than if they were ineffective.

3.9 One general audit approach that auditors may take, if they believe the company's controls are capable of minimising mistakes in the financial statements, is to rely on that assumption and reduce the amount of testing they do on the financial statements. In order to do this, they would have to carry out tests on the controls instead. In addition, they can never eliminate completely audit work on the financial statements (**substantive procedures**).

3.10 If the auditors intend to carry out such a **controls audit**, they are required by SAS 300 to carry out a preliminary assessment of control risk at the planning stage.

POINT TO NOTE

We shall look at company controls and auditors' tests of them in detail in Chapters 9-11.

Detection risk

KEY TERM

Detection risk is the risk that audit procedures will fail to detect material errors in financial statements.

3.11 Detection risk relates to the inability of the auditors to examine all evidence. Audit evidence is usually persuasive rather than conclusive so some detection risk is usually present, allowing the auditors to seek 'reasonable confidence'.

Management of audit risk

3.12 Auditors will want their overall audit risk to be at an acceptable level, or it will not be worth them carrying out the audit. In other words, if the chance of them giving an inappropriate opinion and being sued is high, it might better not to do the audit at all.

3.13 The auditors will obviously consider how risky a new audit client is during the acceptance process, and may decide not to go ahead with the relationship. However, they will also consider audit risk for each individual audit, and will seek to manage the risk.

3.14 As we have seen above, it is not in the auditors' power to affect inherent or control risk. As they are risks integral to the client, the auditor cannot change the level of these risks. SAS 300 states that '**auditors should consider the assessed levels of inherent and control risk in determining the nature, timing and extent of substantive procedures required to reduce audit risk to an acceptable level**'.

3.15 The auditor therefore manages overall audit risk by manipulating detection risk, the only element of audit risk the auditor has control over. This is because, the more audit work the auditors carry out, the lower detection risk becomes, although it can never be entirely eliminated due to the inherent limitations of audit.

3.16 This audit risk management can be shown crudely in a mathematical equation. The auditor will decide what level of overall risk is acceptable, and then determine a level of audit work so that detection risk makes the equation work.

EXAMPLE I

Inherent risk	×	Control risk	×	Detection risk	=	Audit risk
High	×	High	×	Low	=	Acceptable

- Is variable
- Is a high level of audit work

3.17 In Example I, inherent and control risk were both high. This has the following effects on the audit.

- The auditors are unlikely to rely on tests of controls, but will carry out extended substantive tests.
- Detection risk must be rendered low, which will mean carrying out a substantial amount of substantive testing.

3.18 Audits are not all the same, however. A different company could product the following audit risk calculation.

EXAMPLE II

Inherent risk	×	Control risk	×	Detection risk	=	Audit risk
Medium	×	Low	×	Medium	=	Acceptable

3.19 In Example II, as control risk is low, the auditors are likely to carry out tests of controls and seek to rely on the client's system, as we discussed in Paragraph 3.9

3.20 SAS 300 states that '**regardless of the assessed levels of inherent and control risks, auditors should perform some substantive procedures for financial statement assertions of material account balances and transaction classes**'.

3.21 **Substantive procedures can never be abandoned entirely** because control and inherent risk can never be assessed at a low enough level, although substantive procedures may be restricted to analytical procedures if appropriate.

3.22 When both inherent and control risks are assessed as high, the auditors should consider whether substantive procedures can provide sufficient appropriate audit evidence to reduce detection risk, and therefore audit risk, to an acceptably low level. For example, they may not be able to obtain sufficient evidence about the completeness of income in the absence of some internal controls. If sufficient evidence cannot be obtained, auditors may have to qualify their report.

3.23 Misstatements discovered in substantive procedures may cause the auditors to modify their previous assessment of control risk. Where the auditors' assessment of the components of audit risk changes during the audit, they should modify the planned substantive procedures based on the revised risk levels.

3.24 Lastly, it is important to understand that there is not a standard level of audit risk which is considered generally by auditors to be acceptable. This is a matter of audit judgement, and so will vary from firm to firm and audit to audit. Audit firms are likely to charge higher fees for higher risk clients.

POINT TO NOTE

Materiality and audit risk are closely connected. Materiality will be discussed in the next section.

Use of information technology

3.25 The types of mathematical equations discussed above are often calculated by auditors on specialised computer programmes to identify appropriate levels of risk, materiality and sample sizes. However, this does not eliminate the need for audit judgement. A computer will need to be told whether an inherent risk is high or medium, and be told an acceptable level of overall audit risk before it can calculate detection risk.

Question: Audit risk

Hippo Ltd is a long established client of your firm. It manufactures bathroom fittings and fixtures, which it sells to a range of wholesalers in the UK, on credit.

You are the audit senior and have recently been sent the following extract from the draft balance sheet by the finance director.

	Budget		*Actual*	
	£'000s	£'000s	£'000s	£'000s
Fixed assets		453		367
Current assets				
Trade debtors	1,134		976	
Bank	-		54	
Current liabilities				
Trade creditors	967		944	
Bank overdraft	9		-	
Net current assets		158		86
Total assets		611		453

During the course of conversation with the finance director, you establish that a major new customer the company had included in its budget went bankrupt during the year.

Required

Identify any potential risks for the audit of Hippo and explain why you believe they are risks.

Answer

Potential risks relevant to the audit of Hippo

(1) **Credit sales**. Hippo makes sales on credit. This increases the risk that Hippo's sales will not be converted into cash. Debtors is likely to be a risky area and the auditors will have to consider what the best evidence that debtors are going to pay their debts is likely to be.

(2) **Related industry**. Hippo manufactures bathroom fixtures and fittings. These are sold to wholesalers, but it is possible that Hippo's ultimate market is the building industry. This is a notoriously volatile industry, and Hippo may find that their results fluctuate too, as demand rises and falls. This suspicion is added to by the bankruptcy of the wholesaler in the year. The auditors must be sure that accounts which present Hippo as a viable company are in fact correct.

(3) **Controls**. The fact that a major new customer went bust suggests that Hippo did not undertake a very thorough credit check on that customer before agreeing to supply them. This implies that the controls at Hippo may not be very strong.

(4) **Variance**. The actual results are different from budget. This may be explained by the fact that the major customer went bankrupt, or it may reveal that there are other errors and problems in the reported results, or in the original budget.

(5) **Debtors**. There is a risk that the result reported contains debt from the bankrupt wholesaler, which is likely to be irrecoverable.

---

4 MATERIALITY 6/02

4.1 We discussed materiality briefly in Chapter 1. Remember it relates to the level of error that affects the decisions of users of the accounts. SAS 220 *Materiality* required that auditors '**consider materiality when determining the nature, timing and extent of audit procedures**'.

4.2 Materiality considerations during **audit planning** are extremely important. The assessment of materiality at this stage should be based on the most recent and reliable financial information and will help to determine an effective and efficient audit approach. Materiality assessment will help the auditors to decide:

- **How many** and **what items** to examine
- Whether to use **sampling techniques**
- What **level of error** is likely to lead to a qualified audit opinion

4.3 The resulting combination of audit procedures should help to reduce audit risk to an appropriately low level. This is how risk and materiality are closely connected. A level of error lower than would cause a qualification is known as **tolerable error**. The value of discovered errors should be aggregated at the end of the audit to ensure the total is still below the tolerable error.

4.4 The effect of planning materiality on the audit process is shown in the diagram below.

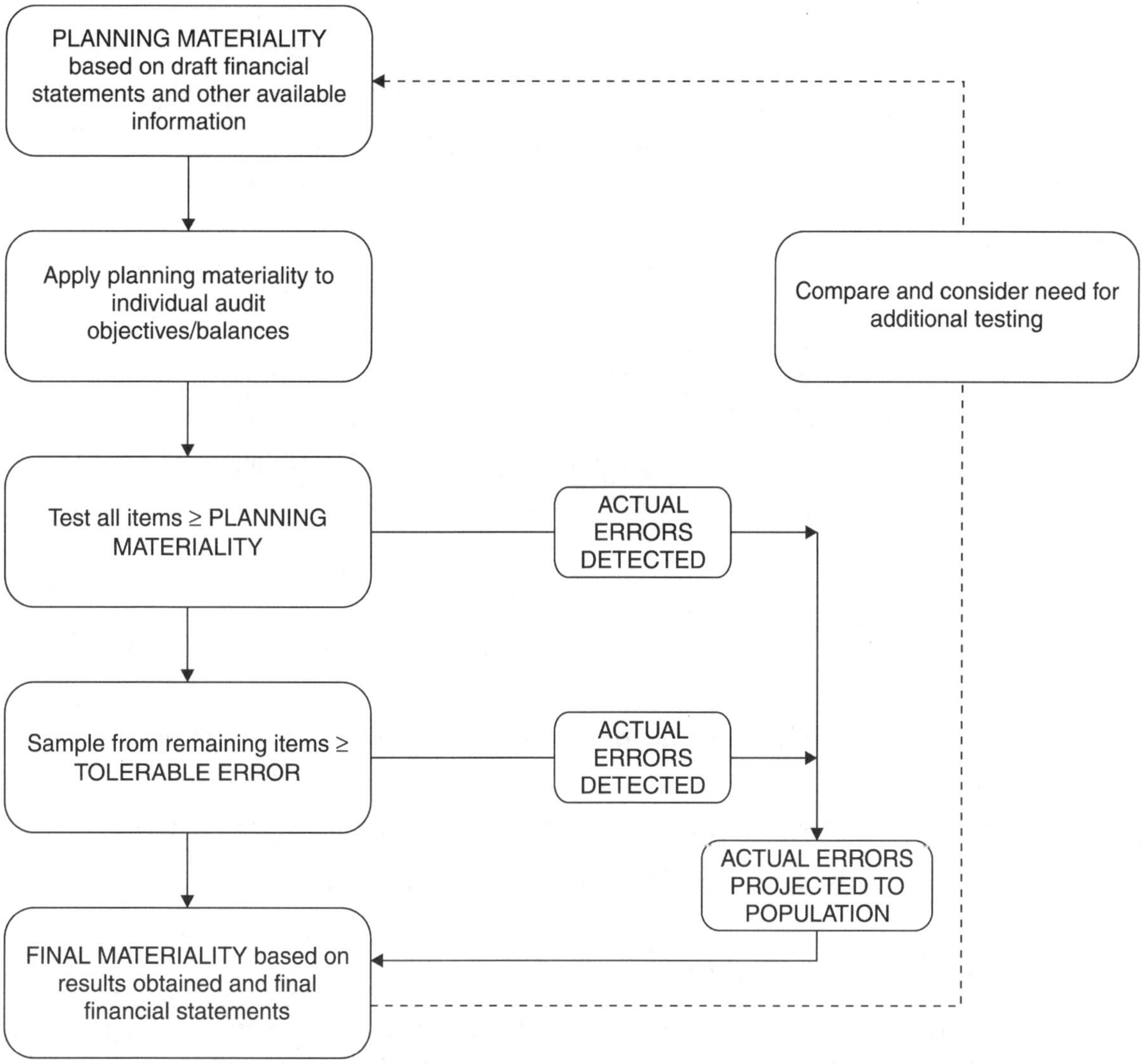

4.5 To set the materiality level the auditors need to decide the level of error which would distort the view given by the accounts. Because many users of accounts are primarily interested in the profitability of the company, the level is often expressed as a proportion of its **profits**.

4.6 Materiality can be thought of in terms of the **size** of the business. Hence, if the company remains a fairly constant size, the materiality level should not change; similarly if the business is growing, the level of materiality will increase from year to year.

4.7 The size of a company can be measured in terms of turnover and total assets before deducting any liabilities (sometimes referred to in legislation as 'the balance sheet total') both of which tend not to be subject to the fluctuations which may affect profit.

4.8 Note that the auditors will often calculate a range of values, such as those shown below, and then take an average or weighted average of all the figures produced as the materiality level.

Value	%
Profit before tax	5
Gross profit	½ - 1
Turnover	½ - 1
Total assets	1 - 2
Net assets	2 - 5
Profit after tax	5 – 10

POINT TO NOTE

However, bear in mind that materiality has qualitative, as well as quantitative, aspects. You must not simply think of materiality as being a percentage of items in the financial statements.

4.9 **Tolerable error** may be set at planning materiality, but it is usually reduced to, say 75% or even 50% of planning materiality so as to take account of sampling risk. The tolerable error is used to determine sample size.

POINT TO NOTE

Tolerable error and sampling risk are discussed in more detail in Chapter 8.

Review of materiality

4.10 The level of materiality must be reviewed constantly as the audit progresses and changes may be required because:

- **Draft accounts** are **altered** (due to material error and so on) and therefore overall materiality changes.
- **External factors cause changes** in the control or inherent risk estimates.
- Such changes are caused by errors found during testing.

5 PLANNING A REVIEW

5.1 There is no UK guidance specifically relating to a review. A review is an exercise similar to audit. It is a matter of professional judgement for a UK accountant as to what planning he does in order to carry out a review. However, he may choose to follow the recommendations given in International Standard of Review Engagements 2400 as good practice.

5.2 ISRE 2400 states that the auditor 'should plan the work so that an effective engagement will be performed'. The standard therefore leaves this as a matter of judgement for the auditor to consider.

5.3 However, the standard also states that 'the auditor should obtain or update the knowledge of the business'. This should include consideration of the following factors:

- The entity's organisation
- The accounting systems
- The operating characteristics of the entity
- The nature of its assets, liabilities, revenues and expenses

5.4 The standard requires that the auditor have sufficient understanding of the business to be able to make appropriate enquiries as part of the review exercise.

6 PLANNING AN INTERNAL AUDIT

6.1 **Main purposes of internal audit planning**

- Determine priorities
- Establish the most cost-effective way of doing the work
- Assist in the direction and control of work
- Ensure that attention is devoted to critical aspects of work
- Ensure that work is completed in accordance with pre-determined targets

6.2 **Nature of work plans**

- Strategic
- Periodic
- Operational

KEY TERMS

The **strategic plan** is a long term plan covering a period of between 2 and 5 years. During this time, all major systems should be audited. The plan should set out the audit objectives, areas, types of activity, frequency of audit and resources to be applied.

The **periodic plan** is typically set out for a financial year and it translates the strategic plan for that year into a schedule of assignments to be carried out, allocating staff and resources. It is likely to be approved by management.

Operational work plans are those plans produced for each audit assignment. They should cover the objectives and scope of the audit, include time budgets and outline procedures and methods.

6.3 All of the types of plan outlined above should be flexible, so that the plans can be adapted to the changing needs of the business.

The internal audit planning process

6.4 When the audit plans (above) are formulated, the following stages should be followed:

Stage 1. Identify the objectives of the organisation

Stage 2. Define internal audit objectives

Stage 3. Take account of relevant legal and regulatory changes

Stage 4. Obtain a comprehensive understanding of the systems, structure and operations

Stage 5. Identify, evaluate and rank risks to which the company is exposed

The issue of risk management has already been discussed in Chapter 3. The internal auditors will incorporate their knowledge and understanding of risk into all the strategic audit plans they prepare.

Stage 6. Take account of changes in structure or systems during the period, known strengths and weaknesses in the system, management concerns and expectations

Stage 7. Identify audit areas by service, function and major systems

For example, the team might audit divisions of the business separately, or focus on the Human Resources department, or the sales systems.

Stage 8. Determine the type of audit, for example, systems, verification, value for money

A systems audit might be conducted on the sales or purchase system, for example. If the internal auditors were investigating a fraud, they might use a verification or substantive approach, trying to substantiate financial results to third party evidence. Value for money audits were discussed in Chapter 3.

Stage 9. Take account of any external audit or review plans

The company will not want internal audit to carry out work that the external audit team plan to carry out as part of their audit as this is not cost-effective. On the other hand, the external audit team might make use of work performed by internal audit (see Chapter 7) which might be cheaper for the company.

Stage 10. Assess staff resources and match to requirements

We will discuss staffing in Chapter 7.

Question: Audit plan

You are the manager in charge of the audit of Ruddington Furniture plc for the year ended 31 July 20X2, and you have been asked to describe the work which should be carried out in planning the statutory audit and in monitoring its progress.

Ruddington Furniture plc buys domestic furniture from manufacturers and sells it to the general public. The company's head office and main warehouse are on the same site, and there are sales branches with associated warehouses in different parts of the country.

Your firm has been auditor of the company for a number of years. All the company's accounting records are maintained on the computer at head office. When a sale takes place at the branch, the salesman checks that the furniture the customer requires is in stock, and if it is, the customer pays for the items by cash, cheque or credit card (or charge card) and collects them from the warehouse. Where the items are not in stock, it is possible to find whether they are available at another local branch, or an order can be placed for the stock.

In previous years' audits there have been problems at branches of the actual stock being less than the computer book stock quantities. Also, problems have been experienced in identifying and valuing damaged stock and goods returned by customers. The company has a small internal audit department and their work includes periodic visits to branches.

The company was subject to a management buy-out in February 20X0 which resulted in high gearing. You understand that because of a recession in the furniture trade the company has liquidity problems and that currently it is negotiating with the bank to obtain additional finance.

Required

List and describe the matters you will consider and the work you will carry out in planning the audit.

Answer

(a) Examine the audit files for the previous year and consider any important matters which might have a bearing on the current year's audit.

(b) Consider any recent changes in legislation or accounting standards which might affect the financial statements of Ruddington Furniture plc.

(c) If possible, obtain the management accounts for the year and examine them to gain information about the trading performance of the company and compare them with the budget.

(d) Note any significant changes in the management or key employees of the company and in the accounting system and procedures.

(e) Agree the timings of the audit with management . In particular:

  (i) The stocktake and the auditors' attendance
  (ii) The preparation of the financial statements
  (iii) The extent to which analyses and summaries can be prepared by the company's employees
  (iv) The relevance of any work to be carried out by the enterprise's internal auditors

(f) Review the stocktaking procedures in detail and obtain the results of any stock counts during the year, considering whether problems still exist in the comparison between book and actual stock levels.

(g) In the light of the known liquidity problems of the company, obtain any forecasts and budgets for the following year or years. This may be useful in performing any post balance sheet review, particularly if there is any considerable period between the end of the audit and the date the directors plan to sign the accounts (and the AGM).

(h) Examine the work of internal auditors to determine whether it is reliable and relevant, and some of the tests they have performed should be reperformed for this purpose. If it is decided that their work can be relied upon, this may reduce some of the testing the external auditors can perform. The internal audit work should highlight problem areas within the company and reduce the risks of the external auditor missing any fraud or errors.

(i) Decide what the general audit approach is to be. A risk-based audit approach is most likely.

(j) Determine which audit staff are to be used. The staff chosen should be suitably qualified and experienced. The number of staff needs to be determined, particularly in relation to the number of stocktake visits the auditors will undertake. Larger branches should be visited and smaller branches in rotation over a few years.

(k) Prepare a timetable for the audit, including the items for the principal phases of the audit, the date the audit report will be signed and an estimate of fees, costs and profit.

Exam focus point

Exam questions on planning an audit commonly give the circumstances of a particular client, and ask you to consider what factors would influence planning and what the auditors need to do in response to those factors.

Chapter roundup

- The auditors will formulate an **overall audit plan** which will be translated into a **detailed audit programme** for audit staff to follow.
- In formulating the audit plan the auditors will consider:
  - Knowledge of the entity's business
  - Risk and materiality
  - Nature, timing and extent of procedures
  - Co-ordination, direction, supervision and review
- Important aspects of **knowledge of the business** are:
  - The industry
  - Directors, managers and ownership
  - Products, markets, suppliers, expenses and operations
  - Financial performance
  - Reporting environment
- **Audit risk** is the risk that the auditors may give an inappropriate opinion on the financial statements. A risk-based audit will make use of the risk model to determine the amount and extent of audit testing. Audit risk comprises **inherent, control** and **detection risk**.
- **Analytical procedures** are very useful at the planning stage, allowing risk areas to be identified.
- **Materiality** should be calculated at the planning stages of all audits. The calculation or estimation of materiality should be based on experience and judgement. The materiality level chosen should be reviewed during the audit.
- Planning an external review plan is a matter of professional judgement, but should include obtaining a knowledge of the business.
- **Internal audit** departments need to plan also, both on an **annual department level**, which should focus on the objectives of the entity and the department, and on an **individual assignment level**, which should focus on the objectives and risks of the function being reviewed.

Quick quiz

1 Fill in the **blanks.**

The three objectives of planning are:

- Ensuring that appropriate .... is devoted to key .... of the audit.
- Ensuring that .... are identified.
- Facilitating ....

2 Complete the table, giving three examples from each source of knowledge of the business.

Knowledge of the business	
General economic factors	1 2 3
The industry	1 2 3
The entity	1 2 3
The entity's business	1 2 3
Financial performance	1 2 3
Information technology	1 2 3
Reporting environment	1 2 3

3 If control and inherent risk as assessed as sufficiently low, substantive procedures can be abandoned completely.

True ☐

False ☐

4 Match the percentages to the values for a correct calculation of materiality

	%
Profit before tax	5
Gross profit	5-10
Turnover	1-2
Total assets	$^1/_2$-1
Net assets	2-5
Profit after tax	$^1/_2$-1

5 Give two reasons for using analytical procedures at the audit planning stage.

1 ……………………………………………………………………………………..

2 ……………………………………………………………………………………..

6 Complete the definitions.

…………………… risk is the risk that ……………. may give an …………………..opinion on the financial statements. It has three components.

…………………… risk is the …………………… of an account balance or ………………………… .. ………………….. to material ………………………… .

7 The audit programme is a standardised document.

True ☐

False ☐

Answers to quick quiz

1 attention, areas
potential problems
review

2 Turn to the mindmap on page 105.

3 False.

4

	%
Profit before tax	5
Gross profit	1/2-1
Turnover	1/2-1
Total assets	1-2
Net assets	2-5
Profit after tax	5-10

5 1 To identify areas of potential audit risk
2 To help in planning the nature, timing and extent of other audit procedures

6 Audit, auditors, inappropriate
Inherent, susceptibility, class of transactions, misstatement

7 False

Now try the question below from the Exam Question Bank

Number	Level	Marks	Time
6	Exam	20	36 mins

Chapter 7

USING THE WORK OF OTHERS

Topic list		Syllabus reference	Study guide
1	Using the work of internal audit	4	11
2	Using the work of an expert	4	11
3	Service organisations	4	11
4	Reporting	4	11
5	External audit staff issues	4	11
6	Internal audit staff issues	4	11

Introduction

Internal auditors can, and often do, carry out similar audit tests to external auditors. In fact, some companies maintain internal audit departments to seek to reduce the audit fee. As mentioned in Chapter 6, the external auditors will sometimes seek to use the work of internal audit.

Section 1 of this chapter looks at the extent to which external auditors can use and rely on the work of internal auditors. It outlines the APB's guidance in this matter, which is found in SAS 500.

While auditors are highly trained individuals, it is possible that when conducting an audit or review they encounter issues which are outside the scope of their expertise, for example, valuation of buildings. In such circumstances an auditor will have to consult an expert. SAS 520, *Using the work of an expert*, outlines the factors an auditor should bear in mind, as we see in section 2.

It is increasingly common for companies to outsource specific functions to service organisations who have more expertise in that function, for example IT or payroll, than the business. If functions relevant to the audit have been outsourced, the auditor must consider how to obtain the audit evidence he requires to come to his opinion. In section 3, we look at the guidance in SAS 480, *Service Organisations.*

Finally, we consider the staffing issues in relation to both internal and external audit.

The relationship between internal and external auditors could be examined as they are both important syllabus areas. Using the work of experts or auditing areas which have been outsourced could be examined in conjunction with a balance sheet area, for example, fixed assets.

1 USING THE WORK OF INTERNAL AUDIT 12/02, 6/03

1.1 The objectives of internal audit will differ from those of the external auditors. However, some of the means of achieving their respective objectives are often similar, and so some of the internal auditors' work may be used by the external auditors.

1.2 Guidance about using the work of internal audit is given to external auditors in SAS 500, *Considering the work of internal audit*, which states that '**external auditors should consider the activities of internal audit and their effect, if any, on external audit procedures**'.

1.3 They should also '**obtain sufficient understanding of internal audit activities to assist in planning the audit and developing an effective audit approach**'.

1.4 An effective IA function may reduce, modify or alter the timing of external audit procedures, but it can **never** eliminate them entirely. Where the IA function is deemed ineffective, it may still be useful to be aware of the IA conclusions.

1.5 The effectiveness of IA will have a great impact on how the external auditors' assess the whole control system and the assessment of audit risk. SAS 500 says '**during the course of their planning the external auditors should perform an assessment of the internal audit function if they consider that it may be possible and desirable to rely on certain internal audit work in specific audit areas for the purpose of the external audit of the financial statements**'.

ASSESSMENT OF INTERNAL AUDIT	
Organisational status	Consider **to whom** internal audit **reports** (should be board), whether internal audit has any **operating responsibilities** and constraints or restrictions on the function
Scope of function	Consider **extent** and **nature** of **assignments** performed and the action taken by management as a result of internal audit reports.
Technical competence	Consider whether internal auditors have adequate **technical training** and proficiency
Due professional care	Consider whether internal audit is **properly planned, supervised, reviewed** and **documented**

1.6 External auditors should liaise with the internal auditors at regular intervals throughout the audit. Information on tests and conclusions should be passed both to and from IA. The internal auditors should liase with the external auditors as part of their planning process.

Evaluating specific internal audit work

1.7 '**When the external auditors use specific internal audit work to reduce the extent of their audit procedures, they should evaluate that work to confirm its adequacy for their purposes.**' The evaluation here will consider the scope of work and related audit programmes and whether the assessment of the IA function remains appropriate.

Evaluation	
Training and proficiency	Have the internal auditors had sufficient and adequate technological training to carry out the work? Are the internal auditors proficient?
Supervision	Is the work of assistants properly supervised, reviewed and documented?
Evidence	Has sufficient, appropriate audit evidence been obtained to afford a reasonable basis for the conclusions reached?
Conclusions	Are the conclusions reached appropriate, given the circumstances?
Reports	Are any reports produced by internal audit consistent with the result of the work performed?
Unusual matters	Have any unusual matters or exceptions arising and disclosed by internal audit been resolved properly?
Plan	Are any amendments to the external audit programme required as a result of the matters identified by internal audit?
Testing	Has the work of internal audit been sufficiently tested by the external auditor to confirm its adequacy?

1.8 If the external auditors decide that the IA work is not adequate, they should extend their procedures in order to obtain appropriate evidence.

Using the work of others as part of a review

1.9 ISRE 2400 states that when the auditor uses work carried out by another party (expert or internal auditor) as part of a review, he must be satisfied that the work is satisfactory for the purposes of the report he is issuing. This will be a matter of judgement.

Internal audit using the work of others

1.10 The situation where internal auditors use the work of experts or service organisations is different to when external auditors use them. The experts etc are **contracted** to provide the service to the organisation (of which the IA function is part).

1.11 This gives the company contractual rights when they rely on the work. If the directors permit the internal auditors to use the services of an expert, the internal auditors may seek to rely on their work and may be able to sue for negligence if the work is not of a satisfactory quality.

2 USING THE WORK OF AN EXPERT

KEY TERM

An **expert** is a person or firm possessing special skill, knowledge and experience in a particular field other than auditing.

2.1 Professional audit staff are highly trained and educated, but their experience and training is limited to accountancy and audit matters. In certain situations auditors will need to use someone else with different expert knowledge. An expert may be engaged by:

- A **client** to provide **specialist advice** on a particular matter which affects the financial statements
- **The auditors** in order to obtain **sufficient audit evidence** regarding certain financial statement assertions

Determining the need to use the work of an expert

2.2 SAS 520 *Using the work of an expert* gives guidance.

- **'When using the work performed by an expert, auditors should obtain sufficient appropriate audit evidence that such work is adequate for the purposes of an audit.'**
- **'When planning to use the work of an expert, the auditors should assess the objectivity and professional qualifications, experience and resources of the expert.'**
- **'The auditors should obtain sufficient appropriate audit evidence that the expert's scope of work is adequate for the purposes of their audit.'**
- **'The auditors should assess the appropriateness of the expert's work as audit evidence regarding the financial statement assertions being considered.'**

2.3 **Examples given in the SAS**

- **Valuations of certain types of assets**, for example, land, buildings, plant, machinery
- **Determination of quantities or physical condition of assets**
- **Determination of amounts** using specialised techniques, for example, pensions
- **The measurement of work completed** and **work in progress** on contracts
- **Legal opinions**

2.4 When considering whether to use the work of an expert, the auditors should review:

- The **importance** of the matter being considered in the context of the accounts
- The **risk of misstatement** based on the nature and complexity of the matter
- The **quantity** and **quality** of other available **relevant audit evidence**

2.5 If they decide that an expert is required, they should discuss it with management. Where management is unwilling or unable to engage an expert, the auditors should consider engaging an expert themselves unless sufficient alternative audit evidence can be obtained.

Competence and objectivity of the expert

2.6 The auditor must consider:

- The expert's **professional certification**, or licensing by, or membership of, an appropriate professional body
- The expert's **experience and reputation** in the field in which the auditors are seeking audit evidence

2.7 The risk that an expert's **objectivity is impaired** increases when the expert is:

- **Employed** by the entity
- **Related** in some other manner to the entity, for example, by being financially dependent upon, or having an investment in, the entity

2.8 If the auditors have **reservations** about the competence or objectivity of the expert they may need to carry out other procedures to obtain evidence from another expert.

The expert's scope of work

2.9 The expert's terms of reference are usually set out in writing and could include:

- The **objectives** and **scope** of the expert's work
- A **general outline** as to the specific matters the expert's report is to cover
- The **intended use** of the expert's work including the possible communication to third parties of the expert's identity and extent of involvement
- The **extent** of the **expert's access** to appropriate records and files
- Information regarding the **assumptions and methods intended** to be used by the expert and their consistency with those used in prior periods

Assessing the work of the expert

2.10 Auditors should assess whether the expert's findings are properly reflected in the financial statements or supports the financial statement assertions. They should also consider:

- The **source data used**
- The **assumptions and methods used**
- **When** the expert carried out the work
- The reasons for any **changes in assumptions and methods**
- The **results** of the expert's work in the light of the auditors' overall knowledge of the business and the results of other audit procedures

2.11 The auditors do **not** have the expertise to judge the assumptions and methods used; these are the responsibility of the expert. However, the auditors should seek to obtain an understanding of these assumptions etc, to consider their reasonableness based on other audit evidence, knowledge of the business and so on.

2.12 Where inconsistencies arise between the expert's work and other audit evidence, then the auditors should attempt to resolve them by discussion with both the entity and the expert. Additional procedures (including use of another expert) may be necessary.

2.13 Where the audit evidence from the expert is insufficient, and there is no satisfactory alternative source of evidence, then the auditors should consider whether they may have a limitation with regard to their audit report.

3 SERVICE ORGANISATIONS

KEY TERM

A **service organisation** is an organisation that provides services to another organisation.

3.1 Some companies outsource certain business activities to service organisations.

3.2 Auditors need to obtain **sufficient, appropriate audit evidence** to express an opinion on financial statements. They therefore need to consider an approach towards the parts of the audit and the financial statements affected by the service organisation.

Audit planning

3.3 As part of their audit planning, auditors need to obtain a knowledge of the business. Understanding what functions are outsourced is a part of that. SAS 480 *Service organisations* says '**in planning the audit, user entity auditors should determine whether activities undertaken by service organisations are relevant to the audit**'.

KEY TERM

The **user entity** is the organisation which is outsourcing any of its activities to the service organisation.

3.4 The SAS lists the following activities as relevant activities. (This is not an exclusive list.)

- Maintenance of accounting records
- Other finance functions
- Management of assets
- Undertaking or making arrangements for transactions as agent of the user entity.

3.5 SAS 480 requires the auditor to understand the terms of the agreement between the service organisation and the user entity. '**User entity and auditors should obtain and document an understanding of:**

(a) **The contractual terms which apply to relevant activities undertaken by service organisations and**

(b) **The way that the user entity monitors those activities so as to ensure that it meets its fiduciary and other legal responsibilities.**'

3.6 The SAS requires the auditor to consider:

- Whether the terms contain an adequate specification of the information to be provided to the user entity and responsibilities for initiating transactions relating to the activity undertaken by the service organisation.
- The way that accounting records relating to relevant activities are maintained.
- Whether the user entity has right to access to accounting records prepared by the service organisation concerning the activities undertaken, and relevant underlying information held by it, and the conditions in which such access may be sought.
- Whether the terms take proper account of any applicable requirements of regulatory bodies concerning the form of records to be maintained, or access to them.
- The nature of relevant performance standards.
- The way in which the use entity monitors performance of relevant activities and the extent to which its monitoring process relies on controls operated by the service organisation.
- Whether the service organisation has agreed to indemnify the user entity in the event of a performance failure.
- Whether the contractual terms permit the user entity auditors access to source of audit evidence including accounting records of the user entity and the information necessary for the conduct of the audit.

Assessing audit risk and designing audit procedures

3.7 SAS 480 requires auditors to '**determine the effect of relevant activities on their assessment of inherent risk and the user entity's control environment**'.

3.8 The auditor should consider:

- The nature of the service
- The degree of authority delegated
- The arrangements for ensuring quality
- Whether assets prone to loss or misappropriation are involved
- The reputation of the service organisation

3.9 In relation to control risk, the auditor should consider the monitoring that the user entity has in place over the service organisation's activities.

3.10 Because it is a legal requirement that the **directors** are **responsible** for maintaining accounting records, '**if a service organisation maintains all or part of a user entity's accounting records, user entity auditors should assess whether the arrangements affect their reporting responsibilities in relation to accounting records arising form law or regulations**'.

3.11 Having considered the risk attached to the use of the service organisation, the auditor should design audit procedures to obtain sufficient, appropriate audit evidence.

Obtaining audit evidence

3.12 The SAS states that '**based on their understanding of the aspects of the user entity's accounting system and control environment relating to relevant activities, user entity auditors should:**

(a) **Assess whether sufficient appropriate audit evidenced concerning the relevant financial statement assessment is available from records held at the user entity; and if not**

(b) **Determine effective procedures to obtain evidence necessary for the audit, either by direct access to records kept by service organisations or through information obtained from the service organisations or their auditors**'.

3.13 It also outlines a series of audit procedures

- Inspecting records and documents held by the user entity
- Establishing the effectiveness of controls
- Obtaining representations to confirm balance and transactions from the service organisation
- Performing analytical review on
  - The records maintained by the user entity, or
  - The returns received from the service organisation
- Inspecting records and documents held by the service organisation
- Requesting specified procedures re performed by
  - The service organisation
  - The user entity's internal audit department

- Reviewing information from the service organisation or its auditors concerning the design and operation of its control systems.

Using reports

3.14 **'When using a report issued by the service organisation's auditors, the user entity's auditors should consider the scope of the work performed and assess whether the report is sufficient and appropriate for its intended use.'**

3.15 The new entity's auditors should consider whether the information contained in the report is:

- Relevant
- Adequate
- Covers the right time period

Exam focus point

The examiner has published an article in **Student Accountant** about service organisations which you should ensure you read.

4 REPORTING

4.1 The auditor is always **solely responsible** for the audit opinion. He must be assured that he has gained sufficient, appropriate advice to have an opinion on the financial statements, he must then express his opinion.

4.2 It would therefore be **inappropriate to refer to the work of others in his final report**. His thoughts on the work of others should, however, be adequately documented in the audit file.

4.3 However, if the user entity auditor judges that there is insufficient audit evidence concerning the activity undertaken by the service organisation, then he will have to mention the service organisation in his reasoning for qualifying the audit report.

POINT TO NOTE

Qualified audit reports will be discussed in detail in Chapter 19.

5 EXTERNAL AUDIT STAFF ISSUES

5.1 When planning the audit the partner or manager must decide how many staff are to be allocated to the assignment, how experienced (which grade) and whether any of them will require special knowledge, skills or experience.

5.2 EXAMPLE

The client may undertake complicated leasing transactions, so an auditor with some experience of leasing would be required.

5.3 The partner will look at the staffing of the audit in previous years and he will need to decide whether that level of staffing was acceptable. He might judge this by looking at the amount of overtime worked last year and whether the actual cost was over or under budget. This must be gauged with reference to any unexpected problems which arose in the previous year and whether they are likely to recur.

5.4 The audit partner is in charge of the audit and it is his opinion that will be given in the audit report.

5.5 Audit engagement partners should ensure that audit work is directed, supervised and reviewed in a manner that provides reasonable assurance that the work has been performed competently. This can be achieved by:

- Good audit planning which is communicated properly to audit staff
- Allocating work to appropriate members of staff
- Supervising work done by keeping in contact with the audit team
- Reviewing the audit file prior to expressing an opinion

6 INTERNAL AUDIT STAFF ISSUES

6.1 An internal audit department should have a well-qualified head who should plan how to use the resources available to him. A good IA department will have a breadth of skills employed.

6.2 The head of internal audit should also ensure the ongoing training needs of his department are met so that they can carry out their duties.

Chapter roundup

- External auditors may use the work of a variety of other people in forming their opinion on financial statements.
- SAS 500 governs using the work of internal audit. The main provisions are:
  - Obtain sufficient understanding
  - Evaluate internal audit function
  - Evaluate specific work
- SAS 520 governs using the work of an expert. The main provisions are:
  - Obtain sufficient, appropriate evidence
  - Assess objectivity and qualifications of expert
  - Assess appropriateness of expert's work
- SAS 480 governs the approach to audits of entities that use service organisations. The main provisions are:
  - Determine if service organisation's activities are relevant to the audit
  - Obtain understanding of the service and assess risk arising from it
  - Design audit procedures to obtain a sufficient, appropriate evidence
- The auditor's report is the sole responsibility of the auditor.
- Audit partners should use appropriate audit staff for each assignment. They should also undertake direction, supervision and review.
- A suitably qualified head of internal audit should be appointed to manage the resources of the department. He should also ensure the ongoing training needs of the department are met.

Quick quiz

1 An effective internal audit function may eliminate the need for external audit procedures.

True ☐

False ☐

2 Name **four** things the external audit function may consider when evaluating the work of internal audit.

1 ....

2 ....

3 ....

4 ....

3 Complete the definitions using the words given below.

An .... is a person or firm possessing ...., knowledge and .... in a particular field other than auditing.

A .... is an organisation that provides .... to another organisation.

services, special, expert, experience, service, skills, organisation

4 The auditor may not use the work of an expert employed by the organisation being audited.

True ☐

False ☐

5 Give two examples of services which may be outsourced.

1 ....

2 ....

6 If the auditor relies on the work of an expert or service organisation, he may refer to that person/organisation in his report and share responsibility with them.

True ☐

False ☐

7 Complete the sentence, using the words given below.

Audit engagement .... should ensure that work is ...., ... and .... in a manner that provides .... assurance that the work has been performed ....

competently, partners, reviewed, supervised, reasonable, directed

8 There are four criteria for assessing the internal audit function. Name two.

1 .... 2 ....

Answers to quick quiz

1 False

2 Have the internal auditors had sufficient and adequate technological training to carry out the work?

Are the internal auditors proficient?

Is the work of assistants properly supervised, reviewed and documented?

Has sufficient, appropriate audit evidence been obtained to afford a reasonable basis for the conclusions reached?

Are the conclusions reached appropriate, given the circumstances?

Are any reports produced by internal audit consistent with the result of the work performed?

Have any unusual matters or exceptions arising and disclosed by internal audit been resolved properly?

Are any amendments to the external audit programme required as a result of the matters identified by internal audit?

Has the work of internal audit been sufficiently tested by the external auditor to confirm its adequacy?

3 expert, special skill, experience
service organisation, services

4 False

5
- Information processing
- Maintenance of accounting records
- Facilities management
- Asset management (for example, investments)
- Initiation or execution of transactions on behalf of the other entity

6 False

7 Partners, directed, supervised, reviewed, reasonable, competently

8 (1) Organisational status
(2) Scope of function
(3) Technical competence
(4) Due professional care

Now try the question below from the Exam Question Bank

Number	Level	Marks	Time
7	Exam	20	36 mins

Chapter 8

AUDIT EVIDENCE AND SAMPLING

Topic list		Syllabus reference	Study guide
1	Audit evidence	6	17
2	Audit sampling	6	23
3	Computer Assisted Audit Techniques (CAATs)	6	23
4	Audit documents	4	10

Introduction

Before auditors start the detailed audit work, they must determine what kind of **evidence** they want. Certain kinds of evidence will satisfy an auditor and certain kinds will not. In the exam you might be asked to make judgements on the strengths of particular types of evidence.

In this chapter, we introduce the **financial statement assertions**. These will be particularly important when we consider balance sheet testing in Part D, since substantive procedures are designed to obtain **sufficient, appropriate** evidence about the assertions in each area.

Auditors need to decide **how they will select the items to be tested** from the whole population.

This is not as simple as it sounds. The auditors will want to **select a sample** which reflects, as closely as possible, the characteristics of the population from which the sample has been selected.

We will explain the practical aspects of sampling as simply as possible as you are not expected to understand the more complicated aspects of sampling theory.

Sampling theory is closely associated with the definition of **audit risk** and you should refer back to Chapter 6 to remind yourself of the relevant definitions.

Once we have established what to test, we must determine **how to test the sample** we have chosen. **CAATs** are a way of carrying out a variety of audit tests using computer-assisted techniques.

Lastly in this Chapter we shall look at **why auditors and reviewers document** their work.

The issues of sampling and evidence will underpin questions about balance sheet areas discussed in Part D.

1 AUDIT EVIDENCE 12/02

KEY TERM

Audit evidence is the information auditors obtain in arriving at the conclusions on which their report is based.

1.1 In order to express a professional opinion as regards truth and fairness of financial statements, the auditors need to gather evidence from various sources. They may carry out two types of test.

KEY TERMS

Tests of control are tests to obtain audit evidence about the effective operation of the accounting and internal control systems, that is, that properly designed controls identified in the preliminary assessment of control risk exist in fact and have operated effectively throughout the relevant period.

Substantive procedures are tests to obtain audit evidence to detect material misstatements in the financial statements. They are generally of two types:

(a) Analytical procedures

(b) Other substantive procedures such as tests of detail of transactions and balances, review of minutes of directors' meetings and enquiry.

1.2 SAS 400 *Audit evidence* states **'auditors should obtain sufficient appropriate audit evidence to be able to draw reasonable conclusions on which to base the audit opinion'**.

Sufficient appropriate audit evidence

1.3 'Sufficiency' and 'appropriateness' apply to both tests of controls and substantive procedures.

- **Sufficiency** is the measure of the **quantity** of audit evidence.
- **Appropriateness** is the measure of the **quality** or **reliability** of the audit evidence.

1.4 Auditors are essentially looking for **enough reliable audit evidence**. Auditors usually examine different sources of evidence because evidence indicates what is probable, not certain. However, auditors will not test all the evidence available.

1.5 The auditors' judgement as to what is sufficient appropriate audit evidence is influenced by:

- **Risk assessment**
- The **nature** of the **accounting and internal control systems**
- The **materiality** of the item being examined
- The **experience gained during previous audits**
- The auditors' **knowledge of the business** and **industry**
- The **results of audit procedures**
- The **source** and **reliability of information** available

1.6 SAS 400 states '**in seeking to obtain audit evidence from tests of control, auditors should consider the sufficiency and appropriateness of the audit evidence to support the assessed level of control risk**'.

1.7 There are two aspects of the relevant parts of the accounting and internal control systems about which auditors should seek to obtain audit evidence.

- **Design**: the accounting and internal control systems are capable of preventing or detecting material misstatements.
- **Operation**: the systems exist and have operated effectively throughout the relevant period.

1.8 Substantive procedures are designed to obtain evidence about the financial statement assertions. SAS 400 states '**in seeking to obtain audit evidence from substantive procedures, auditors should consider the extent to which that evidence together with any evidence from tests of controls supports the relevant financial statement assertions**'.

KEY TERMS

Financial statement assertions are the representations of the directors that are embodied in the financial statements. By approving the financial statements, the directors are making representations about the information therein. These representations or assertions may be described in general terms in a number of ways, one of which is as follows.

Existence An asset or liability exists at a given date

Rights and obligations An asset or liability pertains to the entity at a given date

Occurrence A transaction or event took place which pertains to the entity during the relevant period

Completeness There are no unrecorded assets, liabilities, transactions or events, or undisclosed items

Valuation An asset or liability is recorded at an appropriate carrying value

Measurement A transaction or event is recorded in the proper amount and revenue or expense is allocated to the proper period

Presentation and disclosure An item is disclosed, classified and described in accordance with the applicable reporting framework (for example, relevant legislation and applicable accounting standards)

Exam focus point

When designing audit programmes, focus on the financial statement assertions listed above.

1.9 Audit evidence is usually obtained to support each financial statement assertion and evidence for one does not compensate for failure to obtain evidence for another. However, tests may provide audit evidence of more than one assertion.

1.10 The following generalisations may help in assessing the **reliability** of audit evidence.

QUALITY OF EVIDENCE	
External	Audit evidence from **external sources** is more reliable than that obtained from the entity's records.
Auditor	Evidence obtained **directly by auditors** is more reliable than that obtained by or from the entity
Entity	Evidence obtained from the entity's records is more reliable when accounting and internal **control system operates effectively**
Written	Evidence in the form of **documents** or **written representations** are more reliable than oral representations
Originals	Original documents are more realistic than photocopies, or facsimiles

1.11 **Consistency** of audit evidence from different sources will have a **corroborating effect**, making the evidence more persuasive. Where such evidence is **inconsistent**, the auditors must determine what additional procedures are necessary to resolve the inconsistency.

1.12 Auditors must consider the cost-benefit relationship of obtaining evidence but any difficulty or expense is not in itself a valid basis for omitting a necessary procedure.

Exam focus point

You may be asked to consider how strong certain evidence is from the auditor's viewpoint, for example debtors' circularisation or third party valuation of assets.

1.13 Auditors obtain evidence by one or more of the following procedures.

PROCEDURES	
Inspection of assets	Inspection of assets that are recorded in the accounting records confirms **existence**, gives evidence of **valuation**, but does not confirm **rights and obligations** Confirmation that assets seen are recorded in accounting records gives evidence of **completeness**
Inspection of documentation	Confirmation to documentation of items recorded in accounting records confirms that an asset **exists** or a transaction **occurred**. Confirmation that items recorded in supporting documentation are recorded in accounting records tests **completeness** Cut-off can be verified by inspecting reverse population ie checking transactions recorded **after** the balance sheet date to supporting documentation to confirm that they occurred after the balance sheet date Inspection also provides evidence of **valuation/measurement**, **rights and obligations** and the nature of items (**presentation and disclosure**). It can also be used to **compare** documents (and hence test **consistency** of audit evidence) and confirm **authorisation**

PROCEDURES	
Observation	Involves watching a procedure being performed (for example, post opening) Of limited use, as only confirms procedure took place when auditor watching
Enquiries	Seeking information from **client staff** or **external sources** Strength of evidence depends on knowledge and integrity of source of information
Confirmation	Seeking confirmation from another source of details in client's accounting records for example, confirmation from bank of bank balances
Computations	Checking arithmetic of client's records for example, adding up ledger account
Analytical procedures	See Chapter 12

Question: Audit evidence

(a) Discuss the quality of the following types of audit evidence, giving two examples of each form of evidence.

(i) Evidence originated by the auditors
(ii) Evidence created by third parties
(iii) Evidence created by the management of the client

(b) Describe the general considerations which the auditors must bear in mind when evaluating audit evidence.

Answer

(a) (i) In general, evidence originated by the auditors is the most reliable type of audit evidence as there is little risk that it can be manipulated by management. Examples:

(1) Analytical procedures, such as the calculation of ratios and trends in order to examine unusual variations

(2) Physical inspection or observation, such as attendance at physical stocktakes or inspection of a fixed asset

(3) Re-performance of calculations making up figures in the accounts, such as the computation of total stock values

(ii) Third party evidence is more reliable than client-produced evidence because it is obtained from sources independent of the client. If it is obtained from sources which are not independent, or if there is a risk that client personnel may be able to and have reason to suppress or manipulate it, it is less reliable. This, for instance, is an argument against having replies to circularisations sent to the client instead of the auditors.

Examples:

(1) Circularisation of debtors or creditors and other requests from the auditors for confirming evidence, such as requests for confirmation of bank balances.

(2) Reports produced by experts, such as property valuations, actuarial valuations, legal opinions.

(3) Documents held by the client which were issued by third parties, such as invoices, price lists and statements. These may sometimes be manipulated by the client, to the extent that items may be suppressed or altered, and to this extent they are less reliable than confirmations received direct.

(iii) The auditors cannot place the same degree of reliance on evidence produced by client management as on that produced outside the client organisation, although it will often be necessary to place some reliance on the client's evidence. Auditors need to apply judgement, taking into account previous experience of the client's reliability and the extent to which the client's representations appear compatible with other audit findings, as well as the materiality of the item under discussion. Examples:

(1) The company's accounting records and supporting schedules. Although these are prepared by management, the auditors have a statutory right to examine such records in full: this right enhances the quality of this information.

(2) The client's explanations of, for instance, apparently unusual fluctuations in results. Such evidence requires interpretation by the auditors and, being oral evidence, only limited reliance can be placed upon it.

(3) Information provided to the auditors about the internal control system. The auditors need to check that this information is accurate and up-to-date, and that it does not simply describe an idealised system which is not adhered to in practice.

(b) Audit evidence will often not be wholly conclusive. The auditors must obtain evidence which is **sufficient** and **appropriate** to form the basis for their audit conclusions. The evidence gathered should also be **relevant** to those conclusions, and sufficiently **reliable** ultimately to form the basis for the audit opinion. The auditors must exercise skill and judgement to ensure that evidence is correctly interpreted and that only valid inferences are drawn from it.

There are certain general principles. Written evidence is preferable to oral evidence; independent evidence obtained from outside the organisation is more reliable than that obtained internally; and that evidence generated by the auditors is more reliable than that obtained from others.

2 AUDIT SAMPLING 6/03

2.1 SAS 430 *Audit sampling* is based on the premise that auditors do not normally examine all the information available to them. It would be impractical to do so. Using audit sampling will produce valid conclusions.

2.2 The SAS states '**when using either statistical or non-statistical sampling methods auditors should design and select an audit sample, perform audit-procedures thereon and evaluate sample results so as to obtain appropriate audit evidence**'.

KEY TERMS

Audit sampling is the application of audit procedures to less than 100% of the items within an account balance or class of transactions. It enables auditors to obtain and evaluate evidence about some characteristic of the items selected in order to form a conclusion about the population sampled.

Sampling units are the individual items that make up the population.

Error is an unintentional mistake in the financial statements.

2.3 The SAS points out that some testing procedures do not involve sampling, such as:

- Testing 100% of items in a population (this should be obvious)
- Testing all items with a certain characteristic (for example, over a certain value) as selection is not representative

2.4 The SAS distinguishes between **statistically based sampling**, which involves the use of random selection techniques from which mathematically constructed conclusions about the population can be drawn, and **non-statistical sampling methods**, from which auditors draw a judgemental opinion about the population. However the principles of the SAS apply to both methods.

Design of the sample

Audit objectives

2.5 Auditors must consider the **specific audit objectives** to be achieved and the audit procedures which are most likely to achieve them. The auditors also need to consider the **nature and characteristics of the audit evidence** sought and **possible error conditions**. This will help them to define what constitutes an error and what population to use for sampling.

Population

2.6 The population from which the sample is drawn must be **appropriate** and **complete** for the specific audit objectives. The population may be divided into **sampling units** in a variety of ways, for example, an individual debtors balance or, in monetary unit sampling, £1 of the total debtors balance. Auditors must define the sampling unit in order to obtain an efficient and effective sample to achieve the particular audit objectives.

Setting a sample size

2.7 The SAS requires auditors to consider sampling risk, acceptable levels of error and their expectation of finding errors.

Sampling risk

KEY TERM

Sampling risk is the risk that the auditors' conclusion, based on a sample, may be different from the conclusion that would be reached if the entire population was subject to the same audit procedure.

2.8 Auditors encounter sampling risk in both tests of control and substantive procedures. It is the part of detection risk and is the risk of drawing a wrong conclusion from audit sampling. It affects different types of tests as follows:

(a) **Tests of control**

(i) Auditors may place a **higher than necessary assessment** on control risk, because the error in the sample is greater than the error in the total population

(ii) Auditors may place a **lower than required assessment** on control risk, because the error in the sample is less than the error in the population as a whole

(b) **Substantive tests**

(i) Auditors may conclude that a recorded account balance or class of transactions is **materially misstated when** it is **not**, because the error in the sample is greater than the error in the population as a whole

(ii) Auditors may conclude that a recorded account balance or class of transactions is **acceptable when** it is **materially misstated,** because the error in the sample is less than the error in the population as a whole

2.9 The more auditors rely on the results of the procedure in question, the **lower** the sampling risk they will be willing to accept and therefore the **larger** the sample size needs to be. Sample size should be considered in the context of overall risk assessment.

2.10 In contrast, **non-sampling risk** is detection risk unconnected with sampling, for example, that auditors choose to carryout the wrong type of test. Auditors try and reduce non-sampling risk by appropriate planning and review.

Tolerable error

KEY TERM

Tolerable error is the maximum error in the population that the auditors are willing to accept and still conclude that the audit objective has been achieved.

2.11 This will be considered during the planning stage.

(a) In tests of control, the **tolerable error** is the **maximum rate of deviation from a prescribed control procedure** that auditors are willing to accept in the population and still conclude that the preliminary assessment of control risk is valid. Often this rate will be very low since the auditor is likely to be concentrating on testing important controls. So for example, an auditor might only accept one or two errors, or a low percentage

(b) In substantive procedures, the **tolerable error** is the **maximum monetary error** in an account balance or class of transactions that auditors are willing to accept so that, when the results of all audit procedures are considered, they are able to conclude, with reasonable assurance, that the financial statements are not materially misstated. Sometimes the tolerable error for substantive tests will be the materiality rate. Some accountancy firms set tolerable error as being a fixed percentage of materiality, say 50% or 70%, for reasons of safety.

Expected error

2.12 Auditors require larger samples when errors are expected than if none are expected, in order to conclude that the **actual** error is **less** than the **tolerable** error. If the expected error rate is high then sampling may not be appropriate and auditors may have to examine 100% of the population.

Setting the sample size

2.13 Auditors will usually calculate sample sizes by using computer programmes.

Selecting the sample

2.14 The SAS says 'auditors should select sample items in such a way that the sample can be expected to be representative of the population in respect of the characteristics being tested' and observes that 'for a sample to be representative of the population, all items in the population are required to have an equal or known probability of being selected'.

2.15 The SAS identifies three methods of selection that are commonly used.

(a) **Random selection** ensures that all items in the population have an equal chance of selection, for example, by use of random number tables.

(b) **Systematic selection** involves selecting items using a constant interval between selections, the first interval having a random start. When using systematic selection auditors must ensure that the population is not structured in such a manner that the sampling interval corresponds with a particular pattern in the population.

(c) **Haphazard selection** may be an acceptable alternative to random selection provided auditors are satisfied that the sample is representative of the entire population. This method requires care to guard against making a selection which is biased, for example towards items which are easily located, as they may not be representative.

2.16 In addition the auditors may also consider:

(a) **Stratification.** This means dividing the population being sampled into sub-populations of items with similar characteristics. By stratifying, auditors can concentrate on particular sections of the population which they feel may be vulnerable to error (for example the transactions processed by a new purchase ledger clerk).

(b) **Sequence or block sampling.** Sequence sampling may be used to check whether certain items have particular characteristics. For example an auditor may use a sample of 50 consecutive cheques to check whether cheques are signed by authorised signatories rather than picking 50 single cheques throughout the year. Sequence sampling may however produce samples that are not representative of the population as a whole particularly if errors occurred only during a certain part of the period.

(c) **Monetary Unit Sampling (MUS).** This is a selection method which ensures that every £1 in a population has an equal chance of being selected for testing. How MUS works is shown in the example below. The advantage of this selection method are that it is easy when computers are used, and that every material item will automatically be sampled. Disadvantages include the fact that if computers are not used, it can be time consuming to pick the sample, MUS does not cope well with errors of understatement or negative balances.

2.17 EXAMPLE: MUS

You are auditing creditors. Total creditors is £500,000 and materiality is £50,000. You will select the balances containing the 50,000th £1 from the ledger below.

CREDITOR	BALANCE	CUMULATIVE TOTAL	SELECTED
A	30,000	30,000	
B	35,000	65,000	Yes
C	45,000	110,000	Yes
D	**52,500**	162,500	**Yes**
E	13,000	175,000	
F	**50,000**	225,000	**Yes**
G	23,000	248,000	
H	500	248,500	
I	42,000	290,000	Yes
J	47,000	337,000	Yes
K	**54,000**	391,000	**Yes**
L	17,000	408,000	Yes
M	**80,000**	488,000	**Yes**
N	12,000	500,000	Yes
	500,000		

Material items are shown in bold and have all been selected. The cumulative column shows you when the next 50,000th £1 has been reached.

Evaluating sample results

Analysis of errors in the sample

2.18 The auditors must consider whether the items in question are **true errors**. For example, a misposting between customer accounts will not affect the total debtors. When the expected audit evidence regarding a specific sample item cannot be found, the auditors may be able to obtain sufficient appropriate audit evidence by performing alternative procedures. In such cases, the item is not treated as an error.

2.19 They should also consider the **qualitative** aspects of errors, including the nature and cause of the error and any possible effects the error might have on other parts of the audit.

2.20 Where common features are discovered in errors, the auditors may decide to identify all items in the population which possess the common feature (for example, location), thereby producing a sub-population. Audit procedures could then be extended in this area and separate analysis could then be performed based on the items examined for each sub-population.

Inferences to be drawn from the population as a whole

2.21 The auditors should project the error results from the sample on to the relevant population. The projection method should be consistent with the method used to select the sampling unit. The auditors will **estimate the probable error** in the population by extrapolating the errors found in the sample.

2.22 The auditors should then compare the projected population error (net of adjustments made by the entity in the case of substantive procedures) to the tolerable error, taking account of other audit procedures relevant to the specific control or financial statement assertion.

2.23 If the projected population error **exceeds** tolerable error, then the auditors should re-assess sampling risk. If it is unacceptable, they should consider extending auditing procedures or performing alternative procedures, either of which may result in a proposed adjustment to the financial statements.

Question: Statistical sampling

What are the benefits and disadvantages of statistical sampling in auditing?

Answer

Auditors examine a sample of items and thereby seek to obtain assurance that the whole group is acceptable.

Advantages of statistical sampling

Certain conditions favour the use of statistical sampling, for example:

(a) Existence of large and homogeneous groups of items
(b) Low expected error rate and clear definition of error
(c) Reasonable ease of identifying and obtaining access to items selected

If these conditions are present, statistical sampling is likely to have the following advantages.

(a) At the conclusion of a test the auditors are able to state a definite level of confidence they may have that the whole population conforms to the sample result, within a stated precision limit.

(b) Sample size is objectively determined, having regard to the degree of risk the auditors are prepared to accept for each application.

(c) It may be possible to use smaller sample sizes, thus saving time and money.

(d) The process of fixing required precision and confidence levels compels the auditors to consider and clarify their audit objectives.

(e) The results of tests can be expressed in precise mathematical terms.

(f) Bias is eliminated.

Disadvantages of statistical sampling

(a) The technique may be applied blindly without prior consideration of the suitability of the statistical sampling for the audit task to be performed, although firm standards on sampling should overcome this.

(b) Unsuspected patterns or bias in sample selection may invalidate the conclusions. The probability of these factors before they decide to adopt statistical sampling.

(c) Statistical sampling frequently requires further tests within the population reviewed: large items, non-routine items, sensitive items like directors' transactions.

(d) At the end of a statistical sampling-based test the auditors may fail to appreciate the further action necessary based on the results obtained, but again, training should overcome this.

(e) Statistical sampling may be applied carelessly, without due confirmation that the sample selected is acceptably random.

(f) The selection exercise can be time consuming.

(g) The degree of tolerance of acceptable error must be predetermined.

Statistical techniques should be used when they are convenient and of positive use to the auditors in achieving a level of reliability in their results.

3 COMPUTER ASSISTED AUDIT TECHNIQUES (CAATS)

Exam focus point

Use of computers on audits is now common practice. The examiner expects you to consider the computer aspects of auditing as a matter of course. Therefore in answering questions on obtaining evidence, remember to include reference to CAATs if they seem relevant.

3.1 There is no mystique about using a computer to help with auditing.

(a) Most modern accounting systems allow data to be manipulated in various ways and extracted into a **report**.

(b) Even if reporting capabilities are limited, the data can often be exported directly into a **spreadsheet** package (sometimes using simple Windows-type cut and paste facilities in very modern systems) and then analysed.

(c) Most systems have **searching** facilities that are much quicker to use than searching through print-outs by hand.

3.2 There are a variety of packages specially designed either to ease the auditing task itself or to carry out audit **interrogations** of computerised data automatically. Auditors can use PCs such as laptops that are independent of the organisation's systems when performing CAATs.

Audit software

3.3 Audit software performs the sort of checks on data that auditors might otherwise have to perform by hand. Examples of uses of audit software are:

- Interrogation software, which accesses the client's data files
- Comparison programs which compare versions of a program

- Interactive software for interrogation of on-line systems
- Resident code software to review transactions as they are processed

3.4 Although audit interrogation software may be used during many tests of controls and substantive procedures, its use is particularly appropriate during substantive testing of transactions and especially balances. By using audit software, the auditors may **scrutinise large volumes of data** and concentrate skilled manual resources on the investigation of results, rather than on the extraction of information and **selection** of **samples**.

3.5 Major considerations when deciding whether to use file interrogation software are as follows.

(a) As a minimum auditors will require a **basic understanding** of data processing and the enterprise's computer application, together with a detailed knowledge of the audit software and the computer files to be used.

(b) Depending on the complexity of the application, the auditors may need to have a sound appreciation of **systems analysis**, operating systems and, where program code is used, experience of the programming language to be utilised.

(c) Auditors will need to consider how easy it is to **transfer** the **client's data** onto the auditors' PC.

(d) The client may **lack full knowledge** of the **computer system**, and hence may not be able to explain fully all the information it produces.

Test data

3.6 An obvious way of seeing whether a system is **processing** data in the way that it should be is to input some valid test data and see what happens. The expected results can be calculated in advance and then compared with the results that actually arise.

3.7 Test data can also be used to check the controls that prevent processing of **invalid data** by entering data with say a non-existent customer code or worth an unreasonable amount, or transactions which may if processed breach limits such as customer credit limits.

3.8 A significant problem with test data is that any resulting corruption of the data files has to be corrected. This is difficult with modern real-time systems, which often have built in (and highly desirable) controls to ensure that data entered **cannot** easily be removed without leaving a mark.

3.9 Other problems with **test data** are that it only tests the operation of the system at a **single point of time**, and auditors are only testing controls in the programs being run and controls which they know about. The problems involved mean that test data is being used less as a CAAT.

Embedded audit facilities

3.10 The results of using test data would, in any case, be completely distorted if the programs used to process it were not the ones **normally** used for processing. For example a fraudulent member of the IT department might substitute a version of the program that gave the correct results, purely for the duration of the test, and then replace it with a version that syphoned off the company's funds into his own bank account.

3.11 To allow a **continuous** review of the data recorded and the manner in which it is treated by the system, it may be possible to use CAATs referred to as 'embedded audit facilities'.

3.12 An embedded facility consists of audit modules that are incorporated into the computer element of the enterprise's accounting system. Two frequently encountered examples are Integrated Test Facility (ITF) and Systems Control and Review File (SCARF).

EXAMPLES OF EMBEDDED AUDIT FACILITIES	
Integrated test facility (ITF)	Creates a **fictitious entity** within the company application, where transactions are posted to it alongside regular transactions, and actual results of fictitious entity compared with what it should have produced
Systems control and review file (SCARF)	Allows auditors to have transactions above a **certain amount** from **specific ledger account** posted to a file for later auditor review

Simulation

3.13 Simulation (or 'parallel simulation') entails the preparation of a separate program that simulates the processing of the organisation's real system. Real data can then be passed not only through the system proper but also through the simulated program. For example the simulation program may be used to re-perform controls such as those used to identify any missing items from a sequence.

Knowledge-based systems

3.14 Decision support systems and expert systems can be used to assist with the auditors' own judgement and decisions.

4 AUDIT DOCUMENTS 12/03

4.1 Working papers are the tangible evidence of the work done in support of the opinion given. SAS 230 *Working papers* states 'auditors should document in their working papers matters which are important in supporting their report'.

> **KEY TERM**
>
> **Working papers** are the material the auditors prepare or obtain, and retain in connection with the performance of the audit. Working papers may be in the form of data stored on paper, film, electronic media or other media.

4.2 **Why auditors record their work**

(a) The **reporting partner** needs **to be able to satisfy himself that work delegated** by him has been **properly performed**. The reporting partner can generally only do this by having available detailed working papers prepared by the audit staff who performed the work.

(b) **Working papers** will **provide**, for future reference, **details of audit problems** encountered, together with evidence of work performed and conclusions drawn in arriving at the audit opinion. This can be invaluable if either the client or some third party sues the auditor.

(c) Good working papers will not only **assist** in the **control** of the **current audit**, but will also be invaluable in the **planning** and **control** of **future audits**.

(d) The preparation of working papers **encourages** the auditors to adopt a **methodical approach** to their audit work, which in turn is likely to improve the quality of that work.

4.3 **What auditors record**

Auditors cannot record everything they consider. Therefore judgement must be used as to the extent of working papers, based on:

General rule for documenting the audit process
'What would be necessary to provide an experienced auditor, with no previous connection with the audit, with an understanding of the work performed and the basis of the decisions taken.'

4.4 The same general rule should be applied to the internal auditors' work.

4.5 The form and content of working papers are affected by matters such as:

- The nature of the engagement
- The form of the auditors' report
- The nature and complexity of the entity's business
- The nature and condition of the entity's accounting and internal control systems
- The needs in the particular circumstances for direction, supervision and review of the work of members of the audit team
- The specific methodology and technology the auditors use

Examples of working papers

4.6 These include the following.

- Information concerning the legal and organisational structure of the client
- Information concerning the client's industry, economic and legal environment
- Evidence of the planning process and any changes thereto
- Evidence of the auditors' understanding of the accounting and internal control systems
- Evidence of inherent and control risk assessments and any revisions
- Analyses of transactions and balances
- Analyses of significant ratios and trends
- A record of the nature, timing, extent and results of auditing procedures
- Copies of communications with other auditors, experts and other third parties
- Copies of correspondence with the client
- Reports to directors or management
- Notes of discussions with the entity's directors or management
- A summary of the significant aspects of the audit
- Copies of the approved financial statements and auditors' reports

4.7 Working papers should also show:

- The **objective** of the work done
- The **source of information**
- How any **sample was selected** and the sample size determined

- The **work done**
- A **key** to any audit ticks or symbols
- Appropriate **cross-referencing**
- The **results obtained**
- **Analysis of errors** or other significant observations
- The **conclusions drawn**
- The **key points highlighted**

4.8 Working papers should always contain key references:

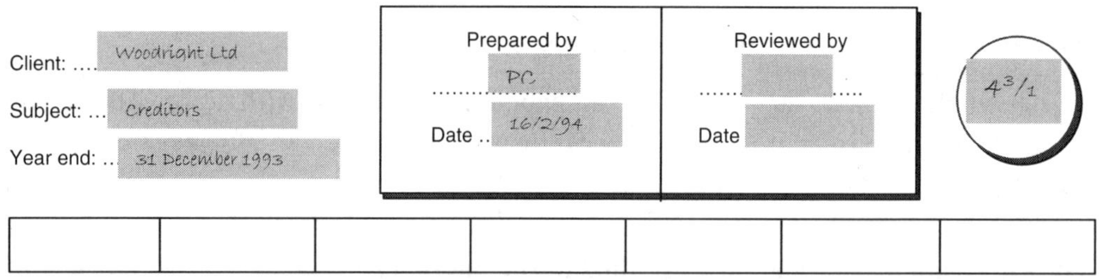

4.9 Firms should have standard **referencing** and **filing** procedures for working papers, to facilitate their review.

4.10 For recurring audits, working papers may be split between permanent and current audit files.

(a) **Permanent audit files** contain information of **continuing importance** to the audit.

- Engagement letters
- New client questionnaire
- The memorandum and articles
- Other legal documents such as prospectuses, leases, sales agreement
- Details of the history of the client's business
- Board minutes of continuing relevance
- Previous years' signed accounts, analytical review and management letters
- Accounting systems notes, previous years' control questionnaires

(b) **Current audit files** contain information of relevance to the current year's audit.

- Financial statements
- Accounts checklists
- Management accounts details
- Reconciliations of management and financial accounts
- A summary of unadjusted errors
- Report to partner including details of significant events and errors
- Review notes
- Audit planning memorandum
- Time budgets and summaries
- Letter of representation
- Management letter
- Notes of board minutes
- Communications with third parties such as experts or other auditors

4.11 Current audit files also contain working papers covering each audit area. These should include the following.

- A lead schedule including details of the figures to be included in the accounts,
- Problems encountered and conclusions drawn
- Audit programmes
- Risk assessments
- Sampling plans
- Analytical review
- Details of substantive tests and tests of control

4.12 **Standardised** working papers, for example, checklists, specimen letters may be efficient to use, but a mechanical approach should never be adopted by the auditor.

4.13 Auditors may use schedules and analyses **prepared by the entity** but they require evidence that such information is properly prepared.

4.14 **Automated** working paper packages make documenting audit work much easier. Such programs aid preparation of working papers, lead schedules, trial balance and the financial statements themselves. These are automatically cross referenced, adjusted and balanced by the computer.

4.15 **Advantages of automated working papers**

- Risk of errors is reduced.
- Working papers will be neater and easier to review.
- Substantial time will be saved as adjustments can be made easily to all working papers, including working papers summarising the key analytical information.
- Standard forms do not have to be carried to audit locations.
- Audit working papers can be transmitted for review via a modem, or fax facilities.

Question: Working papers

The auditing standard SAS 230 *Working Papers* contains the following statement on working papers.

'Auditors base their judgement as to the extent of working papers upon what would be necessary to provide an experienced auditor, with no previous connection with the audit, with an understanding of the work performed and the basis of the decisions taken.'

Describe four benefits that auditors will obtain from working papers that meet the above requirement in SAS 230.

Answer

- The reporting partner can be satisfied that work delegated by him has been completed adequately.
- Working papers are a record of work performed and conclusions drawn which might be necessary in the future, for example, in litigation.
- Good working papers and the planning and control of future audits.
- Preparing working papers encourages auditors to adopt a methodical approach. This is likely to improve quality.

Confidentiality, safe custody and ownership

4.16 Statute does not set down the period of retention of audit working papers; judgement must be used, and further consideration should be given to the matter before their destruction. The ACCA recommends seven years as a minimum period. Working papers are the property of the auditors. They are not a substitute for, nor part of, the entity's accounting records. The SAS requires auditors to adopt appropriate procedures to keep working papers safe and confidential.

Chapter roundup

- The auditors must be able to evaluate all types of audit evidence in terms of its sufficiency and appropriateness.
- Evidence can be in the form of tests of controls or substantive procedures.
- Tests of control concentrate on the design and operation of controls.
- Substantive testing aims to test all the financial statement assertions.
  - Existence
  - Rights and obligations (ownership)
  - Occurrence
  - Completeness
  - Valuation
  - Measurement
  - Presentation and disclosure
- The **reliability** of audit evidence is influenced by its **source** and by its **nature.**
- Audit evidence can be obtained by the following techniques.
  - Inspection
  - Observation
  - Enquiry and confirmation
  - Computation
  - Analytical procedures
- The main stages of sampling are:
  - Design of the sample
  - Selection of the sample
  - Evaluation of sample results
- **Sample sizes for tests of control** are influenced by:
  - Sampling risk
  - Tolerable error rate
  - Expected error rate
- **Sample sizes for substantive tests** are influenced by:
  - Inherent, control and detection risk
  - Tolerable error rate
  - Expected error rate
  - Population value
  - Stratification
- **Sample sizes** can be chosen by a variety of means including:
  - Random selection
  - Systematic selection
  - Haphazard selection

- When evaluating results, auditors should:
  - Analyse any errors considering their amount and the reasons why they have occurred
  - Draw conclusions for the population as a whole.
- **Monetary unit sampling (MUS)** makes it much easier to test populations substantively, by adopting many of the techniques in attribute sampling.
- Auditors may use a number of computer assisted audit techniques including:
  - Audit interrogation software
  - Test data
  - Embedded audit facilities
- Audit work is documented in working papers to:
  - Enable reporting partner to ensure all planned work has been completed adequately
  - Provide details of work done for future reference
  - Assist is planning and control of future audits
  - Encourage a methodical approach and therefore quality

Quick quiz

1 Define sufficiency and appropriateness of evidence in one line each.

2 Name seven financial statement assertions.

3 Fill in the **blanks**

Audit evidence from external sources is .... than that obtained from the entity's records.

Evidence obtained directly .... is more .... than that obtained by or from the entity.

4 Match the definitions to the terms

(a) Sampling risk
(b) Non-sampling risk

(i) The risk that the auditors' conclusion, based on a sample, may be different from the conclusions that would be reached if the entire population was subject to the same audit procedure.

(ii) The risk that the auditors might use inappropriate procedures or might misinterpret evidence and thus fail to recognise an error.

5 Name three methods of sample selection

1 ....

2 ....

3 ....

6 Name two types of audit software

1 ....

2 ....

7 Give two advantages and one disadvantage of standardised working papers.

1 .... 1 ....

2 ....

8 Complete the table, using the working papers given below.

Current audit file	Permanent audit file

engagement letters	new client questionnaire
financial statements	management letter
accounts checklists	audit planning memo
board minutes of continuing relevance	accounting systems notes

Answers to quick quiz

1 Sufficiency is the measure of the quantity of audit evidence.
Appropriateness is the measure of the quality/reliability of audit evidence.

2 Existence, right and obligations, occurrence, completeness, valuation, measurement, presentation and disclosure.

3 More reliable
By auditors, reliable

4 (a) (i)
(b) (ii)

5 Random
Haphazard
Systematic

6
- Interrogation software, which accesses the client's data files
- Comparison programs which compare versions of a program
- Interactive software for interrogation of on-line systems
- Resident code software to review transactions as they are processed

7 **Advantages**

1 Facilitate the delegation of work
2 Means to control quality

Disadvantage

1 Detracts from proper exercise of profession judgement

8

Current audit file	Permanent audit file
financial statements	engagement letters
management letter	new client questionnaire
accounts checklists	board minutes of continuing relevance
audit planning memo	accounting systems notes

Now try the question below from the Exam Question Bank

Number	Level	Marks	Time
8	Exam	20	36 mins

Part C
Internal controls

Chapter 9

INTERNAL CONTROL AND AUDIT RISK EVALUATION

Introduction

Modern auditors often rely on internal controls in order to reduce the amount of testing of final balances.

Auditors evaluate, record and assess a client's system at the planning stage. If the auditors wish to rely on the **internal controls** within the system, they then test these controls.

We shall examine the detailed controls that businesses operate in Chapters 10 and 11. You should bear in mind the principles discussed in this chapter when considering the controls needed over specific accounting and other system areas.

There are regularly questions on internal controls in the exam. Remember exam questions can cover the controls that ought to be operating, or how auditors should test the controls that are in place.

1 FEATURES OF ACCOUNTING AND CONTROL SYSTEMS

REMEMBER

An **internal control system** comprises the control environment and control procedures. It includes all the policies and procedures (internal controls) adopted by the directors and management of an entity to ensure, as far as practicable, the orderly and efficient conduct of its business, including adherence to internal policies, the safeguarding of assets, the prevention and detection of fraud and error, the accuracy and completeness of the accounting records, and the timely preparation of reliable financial information. Internal controls may be incorporated within computerised accounting systems. However the internal control system extends beyond those matters which relate directly to the accounting system.

Control environment

1.1 Control environment is the framework within which controls operate. The control environment is very much determined by the management of a business.

KEY TERM

Control environment is the overall attitude, awareness and actions of directors and managers regarding internal controls and their importance in the entity. The control environment encompasses the management style, and corporate culture and values shared by all employees. It provides the background against which the various other controls are operated.

1.2 SAS 300 *Accounting and internal control systems and audit risk assessments* adds to the definition of the control environment that a strong control environment does not, by itself, ensure the effectiveness of the overall internal control system. However, aspects of the control environment (such as management attitudes towards control) will be a significant factor in determining **how controls operate**.

1.3 Controls are more likely to operate well in an environment where they are treated as being important. In addition consideration of the control environment will, as shown above, mean considering whether certain controls (internal audits, budgets) actually exist.

CONTROL ENVIRONMENT	
Philosophy and **operating style** of management	Consider attitude towards controls - do management override controls? Do they neglect controls? Do they concentrate solely on results and targets and encourage employees to do likewise? Examine attitudes to financial reporting and how these are manifest, for example in choice of accounting policies and view of accounting function Consider also attitudes to business risk and ethics – does management set a clear example? Is there a formal code of ethics? Does management have a clear commitment to maintaining and enhancing competence of all employees?
Organisation structure and segregation of duties	Consider delegation of authority and accountability. Segregation of duties - the principle that no single person should record and process all stages of a transaction - is vital
Directors' methods of imposing controls	Consider extent to which management supervise operations and how control is exercised (whether management solely use informal methods or have formal procedures such as budgets, management accounts, audit committee and internal audit) Personnel policies including recruitment, training, appraisal, rewards and discipline are also important

Segregation of duties

1.4 **Segregation of duties** is a vital aspect of the control environment. Segregation of duties implies a **number of people** being involved in the accounting process.

1.5 This makes it more difficult for fraudulent transactions to be processed (since a number of people would have to collude in the fraud), and it is also more difficult for accidental errors to be processed (since the more people are involved, the more checking there can be). Segregation should take place in various ways:

(a) **Segregation of function.** The key functions that should be segregated are the **carrying out** of a transaction, **recording** that transaction in the accounting records and **maintaining custody** of assets that arise from the transaction.

(b) The various **steps** in carrying out the transaction should also be segregated. We shall see how this works in practice when we look at the major control cycles in Chapters 10 and 11.

(c) The **carrying out** of various **accounting operations** should be segregated. For example the same staff should not record transactions and carry out the reconciliations at the period-end.

Control procedures

KEY TERM

Control procedures are those policies and procedures in addition to the control environment which are established to achieve the entity's specific objectives.

1.6 The definition of control procedures is extended in the SAS. Control procedures include those designed to **prevent** or to **detect** and **correct errors**.

Specific control procedures	
Approval and control of documents	Transactions should be approved by an appropriate person. For example, overtime should be approved by departmental managers.
Controls over computerised applications	These are discussed in Section 2 in greater detail, but common examples include passwords.
Checking the arithmetical accuracy of records	For example, checking to see if individual invoices have been added up correctly.
Maintaining and reviewing control accounts and trial balances	Control accounts bring together transactions in individual ledgers. Trial balances bring together unusual transactions for the organisation as a whole. Preparing these can highlight unusual transactions or accounts.
Reconciliations	Reconciliations involve comparison of a specific balance in the accounting records with what another source says the balance should be. Differences between the two figures should only be reconciling items. For example, a bank reconciliation.
Comparing the results of cash, security and stock counts with accounting records	For example, a physical count of petty cash. The balance shown in the cash book should be the same amount as is in the tin.
Comparing internal data with external sources of information	For example, comparing records of goods despatched to customers with customers acknowledgement if goods that have been received.
Limiting physical access to assets and records	Only authorised personnel should have access to certain assets (particularly valuable or portable ones). For example, ensuring that the stock store is only open when the store personnel are there and is otherwise locked. This can be a particular problem in computerised systems.

Small companies – the problem of control

1.7 Many of the controls which would be relevant to a large enterprise are neither practical nor appropriate for the small enterprise. For these the most important form of internal control is generally the **close involvement** of the **directors or proprietors**. However, that very involvement will enable them to **override controls** and, if they wish, to **exclude transactions** from the records.

1.8 Auditors can have difficulties not because there is a general lack of controls but because the evidence available as to their operation and the completeness of the records is insufficient.

1.9 **Segregation of duties** will often appear inadequate in enterprises having a small number of staff. Similarly, because of the scale of the operation, organisation and management controls are likely to be rudimentary at best.

1.10 The onus is on the proprietor, by virtue of his day-to-day involvement, to compensate for this lack. This involvement should encompass physical, authorisation, arithmetical and accounting checks as well as supervision.

1.11 However it is important to stress that in a well run small company there will be a system of internal control. In any case, all companies must comply with the provisions of the Companies Act concerning the maintenance of a proper accounting system.

1.12 Where the manager of a small business is not himself the owner, he may not possess the same degree of commitment to the running of it as an owner-manager would. In such cases, the auditors will have to consider the adequacy of controls exercised by the shareholders over the manager in assessing internal control.

2 INTERNAL CONTROLS AND THEIR INHERENT LIMITATIONS

2.1 SAS 300 states that the directors of an entity will set up internal controls in the accounting system to ensure:

- **Transactions** are executed in accordance with **proper authorisation**.
- All transactions and other events are **promptly recorded** at the **correct amount**, in the **appropriate accounts** and in the **proper accounting period**.
- **Access to assets** is permitted only in accordance with proper authorisation.
- **Recorded assets** are **compared** with the **existing assets** at reasonable intervals and appropriate action is taken with regard to any differences.

2.2 However, any internal control system can only provide the directors with **reasonable assurance** that their objectives are reached, because of **inherent limitations** which is why auditors cannot obtain all their evidence from tests of the systems of internal control. The limitations include

- The **costs** of control **not outweighing** their **benefits**
- The **potential** for **human error**
- **Collusion** between employees
- The possibility of **controls** being **by-passed** or **overridden** by management
- Controls being **designed to cope** with **routine** and **not non-routine transactions**

2.3 **Key factors**

- Human error
- Potential for fraud

2.4 The safeguard of segregation of duties can help deter fraud. However, if employees decide to perpetrate frauds in harness, or management commit fraud by overriding systems, the accounting system will not be able to prevent such frauds. This is one of the reasons that auditors need to be alert to the possibility of fraud and error, as discussed in Chapter 5.

3 ASSESSMENT OF ACCOUNTING AND CONTROL SYSTEMS

3.1 Auditors are only concerned with assessing policies and procedures which are relevant to financial statement assertions. Auditors try to:

- **Assess the adequacy** of the accounting system as a basis for preparing the accounts
- **Identify** the types of **potential misstatements** that could occur in the accounts
- **Consider factors** that affect the **risk of misstatements**
- **Design appropriate audit procedures**

Accounting system and control environment

3.2 Auditors must obtain an **understanding** of the accounting system to enable them to identify and understand:

- **Major classes of transactions** in the entity's operations
- **How such transactions** are initiated
- **Significant accounting records**, supporting documents and accounts
- The **accounting and financial reporting process**

3.3 The factors affecting the **nature, timing and extent** of the **procedures** performed in order to understand the systems include:

- **Materiality** considerations
- The **size and complexity** of the entity
- Their **assessment** of **inherent risk**
- The **complexity** of the entity's computer systems
- The **type of internal controls** involved
- The **nature of the entity's documentation** of specific internal controls

3.4 The auditors will normally update previous knowledge of the systems in the following ways.

- **Enquiries** of appropriate supervisory and other personnel
- **Inspection** of relevant documents and records produced by the systems
- **Observation** of the entity's activities and operations

3.5 Auditors must also make an assessment of whether accounting records fulfil Companies Act requirements.

3.6 The **responsibility for installing and maintaining** a satisfactory **accounting system** rests, in the case of a company, with the **directors**. The Companies Act 1985 requires that companies shall keep accounting records which are sufficient to show and explain the company's transactions and are such that they:

- Disclose with reasonable accuracy, at any time, the financial position of the company at that time

- Enable the directors to ensure that any balance sheet and profit and loss account prepared under this Part complies with the requirements of this Act

3.7 S 221 goes on to state that the accounting records should show how **monies** have been **received** and **expended** and **record** the **assets** and **liabilities** of the company. If the company deals in goods, records should show **statements** of **stock held** at the **year end** and also **stocktake records** that form the basis of statements of stock held.

3.8 Officers of a company are liable to imprisonment or a fine (or both) if found guilty of knowingly failing to comply with the above sections.

Walk-through tests

3.9 During their assessment of the systems, the auditors will obtain knowledge of the design and operation of the systems. To confirm this knowledge, '**walk-through tests**' are often performed.

> **KEY TERM**
>
> **Walk-through tests** involve tracing one or more transactions through the accounting system and observing the application of relevant aspects of the control system on these transactions.

3.10 Having assessed the accounting system and control environment, as discussed in Chapter 6, the auditors can make a **preliminary assessment** of whether the system is capable of producing reliable financial statements and of the likely mix of tests of control and substantive procedures.

3.11 Assessment of control risk is not necessary when the auditors decide it is likely to be **impossible** to rely on any assessment to reduce their substantive testing. In such cases control risk is assumed to be **high**. It may also be inefficient to test controls if for example the population consists of a few large items which can be tested quickly by substantive tests.

4 ACTING ON ASSESSMENT OF ACCOUNTING AND CONTROL SYSTEMS

Tests of control

4.1 Tests of controls are used to confirm auditors' assessments of the operation of control systems. Remember, tests of control are tests to obtain audit evidence about the effective operation of the accounting and internal control systems.

4.2 Tests of control may include the following.

Enquiries about, and observation of, internal control functions
Inspection of documents supporting controls or events to gain audit evidence that internal controls have operated properly, for example verifying that a transaction has been authorised or a reconciliation approved
Examination of evidence of **management views**, for example minutes of management meetings
Reperformance of control procedures, for example reconciliation of bank accounts, to ensure they were correctly performed by the entity
Testing of the internal controls operating on **specific computerised systems**
Observation of controls. Auditors will consider the manner in which the control is being operated.

4.3 Auditors should consider:

- **How** controls were **applied**
- The **consistency** with which they were applied during the period
- **By whom** they were applied

4.4 **Changes** in the **operation** of **controls** (caused by change of staff etc) may increase control risk and tests of control may need to be modified to confirm effective operation during and after any change. Radical changes in controls, including a periodic breakdown in controls, should be considered as **separate periods** by the auditors.

Interim testing

4.5 If the auditors have tested controls at an **interim audit**, before the period end, and they intend to rely on the system and reduce substantive testing they must obtain appropriate evidence about the operation of the system between the interim audit and the period end.

Final assessment of control risk

4.6 When the auditors have carried out tests of controls, they should assess whether the results justify their original assessment of control risk.

4.7 Failures of controls to operate should be investigated, but in such cases the preliminary assessment may still be supported if the failure is isolated. More frequent failures may require the level of control risk to be revised. When control risk assessment is revised, the nature, timing and extent of the auditors' planned substantive procedures should be modified.

Communication of weaknesses

4.8 The auditors may become aware of weaknesses in the system as a result of obtaining an understanding of those systems. Such weaknesses should be reported to management.

POINT TO NOTE

Reporting control weakness shall be discussed in Chapter 20. Examples of control weakness are discussed in Chapters 10 and 11.

Question: Internal control system

An internal control system has been described as comprising 'the control environment and control procedures. It includes all the policies and procedures (internal controls) adopted by the directors and management of an entity to assist in achieving their objective of ensuring, as far as practicable, the orderly and efficient conduct of its business, including adherence to internal policies, the safeguarding of assets, the prevention and detection of fraud and error, the accuracy and completeness of the accounting records, and the timely preparation of reliable financial information'.

Explain the meaning and relevance to the auditors giving an opinion on financial statements of each of the management objectives above.

Answer

Auditors evaluate and test internal controls to determine how much they can rely on the information contained in the accounting records. If tests of control provide reasonable assurance that the internal control system is effective in ensuring the completeness and accuracy of the accounting records, they may limit the extent of their substantive procedures.

(a) *'the orderly and efficient conduct of its business'*

An organisation which is efficient and conducts its affairs in an orderly manner is much more likely to be able to supply the auditors with sufficient appropriate audit evidence on which to base their audit opinion. More importantly, the level of inherent and control risk will be lower, giving extra assurance that the financial statements do not contain material errors.

(b) *'adherence to internal policies'*

Management is responsible for setting up an effective system of internal control and management policy provides the broad framework within which internal controls have to operate. Unless management does have a pre-determined set of policies, then it is very difficult to imagine how the company could be expected to operate efficiently. Management policy will cover all aspects of the company's activities and will range from broad corporate objectives to specific areas such as determining selling prices and wage rates.

Given that the auditors must have a sound understanding of the company's affairs generally, and of specific areas of control in particular, then the fact that management policies are followed will make the task of the auditors easier in that they will be able to rely more readily on the information produced by the systems established by management.

(c) *'safeguarding of assets'*

This objective may relate to the physical protection of assets (for example locking monies in a safe at night) or to less direct safeguarding (for example ensuring that there is adequate insurance cover for all assets). It can also be seen as relating to the maintenance of proper records in respect of all assets.

The auditors will be concerned to ensure that the company has properly safeguarded its assets so that they can form an opinion on the existence of specific assets and, more generally, on whether the company's records can be taken as a reliable basis for the preparation of financial statements. Reliance on the underlying records will be particularly significant where the figures in the financial statements are derived from such records rather than as the result of physical inspection.

(d) *'prevention and detection of fraud and error'*

The directors are responsible for taking reasonable steps to prevent and detect fraud. They are also responsible for preparing financial statements which give a true and fair view of the entity's affairs. However, the auditors must plan and perform their audit procedures and evaluate and report the results thereof, recognising that fraud or error may materially affect the financial statements. A strong system of internal control will give the auditors some assurance that frauds and errors are not occurring, unless management are colluding to overcome that system.

(e) *'accuracy and completeness of the accounting records'/timely preparation of reliable financial information'*

This objective is most clearly related to statutory requirements relating to both management and auditors. The company has an obligation under the Companies Act 1985 to maintain proper accounting records. The auditors must form an opinion on whether the company has fulfilled this obligation and also conclude whether the financial statements are in agreement with the underlying records.

5 RECORDING OF ACCOUNTING AND CONTROL SYSTEMS

5.1 There are several techniques for recording the assessment of control risk, that is, the system. One or more may be used depending on the complexity of the system.

- Narrative notes
- Questionnaires
- Checklists
- Flowcharts

5.2 Whatever method of recording the system is used, the record will usually be retained on the permanent file and updated each year. Your syllabus focuses on the use of questionnaires.

Questionnaires

5.3 We can look at two types of questionnaire here, each with a different purpose.

- **Internal Control Questionnaires (ICQs)** are used to ask whether controls exist which meet specific control objectives.
- **Internal Control Evaluation Questionnaires (ICEQs)** are used to determine whether there are controls which prevent or detect specified errors or omissions.

Internal Control Questionnaires (ICQs)

5.4 The major question which internal control questionnaires are designed to answer is 'How good is the system of controls?'

5.5 Where strengths are identified, the auditors will perform work in the relevant areas. If, however, weaknesses are discovered they should then ask:

- What errors or irregularities could be made possible by these weaknesses?
- Could such errors or irregularities be material to the accounts?
- What substantive procedures will enable such errors or irregularities to be discovered and quantified?

5.6 Although there are many different forms of ICQ in practice, they all conform to the following basic principles:

(a) They comprise a list of questions designed to determine whether desirable controls are present.

(b) They are formulated so that there is one to cover each of the major transaction cycles.

5.7 Since it is the primary purpose of an ICQ to evaluate the system rather than describe it, one of the most effective ways of designing the questionnaire is to phrase the questions so that all the answers can be given as 'YES' or 'NO' and a 'NO' answer indicates a weakness in the system. An example would be:

Are purchase invoices checked to goods received notes before being passed for payment?	YES/NO/Comments

A 'NO' answer to that question clearly indicates a weakness in the company's payment procedures.

5.8 The ICQ questions below dealing with goods inward provide additional illustrations of the ICQ approach.

Goods inward

(a) Are supplies examined on arrival as to quantity and quality?

(b) Is such an examination evidenced in some way?

(c) Is the receipt of supplies recorded, perhaps by means of goods inwards notes?

(d) Are receipt records prepared by a person independent of those responsible for:

 (i) Ordering functions

 (ii) The processing and recording of invoices

(e) Are goods inwards records controlled to ensure that invoices are obtained for all goods received and to enable the liability for unbilled goods to be determined (by pre-numbering the records and accounting for all serial numbers)?

(f) (i) Are goods inward records regularly reviewed for items for which no invoices have been received?

 (ii) Are any such items investigated?

(g) Are these records reviewed by a person independent of those responsible for the receipt and control of goods?

Internal Control Evaluation Questionnaires (ICEQs)

5.9 In recent years many auditing firms have developed and implemented an evaluation technique more concerned with assessing whether specific errors (or frauds) are possible rather than establishing whether certain desirable controls are present.

5.10 This is achieved by reducing the control criteria for each transaction stream down to a handful of key questions (or control questions). The characteristic of these questions is that they concentrate on the significant errors or omissions that could occur at each phase of the appropriate cycle if controls are weak.

5.11 The nature of the key questions may best be understood by reference to the examples on the following pages.

Internal control evaluation questionnaire: control questions

The sales (revenue) cycle

Is there reasonable assurance that:

(a) Sales are properly authorised?
(b) Sales are made to reliable payers?
(c) All goods despatched are invoiced?
(d) All invoices are properly prepared?
(e) All invoices are recorded?
(f) Invoices are properly supported?
(g) All credits to customers' accounts are valid?
(h) Cash and cheques received are properly recorded and deposited?
(i) Slow payers will be chased and that bad and doubtful debts will be provided against?
(j) All transactions are properly accounted for?
(k) Cash sales are properly dealt with?
(l) Sundry sales are controlled?
(m) At the period end the system will neither overstate nor understate debtors?

The purchases (expenditure) cycle

Is there reasonable assurance that:

(a) Goods or services could not be received without a liability being recorded?
(b) Receipt of goods or services is required in order to establish a liability?
(c) A liability will be recorded:
    (i) Only for authorised items
    (ii) At the proper amount?
(d) All payments are properly authorised?
(e) All credits due from suppliers are received?
(f) All transactions are properly accounted for?
(g) At the period end liabilities are neither overstated nor understated by the system?
(h) The balance at the bank is properly recorded at all times?
(i) Unauthorised cash payments could not be made and that the balance of petty cash is correctly stated at all times?

Wages and salaries

Is there reasonable assurance that:

(a) Employees are only paid for work done?
(b) Employees are paid the correct amount (gross and net)?
(c) The right employees actually receive the right amount?
(d) Accounting for payroll costs and deductions is accurate?

Stock

Is there reasonable assurance that:

(a) Stock is safeguarded from physical loss (eg fire, theft, deterioration)?
(b) Stock records are accurate and up to date?
(c) The recorded stock exists?
(d) The recorded stock is owned by the company?
(e) The cut off is reliable?
(f) The costing system is reliable?
(g) The stock sheets are accurately compiled?
(h) The stock valuation is fair?

Fixed tangible assets

Is there reasonable assurance that:

(a) Recorded assets actually exist and belong to the company?
(b) Capital expenditure is authorised and reported?
(c) Disposals of fixed assets are authorised and reported?
(d) Depreciation is realistic?
(e) Fixed assets are correctly accounted for?
(f) Income derived from fixed assets is accounted for?

> *Investments*
>
> Is there reasonable assurance that:
>
> (a) Recorded investments belong to the company and are safeguarded from loss?
> (b) All income, rights or bonus issues are properly received and accounted for?
> (c) Investment transactions are made only in accordance with company policy and are appropriately authorised and documented?
> (d) The carrying values of investments are reasonably stated?
>
> *Management information and general controls*
>
> Is the nominal ledger satisfactorily controlled?
> Are journal entries adequately controlled?
> Does the organisation structure provide a clear definition of the extent and limitation of authority?
> Are the systems operated by competent employees, who are adequately supported?
> If there is an internal audit function, is it adequate?
> Are financial planning procedures adequate?
> Are periodic internal reporting procedures adequate?

5.12 Each key control question is supported by detailed control points to be considered. For example, the detailed control points to be considered in relation to key control question (b) for the expenditure cycle (Is there reasonable assurance that receipt of goods or services is required to establish a liability?) are as follows.

> (1) Is segregation of duties satisfactory?
>
> (2) Are controls over relevant master files satisfactory?
>
> (3) Is there a record that all goods received have been checked for:
>
> - Weight or number?
> - Quality and damage?
>
> (4) Are all goods received taken on charge in the detailed stock ledgers:
>
> - By means of the goods received note?
> - Or by means of purchase invoices?
> - Are there, in a computerised system, sensible control totals (hash totals, money values and so on) to reconcile the stock system input with the creditors system?
>
> (5) Are all invoices initialled to show that:
>
> - Receipt of goods has been checked against the goods received records?
> - Receipt of services has been verified by the person using it?
> - Quality of goods has been checked against the inspection?
>
> (6) In a computerised invoice approval system are there print-outs (examined by a responsible person) of:
>
> - Cases where order, GRN and invoice are present but they are not equal ('equal' within predetermined tolerances of minor discrepancies)?
> - Cases where invoices have been input but there is no corresponding GRN?
>
> (7) Is there adequate control over direct purchases?
>
> (8) Are receiving documents effectively cancelled (for example cross-referenced) to prevent their supporting two invoices?

5.13 Alternatively, ICEQ questions can be phrased so that the weakness which should be prevented by a key control is highlighted, such as the following.

Question	Answer	Comments or explanation of 'yes' answer
Can goods be sent to unauthorised suppliers?		

5.14 In these cases a 'yes' answer would require an explanation, rather than a 'no' answer.

5.15 **ICQs: advantages**

(a) If drafted thoroughly, they can ensure **all controls** are **considered.**
(b) They are **quick** to **prepare.**
(c) They are **easy** to **use** and **control.**

5.16 **ICQs: disadvantages**

(a) The client may be able to **overstate controls.**

(b) They may contain a large number of **irrelevant controls.**

(c) They may not include **unusual controls,** which are nevertheless effective in particular circumstances.

(d) They can give the impression that all controls are of **equal** weight. In many systems one NO answer (for example lack of segregation of duties) will cancel out a string of YES answers.

5.17 **ICEQs: advantages**

(a) Because they are drafted in terms of **objectives** rather than specific controls, they are easier to apply to a variety of systems than **ICQs**.

(b) Answering ICEQs should enable auditors to **identify the key controls** which they are most likely to test during control testing.

(c) ICEQs can **highlight areas of weakness** where extensive substantive testing will be required.

5.18 **ICQs: disadvantage**

That they can be **drafted vaguely**, hence **misunderstood** and important controls not identified.

Question: Segregation of duties

Explain the importance of segregation of duties

Answer

Segregation of duties is important because the more people that are involved in all the stages of processing a transaction, the more likely it is that fraud or error by a single person will be identified. In addition the more people that are involved, the less the chances all of them colluding in fraud.

6 CONTROLS IN A COMPUTER ENVIRONMENT

Management policy

6.1 It is important for management to have a clear overall policy on the use of computers. A policy statement should include the following:

- Commitment to information security
- Procedures including passwords, data protection and information distribution
- Legal requirements (data protection legislation) and licensing agreements
- Overall supervision by senior management
- Consequences of disobeying the rules

6.2 A policy statement is of particular importance if users are operating on personal computers. Instructions should include policies on:

- Environmental protection
- Security
- Anti-virus checks
- Training
- Documentation standards
- Error correction procedures
- Back-up procedures

Controls

6.3 Auditors must understand and be able to assess computer controls. There are two types of interrelated controls, application controls and general controls. Strong general controls add to an auditors' assurance obtained about application controls, but poor general controls **may undermine** strong application controls.

KEY TERMS

Application controls relate to the transactions and standing data appertaining to each computer-based accounting system and are therefore specific to each such application. The objectives of application controls, which may be manual or programmed, are to ensure the completeness and accuracy of the accounting records and the validity of the entries made in these records resulting from both manual and programmed processing.

General controls are controls, other than application controls, which relate to the environment within which computer based accounting systems are developed, maintained and operated, and which are therefore applicable to all the applications. The objectives of general controls are to ensure the proper development and implementation of applications and the integrity of program and data files and of computer operations. Like application controls, general controls may be either manual or programmed.

6.4 **Auditors' approach**

(a) Before auditors place reliance on application controls which involve computer programs, they need to obtain reasonable assurance that the programs have **operated properly**.

(b) Often transactions will be generated automatically without the need for human agency. Sometimes a programmed accounting procedure may not be subject to effective application controls. In such circumstances, in order to put themselves in a position to limit the extent of substantive procedures, the auditors may choose to perform tests of controls by **testing** the **relevant general controls**.

(c) Computer systems are generally more reliable than manual systems, but in a computer environment there is the possibility of **systematic errors**. This may take place because of program faults or hardware malfunction in computer operations. However, many such potential recurrent errors should be prevented or detected by general controls over the development and implementation of applications and the integrity of the program and data files.

(d) The extent to which the auditors can rely on general controls may be **limited** because many of these controls might not be evidenced, or because they could have been performed inconsistently.

(e) There may be a lack of **segregation of duties**, with users authorised to perform various accounting functions.

(f) Detailed knowledge of computer **operations, programs** and **files** may be confined to a few people or even a single person. This may increase the opportunity to commit an undiscovered fraud by changing **programs** or **data.**

Examples of application controls

6.5 To achieve the overall objectives of application controls identified above, the specific requirements are controls over:

- **Completeness, accuracy** and **authorisation** of **input**
- **Completeness** and **accuracy** of **processing**
- **Maintenance** of **master files** and the **standing data contained therein**.

Standing data is data that will be used over and over again, for example, staff grades, or rates of pay. Master files use this data and store an accumulation of transactions.

Application controls	
Controls over **input**: **completeness**	Manual or programmed agreement of control totals Document counts One for one checking of processed output to source documents Programmed matching of input to a expected input control file Procedures over resubmission of rejected controls
Controls over **input: accuracy**	Programmes to check data fields (for example value, reference number, date) on input transactions for plausibility: Digit verification (eg reference numbers are as expected) Reasonableness test (eg VAT to total value) Existence checks (eg customer name) Character checks (no unexpected characters used in reference) Necessary information (no transaction passed with gaps) Permitted range (no transaction processed over a certain value) Manual scrutiny of output and reconciliation to source Agreement of control totals (manual/programmed)
Controls over **input: authorisation**	Manual checks to ensure information input was - Authorised - Input by authorised personnel
Controls over **processing**	Similar controls to input must be completed when input is completed, for example, batch reconciliations. Screen warnings can prevent people logging out before processing is complete
Controls over **master files and standing data**	One to one checking Cyclical reviews of all master files and standing data Record counts (number of documents processed) and hash totals (for example, the total of all the payroll numbers) used when master files are used to ensure no deletions Controls over the deletion of accounts that have no current balance

Examples of general controls

6.6 To achieve the overall objectives of general controls identified above, controls may be needed in the following areas.

General controls	
Development of computer applications	Standards over **systems design, programming and documentation** Full **testing procedures** using test data Approval by **computer users** and **management** **Segregation of duties** so that those responsible for design are not responsible for testing **Installation procedures** so that data is not corrupted in transition **Training** of staff in new procedures and availability of adequate documentation
Prevention of unauthorised changes to programs	**Segregation of duties** **Full records** of program **changes** **Password protection** of programs so that access is limited to computer operations staff **Restricting access** to **central computer** by locked doors, keypads and other access controls **Maintenance of programs logs** **Virus checks** on software, use of anti-virus software and policy prohibiting use of non-authorised programs or files **Back-up copies** of programs being taken and stored in other locations **Control copies** of programs being preserved and regularly **compared** with **actual programs** **Stricter controls** over certain programs (utility programs) by use of **read only memory** and file **libraries**
Testing and documentation of program changes	Complete **testing procedures** **Documentation standards** **Approval** of changes by computer users and management **Training** of staff using programs
Prevention of use of wrong programs or files being used	**Operation controls** over programs **Libraries** of programs **Proper job scheduling**
Prevention of unauthorised changes to data files	See section below on real-time systems
Controls to ensure continuity of operation	**Storing extra copies** of programs and data files off site **Protection of equipment** against fire and other hazards **Back-up power sources** **Emergency procedures** **Disaster recovery procedures** eg availability of back-up computer facilities. **Maintenance agreements** and **insurance**

7 CONTROLS IN ON-LINE AND REAL-TIME SYSTEMS

Nature of on-line and real-time systems

7.1 Whilst traditional batch processing is still a common method of using a computer to process accounting data there is a rapid increase in the use of an on-line system, including those in real-time.

KEY TERMS

On-line systems provide the facilities for data to be passed to and from the central computer via remote terminals.

Real-time systems are a further development of on-line systems and permit immediate updating of computer held files. The data input and file update phases are therefore merged and the system accepts individual transactions rather than batches of data.

Controls in real-time systems

7.2 There are certain control problems associated with most real-time systems. We are concerned primarily with larger, multi-user systems. By **terminals** we mean either dumb terminals or networked PCs.

Segregation of duties

7.3 The same person is often responsible for producing **and** processing the same information. To compensate for the reduction in internal check, supervisory controls should be strengthened. The systems administrator is particularly important; he should be responsible for backing up files, authorising users, controlling the file server and investigating problems.

Data file security

7.4 A person using a remote terminal can gain access to databases at will so special controls are required to ensure that files are neither read nor written to (nor destroyed), either accidentally or deliberately, without proper authority.

(a) The controls may be partly **physical**. For example:

(i) **Access to terminals** is **restricted** to authorised personnel.

(ii) The **terminals** and the **rooms** in which they are kept are **locked** when not in use or have entry restricted to authorised cardholders, or by keypad codes.

(b) They may be partly controlled by the **operating system**.

(i) The use of **passwords** (or lockwords), or **special badges** or keys, sometimes linked to a user's personal identification code which must be used before the terminal operator can gain access to the computer/particular files.

In some systems one password or other identification is required before it is possible to read a file, a second before it is possible to write new data and yet a third if both operations are permitted. Obviously, the code given to a particular individual will depend on his job function and status within the organisation.

Passwords are particularly important and there are various procedures that can be implemented to prevent unauthorised use of passwords.

- Passwords should be changed regularly, for example, every month and if possible changed by the user.
- Passwords should be of a reasonable length, and possibly mix numbers and words to minimise the possibility of their being guessed.
- Passwords should not be displayed when being input.
- Re-use of old passwords should not be permitted.
- The system should automatically 'log-off' if a terminal is not used for a certain time.
- If someone tries to log on with the wrong password, the terminal should be disabled after two or three wrong attempts.

More sophisticated controls might include voice and fingerprint recognition.

(ii) **Restriction** by the operating system of **certain users** to **certain files**. For example, the PC in the wages department may only be given access to the wages files.

(iii) **Logging** of all **attempted violations** of the above controls possibly accompanied by the automatic shut down of the PC or terminal used. Obviously all violations should be speedily and thoroughly investigated.

(iv) **Reviews** of **systems records** of entries made to system and files accessed.

(v) **Internet controls**. Unauthorised users may be able to access businesses' internal systems to obtain confidential information, or to launch a virus that disrupts internal systems. Controls include **firewalls** which disable part of the communication technology that normally allows two-way communication, so that external contacts are denied access to part of the system. Other possibilities are **encryption** of data, and **callback** to external customers who wish to access the system.

(c) **Application controls** may include validity checks on input and reporting of unusual transactions.

Server security

7.5 Access controls on the server are particularly important, since interference here can damage the whole system. The server should not also be used as a normal terminal, and it should be in secure accommodation.

Back-ups

7.6 Back-ups must be taken at least **daily**, and separately on a weekly basis. In a real time system it may be necessary to have a cut off time after which no further transactions are ever posted. Attempts to open a file when a back-up is in progress can sometimes corrupt the process. Stray transactions posted after the back-up has been done could be lost if there is some sort of accident and the back-up data has to be restored in full the next day.

7.7 On the other hand, immediate access to files allows more sophisticated checks to be performed. For example it allows more extensive use of computer matching, where the information input may be checked for accuracy against that held on file. Moreover, in spite of the potential for abuse, there is a distinct advantage to enabling users to correct certain types of error immediately.

Database management systems (DBMS)

7.8 DBMS are normally designed for use in real-time environments. They enable elements of data to be accessed by different programs. This avoids the duplication of data which inevitably occurs in a traditional system.

7.9 As data is normally only stored once, and may be accessible to all users that require it, the principal control problems raised concern the authorisation of data amendments and restriction of access to data. Any data amendments must take into account the requirements of all the users.

7.10 An **administration function** should be set up to run and control the day to day operation of the database, thereby enhancing segregation of duties (this function will be independent of the systems development personnel and programmers and data processing manager).

7.11 The audit of DBMS creates particular problems as the two principal CAATs, test data and audit software, tend to work unsatisfactorily in these systems. The auditors may, however, be able to use **embedded audit facilities**. The auditors should if possible be involved at the evaluation, design and development stages so that they are able to determine their audit requirements and identify control problems.

Exam focus point

Watch out in the exam to see whether the systems are on-line or real-time, since this will affect what controls are the most important.

Electronic Data Interchange systems

7.12 Electronic Data Interchange (EDI) systems allow businesses to **transmit** standard business documents such as sales invoices or purchase orders **electronically**.

7.13 EDI systems pose a number of problems for auditors.

(a) **Originating documents** may be **eliminated**, and there may be a **lack of evidence** of the operation of controls.

(b) The **consequences** of **problems** may be **enhanced**. Greater integration between the various aspects of an entity's accounting system is likely, and problems with one business may have a serious impact upon its suppliers or competitors. Computer failures may rapidly lead to material losses.

(c) The **risk of unauthorised access** to data may be **increased**. Not only will a business have to have its own controls, but it will have to rely as well on the controls operated by its business partners.

7.14 Controls over transmission including **acknowledgements**, **agreements** by both parties of amounts transmitted, **authentication codes** and **encryption** are particularly important. Transactions should be monitored continuously by **checking** the **sequence** of transaction numbers and **integrated test facilities** within the computer. **Limitation controls**, such as only allowing transactions with certain businesses, can be built into the organisation's computer system. There should also be **virus protection** and appropriate **insurance**, and **contingency plans** and **back-up arrangements**.

7.15 Auditors are likely to have to place significant reliance on controls and may be able to **test compliance** with agreed **best practice.** Auditors may also be able to obtain assurance on the working of controls of business partners by obtaining a certificate from their auditors.

Chapter roundup

- There are always inherent limitations to internal controls.
- Specific **control procedures** include the following.
  - Approval and control of documents
  - Controls over computerised applications and the information technology environment
  - Checking the arithmetical accuracy of the records
  - Maintaining and reviewing control accounts and trial balances
  - Reconciliations
  - Comparing the results of cash, security and stock counts with accounting records
  - Comparing internal data with external sources of information
  - Limiting direct physical access to assets and records
- The auditors must **understand** the **accounting system** and **control environment** in order to determine the audit approach.
- Learn the CA 1985 requirements relating to the **accounting records**.
- Both **ICQs** and **ICEQs** are used to evaluate control systems.
- A report to directors or management may be sent after both the interim and final audits, or combined in one letter or report at the end. The primary purpose of the report is to inform the management of **weaknesses** in the system of **internal controls** but the letter can also be used for other purposes.
- **Application controls** should ensure:
  - The completeness, accuracy and authorisation of input
  - The completeness and accuracy of processing
  - The proper maintenance of master files and standing data
- **General controls** are required to:
  - Ensure proper application development
  - Prevent or detect unauthorised changes to programs
  - Ensure that all program changes are adequately tested and documented
  - Prevent or detect errors during program execution
  - Prevent unauthorised amendments to data files
  - Ensure that systems software is properly installed and maintained
  - Ensure that proper documentation is kept
  - Ensure continuity of operations
- The majority of modern systems are **real-time systems**, where users have instant and direct access to data. Important real-time controls are:
  - Segregation of duties
  - Data file security
  - Program security
  - Back-ups

Quick quiz

1 Complete the definition taking the words given below.

.... is the overall ...., ... and actions of directors and managers regarding internal .... and their .... in the entity. The .... encompasses the management style and corporate culture and values shared by all .... It provides the background against which various other controls are operated.

employees, controls, attitude, environment, control, awareness, importance, environment, control

2 Name two **key** inherent limitations of an internal control system

1 ....

2 ....

3 Which of the following is not a test of control?

A Inspection of documents
B Reperformance of control procedures
C Observation of controls
D Verification of value to invoice

4 After the controls have been assessed, the audit plan may be modified.

True ☐

False ☐

5 Put the controls below in the correct category

Application controls	**General controls**

one to one checking	virus checks	hash totals
segregation of duties	passwords	program libraries
review of master files	training	controls over account deletions
back-up copies	record counts	back-up power source

Answers to quick quiz

1 Control environment, attitude, awareness, controls, importance, control environment, employees.

2 Human error
Possibility of staff colluding in fraud

3 D

4 True

5

Application controls	General controls
one to one checking hash totals review of master files record counts	virus checks program libraries segregation of duties passwords controls over account deletion training back-up power source back-up copies

Now try the question below from the Exam Question Bank

Number	Level	Marks	Time
9	Exam	20	36 mins

Chapter 10

TESTS OF CONTROLS: SALES, PURCHASES AND WAGES

Topic list		Syllabus reference	Study guide
1	The sales system	5	13
2	The purchases and expenses system	5	13
3	The wages system	5	15
4	Smaller entities	5	13-16

Introduction

In Chapter 9 we stated that the auditors must ascertain the accounting system and the system of internal control. The auditors will then decide which controls, if any, they wish to rely on and plan **tests of controls** to obtain the audit evidence as to whether such reliance can be warranted. For each of the systems listed above we will look at the system **objectives** the auditors will bear in mind while assessing the internal controls and give examples of common controls. We shall then go on to look at a 'standard' programme of tests of controls.

In this chapter we deal with **sales, purchases** and **wages and salaries**. These areas are the areas that are most commonly tested in auditing exams.

For **sales**, businesses want to give credit only to customers who will **pay their debts**. In addition there are various stages of the selling process- **ordering, despatch and charging**, all of which should be **documented** and **matched** so that customers receive what they ordered and are appropriately billed. In order to keep track of who owes what and to be able to identify slow-paying customers, a **sales ledger** should be maintained.

Similarly **purchases** must be controlled. Businesses should ensure that only **properly authorised purchases** which are necessary for the business are made. Again all stages of the purchase process, ordering, receiving goods and being charged for them should be **documented and matched** so that the business gets what it ordered and only pays for what it ordered and received. Businesses also need to keep track of what they owe to each supplier by maintaining a purchase ledger.

For **wages and salaries** businesses are trying to ensure that they only pay for **hours worked** and that they pay the **right staff** the **right amount**. Controls should also be in place to ensure **PAYE and VAT liabilities** are calculated correctly otherwise penalties may be imposed by the tax authorities.

There has always been a compulsory question on controls in the 2.6 exam to date.

1 THE SALES SYSTEM — Pilot paper, 12/02

1.1 Aims of controls

Ordering and granting of credit

- **Goods** and **services** are **only supplied** to **customers** with **good credit ratings**
- **Customers** are encouraged to **pay promptly**
- **Orders** are **recorded correctly**
- **Orders** are **fulfilled**

Despatch and invoicing

- All **despatches** of goods are **recorded**
- All **goods and services** sold are **correctly invoiced**
- All **invoices** raised **relate to goods and services supplied** by the business
- **Credit notes** are only given for **valid reasons**

Recording, accounting and credit control

- All sales that have been **invoiced** are **recorded** in the general and sales ledgers
- All **credit notes** that have been **issued** are **recorded** in the general and sales ledgers
- All **entries** in the sales ledger are **made** to the **correct** sales ledger **accounts**
- **Cut-off** is applied correctly to the sales ledger
- Potentially **doubtful debts** are **identified**

Controls: ordering and granting of credit process

- **Segregation** of duties; credit control, invoicing and stock despatch
- **Authorisation** of **credit terms** to customers
  - References/credit checks obtained
  - Authorisation by senior staff
  - Regular review
- **Authorisation** for changes in **other customer data**
  - Change of address supported by letterhead
  - Deletion requests supported by evidence balances cleared/customer in liquidation
- **Orders** only **accepted** from **customers** who have no credit problems
- **Sequential numbering** of blank pre-printed order documents
- **Correct prices quoted** to **customers**
- **Matching** of **customer orders** with production orders and despatch notes and querying of orders not matched
- **Dealing** with **customer queries**

Controls: despatches and invoice preparation

- **Authorisation** of **despatch** of **goods**
  - Despatch only on sales order
  - Despatch only to authorised customers
  - Special authorisation of despatches of goods free of charge or on special terms
- **Examination** of **goods outwards** as to quantity, quality and condition
- **Recording** of **goods outwards**

• **Agreement** of **goods outwards records** to **customer orders**, **despatch notes** and **invoices**
• **Prenumbering** of despatch notes and delivery notes and regular checks on sequence
• **Condition** of **returns checked**
• Recording of goods returned on **goods returned notes**
• **Signature** of **delivery notes** by customers
• Preparation of invoices and credit notes
  ○ **Authorisation** of **selling prices**/use of **price lists**
  ○ **Authorisation** of **credit notes**
  ○ **Checks on prices, quantities, extensions** and totals on invoices and credit notes
  ○ **Sequential numbering** of blank invoices/credit notes and regular sequence checks
• **Stock records updated**
• **Matching** of sales **invoices** with **despatch** and **delivery notes** and sales orders
• **Regular review** for **despatch notes** not matched by invoices

Controls: accounting, recording and credit problems
• **Segregation of duties:** recording sales, maintaining customer accounts and preparing statements • **Recording** of **sales invoices** sequence and **control** over **spoilt invoices** • **Matching** of **cash receipts** with **invoices** • **Retention** of **customer remittance advices** • **Separate recording** of **sales returns, price adjustments** etc • **Cut-off procedures** to ensure goods despatched and not invoiced (or vice versa) are properly dealt with the correct period • Regular **preparation** of **debtor statements** • **Checking** of **debtors' statements** • **Safeguarding** of **debtor statements** so that they cannot be altered before despatch • **Review** and **follow-up** of **overdue accounts** • **Authorisation** of **writing off** of **bad debts** • **Reconciliation** of **sales ledger control account** • Analytical review of sales ledger and profit margins

Tests of controls

Tests of control: ordering and granting credit
• **Check** that **references** are being **obtained** for **all new customers** • **Check** that all **new accounts** on the sales ledger have been **authorised** by senior staff • **Check** that **orders** are only **accepted** from customers who are **within** their **credit terms** and **credit limits** • **Check** that **customer orders** are being **matched** with **production orders** and **despatch notes**

Tests of control: despatches and invoices
• Verify details of **trade sales** or goods despatched notes with **sales invoices checking** ◦ **Quantities** ◦ **Prices** charged with official price lists ◦ **Trade discounts** have been properly dealt with ◦ **Calculations** and **additions** ◦ **Entries** in sales day book are correctly **analysed** ◦ **VAT**, where chargeable, has been properly **dealt with** ◦ **Postings** to sales ledger • Verify details of trade sales with **entries in stock records** • Verify **non-routine** sales (scrap, fixed assets etc) with: ◦ **Appropriate supporting evidence** ◦ **Approval** by authorised officials ◦ **Entries** in **plant register** • Verify **credit notes** with: ◦ **Correspondence** or other supporting evidence ◦ **Approval** by authorised officials ◦ **Entries** in **stock records** ◦ **Entries** in **goods returned records** ◦ **Calculations** and **additions** ◦ **Entries** in **day book**, checking these are correctly analysed ◦ **Postings** to **sales ledger** • **Test numerical sequence** of **despatch notes** and **enquire** into **missing numbers** • **Test numerical sequence** of **invoices** and **credit notes**, **enquire** into **missing numbers** and **inspect copies** of those cancelled • **Test numerical sequence** of **order forms** and enquire into missing numbers • **Check** that **despatches** of **goods free of charge** or on **special terms** have been **authorised** by management

Tests of control: recording of and accounting for sales
Sales day book • **Check entries** with **invoices** and **credit notes** respectively • **Check additions** and **cross casts** • **Check postings** to **sales ledger control account** • **Check postings** to **sales ledger** Sales ledger • **Check** entries in a **sample of accounts** to sales day book • **Check additions** and **balances** carried down • **Note** and **enquire** into **contra entries** • Check that **control accounts** have been **regularly reconciled** to total of sales ledger balances • **Scrutinise accounts** to see if credit limits have been observed • **Check** that **debtor statements** are **prepared** and **sent out regularly** • **Check** that **overdue accounts** have been **followed up** • **Check** that **all bad debts written off** have been **authorised** by management

Exam focus point

In the exam you may be asked:

(a) What controls are appropriate for a specific situation?
(b) What are the major weaknesses in the system given in the question?
(c) What are the consequences of the failure or non-existence of controls?
(d) What tests would auditors use on the controls given in the question?

If you are asked about appropriate controls or weaknesses, remember the **objectives** for the accounting area. Controls should be in place to **fulfil** the **objectives** given, weaknesses will mean that the objectives are not fulfilled. You should also consider the **documentation** and **staff** involved in each area.

You should give enough detail about the controls you suggest to enable a non-accountant to implement the controls.

You should use a similar thought process when deciding how to test the controls. Think of the **objectives** of the system; assess how the controls given **fulfil** those **objectives**; and set out tests which demonstrate whether the controls are working. Remember that different types of test can be used to test different controls. Inspection for example can be used to test whether different documents are being compared or documents are being properly authorised. Computation can be used to check invoices have been properly completed or reconciliations correctly made.

The examiner may ask you to describe or compile an internal control questionnaire/checklist relating to internal control. An example of this was given in Chapter 9.

Question: Complete recording

What tests of control can give auditors assurance that the company's system of control ensures that sales are completely recorded?

Answer

Tests of control: completeness of recording of sales

(a) Sequence tests on sales orders, despatch notes, invoices and credit notes to ensure that there are no missing numbers or two documents with the same number

(b) Comparisons of despatch notes with order and invoices, checking documents are cross-referenced to each other

(c) Checking posting of sales day book to sales ledger control account and sales ledger

(d) Checking control account reconciliations have been carried out and have been reviewed by senior staff

(e) Controls over computerised input including:

  (i) Control totals
  (ii) Checking of output to source documents
  (iii) Procedure over resubmisson of rejected inputs

Question: Weaknesses and tests of controls

You are the auditor of Arcidiacono Stationery Ltd, and you have been asked to suggest how audit work should be carried out on the sales system.

Arcidiacono Stationery Ltd sells stationery to shops. Most sales are to small customers who do not have a sales ledger account. They can collect their purchases and pay by cash. For cash sales:

(a) The customer orders the stationery from the sales department, which raises a pre-numbered multi-copy order form.

(b) The despatch department make up the order and give it to the customer with a copy of the order form.

(c) The customer gives the order form to the cashier who prepares a hand-written sales invoice.

(d) The customer pays the cashier for the goods by cheque or in cash.

(e) The cashier records and banks the cash.

Required

(a) State the weaknesses in the cash sales system.
(b) Describe the systems based tests you would carry out to check the controls over the system.

Answer

(a) **Weaknesses in the cash system**

(i) The physical location of the despatch department and the cashier are not mentioned here, but there is a risk of the customer taking the goods without paying. The customer should pay the cashier on the advice note and return for the goods, which should only be released on sight of the paid invoice.

(ii) There is a failure in segregation of duties in allowing the cashier to both complete the sales invoice and receive the cash as he could perpetrate a fraud by replacing the original invoice with one of lower value and keeping the difference.

(iii) No-one checks the invoices to make sure that the cashier has completed them correctly, for example by using the correct prices and performing calculations correctly.

(iv) The completeness of the sequence of sales invoices cannot be checked unless they are pre-numbered sequentially and the presence of all the invoices is checked by another person. The order forms should also be pre-numbered sequentially.

(v) There is also no check that the cashier banks all cash received, ie this is a further failure of segregation of duties.

If the sales department prepared and posted the invoices and also posted the cash for cash sales to a sundry sales account, this would solve some of the internal control problems mentioned above. In addition, the sales department could run a weekly check on the account to look for invoices for which no cash had been received. These could then be investigated.

All of these weaknesses, and possible remedies, should be reported to management.

(b) **Tests**

(i) Select a sample of order forms issued to customers during the year. Trace the related sales invoice and check that the details correlate (date, unit amounts etc). The customer should have signed for the goods and this copy should be retained by the despatch department.

(ii) For the sales invoices discovered in the above test, I would check that the correct order form number is recorded on the invoice, that the prices used are correct (by reference to the prevailing price list) and that the castings and cross-castings (ie arithmetic) is correct.

(iii) I will then trace the value of the sales invoices to the cash book and from the cash book that the total receipts for the day have been banked and appear promptly on the bank statement.

(iv) I would check that the sales invoices have been correctly posted to a cash or sundry sales account. For any sales invoices missing from this account (assuming they are sequentially numbered), I will trace the cancelled invoice and check that the cancelled invoice was initialled by the customer and replaced by the next invoice in sequence.

(v) Because of the weaknesses in the system I would carry out the following sequence checks on large blocks of order forms/invoices, eg four blocks of 100 order forms/invoices.

(1) Check all order forms present; investigate those missing.
(2) Check sales invoices raised for all order forms.
(3) Check all sales invoices in a sequence have been used; investigate any missing.
(4) Cash for each sales invoice has been entered into the cash book.

Using the results of the above tests I would decide whether the system for cash sales has operated without material fraud or error. If I am not satisfied that it has then I will consider qualifying my audit report on the grounds of limitation of scope.

2 THE PURCHASES AND EXPENSES SYSTEM 12/01

2.1 Aims of controls

Ordering

- All **orders for goods and services** are properly **authorised**, and are for **goods and services** that are actually **received** and are for the company
- Orders are only made to **authorised suppliers**
- Orders are made at **competitive prices**

Receipt and invoices

- All goods and services received are used for the **organisation's purposes**, and not private purposes
- Goods and services are **only accepted if** they have been **ordered**, and the **order** has been **authorised**
- All **goods** and **services received** are accurately **recorded**
- **Liabilities** are **recognised** for all **goods and services** that have been **received**
- All **credits** to which business is due are **claimed** and **received**
- **Receipt** of **goods** and **services** is **necessary** to establish a **liability to be recorded**

Accounting

- All **expenditure** is for goods that are **received**
- **All expenditure** is **authorised**
- All **expenditure** that is made is **recorded** correctly in the general and purchase ledger
- All **credit notes** that are received are **recorded** in the general and purchase ledger
- All **entries** in the **purchase ledger** are **made** to the **correct purchase ledger accounts**
- **Cut-off** is **applied correctly** to the purchase ledger

Controls: ordering
• **Segregation** of duties; requisition and ordering • **Central policy** for choice of suppliers • Evidence required of **requirements** for purchase before purchase authorised (re-order quantities and re-order levels) • **Order forms** prepared only when a **pre-numbered purchase requisition** has been **received** • **Authorisation** of order forms • **Prenumbered order forms** • **Safeguarding** of **blank order forms** • **Review** for **orders not received** or invoiced • **Monitoring** of **supplier terms** and taking advantage of favourable conditions (bulk order, discount)
Controls: goods and invoices received

• **Examination** of goods inwards
   ◦ Quality
   ◦ Quantity
   ◦ Condition

- **Recording arrival** and **acceptance** of goods (prenumbered goods received notes)
- **Comparison** of **goods received notes** with **purchase orders**
- **Referencing** of supplier invoices; numerical sequence and supplier reference
- **Checking** of **suppliers' invoices**
  - Prices, quantities, accuracy of calculation
  - Comparison with order and goods received note
- **Recording return of goods** (pre-numbered goods returned notes)
- Procedures for **obtaining credit notes** from suppliers

Controls: accounting for purchases

- **Segregation** of **duties:** accounting and checking functions
- Prompt **recording of purchases** and **purchase returns** in day books and ledgers
- **Regular maintenance** of **purchase ledger**
- **Comparison** of **supplier statements** with **purchase ledger balances**
- **Authorisation** of **payments**
  - Authority limits
  - Confirmation that goods have been received, accord with purchase order, and are properly priced and invoiced
- **Review** of **allocation** of expenditure
- **Reconciliation** of **purchase ledger** control account to total of purchase ledger balances
- **Cut-off** accrual of goods received notes not matched by purchases at year-end

Tests of controls

2.2 A most important test of controls is for auditors to check that all **invoices** are **supported** by authorised **purchase invoices** and **purchase orders**. The officials who approve the invoices should be operating within laid-down **authority limits.**

Tests of control: receipts of goods/invoices

- Check invoices for goods, raw materials are:
  - **Supported** by **goods received notes** and **inspection notes**
  - **Entered** in **stock records**
  - **Priced correctly** by checking to **quotations, price lists** to see the price is in order
  - **Properly referenced** with a number and supplier code
  - **Correctly coded** by type of expenditure

  Trace entry in **record of goods returned** etc and see credit note duly received from the supplier, for invoices not passed due to defects or discrepancy
- For invoices of all types:
  - **Check calculations** and **additions**
  - **Check entries in purchase day book** and verify that they are correctly **analysed**
  - **Check posting** to **purchase ledger**
- For credit notes:
  - **Verify** the **correctness** of credit received with correspondence

- **Check entries** in **stock records**
  - **Check entries** in **record of returns**
  - **Check entries** in **purchase day book** and verify that they are correctly analysed
  - **Check postings** to **purchase ledger**
- Check for **returns** that **credit notes** are duly **received** from the suppliers
- Test **numerical sequence** and enquire into missing numbers of:
  - Purchase requisitions
  - Purchase orders
  - Goods received notes
  - Goods returned notes
  - Suppliers' invoices
- **Obtain explanations** for **items** which have been **outstanding** for a long time:
  - Unmatched purchase requisitions
  - Purchase orders
  - Goods received notes (if invoices not received)
  - Unprocessed invoices

Tests of control: recording of purchases

- Verify that invoices and credit notes recorded in the purchase day book are:
  - **Initialled** for prices, calculations and extensions
  - **Cross-referenced** to purchase orders, goods received notes etc
  - **Authorised** for payment
- **Check additions**
- **Check postings** to general ledger accounts and control account
- **Check postings** of entries to purchase ledger

Purchase ledger

- For a sample of accounts recorded in the purchase ledger
  - **Test check entries** back into books of prime entry
  - **Test check additions** and **balances** forward
  - **Note** and **enquire** into all contra entries
- Confirm **control account balancing** has been regularly carried out during the year
- **Examine control account** for unusual entries

Question: Purchase controls

Derek Limited operates a computerised purchase system. Invoices and credit notes are posted to the bought ledger by the bought ledger department. The computer subsequently raises a cheque when the invoice has to be paid.

Required

List the controls that should be in operation:

(a) Over the addition, amendment and deletion of suppliers, ensuring that the standing data only includes suppliers from the company's list of authorised suppliers

(b) Over purchase invoices and credit notes, to ensure only authorised purchase invoices and credit notes are posted to the purchase ledger

Answer

(a) **Controls over the standing data file containing suppliers' details**

(i) All amendments/additions/deletions to the data should be authorised by a responsible official. A standard form should be used for such changes.

(ii) The amendment forms should be input in batches (with different types of change in different batches), sequentially numbered and recorded in a batch control book so that any gaps in the batch numbers can be investigated. The output produced by the computer should be checked to the input.

(iii) A listing of all such adjustments should automatically be produced by the computer and reviewed by a responsible official, who should also check authorisation.

(iv) A listing of suppliers' accounts on which there has been no movement for a specified period (6 months, 12 months) should be produced to allow decisions to be made about possible deletions, thus ensuring that the standing data is current. The buying department manager might also recommend account closures on a periodic basis.

(v) Users should be controlled by use of passwords. This can also be used as a method of controlling those who can amend data.

(vi) Periodic listings of standing data should be produced in order to verify details (for example addresses) with suppliers' documents (invoices/ statements).

(b) **Control over the input of authorised purchase invoices and credit notes**

(i) Authorisation should be evidenced by the signature of the responsible official (say the Chief Accountant). In addition, the invoice or credit note should show initials to demonstrate that the details have been agreed: to a signed GRN; to a purchase order; to a price list; for additions and extensions.

(ii) There should be adequate segregation of responsibilities between the posting function, stock custody and receipt, payment of suppliers and changes to standing data.

(iii) Input should be restricted by use of passwords linked to the relevant site number.

(iv) A batch control book should be maintained, recording batches in number sequence. Invoices should be input in batches using pre-numbered batch control sheets. The manually produced invoice total on the batch control sheet should be agreed to the computer generated total. Credit notes and invoices should be input in separate batches to avoid one being posted as the other.

(v) A program should check calculation of VAT at standard rate and total (net + VAT = gross) of invoice. Non-standard VAT rates should be highlighted.

(vi) The input of the supplier code should bring up the supplier name for checking by the operator against the invoice.

(vii) Invoices for suppliers which do not have an account should be prevented from being input. Any sundry suppliers account should be very tightly controlled and all entries reviewed in full each month.

(viii) An exception report showing unusual expense allocation (by size or account) should be produced and reviewed by a responsible official. Expenses should be compared to budget and previous years.

(ix) There should be monthly reconciliations of purchase ledger balances to suppliers' statements by someone outside the purchasing (accounting) function.

Question: Tests of controls

You have recently been appointed auditor of Dryden Manufacturing Ltd and are commencing the audit of the purchases system for the year ended 31 December 20X6. The company has about 200 employees and generally has sufficient staff for there to be a proper division of duties for internal control purposes.

Required

For the audit of the company's purchases system:

(a) Describe how you would evaluate the controls, and how your audit tests would be affected by the results of this evaluation;

(b) List the audit tests you would perform (your answer should include consideration of:

(i) The number of items you would select for testing

(ii) The basis of selecting the items

(iii) What action you would take if errors are found, and you should consider the effect of the size and frequency of errors)

(c) Describe the general form of your conclusions on the results of testing the purchase system and how these conclusions may influence your work at the final audit.

Answer

(a) Many large audit firms now use a standard method of internal control evaluation questionnaire (ICEQ) based on key control questions. The characteristics of this system are usually as follows.

(i) It is concerned only with the primary or key controls.

(ii) The format of the questionnaires leads to a detailed assessment of each of the primary control areas.

(iii) The ICEQ schedules can normally be linked and cross-referenced to the flowcharts, ICQs or other systems records.

(iv) It encourages the audit staff to design their tests to suit the particular needs of each client's systems. In other words, it ensures that time is not wasted in performing 'standard' audit programme tests that are not relevant to the circumstances, and that there is a direct link between the evaluation of the system of internal control and the tests carried out.

One method of constructing an ICEQ could be by listing under each major control question the answers of the detailed questions relating to that control which appear in the ICQ and then answering the major question on the basis of the subsidiary questions.

It is also important that against each major control question in the ICEQ there should be space for the auditors to cross-reference their answer to the action they have taken (eg modifying the audit programme or advising the client of weaknesses). An ICEQ will be useless unless the appropriate action is taken as a result of the evaluation.

(b) The audit tests necessary in relation to the purchases system will depend very much upon the auditors' evaluation of the strengths of the system. Assuming there to be a sound system of internal control in operation, then it will be necessary to carry out a programme of both tests of controls and substantive procedures and these will be spread over the interim and final audit visits. The sample size will depend on:

(i) The level of tolerable error, the error that the auditor is prepared to tolerate and still conclude that the objectives of the tests have been achieved. For tests of control the level is likely to be low.

(ii) The level of sampling risk. The more I am relying on the tests, the lower will be the level of sampling risk I am prepared to tolerate, and the higher the sample size will be.

(iii) The level of control risk. The lower the level, the lower will be the sample size.

Samples should be selected using a method that ensures samples chosen are representative of the population. Random sampling would be one such method.

Typically the majority of the tests of control will be carried out on the occasion of the interim audit and should cover tests on the following.

(i) Sequence of purchase orders
(ii) Approval of purchase orders
(iii) Adherence to authority limits
(iv) Sequence of goods received records
(v) Sequence of goods returned records
(vi) Authorisation of adjustments to purchase ledger balances
(vii) Serial numbering of purchase orders
(viii) Sequence of purchase invoices
(ix) Correlation of purchase invoices with purchase orders and goods received records
(x) Correlation of credit notes with goods returned records
(xi) Checking of castings and extensions on purchase invoices
(xii) Coding of purchase invoices for accounting classification purposes

(xiii) Correct segregation of VAT
(xiv) Initialling of purchase invoice 'grid' for work done
(xv) Approval of purchase invoices for processing into accounting system

Since the main aim of the testing at the interim stage is to ensure that the company's laid down procedures are being properly applied, it will be necessary to follow up an error on a transaction of £5 in the same way as an error in a transaction of £50,000. Where errors are found further testing will usually be necessary in the area of weakness to confirm whether the error is isolated or recurring. If the errors persist, then management should be informed of the facts and the matters should be noted in the interim comments letter sent by the auditors to the client.

(c) If the results of the auditors' tests on the purchases system are satisfactory they may conclude that it will produce reliable accounting records and this in turn will mean that they may keep substantive testing at the year end to a minimum. If, however, the tests of control reveal weaknesses in the system then at the final audit, the auditors will have to carry out a more extensive programme of substantive tests.

3 THE WAGES SYSTEM 12/03

3.1 Aims of controls

Setting of wages and salaries

- **Employees** are **only paid** for **work** that they have **done**
- **Gross pay** has been **calculated correctly** and **authorised**

Recording of wages and salaries

- **Gross** and **net pay** and **deductions** are **accurately recorded** on the payroll
- **Wages and salaries paid** are **recorded correctly** in the **bank** and **cash records**
- **Wages and salaries** are **correctly recorded** in the **general ledger**

Payment of wages and salaries

- The **correct employees** are **paid**

Deductions

- All **deductions** have been **calculated correctly** and are **authorised**
- The **correct amounts** are **paid** to the **taxation authorities**

3.2 While in practice separate arrangements are generally made for dealing with wages and salaries, the considerations involved are broadly similar and for convenience the two aspects are here treated together.

Controls: general arrangements
Responsibility for the preparation of pay sheets should be delegated to a suitable person, and adequate staff appointed to assist him. The extent to which the staff responsible for preparing wages and salaries may perform other duties should be clearly defined. In this connection full advantage should be taken where possible of the division of duties, and checks available where automatic wage-accounting systems are in use.
Controls: setting of wages and salaries

• **Staffing** and **segregation of duties**
• **Maintenance of personnel records** and regular checking of wages and salaries to details in personnel records
• **Authorisation**
    ○ Engagement and discharge of employees
    ○ Changes in pay rates

◦ Overtime ◦ Non-statutory deductions (for example pension contributions) ◦ Advances of pay • **Recording** of **changes** in **personnel** and **pay rates** • **Recording** of hours worked by **timesheets, clocking** in and out arrangements • **Review** of hours worked • **Recording** of **advances** of **pay** • **Holiday pay** arrangements • **Answering queries** • **Review** of **wages** against **budget**
Controls: payment of cash wages
• **Segregation of duties** ◦ Cash sheet preparation ◦ Filling of pay packets ◦ Distribution of wages • **Authorisation** of **wage cheque** cashed • **Custody** of cash ◦ Encashment of cheque ◦ Security of pay packets ◦ Security of transit ◦ Security and prompt banking of unclaimed wages • **Verification of identity** • **Recording** of distribution
Controls: payment of salaries
• **Preparation** and **authorisation** of cheques and bank transfer lists • Comparison of **cheques** and **bank transfer list** with **payroll** • **Maintenance** and **reconciliation** of wages and salaries bank account
Controls: recording of wages and salaries
• **Bases** for **compilation** of payroll • **Preparation, checking** and **approval** of payroll • Dealing with **non-routine matters**
Controls: deductions from pay
• **Maintenance** of **separate employees' records,** with which pay lists may be compared as necessary • **Reconciliation** of **total pay** and **deductions** between one pay day and the next • **Surprise cash counts** • **Comparison** of actual pay totals with **budget estimates** or standard costs and the investigation of variances • **Agreement** of **gross earnings** and **total tax deducted** with PAYE returns to the Inland Revenue

3.3 Appropriate arrangements should be made for dealing with statutory and other authorised deductions from pay, such as national insurance, PAYE, pension fund contributions, and savings held in trust. A primary consideration is the establishment of adequate controls over the **records** and **authorising** deductions.

Tests of controls: setting of wages and salaries

Auditors should check that the **wages** and **salary summary** is approved for payment. They should confirm that procedures are operating for **authorising changes** in **rates of pay**, overtime, and holiday pay.

A particular concern will be joiners and leavers. Auditors will need to obtain evidence that staff only start being paid when they join the company, and are removed from the payroll when they leave the company. They should check that the **engagement** of **new employees** and **discharges** have been **confirmed in writing**.

Auditors will also wish to check calculations of wages and salaries. This test should be designed to check that the client is carrying out **checks** on **calculations** and also to provide substantive assurance that **wages** and **salaries** are being **calculated correctly**.

For wages, this will involve checking **calculation** of **gross pay** with:

- Authorised rates of pay
- Production records. See that production bonuses have been authorised and properly calculated
- Clock cards, time sheets or other evidence of hours worked. Verify that overtime has been authorised

For salaries, auditors should **verify that gross salaries and bonuses are in accordance with personnel records, letters of engagement** etc and that increases in pay have been properly authorised.

Tests of controls: payment of wages and salaries

Wages paid in cash

- **Arrange to attend** the **pay-out** of wages to confirm that the official procedures are being followed
- Before the wages are paid **compare payroll** with **wage packets** to ensure all employees have a wage packet
- **Examine receipts** given by employees; **check unclaimed wages** are recorded in unclaimed wages book
- **Check** that **no employee receives more than one wage packet**
- **Check entries** in the **unclaimed wages book** with the entries on the payroll
- **Check that unclaimed wages** are **banked regularly**
- **Check** that unclaimed wages books shows **reasons** why wages are unclaimed
- **Check pattern** of **unclaimed wages** in unclaimed wages book; variations may indicate failure to record

Holiday pay

- **Verify** a sample of **payments** with the **underlying records** and **check** the **calculation** of the amounts paid

For salaries, auditors should check that comparisons are being made between payment records and they should themselves **examine paid cheques** or a **certified copy** of the **bank list** for employees paid by cheque of banks transfer.
Tests of control: recording of wages and salaries
A key control auditors will be concerned with is the reconciliation of wages and salaries. For wages, there should have been reconciliations with: • The **previous week's payroll** • **Clock cards/time sheets/job cards** • **Costing analyses, production budgets** The total of **salaries** should be **reconciled** with the **previous week/month** or the **standard payroll.** In addition auditors should confirm that important calculations have been checked by the clients and re-perform those calculations. These include checking for wages for a number of weeks: • **Additions** of **payroll sheets** • **Totals** of **wages sheets** selected to summary • **Additions** and **cross-casts** of summary • **Postings** of **summary** to **general ledger** (including control accounts) • **Casts** of **net cash column** to cash book For salaries they include checking for a number of weeks/months: • **Additions of payroll sheets** • **Totals of salaries sheets** to **summary** • **Additions** and **cross-casts** of **summary** • **Postings** of **summary** to **general ledger** (including control accounts) • **Total** of **net pay column** to cash book
Tests of controls: deductions
Auditors should **check** the **calculations** of **PAYE, National Insurance** and **non-statutory deductions.** For PAYE and NI they should carry out the following tests: • **Scrutinise** the **control accounts** maintained to see **appropriate deductions** have been **made** • **Check** to see that the **employer's contribution** for national insurance has been **correctly calculated** • **Check** that the **payments** to the **Inland Revenue** and other bodies are **correct** They should check other deductions to appropriate records. For voluntary deductions, they should see the authority completed by the relevant employees.

Question: Wages – control objectives and tests

The following questions have been selected from an internal control questionnaire for wages and salaries.

Internal control questionnaire - wages and salaries

		Yes	*No*
1	Does an appropriate official authorise rates of pay?		
2	Are written notices required for employing and terminating employment?		
3	Are formal records such as time cards used for time keeping?		
4	Does anyone verify rates of pay, overtime hours and computations of gross pay before the wage payments are made?		
5	Does the accounting system ensure the proper recording of payroll costs in the financial records?		

Required

(a) Describe the internal control objective being fulfilled if the controls set out in the above questions are in effect.

(b) Describe the audit tests which would test the effectiveness of each control and help determine any potential material error.

(c) Identify the potential consequences for the company if the above controls were not in place.

You may answer in columnar form under the headings:

ICQ question	*Internal control objective*	*Audit tests*	*Consequences*

Answer

	ICQ question	*Internal control objective*	*Audit tests*	*Consequences*
1	Does an appropriate official authorise rates of pay?	Employees are paid amounts authorised	Test rates of pay from payroll to schedule of authorised pay rates (personnel files, board minutes etc)	Incorrect rates of pay could lead to over/under statement of profit
2	Are written notices required for employing and terminating employment?	All employees paid through payroll exist	Check a sample of employees from payroll files for authorisation of employment or termination Check details for cheque or credit transfer salary payments to personnel files	Payroll may include fictitious employees
3	Are formal records such as time cards used for time keeping?	Employees are only paid for work done	Review time records to ensure they are properly completed and controlled Observe procedures for time recording	Overstatement of payroll costs. Employees over/under paid

			Check time records where absences are recorded to payroll to ensure they have been accounted for Review the wages account and investigate any large or unusual amounts	
4	Does anyone verify rates of pay, overtime hours and computation of gross pay before wage payments are made?	Employees are paid the correct amount	Examine payroll for evidence of verification Recompute gross pay (including overtime) Check wage rates to authorised schedule	Misstatement of payroll costs
	ICQ question	*Internal control objective*	*Audit tests*	*Consequences*
5	Does the accounting system ensure the proper recording of payroll costs in the financial records?	Payroll costs are properly recorded	Check posting of payroll costs to the nominal ledger	Misstatement of payroll costs

4 SMALLER ENTITIES

4.1 Remember, the control systems in smaller entities are often not as sophisticated as those in larger entities. The particular area that can be a concern for smaller entities with few staff is **segregation of duties**. It can be impossible to adequately share duties between staff when there are only one or two staff.

4.2 Having established in Chapter 9 that proprietor involvement is the key to internal control in the small enterprise, we need next to be rather more precise and identify the types of control relevant to each principal accounting area. These controls can be referred to as '**minimum business controls**'.

4.3 It is important to appreciate that such controls will not, and **cannot, be evaluated and relied on** by the auditors as in a 'systems' audit approach, but they do **provide overall comfort** to the auditors, particularly when determining whether to seek to rely on management assurances as to the completeness of the accounting records.

4.4 The following checklist provides illustrative examples of minimum control standards.

Mail

- Is all mail received and opened by the proprietor?
- If the proprietor does not himself open the mail, is it opened by a person not connected with the accounts and read by him before it is distributed to the staff?

Receipts

- Are all cheques and postal orders received by post counted by the proprietor before they are passed to the cashier?
- Are all cheques and postal orders crossed to the company's branch of its bankers 'Not negotiable - account payee only'.

- Are cash sales and credit sale receipts over the counter controlled by locked cash register tapes which only the proprietor can open?
- Does the proprietor reconcile the cash register totals with the cash sales receipts daily?
- Is the person performing the duties of cashier barred any responsibility concerning the sales, purchase or nominal ledgers?

Banking

- Is all cash received banked intact at intervals of not more than three days?
- Does the proprietor reconcile all monies received with the copy paying-in slips at regular intervals?

Payments

- Are all payments except sundry expenses made by cheques?
- Does the proprietor sign all cheques?
- Are cheques signed by the proprietor only after he has satisfied himself that:
  - He has approved and cancelled all vouchers supporting the payment?
  - All cheques are crossed not negotiable and account payee only?
  - All cheque numbers are accounted for?
- Are petty cash expenses controlled by the imprest system?
- Does the proprietor review all expenses and initial the petty cash book before reimbursing the cashier?

Bank statements

- Are bank statements and paid cheques sent direct to the proprietor and opened only by him?
- Does the proprietor scrutinise all paid cheques to ensure that he has signed them all before he passes them to the cashier?
- Does the proprietor:
  - Prepare a bank reconciliation each month? or
  - Review in detail a reconciliation produced by the cashier?

Orders

- Are all purchase orders issued:
  - Serially numbered by the printer?
  - Pre-printed duplicate order forms?
- Does the proprietor approve all orders?

Receipt of goods

Are delivery notes:

- Checked with goods?
- Compared with the copy order?
- Compared with the invoice?

Wages

- Is a separate cheque drawn for the exact amount to pay wages and PAYE/National Insurance?
- Does the proprietor either prepare or examine the wages records before signing the cheque?
- Does the proprietor initial the wages records after his examination?

- Does the proprietor oversee the distribution of the wages packets or does he distribute them himself?

Debtors

- If credit is granted to customers does the proprietor:
  - Authorise every extension of credit to a customer?
  - Approve credit limits for each customer?
- Does the proprietor authorise all:
  - Write offs of bad debts?
  - Sales returns and allowances?
  - Discounts other than routine cash discounts?
- Does the proprietor receive a monthly list of debtors, showing the age of the debts?
- Are all authorisations by the proprietor evidenced by his initials?

Goods outwards

- Are pre-numbered despatch notes prepared for all goods leaving the premises?
- Are all despatch notes:
  - Accounted for?
  - Cross referenced with invoices and credit notes?
- Is the proprietor satisfied that all goods leaving the premises have been accounted for?

Stock

Does the proprietor scrutinise the stocks regularly to:

- Keep abreast of what is in stock?
- Discover obsolete items?
- Discover damaged articles?
- Ensure that stock levels are kept under control?

4.5 Although the above types of control are desirable and feasible, they are nevertheless relatively informal. Consequently evidence of their performance tends to be lacking and they may indeed be overridden as there is no check on the proprietor himself.

Exam focus point

In the exam, run the following checklist through your mind when approaching questions about controls in smaller entities.

Are you being logical?

- Consider the number of staff the entity is likely to employ.
- Remember, top management or the owners are likely to be involved on a day to day level
- Bear in mind a general rule: The smaller the entity, the fewer the daybooks and ledgers...

Chapter roundup

- The sales and purchases systems will be the most important components of most company accounting systems.
- The tests of controls of the **sales system** will be based around:
  - **Selling** (authorisation)
  - **Goods outwards** (custody)
  - **Accounting** (recording)
- Similarly, the **purchases systems** tests will be based around:
  - **Buying** (authorisation)
  - **Goods** inwards (custody)
  - **Accounting** (recording)
- Important **tests of control** by auditors include:
  - Checking documentation for correct details, authorisation and calculations
  - Comparing documents
  - Checking completeness of documentation series
- Note that all weaknesses discovered in these tests will be included in a **report to management**. Management reports will be discussed in Chapter ??.
- Obviously, most manufacturing companies will have a large payroll. Wages and salaries are usually dealt with in very different ways, but they are often grouped together for audit testing purposes.
- Key controls over **wages** cover:
  - **Documentation** and **authorisation** of staff changes
  - **Calculation** of wages and salaries
  - **Payment** of wages
  - **Authorisation** of **deductions**
- These three systems are those most likely to come up in the exam, as you can see by how often they have been examined recently.

Quick quiz

1 Complete the table, putting the sales system control considerations under the correct headings.

Ordering/granting of credit	Despatch/invoicing	Recording/accounting

(a) All sales that have been invoiced have been put in the general ledger
(b) Orders are fulfilled
(c) Cut off is correct
(d) Goods are only supplied to good credit risks
(e) Goods are correctly invoiced
(f) Customers are encouraged to pay promptly

2 Name five controls relating to the ordering and granting of credit process.

1 ....

2 ....

3 ....

4 ....

5 ....

3 When checking sales invoicing the auditor should verify ...., ... ,................ and ...., ..., correct analysis in the sales ledger and correct posting and that VAT has been dealt with.

4 Complete the table, putting the purchase system control considerations under the correct headings.

Ordering	Receipt/invoices	Accounting

(a) Orders are only made to authorised suppliers
(b) Liabilities are recognised for all goods and services received
(c) Orders made at competitive prices
(d) All expenditure is authorised
(e) Cut off is correctly applied
(f) Goods and services are only accepted if there is an authorised order

5 (a) Name four examples of purchase documentation on which numerical sequence should be checked

1 ....

2 ....

3 ....

4 ....

(b) Why is numerical sequence checked?

6 Name 6 procedures auditors should carry out if wages are paid in cash.

1 ....

2 ....

3 ....

4 ....

5 ....

6 ....

Answers to quick quiz

1

Ordering/granting of credit	Despatch/invoicing	Recording/accounting
(b) (d) (f)	(e)	(a) (c)

2
- **Segregation** of duties; credit control, invoicing and stock despatch
- **Authorisation** of **credit terms** to customers
  - References/credit checks obtained
  - Authorisation by senior staff
  - Regular review
- **Authorisation** for changes in **other customer data**
  - Change of address supported by letterhead
  - Deletion requests supported by evidence balances cleared/customer in liquidation
- **Orders** only **accepted** from **customers** who have no credit problems
- **Sequential numbering** of blank pre-printed order documents
- **Correct prices quoted** to **customers**
- **Matching** of **customer orders** with production orders and despatch notes and querying of orders not matched
- **Dealing** with **customer queries**

3 quantities, prices, calculations, additions, discounts

4

OrderingReceipt/invoices	Accounting	
(a) (c)	(b) (f)	(d) (e)

5 (a) (1) purchase requisitions, (2) purchase orders, (3) goods received notes, (4) goods returned notes, (5) suppliers invoices

(b) Sequence provides a control that sales are complete. Missing documents should be explained, or cancelled copies available.

6
- **Arrange to attend** the **pay-out** of wages to confirm that the official procedures are being followed
- Before the wages are paid **compare payroll** with **wage packets** to ensure all employees have a wage packet
- **Examine receipts** given by employees; **check unclaimed wages** are recorded in unclaimed wages book
- **Check** that **no employee receives more than one wage packet**
- **Check entries** in the **unclaimed wages book** with the entries on the payroll
- **Check that unclaimed wages** are **banked regularly**
- **Check** that unclaimed wages books shows **reasons** why wages are unclaimed
- **Check pattern** of **unclaimed wages** in unclaimed wages book; variations may indicate failure to record
- **Verify** a sample of holiday pay **payments** with the **underlying records** and **check** the **calculation** of the amounts paid

Now try the question below from the Exam Question Bank

Number	Level	Marks	Time
10	Exam	20	36 mins

Chapter 11

TESTS OF CONTROLS: OTHER AREAS

Introduction

This chapter completes the tests of controls topic begun in Chapter 10.

Controls over **cash and bank balances** cannot be seen in complete isolation from controls over the sales, purchases and wages cycle. In this chapter we concentrate on controls over and testing of the safe **custody and recording** of cash. You should note in particular the emphasis on prompt recording of receipts and payments, and prompt banking of cash and cheques received. Bear in mind also when you work through the section on bank and cash that controlling cheque receipts and payments is significantly easier than controlling cash receipts and payments.

For **stock**, there should be **proper security arrangements** and **prompt recording**. You should note however the other aspects of control of stock, particularly reviews of the condition of stock, and stockholding policies designed to ensure that the business is not holding too much or too little stock. These controls interest auditors since they may impact upon how stock is valued. We shall discuss valuation of stock further in Chapter 14.

For **fixed assets,** it is vital that there are controls in place to ensure that capital items are capitalised as assets and revenue items are charged to the profit and loss account.

In a number of areas discussed in this chapter, auditors will be considering controls at the same time as they are carrying out substantive tests. Thus for example when receiving cash at bank, auditors will be interested in the clients' bank reconciliations as an important control over the custody of cash; they will also re-perform one (or more) reconciliations to gain substantive assurance. Similarly with stock auditors will review stock counts held by the client over the year, and also attend one or more stocktakes themselves to gain the necessary substantive assurance.

Note that weakness reporting is covered in the section on management letters in Chapter 20.

We shall look at some of the wider **operational cycles** of interest to internal auditors which were touched on in Chapter 3, and the aims and operations of controls in these cycles. We shall also consider tests of control which **internal auditors** might carry out on them.

The APB has issued guidance about **providing assurance** on **the effectiveness of internal controls**. We shall consider this guidance briefly in section 5.

Controls testing and substantive testing could both be examined in a question on a specific balance sheet area.

1 THE CASH SYSTEM 6/02

1.1 **Aims of controls**

- **All monies received** are **recorded**
- **All monies received** are **banked**
- **Cash and cheques** are **safeguarded** against loss or theft
- **All payments** are **authorised, made** to the **correct payees** and **recorded**
- **Payments** are **not made twice** for the same liability

1.2 Controls over the **completeness** of **recording** of cash receipts are particularly important. If these controls are inadequate, there may be insufficient audit evidence available when the auditor carries out substantive procedures.

1.3 Segregation of duties is also important. The person responsible for receiving and recording cash when it arrives in the post should not be the same as the person responsible for banking it. Ideally the cash book should be written up by a further staff member, and a fourth staff member should reconcile the various records of amounts received.

1.4 Records of cash are obviously also at the heart of a company's accounting records; therefore if these accounting records are to fulfil Companies Act requirements, cash must be recorded **promptly.**

Controls: cash at bank and in hand - receipts

Segregation of duties between the various functions listed below is particularly important.

Recording of receipts by post

- **Safeguards** to **prevent interception of mail** between receipt and opening
- Appointment of **responsible person** to supervise mail
- **Protection** of **cash and cheques** (restrictive crossing)
- **Amounts received listed** when post opened
- **Post stamped** with date of receipt

Recording of cash sales and collections

- **Restrictions** on **receipt of cash** (by cashiers only, or by salesmen etc)
- **Evidencing** of receipt of cash
  - Serially numbered receipt forms
  - Cash registers incorporating sealed till rolls
- **Clearance** of cash offices and registers
- **Agreement of cash collections with till rolls**
- **Agreement of cash collections with bankings and** cash and sales **records**
- **Investigation** of cash shortages and surpluses

General controls over recording

- Prompt **maintenance of records** (cash book, ledger accounts)
- **Limitation** of **duties** of receiving cashiers
- **Holiday arrangements**
- **Giving** and **recording** of **receipts**
  - Retained copies
  - Serially numbered receipts books
  - Custody of receipt books
  - Comparisons with cash records and bank paying in slips

Banking

- **Daily bankings**
- **Make-up** and **comparison** of **paying-in** slips against initial receipt records and cash book
- **Banking** of receipts **intact**/control of disbursements

Safeguarding of cash and bank accounts

- **Restrictions** on **opening new bank accounts**
- **Limitations** on **cash floats** held
- **Restrictions** on **payments** out of **cash received**
- **Restrictions** on **access** to cash registers and offices
- **Independent checks** on cash floats
- **Surprise cash counts**
- **Custody** of **cash** outside **office hours**
- **Custody** over **supply** and issue of cheques
- **Preparation** of **cheques** restricted
- **Safeguards** over **mechanically signed cheques**/cheques carrying printed signatures
- **Restrictions** on issue of **blank** or **bearer** cheques
- **Safeguarding** of **IOUs**, cash in transit
- **Insurance arrangements**
- **Control of funds** held in trust for employees
- **Bank reconciliations**
    - Issue of bank statements
    - Frequency of reconciliations by independent person
    - Reconciliation procedures
    - Treatment of longstanding unpresented cheques
    - Stop payment notice
    - Sequence of cheque numbers
    - Comparison with cash books

Controls: cash at bank and in hand - payments

The arrangements for controlling payments will depend to a great extent on the nature of business transacted, the volume of payments involved and the size of the company.

Controls: cheque and cash payments generally

The cashier should generally not be concerned with keeping or writing-up books of account other than those recording disbursements nor should he have access to, or be responsible for the custody of, securities, title deeds or negotiable instruments belonging to the company.

The person responsible for preparing cheques or traders' credit lists should not himself be a cheque signatory. Cheque signatories in turn should not be responsible for recording payments.

Cheque payments

- **Cheque requisitions**
    - Appropriate supporting documentation
    - Approval by appropriate staff
    - Presentation to cheque signatories
    - Cancellation (crossing/recording cheque number on requisition)
- **Authority** to sign cheques
    - Signatories should not also approve cheque requisitions
    - Limitations on authority to specific amounts

- Number of signatories
- Prohibitions over signing of blank cheques

- **Prompt despatch** of signed **cheques**
- **Obtaining** of paid **cheques** from **banks**
- Payments **recorded promptly** in **cash book** and **general** and **purchase ledger**

Cash payments

- **Authorisation** of **expenditure**
- **Cancellation** of **vouchers** to ensure cannot be paid
- **Limits** on **disbursements**
- **Rules** on **cash advances** to employees, IOUs and cheque cashing

Tests of controls

1.5 Note that as well as testing controls over receipts, auditors are also obtaining evidence to support the assertion that sales and receipts are **completely recorded**.

Tests of control: receipts received by post

- **Observe procedures** for **post opening** are being followed
- **Observe** that **cheques** received by post are immediately **crossed** in the company's favour of the company
- For items entered in the rough cash book (or other record of cash, cheques etc received by post), **trace entries** to:
  - **Cash book**
  - **Paying-in book**
  - **Counterfoil** or carbon copy receipts
- **Verify amounts entered** as **received** with remittance advices or other supporting evidence

Tests of control: cash sales, branch takings

- For a sample of cash sales summaries/branch summaries from different locations:
  - **Verify with till rolls** or copy cash sale notes
  - **Check to paying-in slip** date-stamped and initialled by the bank
  - **Verify that takings** are banked intact daily
  - **Vouch expenditure** out of takings

Tests of control: collections

- For a sample of items from the original collection records:
  - **Trace amounts** to **cash book** via collectors' cash sheets or other collection records
  - **Check entries** on **cash sheets** or collection records with collectors' receipt books
  - **Verify** that **goods delivered** to travellers/salesmen have been regularly **reconciled** with sales and stocks in hand
  - **Check numerical sequence** of collection records

Tests of control: receipts cash book
• For cash receipts for several days throughout the period: ◦ **Check to entries in rough cash book**, receipts, branch returns or other records ◦ **Check to paying-in slips** obtained direct from the bank, observing that there is no delay in banking monies received ◦ **Check additions** of **paying-in slips** ◦ **Check additions** of **cash book** ◦ **Check postings to the sales ledger** ◦ **Check postings** to the **general ledger**, including control accounts • **Scrutinise the cash book** and **investigate items** of a **special** or **unusual nature**.
Tests of control: payment cash book (authorisation)
• For a sample of payments: ◦ **Compare** with paid cheques to ensure payee agrees ◦ **Note** that **cheques** are **signed** by the **persons authorised** to do so within their authority limits ◦ **Check** to **suppliers' invoices** for goods and services. Verify that supporting documents are signed as having been **checked** and **passed for payment** and have been stamped 'paid' ◦ **Check** to **suppliers' statements** ◦ **Check** to **other documentary evidence**, as appropriate (agreements, authorised expense vouchers, wages/salaries records, petty cash books etc)
Tests of control: payments cash book (recording)
• For a sample of weeks: ◦ **Check the sequence of cheque numbers** and enquire into missing numbers ◦ **Trace transfers** to other bank accounts, petty cash books or other records, as appropriate ◦ **Check additions**, including extensions, and balances forward at the beginning and end of the months covering the periods chosen ◦ **Check postings** to the **purchase ledger** ◦ **Check postings** to the **general ledger**, including the control accounts

1.6 When checking that bank and cash are **secured**, auditors should consider the security arrangements over blank cheques. Bank reconciliations are also a very important control and auditors should carry out the following tests on these.

• For a period which includes a reconciliation date **reperform reconciliation** (see Chapter 16) • **Verify** that **reconciliations have been prepared** at **regular intervals** throughout the year • **Scrutinise reconciliations for unusual items**

1.7 The following tests should be carried out for petty cash

- For a sample of payments:
  - **Check** to supporting vouchers
  - **Check** whether they are properly **approved**
  - **See** that **vouchers** have been **marked and initialled** by the cashier to prevent their re-use
- For a sample of weeks:
  - **Trace amounts** received to **cash books**
  - **Check additions** and **balances carried** forward
  - **Check postings** to the **nominal ledger**

Exam focus point

Questions about the sales or purchases systems may also require consideration of controls over receipts or payments.

2 THE STOCK SYSTEM

2.1 The stock system can be very important in an audit because of the high value of stock or the complexity of its audit. It is closely connected with the sales and purchases systems covered in Chapter 10.

2.2 **Aims of controls**

Recording

- All **stock movements** are **authorised** and **recorded**
- **Stock records** only **include items** that **belong** to the client
- **Stock records include stock** that **exists** and is **held** by the client
- **Stock quantities** have been **recorded correctly**
- **Cut-off procedures** are **properly applied** to stock

Protection of stock

- **Stock** is **safeguarded** against loss, pilferage or damage

Valuation of stock

- The **costing system values stock correctly**
- **Allowance** is **made** for **slow-moving, obsolete** or **damaged stock**

Stock-holding

- **Levels** of **stock held** are **reasonable**

Controls: recording of stock
• **Segregation** of duties; custody and recording of stocks • **Reception, checking** and **recording** of goods inwards • **Stock issues supported** by **appropriate documentation** • **Maintenance** of **stock records** ○ Stock ledgers ○ Bin cards ○ Transfer records
Controls: protection of stock
• **Precautions** against **theft, misuse** and **deterioration** ○ Restriction of access to stores ○ Controls on stores environment (right temperature, precautions against damp etc). • **Security** over **stock** held by third parties, and third party stock held by entity • **Stock-taking** (see also Chapter 14). ○ Regular stock-taking ○ Fair coverage so that all stock is counted at least once a year ○ Counts by independent persons ○ Recording ○ Cut-off for goods in transit and time differences ○ Reconciliation of stock count to book records and control accounts
Controls: valuation of stock
• **Computation** of **stock valuation** ○ Accords with SSAP 9 ○ Checking of calculations • **Review** of **condition** of stock ○ Treatment of slow-moving, damaged and obsolete stock ○ Authorisation of write-offs • **Accounting** for **scrap** and **waste**
Controls: stockholding
• **Control** of **stock levels** ○ Maximum stock limits ○ Minimum stock limits ○ Re-order quantities and levels • Arrangements for dealing with **returnable containers**

Tests of controls

2.3 Most of the testing relating to stock has been covered in the purchase and sales testing outlined in Chapter 10. Auditors will primarily be concerned at this stage with ensuring that the business keeps track of stock. To confirm this, checks must be made on how stock **movements** are **recorded** and how **stock** is **secured**.

- **Select** a sample of **stock movements records** and **agree** to **goods received** and **goods despatched notes**
- **Confirm** that **movements** have been **authorised** as **appropriate**
- **Select** a sample of **goods received** and **goods despatched** notes and agree to **stock movement records**
- **Check sequence** of stock records

2.4 Other tests that auditors are likely to perform include:

- **Test** check **stock counts** carried out from time to time (eg monthly) during the period and confirm:
  - **All discrepancies** between **book** and **actual** figures have been fully investigated
  - **All discrepancies** have been **signed off** by a senior manager
  - **Obsolete, damaged or slow-moving goods** have been **marked accordingly** and written down to net realisable value
- **Observe security arrangements** for stocks
- **Consider environment** in which stocks are held

Auditors will carry out extensive tests on the **valuation** of stock at the substantive testing stage (see Chapter 14).

Question: Cash – control weaknesses

Jonathan is the sole shareholder of Furry Lion Stores Ltd, a company which owns five stores in the west of England. The stores mainly stock food and groceries, and four of the stores have an off-licence as well.

Each store is run by a full-time manager and three or four part-time assistants. Jonathan spends on average ½ a day a week at each store, and spends the rest of his time at home, dealing with his other business interests.

All sales are for cash and are recorded on till rolls which the manager retains. Shop manager wages are paid monthly by cheque by Jonathan. Wages of shop assistants are paid in cash out of the takings.

Most purchases are made from local wholesalers and are paid for in cash out of the takings. Large purchases (over £250) must be made by cheques signed by the shop manager and countersigned by Jonathan.

Shop managers bank surplus cash once a week, apart from a float in the till.

All accounting records including the cash book, wages and VAT records are maintained by the manager. Jonathan reviews the weekly bank statements when he visits the shops. He also has a look at stocks to see if stock levels appear to be about right. All invoices are also kept in a drawer by a manager and marked with a cash book reference, and where appropriate a cheque number when paid.

Required

Discuss the weaknesses in the control systems of Furry Lion Ltd, and how the weaknesses can be remedied.

Answer

Weaknesses in the system, and their remedies are as follows.

Stock

The shops do not appear to have any stock movement records. This would appear to breach the Companies Act s 221 requirement for the company to maintain proper accounting records. Jonathan has also only a very approximate indication of stock levels. Hence it will be difficult to detect whether stock levels are too high, or too low with a risk of running out of stock. Theft of stock would also be difficult to detect. The company should therefore introduce stock movement records, detailing values and volumes.

In addition regular stock counts should be made either by Jonathan or by staff from another shop. Discrepancies between the stock records and the actual stock counted should be investigated.

Cash controls

Too much cash appears to be held on site. In addition the fact that most payments appear to be for cash may mean inadequate documentation is kept. The level of cash on site can be decreased by daily rather than weekly bankings. In addition the need for cash on site can be decreased by paying wages by cheque, and by paying all but the smallest payments by cheque.

The cash book should obviously still be maintained but cheque stubs should also show details of amounts paid. The cash book should be supported by invoices and other supporting documentation, and should be cross-referenced to the general ledger (see below).

Cash reconciliations

There is no indication of the till-rolls that are kept being reconciled to cash takings.

There should be a daily reconciliation of cash takings and till rolls; this should be reviewed if not performed by the shop manager.

Bank reconciliations

There is no mention of bank reconciliations taking place.

Bank reconciliations should be carried out at least monthly by the shop manager, and reviewed by the owner.

Purchases

There is no formal system for recording purchases. Invoices do not appear to be filed in any particular way. It would be difficult to see whether accounting records were complete, and hence it would be difficult to prepare a set of accounts from the accounting records available.

In addition the way records are maintained means that accounts would have to be prepared on a cash basis, and not on an accruals basis, as required by the Companies Act.

A purchase day book should be introduced. Invoices should be recorded in the purchase day book, and filed in a logical order, either by date received or by supplier.

General ledger

There is no general ledger, and again this means that annual accounts cannot easily be prepared (and also management accounts).

A general ledger should be maintained with entries made from the cash book, wages records and purchase day book. This will enable accounts to be prepared on an accruals basis.

Supervision

Jonathan does not take a very active part in the business, only signing cheques over £250, and visiting the shops only half a day each week. This may mean that assets can easily go missing, and Jonathan cannot readily see whether the business is performing as he would wish.

Jonathan should review wage/VAT/cash book reconciliations. Management accounts should also be prepared by shop managers for Jonathan.

Tutorial note. This question deals with controls that are possible given the circumstances of the business. Greater segregation of duties does not appear to be possible as the shops are small, and Jonathan cannot spend more time at the shops (although he can use his time more productively by reviewing reconciliations).

3 REVENUE AND CAPITAL EXPENDITURE 12/01, 6/03

3.1 The nature of a balance sheet and profit and loss account means that it is important to classify capital and revenue expenditure correctly, or profit will be over or understated. You should know the distinction between them from your 2.5 studies.

3.2 The controls and tests outlined below are often considered and performed when during the audit of fixed assets (see Chapter 13) as this is where the main issue of capitalisation occurs.

3.3 **Aims of control**

Authorisation

- All expenditure is authorised

Recording

- All expenditure is classified correctly in the financial statements as capital or revenue expenditure

3.4 The issue of authorisation was considered in Chapter 10 as part of the controls surrounding purchases and expenses. We shall consider the issue of recording briefly here.

Controls
Ordering • Orders for capital items should be authorised • Order should be requisitioned on appropriate (different to revenue) documentation
Invoices • Invoices should be approved by the person who authorised the order • They should be marked with the appropriate general ledger code
Recording • All the standard controls over purchases are relevant here • Capital items should be written up in the fixed asset register • The fixed asset register should be reconciled regularly to the general ledger

Tests of controls

3.5 If the ordering documentation is different for capital purchases, all the standard purchase control tests should be carried out.

3.6 If the documentation is not different, the auditor should enquire as to the client's system for recording and filing capital invoices

3.7 It is likely that capital purchases in the year will be fewer than standard purchases in the year and if the invoices are not segregated it may not be cost efficient to test the controls over this area.

3.8 Alternative substantive procedures include:

Analytical review

- General review between current and prior year figures to ascertain any unexplained differences
- Review of sensitive codes in the general ledger such as repairs or maintenance
- Review of the movements on the fixed asset codes
- Compare budgeted capital purchases with actual capital purchases

Enquiry and review

- Discuss the level of capital purchases in the year with the purchasing manager
- Review the board minutes for authorisation of capital purchases

3.9 These substantive tests are often carried out as part of the substantive audit of fixed assets.

3.10 The auditor should be aware of the risks attaching to the audit of this area. As test of controls might be cost-ineffective, control risk in this area is higher than would have been if they were tested.

3.11 Inherent risk can also be high in this area. Capital and revenue expenditure is treated differently for the purposes of tax, and if the client is sensitive to their tax bill, there may be motivation to creatively account.

4 INTERNAL AUDIT: RELEVANT CYCLES 12/03

4.1 In Chapter 3 we discussed some of the operational cycles that internal auditors might be interested in. These are likely to be of lesser interest to the external auditor, particularly where the cycle does not directly impact on the financial statements.

4.2 In this section we shall consider some of the matters which will affect the work of the internal auditors, in particular, aims of controls in the cycles, the controls themselves, and how the auditor will test those controls.

Procurement

4.3 We have already noted that many of the controls will in this cycles will be the same as in the purchases cycle which the external auditor is interested in. However, as the scope of the internal auditor goes beyond the financial statements, consider these additional factors which he will be interested in.

4.4 A procurement system is likely to have many systems within it (for example, tendering, placing orders, checking goods inwards), which the internal auditor would probably approach separately.

Aims of control

4.5 The following might be aims of a procurement system:

- The business has goods and services when it needs them
- The business does not pay too much for those goods and services
- The business does not make short-term savings on goods and services which lead to longer term inflated costs

- Employees or suppliers do not defraud the company

Controls

4.6 Controls such as the following could be instituted:

- The business always invites tenders for goods and services
- Research is conducted on potential suppliers before they are invited to tender
- Requirements for goods and services are always put in writing
- Use is made of discounting and calculations of long term costs where service is for a prolonged period
- No transactions are carried out with employees and connected persons

Tests of control

4.7 The following related tests of the above controls could be carried out.

- A sample of contracts can be reviewed to confirm research and tender process
- A sample of invoices checked back to written requisition
- For a sample of long term contracts, check long term calculations exist and are correct
- Review central database of suppliers to ensure that none are connected parties

Exam focus point

As usual, there could be various tests of these controls. If required in an exam to suggest tests of controls, you should consider what the objective of the control is, and how you could prove that that objective is being met.

Remember however, that only internal audit would be interested in some of these controls features. In principle, for example, the external auditors are not too concerned if the company pays more than it should do for its goods and services, so long as what it does pay is recorded properly in the financial statements.

Marketing

4.8 Similarly to procurement, 'marketing' covers a wide range of systems, including research, advertising, promotions, sales, after-sales.

Aims of controls

4.9 The objectives of a marketing system might include the following:

- Customer demand should be understood and met
- Customers should be made aware of products
- Products are competitive, not hampered by pricing or promotion tactics
- Goods are sold for valuable consideration

Controls

4.10 Some of the controls will be similar to those discussed in the sales cycle in Chapter 10. However, think again that the internal auditor is interested in objectives beyond the scope of the financial systems. The following controls might be used to meet the above objectives:

- Market research should be commissioned or carried out
- Actual sales should be compared to budgets

- Advertising is targeted
- Promotions are timed to coincide with periods historically linked with sales, eg Christmas
- Competitor prices are monitored
- Terms and conditions are made known to customers
- Credit checks are made

Tests of control

4.11 Some of the tests, particularly those in relation to credit, will be the same as those discussed in the sales system in Chapter 10.

Question: Marketing – tests of controls

Try to think up some ways of testing the controls listed in paragraph 5.10.

Answer

Potential tests of control include:

- Review company policy on commissioning market research
- For a sample of major promotions, check that research was commissioned and used
- Check that actual sales are compared to budget sales and that variances are investigated
- For a sample of major promotions, ensure that timing has been considered and documented
- Ensure that records are maintained of competitor pricing policy
- Review terms and conditions to ensure that they comply with company policy
- Check as sample of contracts/sales to ensure terms and conditions were highlighted

You may have thought of other tests of controls, this list is not definitive. Check that your answers prove that the objective you had in mind is being tested.

Treasury

Aims of controls

4.12 The following will be objectives of the treasury department:

- Money is available to the company when it is required
- Risks in relation to foreign currency and interest rates are managed effectively
- Transactions do not lose the company money over time
- Exposures are highlighted and reported on, on a timely basis

Controls

4.13 These objectives will be met the following controls:

- Cash flow forecasting
- Arrangements with the bank in the event of cash emergencies
- Contingency plans available
- Clear policy on tolerated risk
- Regular review of investment
- Frequent two-way communication

Tests of controls

4.14 The internal auditor may carry out the following tests

- Reviewing cash flow forecasts
- Reading correspondence with the bank
- Reading contingency plans and assessing them for realism
- Discuss review of investments with investment managers
- Seek evidence of such reviews being made (reports, memos)
- Seek evidence of communication

Human resources

Aims of controls

4.15 The objectives of a human resources department will be as follows:

- Sufficiently qualified and capable staff are available when required
- There is no significant over-reliance on key personnel
- Staff are paid the correct remuneration on a timely basis
- Staff are contented and not prone to industrial action or seeking alternative employment
- Employment laws are complied with
- The human resource is handled considerately

Controls

4.16 The following controls will be put into place to meet these objectives:

- The business has a long term human requirement plan
- Salary is benchmarked against the market
- Performance of staff is regularly and formally appraised
- Staff are given adequate training
- Key personnel are not put at risk together
- Long term succession planning is undertaken
- Payroll controls as discussed in Chapter 10
- Relationships with trade unions are well maintained
- Human resources managers receive training in employment law

Tests of control

4.17 The internal auditors may use the following tests:

- Obtain a copy of the long term human resource plan and review it
- Obtain evidence that the HR department monitors pay levels in the market
- Review of appraisal procedure, check that a sample of employees have had appraisals
- Review training records to ensure that training is in accordance with company policy
- Review long term succession plan and any 'apprenticing' schemes are in operation
- Review training procedures within department by discussion with staff

Exam focus point

As you considered each of these cycles more carefully, you will have seen the strong links that they have with the income and asset cycles that the external auditor is interested in. You will also have seen that the internal auditor is interested in risks arising to the company, whereas the external auditor is more interested in risks of errors in the financial statements.

In the exam, you could be asked the difference between the internal and external auditors interest in internal controls. Remember that the difference is in the objectives each is interested in, and the controls and the tests follow on from that.

You might want to re-read the following sections in conjunction with one another, to see how the objectives of the internal auditors (or the company) extend further than the external auditors in each case:

- Purchases/procurement
- Sales/marketing
- Cash/treasury
- Payroll/human resources

5 PROVIDING ASSURANCE ON INTERNAL CONTROLS

5.1 In July 2001, the APB issued a briefing paper on the issue of providing assurance in the effectiveness of internal control. This was issued in the light of previous consultation documents by the APB, but particularly, in the context of the IFAC standards and guidance on *Assurance Engagements*.

5.2 The briefing paper outlines the **APB's thinking in relation to assurance engagements**. **Internal controls** are an area of particular importance in the UK, having been given prominence by the investigations in to **corporate governance** in the 1990s, notably the **Turnbull report**, which concentrated on the risks facing companies, and the need for directors to manage that risk. This was discussed in Chapter 3 in the context of internal audit.

Providing assurance on internal control

5.3 The APB draw a clear distinction between two areas of assurance:

- Assurance on the **design** of internal control systems
- Assurance on the **operation** of the internal control system, in accordance with the design

These are two very distinct issues, and the two assignments should be approached very differently.

Process of internal control

5.4 The APB recognise the following process in relation to internal controls:

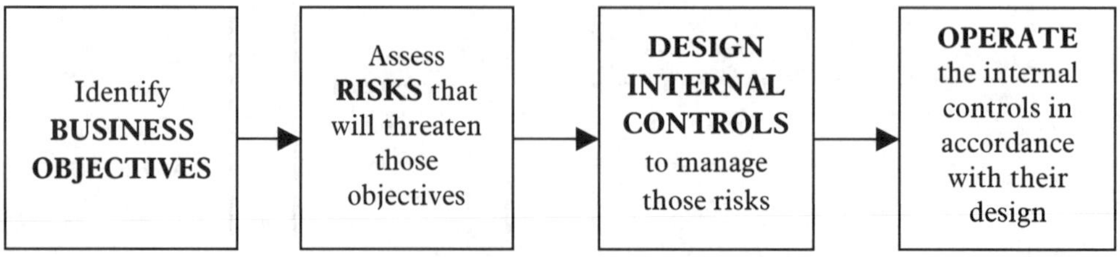

5.5 We have already considered this process from the point of view of internal auditors in Chapter 3. The diagram above also illustrates the points of the process where assurance services can be offered:

- Risk identification
- Design of system
- Operation of system

5.6 In order to carry out an engagement in relation to the internal controls, the practitioners will require sufficient **knowledge of the business** that they can **identify and understand** the events, transactions and practices which will impact on the system of internal control.

Providing assurance on the operation of the system

5.7 The practitioner should establish whether the engagement relates to a period of time or a point of time. The practitioner will only be able to provide a **high level of assurance** on this point if the entity has a detailed description of the design of their system of internal control.

5.8 The **report** arising from such an assignment need not be extensive, but is likely to be narrative. This is because practitioners are likely to include such issues as:

- Isolated control failures
- Observation about the abilities of staff involved in operating the system of control
- Potential weaknesses observed which were not contemplated within the design

Providing assurance on the design and operation of the system

5.9 In such an engagement practitioners will consider two issues:

- The design of the system in addressing a set of identified risks
- The operation of the system (discussed above)

5.10 Such an engagement will involve significant **discussions with management** at the outset, to establish matters such as:

- The desired balance between prevention and detection controls
- The balance between costs and benefits
- The importance of specific control objectives

5.11 The outcome of these discussions will necessarily be included in the assurance **report**, to provide a context for their conclusions. The following things will also be included in the report:

- The applicable risks
- Any framework for design used by either the directors or the practitioners
- A description of the design of the system of internal control.

5.12 The **level of assurance** given by the practitioners will **depend on several factors**, including the nature of the entity, the knowledge of the business the practitioner possesses and the scope of the engagement. It is likely that the report in this instance would be quite long.

Providing assurance on applicable risks and design and operation of the system

5.13 This engagement would include consideration of all the three stages of the internal controls process identified above. The identification of risks is likely to involve a **high degree of judgement** as there are no universally recognised criteria suitable for evaluating the effectiveness of an entity's risk evaluation. This means that practitioners are **unlikely to be** able to provide a **high level of assurance** in this area.

5.14 The starting point for the practitioner would be the entity's business objectives. The key considerations will include:

- The completeness of the applicable identified risks
- The probability of a risk crystallising
- The materiality of the likely impact of the risk
- The time period over which crystallisation is anticipated

5.15 In their **report**, the practitioners would have to outline the business objectives of the entity, a description of the risk identification process and the applicable risks.

Inherent limitations

5.16 Internal control systems have inherent limitations, a key one of which is the chance of staff colluding in fraud to override the system. **Any assurance report on internal controls** systems should **include a mention of these inherent limitations**, in order to prevent an unnecessary expectations gap.

Reports

5.17 The nature of the individual reports has been touched on above. The discussion paper also includes an example report. However, as the APB make the key point that it is difficult to issue a standard report for assurance services, which are largely dependent on the scope and nature of the individual assignment, this has not been reproduced here.

Chapter roundup

- Controls over cash receipts and payments should prevent fraud or theft.
- Key controls over **receipts** include:
  - Proper **post-opening** arrangements
  - **Prompt recording**
  - **Prompt banking**
  - **Reconciliation** of records of cash received and banked
- Key controls over **payments** include:
  - **Restriction of access** to cash and cheques
  - Procedures for **preparation and authorisation** of payments
- A further important control is **regular independent bank reconciliations**
- **Stock controls** are designed to ensure safe custody. These include:
  - **Restriction of access** to stock
  - **Documentation** and **authorisation** of movements
- Other important controls over stock include regular **independent stock-taking** and **review of stock condition**.
- Most of the key controls over capital and revenue expenditure are the general purchase controls, covered in Chapter 10.
- It is also important that they are recorded correctly, so that profit/loss and assets are not misstated.
- It may not be cost-effective to test controls in this area. Alternative substantive procedures include:
  - Analytical review
  - Enquiry of purchasing personnel
  - Review of board minutes
- The **internal auditors are interested in the risks arising to the company in certain cycles**, not simply the risks of errors arising in the financial statements
- The objectives and controls they are interested in are more extensive. However, the following links can be seen:
  - Purchases/procurement
  - Sales/marketing
  - Cash/treasury
  - Payroll/human resources
- The APB has issued guidance on **providing assurance** on the effectiveness of internal controls. Such assurance can be related to the identification of risks, but is more likely to relate to the **design and operation of controls**.

Quick quiz

1 Name the five key aims of controls of the cash system.

1 ....

2 ....

3 ....

4 ....

5 ....

2 Give five examples of tests to be performed on the cash payments book.

1 ....

2 ....

3 ....

4 ....

5 ....

3 Three important controls over the protection of stocks are:

- Restriction of access to stores
- Regular stocktaking
- Reconciliation of book stock to physical stock

True ☐

False ☐

4 Give two examples of **substantive procedures** that can be used to test capital and revenue expenditure.

Answers to quick quiz

1 (1) **All monies received** are **recorded**
(2) **All monies received** are **banked**
(3) **Cash and cheques** are **safeguarded** against loss or theft
(4) **All payments** are **authorised**, **made** to the **correct payees** and **recorded**
(5) **Payments** are **not made twice** for the same liability

2 (1) **Compare** with paid cheques to ensure payee agrees

(2) **Note** that **cheques** are **signed** by the **persons authorised** to do so within their authority limits

(3) **Check** to **suppliers' invoices** for goods and services. Verify that supporting documents are signed as having been **checked** and **passed for payment** and have been stamped 'paid'

(4) **Check** to **suppliers' statements**

(5) **Check** to **other documentary evidence**, as appropriate (agreements, authorised expense vouchers, wages/salaries records, petty cash books etc)

3 True

4 Two from:

- General review between current and prior year figures to ascertain any unexplained differences
- Review of sensitive codes in the general ledger such as repairs or maintenance
- Review of the movements on the fixed asset codes
- Compare budgeted capital purchases with actual capital purchases
- Discuss the level of capital purchases in the year with the purchasing manager
- Review the board minutes for authorisation of capital purchases

Now try the questions below from the Exam Question Bank

Number	Level	Marks	Time
11	Exam	20	36 mins

Part D
Balance sheet audit

Chapter 12

THE SUBSTANTIVE AUDIT

Topic list		Syllabus reference	Study guide
1	**Substantive testing**	6	17
2	**Directional testing**	6	17
3	**Analytical procedures**	6	17
4	**Accounting estimates**	6	17
5	**Opening balances and comparatives**	6	17

Introduction

Having looked at tests of control in detail, we now move onto substantive testing. In the following chapters we shall consider substantive testing in each of the major audit areas. In this chapter however we consider general auditing issues that affect substantive tests generally, directional testing, analytical review and the audit of estimates.

Analytical review impacts upon the whole audit process. We mentioned briefly in Chapter 6 that auditors are required to carry out analytical procedures when **planning** an audit; this chapter goes into more detail. We then go on to discuss how substantive analytical review can provide **audit evidence**.

Lastly analytical review is required at the final stage of the audit, as a key part of the **overall review** of the final accounts. The purpose of analytical review at this stage is to answer the question 'Do the figures make sense?'

In the second part of this chapter we examine **accounting estimates**. We have mentioned in previous chapters that judgement has to be used in accounting for several figures in the accounts. Often these judgements depend on uncertain future events - what percentage of outstanding debtors will fail to pay their debts, or for how much will stock which has been in the warehouse eventually sell.

Since there may be a range of plausible answers to questions such as these, estimates can cause problems for auditors. We shall see that there are a number of possible ways in which estimates can be tested, and auditors will often wish to use a combination of procedures to obtain the required assurance.

Lastly, we look at the work that the auditor has to do on **opening balances and comparatives**. Substantiating the opening position is a key feature of any substantive audit.

This chapter forms a basis for the rest of the chapters in this Part of the Text, so the topics covered here are likely to be examined in that context.

1 SUBSTANTIVE TESTING

1.1 As discussed in Chapter 8, the auditors need to obtain **sufficient and appropriate audit evidence** to support the financial statement assertions. Substantive procedures aim to obtain that evidence.

REMEMBER

Substantive procedures are tests to obtain audit evidence to detect material misstatements in the financial statements. They are generally of two types:

(a) Analytical procedures

(b) Other substantive procedures such as tests of detail of transactions and balances, review of minutes of directors' meetings and enquiry.

1.2 The types of substantive tests carried out to obtain evidence about the assertions are outlined in the table below.

Audit objective	*Typical audit tests*
Completeness	(a) Review of post balance sheet items (b) Cut off (c) Analytical review (d) Confirmations (e) Reconciliations to control account (f) Sequence checks (g) Review of reciprocal populations
Rights and obligations	(a) Checking invoices for proof that item belongs to the company (b) Confirmations with third parties
Valuation	(a) Checking to invoices (b) Recalculation (c) Confirming accounting policy consistent and reasonable (d) Review of post balance sheet payments and invoices
Existence	(a) Physical verification (b) Third party confirmations (c) Cut off testing
Occurrence	(a) Inspection of supporting documentation (b) Confirmation from directors that transactions relate to business (c) Inspection of items purchased
Measurement	(a) Re-calculation of correct amounts (b) Third party confirmation (c) Expert valuation (d) Analytical review
Disclosure	(a) Check compliance with CA 1985 and SSAPs and FRSs (b) True and fair override invoked

1.3 Use the following model for drawing up an audit programme.

- **Agree opening balances** with **previous year's working papers** (see section 5)
- **Review general ledger** for unusual records
- **Check schedules** provided by client **to and from accounting records** to ensure completeness
- Carry out **analytical review**
- **Test transactions in detail**
- **Test balances in detail**
- **Review presentation** and **disclosure** in accounts.

Exam focus point

Auditing exams require a good knowledge of how the **financial statement assertions** determine audit objectives, and the procedures for obtaining audit evidence. You should be aiming to produce a description of procedures that could be followed by an inexperienced staff member.

2 DIRECTIONAL TESTING

2.1 Broadly speaking, **substantive procedures** can be said to fall into **two categories:**

- Tests to discover **errors** (resulting in over- or under-statement)
- Tests to discover **omissions** (resulting in under-statement)

We have already mentioned over- and under-statement in previous chapters, but such matters are particularly relevant in the next few chapters.

Tests designed to discover errors

2.2 These tests will start with the **accounting records** in which the transactions are recorded and check from the entries to supporting documents or other evidence. Such tests should detect any over-statement and also any under-statement through causes other than omission.

Case example: test for errors

If the test is designed to ensure that sales are priced correctly, the test would begin with a sales invoice selected from the sales ledger. Prices would then be checked to the official price list.

Tests designed to discover omissions

2.3 These tests must start from **outside the accounting records** and then check back to those records. Understatements through omission will never be revealed by starting with the account itself as there is clearly no chance of selecting items that have been omitted from the account.

Case example: tests for omission

If the test is designed to discover whether all raw material purchases have been properly processed, the test would start, say, with goods received notes, to be checked to the stock records or purchase ledger.

Directional testing

2.4 For most systems auditors would include tests designed to discover both errors and omissions. The type of test, and direction of the test, should be recognised before selecting the test sample. If the sample which tested the accuracy and validity of the sales ledger were chosen from a file of sales invoices then it would not substantiate the fact that there were no errors in the sales ledger. The approach known as 'directional testing' applies this testing discipline.

2.5 Directional testing is particularly appropriate when testing the financial statement assertions of **existence**, **completeness**, **rights and obligations**, and **valuation**.

2.6 The concept of directional testing derives from the principle of double-entry bookkeeping, in that for every **debit** there is a **corresponding credit**, (assuming that the double entry is complete and that the accounting records balance). Therefore, any **misstatement** of a **debit entry** will result in either a corresponding **misstatement** of a **credit entry** or a **misstatement** in the opposite direction, of **another debit entry**.

2.7 By designing audit tests carefully the auditors are able to use this principle in drawing audit conclusions, not only about the debit or credit entries that they have directly tested, but also about the corresponding credit or debit entries that are necessary to balance the books.

2.8 Tests are therefore designed in the following way.

Test item	Example
Test **debit items** (expenditure or assets) for overstatement by selecting debit entries recorded in the nominal ledger and checking value, existence and ownership	If a fixed asset entry in the nominal ledger of £1,000 is selected, it would be overstated if it should have been recorded at anything less than £1,000 or if the company did not own it, or indeed if it did not exist (eg it had been sold or the amount of £1,000 in fact represented a revenue expense)
Test **credit items** (income or liabilities) for understatement by selecting items from appropriate sources independent of the nominal ledger and ensuring that they result in the correct nominal ledger entry	Select a goods despatched note and check that the resultant sale has been recorded in the nominal ledger sales account. Sales would be understated if the nominal ledger did not reflect the transaction at all (completeness) or reflected it at less than full value (say if goods valued at £1,000 were recorded in the sales account at £900, there would be an understatement of £100).

2.9 A test for the overstatement of an asset simultaneously gives comfort on understatement of other assets, overstatement of liabilities, overstatement of income and understatement of expenses.

Question: Directional audit

Fill in the blank spaces.

(a) Based on double-entry bookkeeping, assets can only be *understated* by virtue of:

(i) Other assets being __________; or
(ii) Liabilities being __________; or
(iii) Income being __________; or
(iv) Expenses being __________.

(b) Similarly, liabilities can only be *overstated* by virtue of:

(i) Assets being __________; or

(ii) Other liabilities being __________; or
(iii) Income being __________; or
(iv) Expenses being __________.

Answer

(a) (i) Overstated
(ii) Understated
(iii) Understated
(iv) Overstated

(b) (i) Overstated
(ii) Understated
(iii) Understated
(iv) Overstated

2.10 So, by performing the primary tests, the auditors obtain audit assurance in other audit areas. Successful completion of the primary tests will therefore result in them having tested all account areas both for overstatement and understatement.

2.11 The **major advantage** of the directional audit approach is its **cost-effectiveness.**

(a) Assets and expenses are tested for overstatement only, and liabilities and income for understatement only, that is, items are not tested for both overstatement and understatement.

(b) It audits directly the more likely types of transactional misstatement, that is, unrecorded income and improper expense (arising intentionally or unintentionally).

3 ANALYTICAL PROCEDURES 6/02, 6/03

KEY TERM

Analytical procedures are the analysis of relationships:

(a) Between items of financial data, or between items of financial and non-financial data, deriving from the same period, or

(b) Between comparable financial information deriving from different periods to identify consistencies and predicted patterns or significant fluctuations and unexpected relationships, and the results of investigation thereof

Nature and purpose of analytical procedures

3.1 SAS 410 *Analytical procedures* states that they include:

(a) The **consideration of comparisons** of this year's financial information with:

- **Similar information** for prior periods
- **Anticipated results** of the client
- **Predictions prepared** by the auditors, such as an estimation of the depreciation charge for the year
- **Industry information**, such as a comparison of the client's ratio of sales to trade debtors with industry averages, or with the ratios relating to other entities of comparable size in the same industry.

(b) Those between **elements of financial information** that are **expected to conform** to a predicted pattern based on experience, such as the relationship of gross profit to sales

(c) Those between **financial information** and **relevant non-financial information**, such as the relationship of payroll costs to number of employees

3.2 A variety of methods can be used to perform the procedures discussed above, ranging from **simple comparisons** to **complex analysis** using statistics, on a company level, branch level or individual account level. The choice of procedures is a matter for the auditors' professional judgement.

Analytical procedures in planning the audit

3.3 The SAS requires analytical procedures to be carried out at the planning stage to understand the business, in risk analysis and in planning audit procedures.

3.4 As well as helping to determine the nature, timing and extent of other audit procedures, such analytical procedures may also indicate aspects of the business of which the auditors were previously unaware.

3.5 Auditors are looking to see if developments in the client's business have had the expected effects. They will be particularly interested in changes in audit areas where problems have occurred in the past.

Analytical procedures as substantive procedures

3.6 The SAS states that auditors must decide whether using available analytical procedures as substantive procedures will be effective and efficient in reducing **detection risk** for specific financial statement assertions.

3.7 The SAS lists a number of factors which the auditors should consider when deciding whether to use analytical procedures as substantive procedures.

Factors to consider	Example
The **plausibility and predictability** of the relationships identified for comparison and evaluation	The strong relationship between certain selling expenses and turnover in businesses where the sales force is paid by commission
The **objectives** of the analytical procedures and the extent to which their results are reliable	
The **detail** to which information can be **analysed**	Analytical procedures may be more effective when applied to financial information on individual sections of an operation such as individual factories or shops
The **availability of information**	Financial: budgets or forecasts Non-financial: eg the number of units produced or sold
The **relevance of the information** available	Whether budgets are established as results to be expected rather than as tough targets (which may well not be achieved)
The **comparability of the information** available	Comparisons with average performance in an industry may be of little value if a large number of companies differ significantly from the average.
The **knowledge gained during previous audits**	The effectiveness of the accounting and internal control systems The types of problems giving rise to accounting adjustments in prior periods

Reliance on analytical procedures

3.8 From our earlier coverage of audit evidence we can see that the information used in analytical procedures will be more reliable if it comes from sources independent from, rather than internal to, the client. Information produced independently outside the accounting function is more reliable than that originating from within it.

3.9 The results of **other audit procedures** will help to determine the reliability of the information used in analytical procedures, as will the importance of the results of the procedure for the auditors' opinion.

3.10 The SAS identifies other factors which should be considered when determining the reliance that the auditors should place on the results of substantive analytical procedures.

Reliability factors	Example
Other audit procedures directed towards the same financial statements assertions	Other procedures auditors undertake in reviewing the collectability of debtors, such as the review of subsequent cash receipts, may confirm or dispel questions arising from the application of analytical procedures to a profile of customers' accounts which lists for how long monies have been owed
Thc **accuracy** with which the expected results of analytical procedures can be predicted	Auditors normally expect greater consistency in comparing the relationship of gross profit to sales from one period to another than in comparing expenditure which may or may not be made within a period, such as research or advertising
The **frequency** with which a relationship is observed	A pattern repeated monthly as opposed to annually

3.11 Reliance on the results of analytical procedures depends on the auditors' assessment of the **risk** that the procedures may identify relationships (between data) do exist, whereas a material misstatement exists (that is, the relationships, in fact, do not exist).

3.12 It depends also on the results of investigations that auditors have made if substantive analytical procedures have highlighted significant fluctuations or unexpected relationships (see below).

Analytical review at the final stage

3.13 SAS 410 goes on to look at analytical procedures as part of the overall review when completing the audit. The key aim of procedures is to see whether the overall accounts appear reasonable. The final review procedures are considered in Chapter 18.

3.14 The conclusions from these analytical procedures should be consistent with the conclusions formed from other audit procedures on parts of the financial statements. However, these analytical procedures may highlight areas which require further investigation and audit.

Investigating significant fluctuations or unexpected relationships

3.15 The SAS requires auditors to investigate significant fluctuations or unexpected relationships and obtain adequate explanations and appropriate evidence about them. Investigations will start with **enquiries** to management and then confirmation of management's responses by:

- **Comparing them** with the auditors' knowledge of the entity's business and with other evidence obtained during the course of the audit, or
- **Carrying out additional audit procedures** where appropriate to confirm the explanations received

3.16 If explanations cannot be given by management, or if they are insufficient, the auditors must determine which further audit procedures to undertake to explain the fluctuation or relationship.

Practical techniques

3.17 When carrying out analytical procedures, auditors should remember that every industry is different and each company within an industry differs in certain respects.

Important accounting ratios

$$\text{Gross profit margin} = \frac{\text{Gross profit}}{\text{Turnover}} \times 100\%$$

This should be calculated in total and by product, area and month/quarter if possible.

$$\text{Debtors turnover period} = \frac{\text{Debtors}}{\text{Sales}} \times 365$$

$$\text{Stock turnover ratio} = \frac{\text{Cost of sales}}{\text{Stock}}$$

$$\text{Current ratio} = \frac{\text{Current assets}}{\text{Current liabilities}}$$

$$\text{Quick or acid test ratio} = \frac{\text{Current assets (excluding stock)}}{\text{Current liabilities}}$$

$$\text{Gearing ratio} = \frac{\text{Loans}}{\text{Share capital and reserves}} \times 100\%$$

$$\text{Return on capital employed} = \frac{\text{Profit before tax}}{\text{Total assets - current - liabilities}}$$

Significant items

Creditors and purchases

Stocks and cost of sales

Fixed assets and depreciation, repairs and maintenance expense

Intangible assets and amortisation

Loans and interest expense

Investments and investment income

Debtors and bad debt expense

Debtors and sales

3.18 Ratios mean very little when used in isolation. They should be calculated for **previous periods** and for **comparable companies**. The permanent file should contain a section with summarised accounts and the chosen ratios for prior years.

3.19 In addition to looking at the more usual ratios the auditors should consider examining **other ratios** that may be **relevant** to the particular **clients' business**, such as revenue per passenger mile for an airline operator client, or fees per partner for a professional office.

3.20 Other analytical techniques include:

(a) **Examining related accounts** in conjunction with each other. Often revenue and expense accounts are related to balance sheet accounts and comparisons should be made to ensure relationships are reasonable.

(b) **Trend analysis**. Sophisticated statistical techniques (beyond the scope of this paper) can be used to compare this period with previous periods.

(c) **Reasonableness tests**. These involve calculating **expected value** of an item and comparing it with its actual value, for example, for straight-line depreciation.

(Cost + Additions – Disposals) × Depreciation % = Charge in P&L A/C

3.21 Other areas that might be investigated as part of the analytical procedures include the following.

- **Examine changes** in **products, customers and levels** of **returns**
- **Assess** the effect of **price and mix changes** on the cost of sales
- **Consider** the effect of **inflation, industrial disputes, changes in production methods** and **changes in activity** on the charge for wages
- **Obtain explanations** for all **major variances** analysed using a standard costing system. Particular attention should be paid to those relating to the over or under absorption of overheads since these may, inter alia, affect stock valuations
- **Compare trends in production and sales** and assess the effect on any provisions for obsolete stocks
- **Ensure** that **changes in the percentage labour or overhead content** of production costs are also reflected in the stock valuation
- **Review other profit and loss expenditure**, comparing:
  - Rent with annual rent per rental agreement
  - Rates with previous year and known rates increases
  - Interest payable on loans with outstanding balance and interest rate per loan agreement
  - Hire or leasing charges with annual rate per agreements
  - Vehicle running expenses to vehicles
  - Other items related to activity level with general price increase and change in relevant level of activity (for example telephone expenditure will increase disproportionately if export or import business increases)
  - Other items not related to activity level with general price increases (or specific increases if known)
- **Review** profit and loss account for **items** which may have been **omitted** (eg scrap sales, training levy, special contributions to pension fund, provisions for dilapidation etc)
- **Ensure expected variations** arising from the following have occurred:
  - Industry or local trends
  - Known disturbances of the trading pattern (for example strikes, depot closures, failure of suppliers)

3.22 Certain of the comparisons and ratios measuring liquidity and longer-term capital structure will assist in evaluating whether the company is a **going concern,** in addition to contributing to the overall view of the accounts. We shall see in Chapter 18, however, that there are factors other than declining ratios that may indicate going concern problems.

3.23 The working papers must contain the completed results of analytical procedures. They should include:

- The **outline programme** of the work
- The **summary of significant figures** and relationships for the period
- A **summary** of **comparisons made** with budgets and with previous years
- Details of all **significant fluctuations** or **unexpected relationships** considered
- Details of the **results of investigations** into such fluctuations/relationships
- The **audit conclusions** reached
- **Information considered necessary** for assisting in the planning of subsequent audits

Exam focus point

In the exam you may be given a set of figures and:

(a) Asked to calculate changes, key ratios etc and hence identify significant areas of the accounts
(b) Asked what audit work will be required on these significant areas

When analysing figures, make sure that the points which you make are consistent with each other.

Factors that indicate possible going concern problems are particularly important.

Mention of analytical procedures will generally be worth a couple of marks in any question on substantive testing.

However you will not get any marks just for saying 'perform analytical procedures'; you will need to give details of the procedures that should be performed.

Analytical procedures in a review

3.24 As we mentioned in Chapter 1, analytical procedures have a key role in a review. It is unlikely that other substantive procedures would be used in a review. Therefore, significant use is made of analytical review and enquiries of client staff.

4 ACCOUNTING ESTIMATES

KEY TERM

An **accounting estimate** is an approximation of the amount of an item in the absence of a precise means of measurement.

4.1 SAS 420 *Audit of accounting estimates* states 'auditors should obtain sufficient appropriate audit evidence regarding accounting estimates'.

4.2 The SAS gives these examples.

- Allowances to reduce stocks and debtors to their estimated realisable value
- Depreciation provisions
- Accrued revenue
- Provision for a loss from a lawsuit

- Profits or losses on construction contracts in progress
- Provision to meet warranty claims

4.3 Accounting estimates may be produced as part of the routine operations of the accounting system, or may be a non-routine procedure at the period end. Where, as is frequently the case, a **formula** based on past experience is used to calculate the estimate, it should be reviewed regularly by management (for example, actual vs estimate in prior periods).

4.4 **Directors and management** are responsible for making accounting estimates included in the financial statements. These estimates are often made in conditions of uncertainty regarding the outcome of events and involve the use of judgement. The risk of a material misstatement therefore increases when accounting estimates are involved.

4.5 **Audit evidence** supporting accounting estimates is **generally less than conclusive** and so auditors need to exercise **significant judgement**.

Audit procedures

4.6 The auditors should gain an understanding of the procedures and methods used by management to make accounting estimates. This will aid the auditors' planning of their own procedures. Auditors must gain evidence that estimates are reasonable and, where applicable, properly disclosed. They do this by one or a combination of the following methods.

(a) Review and test the process used by management or the directors to develop the estimate

(b) Use an independent estimate for comparison with that prepared by management or the directors or

(c) Review subsequent events.

Review and testing the process

4.7 The auditors will carry out the following steps.

- **Consider whether data** is **accurate, complete and reliable**
- **Seek appropriate evidence from outside client** (for example, industry sales projections to confirm internal estimates of future sales orders)
- **Check** whether **data is appropriately analysed** and **projected** (for example, age analysis of accounts receivable)
- **Evaluate** whether **base used** for assumptions is **appropriate**
- **Evaluate** whether **assumptions** are **reasonable** in light of **prior period results**
- **Consider** whether **formulae** used remain **appropriate** in the light of current conditions
- Consider whether **assumptions** are **consistent**
  - With those used for other accounting estimates
  - With management's plans
- **Consider** whether **expert opinion** is required if estimates are complex
- **Test calculations** involved in the estimate considering:
  - Complexity of calculation
  - Procedures and methods used by the client
  - Materiality of estimate

- **Compare previous estimates** with actual results, aiming to obtain evidence about:
  - General reliability of the client's estimating procedures
  - Whether adjustments to estimating formulae will be required
  - Whether differences between previous estimates and actual figures ought to be disclosed
- Consider management's approval procedures, confirming it is performed by the **appropriate level of management** and **evidenced**

Use of an independent estimate

4.8 Such an estimate (made or obtained by the auditors) may be compared with the accounting estimate. The auditors should **evaluate the data**, **consider the assumptions** and **test** the **calculation procedures** used to develop the independent estimate. Prior period independent assessments and actual results could also be compared.

Review of subsequent events

4.9 The auditors should review transactions or events after the period end which may reduce or even remove the need to test accounting estimates (as described above).

Evaluation of results of audit procedures

4.10 The SAS states 'auditors should make a final assessment of the reasonableness of the accounting estimate based on their knowledge of the business and whether the estimate is consistent with other audit evidence obtained during the audit'.

4.11 Auditors must assess the difference between the amount of an estimate supported by evidence and the estimate calculated by management.

- If the auditors believe that the difference is unreasonable then an adjustment should be made.
- If the directors or management refuse to revise the estimate, then the difference is considered a misstatement and will be treated as such.

5 OPENING BALANCES AND COMPARATIVES

KEY TERMS

Opening balances are those account balances that exist at the beginning of the period. Opening balances are based upon the closing balances of the preceding period and reflect the effect of transactions of preceding periods and accounting policies applied in the preceding period.

Comparatives are the corresponding amounts and other related disclosures from the preceding period which are part of the current period's financial statements as required by relevant legislation and applicable accounting standards. Such comparatives are intended to be read in relation to the amounts and other disclosures related to the current period.

5.1 It is appropriate to consider such matters at the planning stage and early in the audit process as the **outcome of the relevant audit procedures could have a substantial impact on the audit of current year transactions and balances**.

5.2 SAS 450 *Opening balances and comparatives* states 'auditors should obtain sufficient appropriate audit evidence that amounts derived from the preceding period's financial statements are free from material misstatements and are appropriately incorporated in the financial statements for the current period'.

5.3 Note that the preceding period accounts, when new auditors are appointed, may have been reported on by the predecessor auditors or they may have been **unaudited**.

Opening balances

5.4 The SAS says 'auditors should obtain sufficient appropriate audit evidence that:

(a) Opening balances have been appropriately brought forward

(b) Opening balances do not contain errors or misstatements which materially affect the current period's financial statements and

(c) Appropriate accounting policies are consistently applied or changes in accounting policies have been properly accounted for and adequately disclosed'.

5.5 If the auditors are unable to obtain sufficient appropriate audit evidence, then they should consider the implications for their audit report. The reporting implications of this are discussed in Chapter 19.

5.6 The SAS goes on to look at opening balances from the point of view of both **continuing auditors** and **incoming auditors**.

KEY TERMS

Continuing auditors are the auditors who audited and reported on the preceding period's financial statements and continue as the auditors for the current period.

Predecessor auditors are the auditors who previously audited and reported on the financial statements of an entity, and who have been replaced by the incoming auditors.

Incoming auditors are the auditors who are auditing and reporting on the current period's financial statements, not having audited and reported on those for the preceding period.

Continuing auditors

5.7 Audit procedures need not extend beyond ensuring that opening balances have been **appropriately brought forward** and the current accounting policies have been consistently applied, **if**:

- The continuing auditors issued an unqualified report on the preceding periods' financial statements.
- The audit of the current period does not reveal any matters which cast doubt on those financial statements.

5.8 If a **qualified audit report** was issued on the preceding period's financial statements then the auditors should consider whether the matter which gave rise to the qualification has been **adequately resolved** and properly dealt with in the **current period's financial statements**. This is in addition to the procedures above.

Incoming auditors

5.9 This situation is obviously more difficult. Appropriate and sufficient audit evidence is required on the opening balances and this depends on matters such as the following.

- The **accounting policies** followed by the entity
- Whether the **preceding period's financial statements were audited** and, if so, whether the auditors' report was **qualified**
- The **nature of the opening balances**, including the risk of their misstatement
- The **materiality of the opening balances** relative to the current period's financial statements

5.10 The **procedures given** for continuing auditors should be carried out. Other procedures suggested by the SAS are as follows.

- **Consultations with management** and review of records, working papers and accounting and control procedures for the preceding period
- **Substantive testing of any opening balances** in respect of which the results of other procedures are considered unsatisfactory

5.11 Consultations with predecessor auditors will not normally be necessary as the above procedures will be sufficient. Predecessor auditors have no legal or ethical duty to provide information and would not normally be expected to release relevant working papers but are expected to cooperate with the incoming auditors on specific issues.

Comparatives

5.12 Opening balances will, in the current year's financial statements, become comparative figures which must be disclosed. The SAS states 'auditors should obtain sufficient appropriate audit evidence that:

(a) The accounting policies used for the comparatives are consistent with those of the current period and appropriate adjustments and disclosures have been made where this is not the case

(b) The comparatives agree with the amounts and other disclosures presented in the preceding period and are free from errors in the context of the financial statements of the current period and

(c) Where comparatives have been adjusted as required by relevant legislation and accounting standards, appropriate disclosures have been made'.

5.13 Comparative figures are a part of the financial statements on which the auditor report, although they do not comment on them directly.

Continuing auditors

5.14 The extent of audit procedures for comparatives will be significantly less then those for current year balances; normally they will be limited to a **check that balances have been**

brought forward correctly. Materiality of any misstatements should be considered in relationship to **current** period figures.

5.15 The auditors' report on the previous period financial statements may have been qualified. Where the qualification matter is still **unresolved,** two situations may apply.

(a) If the matter is material in the context of the current period's opening balances as well as comparatives, the report on the current period's financial statements should be **qualified regarding opening balances and comparatives.**

(b) If the matter does not affect opening balances but is material in the context of the current period's financial statements, the report on the current period's financial statements should **refer to the comparatives.**

(i) If comparatives are **required by law or regulation,** the reference will be in the form of a **qualification on the grounds of non-compliance** with that requirement.

(ii) If comparatives are presented solely as **good practice,** the reference should be in the form of an **explanatory paragraph.**

5.16 Where a previous qualification has been resolved and dealt with properly in the financial statements then no mention of the qualification needs to be made in the current audit report.

5.17 If, however, the matter was material to the current period, then it should be mentioned in the current report, including an explanation of how it has been resolved. It is also possible that a qualification will still be necessary, for example, if a provision has been made in the current year which should have been made in the previous period.

Incoming auditors: audited comparatives

5.18 In this situation, the preceding period's financial statements have been audited by other auditors. The **incoming auditors only bear audit responsibility for the comparatives in the context of the financial statements as a whole**.

5.19 The incoming auditors will use the knowledge gained in the current audit to decide whether the previous period's financial statements have been properly reflected as comparatives in the current period's financial statements.

5.20 The procedures described above should be considered should such a situation arise.

Incoming auditors: unaudited comparatives

5.21 In this situation (for example, where the company took advantage of the small company audit exemption in the previous period) the auditors should check that there is clear **disclosure** in the current financial statements that the **comparatives are unaudited**. They must still undertake the duties mentioned above as far as is appropriate.

5.22 If there is not sufficient appropriate evidence, or if disclosure is inadequate, the auditors should consider the implications for their reports.

Question: Opening balances and comparatives

You have recently been appointed auditor of Lowdham Castings Ltd, a company which has been trading for about thirty years, and are carrying out an audit for the year ended 30 September 20X6. The company's turnover is about £500,000 and its normal profit before tax is about £30,000.

Required

Discuss your responsibilities in relation to the comparatives included in the accounts for the year ended 30 September 20X6. You should also consider the information you would require from the retiring auditors.

Answer

Consideration of the financial statements of the preceding period is necessary in the audit of the current period's financial statements in relation to three main aspects.

(a) *Opening position:* obtaining satisfaction that those amounts which have a direct effect on the current period's results or closing position have been properly brought forward

(b) *Accounting policies:* determining whether the accounting policies adopted for the current period are consistent with those of the previous period

(c) *Comparatives:* determining that the comparatives are properly shown in the current period's financial statements

The auditors' main concern will therefore be to satisfy themselves that there were no material misstatements in the previous year's financial statements which may have a bearing upon their work in the current year.

The new auditors do not have to 're-audit' the previous year's financial statements, but they will have to pay more attention to them than would normally be the case where they had themselves been the auditors in the earlier period. A useful source of audit evidence will clearly be the previous auditors, and, with the client's permission, they should be contacted to see if they are prepared to co-operate. Certainly, any known areas of weakness should be discussed with the previous auditors and it is also possible that they might be prepared to provide copies of their working papers (although there is no legal or ethical provision which requires the previous auditors to co-operate in this way).

Chapter roundup

- **Analytical procedures** cover comparisons of financial data with other financial or non-financial data of the same or previous periods, also comparisons of financial data with expected data.
- Analytical procedures aim to **identify inconsistencies** or **significant fluctuations**.
- Analytical procedures must be undertaken at the **planning** stage of audits.
- Analytical procedures can be used as substantive procedures, depending on the **available information** and the plausibility and predictability of the relationships.
- Analytical review should be undertaken at the **final stage** of an audit on the final accounts.
- **Significant fluctuations** and **unexpected variations** should be investigated by enquiries of management, comparisons with other evidence and further audit procedures as required.
- Accounts may contain **accounting estimates** in a number of areas.
- Auditors can test accounting estimates by:
  - **Reviewing** and **testing** the management process
  - **Using an independent estimate**
  - **Reviewing subsequent events**
- Specific procedures must be applied to **opening balances** at a new audit client.
- The auditors' responsibilities for **comparatives** relate mainly to **consistency**, although comparatives and opening balances can have an impact on current results.

Quick quiz

1 Link the type of account with the purpose of the primary test in directional testing.

(a)	Assets	(i)	Overstatement
(b)	Liabilities	(ii)	Overstatement
(c)	Income	(iii)	Understatement
(d)	Expense	(iv)	Understatement

2 Name four sources of analytical information which can be used at the planning stage of the audit.

1 ....

2 ....

3 ....

4 ....

3 Identify the significant relationships in the list of items below

(a) creditors	(b) interest	(c) purchases	(d) sales
(e) amortisation	(f) loans	(g) debtors	(h) intangibles

4 Complete the definition.

An accounting estimate is an .... of the .... of an item in the absence of a .... of measurement.

5 Give three examples of an accounting estimate.

1 ....

2 ....

3 ....

6 Auditors are responsible for making accounting estimates to be used in the accounts.

True ☐

False ☐

7 Give three steps in the review and test the stage of auditing accounting estimates.

1 ....

2 ....

3 ....

8 The audit report covers the comparatives as well as the current year figures

True ☐

False ☐

Answers to quick quiz

1 (a) (i)
(b) (iii)
(c) (ii)
(d) (iv)

2
- Interim financial information
- Budgets
- Management accounts
- Non-financial information
- Bank and cash records
- VAT returns
- Board minutes
- Discussions or correspondence with the client at the year-end.

3 (a) (c)
(b) (f)
(d) (g)
(e) (h)

4 approximation, amount, precise means

5
- Allowances to reduce stocks and debtors to their estimated realisable value
- Depreciation provisions
- Accrued revenue
- Provision for a loss from a lawsuit
- Profits or losses on construction contracts in progress
- Provision to meet warranty claims

6 False

7 **Three** from:
- **Consider whether data** is **accurate, complete and reliable**
- **Seek appropriate evidence from outside client** (for example, industry sales projections to confirm internal estimates of future sales orders)
- **Check** whether **data is appropriately analysed** and **projected** (for example, age analysis of accounts receivable)
- **Evaluate** whether **base used** for assumptions is **appropriate**
- **Evaluate** whether **assumptions** are **reasonable** in light of **prior period results**
- **Consider** whether **formulae** used remain **appropriate** in the light of current conditions
- Consider whether **assumptions** are **consistent**
  - With those used for other accounting estimates
  - With management's plans
- **Consider** whether **expert opinion** is required if estimates are complex
- **Test calculations** involved in the estimate considering:
  - Complexity of calculation
  - Procedures and methods used by the client
  - Materiality of estimate
- **Compare previous estimates** with actual results, aiming to obtain evidence about:
  - General reliability of the client's estimating procedures
  - Whether adjustments to estimating formulae will be required
  - Whether differences between previous estimates and actual figures ought to be disclosed
- Consider management's approval procedures, confirming it is performed by the **appropriate level of management** and **evidenced**

8 True

Now try the question below from the Exam Question Bank

Number	Level	Marks	Time
12	Introductory	n/a	30 mins

Chapter 13

FIXED ASSETS

Topic list		Syllabus reference	Study guide
1	**Tangible fixed assets**	**6**	**22**
2	**Other fixed assets**	**6**	**22**

Introduction

The final audit will concentrate on the balance sheet to a great extent. The following chapters cover the audit of the key balance sheet areas.

Although each audit client is different, most of the assets in this and the next two chapters will be present in the final accounts. The importance of each balance sheet component will vary from client to client.

The chapter highlights the key objectives for each major component. You must understand what **objectives** the various audit tests are designed to achieve. Objectives of particular significance for tangible fixed assets are **rights and obligations** (that is ownership), **existence and valuation**. You should note it is generally necessary to carry out different tests on ownership and existence.

Valuation is the other important assertion. The auditors will concentrate on testing any valuations made during the year, and also whether other values appear reasonable given asset usage and condition. A very important aspect of testing valuation is reviewing depreciation rates.

A topic which we covered in an earlier chapter may well be important in the audit of fixed assets, using the work of an expert (which we covered in Chapter 7). You should refer back to your notes in this subject.

Exam questions on any balance sheet area may either focus on:

- Audit work required
- Accounting treatment problems
- Both the above

Tangible fixed assets are often financed by long term loans (for instance a mortgage or lease). Therefore these areas could be examined together. Fixed assets were examined on the pilot paper.

1 TANGIBLE FIXED ASSETS **Pilot Paper**

Internal control considerations

1.1 The **fixed asset register** is a very important aspect of the internal control systems. It enables assets to be identified, and comparisons between the general ledger, fixed asset register and the assets themselves provide **evidence** that the assets are **completely recorded**.

1.2 Another significant control is procedures over acquisitions and disposals, that acquisitions are properly **authorised**, and **disposals** are **authorised** and **proceeds accounted for**.

1.3 Other significant aspects are:

- **Security arrangements** over fixed assets are **sufficient**.
- **Fixed assets** are **maintained properly.**
- **Depreciation** is **reviewed every year.**
- **All income** is **collected** from **income-yielding assets.**

Completeness

AUDIT PROGRAMME: TANGIBLE FIXED ASSETS - COMPLETENESS
• **Obtain** or **prepare** a **summary** of tangible fixed assets showing how: ○ **Gross book value** ○ **Accumulated depreciation** ○ **Net book value** **reconcile** with the **opening position**. • **Compare fixed assets** in the general ledger with the **fixed assets register** and **obtain explanations** for **differences** • **Check** whether **assets** which **physically exist** are **recorded** in **fixed asset register** • If a fixed asset register is not kept, **obtain** a **schedule** showing the original costs and present depreciated value of major fixed assets • **Reconcile** the **schedule** of fixed assets with the **general ledger**

Existence

AUDIT PROGRAMME: TANGIBLE FIXED ASSETS – EXISTENCE
• **Confirm** that the **company physically inspects** all items in the fixed asset register each year • **Inspect assets,** concentrating on high value items and additions in year. Confirm items inspected: ○ Exist ○ Are in use ○ Are in good condition ○ Have correct serial numbers • **Review records** of **income yielding assets** • **Reconcile** opening and closing **vehicles** by numbers as well as amounts

Valuation

AUDIT PROGRAMME: TANGIBLE FIXED ASSETS - VALUATION

• **Verify valuation** to valuation certificate
• **Consider reasonableness** of **valuation**, reviewing:
   ° Experience of valuer
   ° Scope of work
   ° Methods and assumptions used
   ° Valuation bases are in line with FRS 15
• **Check revaluation** surplus has been **correctly calculated**
• Check valuations of all assets that have been revalued have been **updated regularly** (full valuation every five years and an interim valuation in year three generally)
• Check that client has **recognised** in the **profit and loss account** revaluation losses which relate to clear consumption of economic benefits or which take the valuation below depreciated historical cost, and client has **recognised all other gains and losses** in **statement of total recognised gains and losses**

Depreciation

• **Review depreciation rates** applied in relation to:
   ° Asset lives
   ° Residual values
   ° Replacement policy
   ° Past experience of gains and losses on disposal
   ° Consistency with prior years and accounting policy
   ° Possible obsolescence
• **Check depreciation** has been **charged on all assets** with a limited useful life
• For **revalued assets**, ensure that the charge for **depreciation** is **based** on the **revalued amount**
• **Check calculation** of depreciation rates
• **Compare ratios** of depreciation to fixed assets (by category) with:
   ° Previous years
   ° Depreciation policy rates
• **Ensure no further depreciation** provided on **fully depreciated assets**
• **Check** that **depreciation policies and rates are disclosed** in the accounts

Insurance
• **Review insurance policies** in force for all categories of tangible fixed assets and consider the adequacy of their insured values and check expiry dates

Rights and obligations

AUDIT PROGRAMME: TANGIBLE FIXED ASSETS – RIGHTS AND OBLIGATIONS

• **Verify title** to land and buildings by inspection of:
  ◦ Title deeds
  ◦ Land registry certificates
  ◦ Leases
• Obtain a certificate from solicitors/bankers:
  ◦ **Stating purpose** for which the deeds are being held (custody only)
  ◦ **Stating deeds** are **free** from **mortgage** or **lien**
• **Inspect registration documents** for vehicles held, checking that they are in client's name
• **Confirm** all vehicles used for the **client's business**
• **Examine documents** of **title** for other assets (including purchase invoices, architects' certificates, contracts, hire purchase or lease agreements)
Charges and commitments
• **Review for evidence** of charges in statutory books and by company search
• **Review leases** of leasehold properties to ensure that company has fulfilled covenants therein
• **Examine invoices received after year-end, orders and minutes** for evidence of capital commitments

1.4 Inspection of building's title deeds does not give audit evidence about **existence** and if there is doubt that a building actually exists, the auditors should physically inspect it.

Additions

1.5 These tests are to confirm **rights and obligations**, **valuation** and **completeness**

AUDIT PROGRAMME: TANGIBLE FIXED ASSETS - ADDITIONS

• **Verify additions** by inspection of architects' certificates, solicitors' completion statements, suppliers' invoices etc.
• **Check capitalisation** of **expenditure** is correct by considering for fixed assets additions and items in relevant expense categories (repairs, motor expenses, sundry expenses) whether:
  ◦ Capital/revenue distinction is correctly drawn
  ◦ Capitalisation is in line with consistently applied company policy
• **Check purchases** have been **properly allocated** to correct fixed asset accounts
• **Check purchases** have been **authorised** by directors/senior management
• **Ensure** that appropriate **claims** have been made for **grants**, and grants received and receivable have been received
• **Check additions** have been **recorded** in fixed asset register and general ledger

Self-constructed assets

1.6 These tests are to confirm **valuation** and **completeness**

AUDIT PROGRAMME: TANGIBLE FIXED ASSETS – SELF CONSTRUCTED ASSETS
• **Verify material** and **labour** costs and **overheads** to invoices, wage records etc
• **Ensure expenditure** has been **analysed correctly** and **properly charged** to capital
• **Check no profit element** has been included in costs
• Check **finance costs** have been **capitalised** (or not) on a consistent basis and costs capitalised in period do not exceed total finance costs

Disposals

1.7 These tests are to confirm **rights and obligations, completeness, occurrence** and **measurement**.

AUDIT PROGRAMME: TANGIBLE FIXED ASSETS - DISPOSALS
• **Verify disposals** with supporting documentation, checking transfer of title, sales price and dates of completion and payment
• **Check calculation** of profit or loss is accurate and is in **accordance** with FRS 3
• **Check** that **disposals** have been **authorised**
• **Consider** whether **proceeds** are **reasonable**
• If the asset was **used as security**, ensure **release from security** has been correctly made

Question: Fixed assets

You are the manager in charge of the audit of Maurice plc, a building and construction company, and you are reviewing the fixed asset section of the current audit file for the year ended 30 September 20X5. You find the following five matters which the audit senior has identified as problem areas. He is reviewing the company's proposed treatment of the five transactions in the accounts and is not sure that he has yet carried out sufficient audit work.

The five matters are as follows.

(a) During the year Maurice plc built a new canteen for its own staff at a cost of £450,000. This amount has been included in buildings as at 30 September 20X5.

(b) Loose tools included in the financial statements at a total cost of £166,000 are tools used on two of the construction sites on which Maurice operates. They are classified as fixed assets and depreciated over two years.

(c) A dumper truck, previously written off in the company's accounting records has been refurbished at a cost of £46,000 and this amount included in plant and machinery as at 30 September 20X5.

(d) The company's main office block has been revalued from £216,000 to £266,000 and this amount included in the balance sheet as at 30 September 20X5.

(e) A deposit of £20,000 for new equipment has been included under the heading plant and machinery although the final instalment of £35,000 was not paid over until 31 October 20X5 which was the date of delivery of the plant.

You are required, for each of the above matters to:

(a) Comment on the acceptability of the accounting treatment and disclosure as indicated above.
(b) Outline the audit work and evidence required to substantiate the assets.

Answer

(a) **Acceptability of accounting treatment and disclosure**

(i) *New staff canteen.* The costs of building a new staff canteen can quite properly be capitalised and treated as part of buildings in the balance sheet. The company's normal depreciation policy should be applied, subject only to the canteen being completed and in use at the year end.

(ii) *Loose tools.* Loose tools tend to have a very limited life and individually not to be material in value. For these reasons any capitalisation policy must be extremely prudent. The acceptability of this accounting treatment would depend on the policy in previous years and normal practice within the industry.

(iii) *Dumper truck.* The refurbishment costs have obviously extended the useful life of this asset and it therefore seems reasonable to capitalise the expenditure. Depreciation should be charged on the refurbishment costs over the estimated remaining useful life.

(iv) *Revaluation of office block.* The revaluation of property is acceptable, but the auditors will need to ensure that the company complies with a number of disclosure requirements. A note to the accounts should give details of the revaluation and the name of the valuer. The surplus on revaluation should be transferred to a separate non-distributable reserve in the balance sheet as part of shareholders' funds. In addition, the audit report will make reference to this modification of the use of the historical cost convention used in the preparation of the financial statements.

(v) *Deposit for new equipment.* As the equipment was not actually in the company's possession and use at the year end, the deposit should not have been shown as plant and machinery, but rather as a payment on account. If the amount was considered to be material a note to the accounts should give details of this prepayment.

(b) **Audit work and evidence required**

(i) *New staff canteen*

(1) Physically confirm existence of the asset.

(2) Confirm title to building by reference to Land Registry Certificate.

(3) Ascertain and confirm the details of any security granted over the asset, ensuring that this is properly recorded and disclosed.

(4) Test the detailed costings of the building and obtain explanations for any material variances from the original budget. Particular care should be taken in assessing the reasonableness of any overheads included as an element of cost.

(5) Review the depreciation policy for adequacy and consistency.

(ii) *Loose tools*

(1) Visit the two sites where the loose tools are used to confirm the existence and condition of a sample of them.

(2) Vouch the cost and ownership of the loose tools to purchase invoices and the company's asset register.

(3) Confirm the company's estimate of a two year life for these assets.

(4) Review control procedures for safe custody of the loose tools.

(5) Review the company's policy with regard to scrapping and/or sale of tools no longer required to ensure that any proceeds are properly recorded and the assets register appropriately updated and tools are completely recorded.

(iii) *Dumper truck*

(1) Inspect the truck to confirm its existence and to gain evidence of its valuation by reviewing its condition and the fact that it is still being used.

(2) If the vehicle is used at all on public roads then the vehicle registration document should be inspected as some evidence of title.

(3) Inspect the insurance policy for the truck as evidence of valuation.

(4) Vouch the expenditure on refurbishment to suppliers' invoices or company's payroll records where any of the work has been done by the client's own staff.

(5) Review the depreciation policy and assess for reasonableness by discussion with management and past experience of similar vehicles.

(iv) *Revaluation of office block*

(1) Inspect the building to confirm its existence and state of repair.

(2) Examine documents of title to confirm ownership.

(3) Enquire about any charges on the building and confirm that these have been properly recorded and disclosed.

(4) Review the valuer's certificate and agree to the amount used in the financial statements, with consideration also being given to his qualifications, experience and reputation.

(5) Assess the reasonableness of the valuation by comparison with any similar properties which may have recently changed hands on the open market.

(v) *Deposit for new equipment*

(1) Agree the payment of the deposit to the contract for purchase of the equipment.

(2) Confirm the existence of the plant following its delivery on 31 October 20X5 as it is unlikely that the audit work will have been completed by that date.

2 OTHER FIXED ASSETS

2.1 The key assertions relating to intangibles are **existence** (not so much 'do they exist?', but, 'are they genuinely assets?') and **valuation**. They will therefore be audited with reference to criteria laid down in the financial reporting standards. As only purchased goodwill or intangibles or intangibles with a readily ascertainable market value can be capitalised, **audit evidence should be available** (purchase invoices or specialist valuations). Audit of **amortisation** will be similar to the audit of depreciation.

AUDIT PROGRAMME: OTHER FIXED ASSETS

Goodwill

- Agree the consideration to sales agreement
- Check that asset valuation is reasonable
- Agree that the calculation is correct
- Review the amortisation calculation and check it is correct
- Ensure valuation of goodwill is reasonable/there has been no impairment

Intangibles

- Agree purchased intangibles to purchase documentation
- Review specialist valuation of intangibles and ensure they are reasonable
- Review amortisation calculations and ensure they are correct

Research and development costs

- Check that capitalised development costs conform to SSAP 13 criteria
- Confirm feasibility and viability by reference to budgets
- Check amortisation calculation, to ensure it commences with production/is reasonable

Chapter roundup

- The disclosure and valuation requirements for all fixed assets under CA 1985 are relevant here.
- Key areas when testing **tangible fixed assets** are:
  - **Confirmation** of ownership
  - **Inspection** of fixed assets
  - **Valuation** by third parties
  - **Adequacy** of **depreciation** rates

Quick quiz

1 Complete the control procedures.

(a) Acquisitions are properly ....

(b) Disposals are .... and proceeds ....

(c) Security .... over fixed assets are ....

(d) .... is reviewed ....

2 Complete the table, showing which tests are designed to provide evidence about which financial statement assertion.

Completeness	**Existence**
Valuation	**Rights and obligations**

(a) Inspect assets

(b) Verify to valuation certificate

(c) Refer to title deeds

(d) Compare assets in ledger to fixed asset register

(e) Review depreciation rates

(f) Verify material on self-constructed asset to invoices

(g) Examine invoices after the year end

(h) Review repairs in general ledger

3 Name two tests to confirm rights and obligations concerning charges and commitments.

1 ....

2 ....

Answers to quick quiz

1 (a) authorised
(b) authorised, accounted for
(c) arrangements, sufficient
(d) depreciation, every year

2

Completeness	Existence
(d) Compare assets in ledger to register (h) Review repairs in general ledger	(a) Inspect assets
Valuation	**Rights and obligations**
(b) Verify to valuation certificate (e) Review valuation rates (f) Verify material on self-constructed assets to invoice	(c) Refer to title deeds (g) Examine invoices after the year end

3
- **Review for evidence** of charges in statutory books and by company search
- **Review leases** of leasehold properties to ensure that company has fulfilled covenants therein
- **Examine invoices received after year-end, orders and minutes** for evidence of capital commitments

Now try the question below from the Exam Question Bank

Number	Level	Marks	Time
13	Exam	20	36 mins

Chapter 14

STOCKS AND WORK IN PROGRESS

Introduction

No balance sheet audit area creates more potential problems for the auditors than that of stock.

Closing stock does not normally form an integrated part of the double entry bookkeeping system and hence an under or overstatement may not be detected from tests in other audit areas. Also:

(a) Stock and work in progress often represent a significant asset on the balance sheet.

(b) The value of closing stock and work in progress has a direct impact on profit.

(c) Stock is often made up of a large number of diverse items with different unit values.

(d) The valuation of work in progress and allocation of overheads to stock is often a subjective process

(e) Verification of existence involves attendance at the stock-take and extensive follow-up.

(f) The provision for slow-moving and obsolete stock is another subjective area.

(g) The physical control of stock is often difficult because of multiple locations, stock held by third parties and so on.

(h) Different valuation methods are allowed under SSAP 9 *Stocks and long-term contracts*, although they must be applied consistently.

The four main elements of the audit of stocks (completeness, existence, rights and obligations (ownership) and valuation) require careful consideration.

As stock is often the most difficult area in practice for auditors it is also very important in exams. Questions could be on any area covered in this chapter, or a combination of them. The stocktake and valuation were examined in the pilot paper.

1 REGULATORY ASPECTS OF STOCK

1.1 Three sources of rules

- Companies Act 1985 (disclosure, basis of valuation)
- SSAP 9 *Stocks and long-term contracts* (departure, disclosure and valuation)
- Auditing standards/guidelines (audit approach, valuation)

Companies Act 1985

1.2 In terms of **valuation**, CA 1985 states that all current assets should be stated at the lower of their **purchase price** and their **net realisable value**. 'Purchase price' can be interpreted as 'fair value'. 'Production cost' is determined according to the provision of SSAP 9.

1.3 CA 1985 allows certain methods of identifying cost, because it recognises that it can be impossible to identify cost for each item individually. The methods allowed are:

- First in first out (FIFO)
- Last in first out (LIFO)
- Weighted average cost
- Other similar methods, such as standard cost

SSAP 9 does **not** allow LIFO as a method of valuation.

SSAP 9 *Stocks and long-term contracts*

KEY TERMS

Cost is defined by SSAP 9 as that expenditure which has been incurred in the normal course of business in bringing the product or service to its present location and condition. This includes the purchase price plus production costs (costs of conversion) appropriate to the location and condition of the stock.

Net realisable value as the estimated or actual selling price, (net of trade discounts but before settlement discounts,) less all further costs to completion and all cost to be incurred in marketing, selling and distributing the good or service.

1.4 Production costs (costs of conversion) include:

- Costs specifically attributable to units of production
- Production overheads
- Other overheads attributable to bringing the product or service to its present location and condition

Question: Difficulties of auditing stock

Give some of the main reasons why stock and work in progress is one of the most difficult areas of the audit.

Answer

See Introduction.

2 THE STOCKTAKE

Pilot paper, 6/03

Exam focus point

You **must** have a thorough knowledge of audit procedures before, during and after the stocktake

Responsibilities in relation to stock	
Management	Ensure stock figure in accounts • Represents stock that **exists** • Includes all stock **owned** Ensure accounting records include **stocktaking statements.**
Auditors	**Obtain sufficient audit evidence** about stock figure from • Stock records • Stock control systems • Results of stocktaking • Test counts by auditors **Attend stocktaking if** stock is material and evidence of existence is provided by management stocktake.

Methods of stocktaking

2.1 A business may take stock by one or a combination of the following methods.

(a) **Stocktaking** at the **year-end**

From the viewpoint of the auditor, this is often the best method.

(b) **Stocktaking before** or **after** the **year-end**

This will provide audit evidence of varying reliability depending on:

- The **length of time** between the stocktake and the year-end; the greater the time period, the less the value of audit evidence
- The **business's system** of **internal controls**
- The **quality of records** of stock movements in the period between the stocktake and the year-end

(c) **Continuous stocktaking** where management has a programme of stock-counting throughout the year

2.2 If continuous stocktaking is used, auditors will check that management:

(a) Ensures that **all stock lines** are **counted at least once a year.**

(b) Maintains **adequate stock records** that are kept up-to-date. Auditors may compare sales and purchase transactions with stock movements, and carry out other tests on the stock records, for example checking casts and classification of stock.

(c) Has **satisfactory procedures** for **stocktaking** and **test-counting**. Auditors should confirm the stocktaking arrangements and instructions are as rigorous as those for a year-end stocktake by reviewing instructions and observing counts. Auditors will be particularly concerned with **cut-off**, that there are no stock movements whilst the count is taking place, and stock records are updated up until the time of the stocktakes.

(d) **Investigates** and **corrects** all **material differences**. Reasons for differences should be recorded and any necessary corrective action taken. All corrections to stock movements should be **authorised** by a manager who has not been involved in the detailed work; these procedures are necessary to guard against the possibility that stock records may be adjusted to conceal shortages. Auditors should check that the procedures are being operated.

AUDIT PROGRAMME: CONTINUOUS STOCKTAKING
Attend one of the stock counts (to observe and confirm that instructions are being adhered to)
Follow up the **stock counts attended** to compare quantities counted by the auditors with the stock records, obtaining and verifying explanations for any differences, and checking that the client has reconciled count records with book stock records
Review the **year's stock counts** to confirm the extent of counting, the treatment of discrepancies and the overall accuracy of records, if matters are not satisfactory, auditors will only be able to gain sufficient assurance by a full count at the year-end
Assuming a full count is not necessary at the year-end, **compare** the **listing of stock with** the **detailed stock records**, and carry out other procedures (**cut-off, analytical review**) to gain further comfort

The main stocktaking procedures

2.3 Attendance at a stocktake gives evidence of the **existence** and **apparent ownership** of stock. It also gives evidence of the **completeness** of stock, as do the followup tests to ensure all stock sheets were included in the final count.

PLANNING STOCKTAKE	
Gain knowledge	**Review** previous year's **arrangements** **Discuss** with **management stock-taking arrangements** and **significant changes**
Assess key factors	The **nature** and **volume** of the **stocks** The **identification** of **high value items** **Method of accounting for stocks** **Location** of stock and how it affects stock control and recording **Internal control** and **accounting systems** to identify potential areas of difficulty
Plan procedures	**Ensure** a **representative selection** of **locations, stocks** and **procedures** are covered Ensure sufficient attention is given to **high value items** **Arrange to obtain** from **third parties confirmation** of stocks they hold Consider the need for **expert help**

REVIEW OF STOCK-TAKING INSTRUCTIONS	
Organisation of count	**Supervision** by senior staff including senior staff not normally involved with stock **Tidying** and **marking** stock to help counting **Restriction** and **control** of the production process and stock movements during the count **Identification of damaged, obsolete, slow-moving, third party** and **returnable** stock
Counting	**Systematic counting** to ensure all stock is counted Teams of **two counters,** with one counting and the other checking or two **independent counts**
Recording	**Serial numbering, control** and **return** of all stock sheets Stock sheets being **completed** in **ink** and **signed** **Information** to be recorded on the **count records** (location and identity, count units, quantity counted, conditions of items, stage reached in production process) Recording of **quantity, conditions** and **stage of production** of **work-in-progress** Recording of last numbers of **goods inwards** and **outwards** records and of internal transfer records **Reconciliation** with **stock records** and **investigation** and correction of any **differences**

AUDIT PROGRAMME: ATTENDANCE AT STOCKTAKING

- **Check** the **client's staff** are following instructions
- **Make test counts** to ensure procedures and internal controls are working properly, if the results of the test counts are not satisfactory, the auditors may request stock be recounted
- **Ensure** that the **procedures** for **identifying damaged, obsolete** and **slow-moving** stock **operate** properly; the auditors should obtain information about the stocks' condition, age, usage and in the case of work in progress, its stage of completion
- **Confirm** that **stock held** on behalf of **third parties** is separately identified and accounted for
- **Conclude** whether the **stocktaking** has been **properly carried out** and is sufficiently reliable as a basis for determining the existence of stocks
- **Consider** whether any **amendment** is **necessary** to subsequent **audit procedures**
- **Gain** an **overall impression** of the levels and values of stocks held so that the auditors may, in due course, judge whether the figure for stocks appearing in the financial statements is reasonable

2.4 When carrying out test counts the auditors should select items from the count records and from the physical stocks and check one to the other, to confirm the accuracy of the count records. The auditors should concentrate on high value stock.

2.5 The auditors' working papers should include:

- Details of their **observations** and **tests**
- The manner in which **points** that are **relevant** and **material** to the stocks being counted or measured have been dealt with by the client
- Instances where the **client's procedures** have **not been satisfactorily carried out**
- **Items for subsequent testing,** such as photocopies of (or extracts from) rough stocksheets
- **Details** of the **sequence** of **stocksheets**
- The **auditors' conclusions**

2.6 After the stocktaking, the matters recorded in the auditors' working papers at the time of the count or measurement should be followed up. Key tests include the following.

AUDIT PROGRAMME: FOLLOWING UP THE STOCKTAKE
• **Trace items** that were **test counted** during the stocktake to final stocksheets
• **Check all count** records have been **included** in final stocksheets
• **Check final stocksheets** are **supported by** count records
• **Ensure** that **continuous stock records** have been **adjusted** to the amounts physically counted or measured, and that differences have been investigated
• **Confirm cut-off** by using details of the last serial number of goods inward and outwards notes; and of movements during the stocktake
• **Check replies** from **third parties** about stock held by or for them
• **Confirm** the client's final **valuation** of stock has been calculated correctly
• **Follow up queries** and **notifying problems** to management

Question: Stocktake

In connection with your examination of the financial statements of Camry Products Ltd for the year ended 31 March 20X9, you are reviewing the plans for a physical stock count at the company's warehouse on 31 March 20X9. The company assembles domestic appliances, and stocks of finished appliances, unassembled parts and sundry stocks are stored in the warehouse which is adjacent to the company's assembly plant. The plant will continue to produce goods during the stock count until 5pm on 31 March 20X9. On 30 March 20X9, the warehouse staff will deliver the estimated quantities of unassembled parts and sundry stocks which will be required for production for 31 March 20X9; however, emergency requisitions by the factory will be filled on 31 March. During the stock count, the warehouse staff will continue to receive parts and sundry stocks, and to despatch finished appliances. Appliances which are completed on 31 March 20X9 will remain in the assembly plant until after the physical stock count has been completed.

Required

(a) List the principal procedures which the auditors should carry out when planning attendance at a company's stocktake.

(b) Describe the procedures which Camry Products Ltd should establish in order to ensure that all stock items are counted and that no item of stock is counted twice.

Answer

(a) **Planning attendance**

(i) Review previous year's audit working papers and discuss any developments in the year with management.

(ii) Obtain and review a copy of the company's stocktaking instructions.

(iii) Arrange attendance at stockcount planning meetings, with the consent of management.

(iv) Gain an understanding of the nature of the stock and of any special stocktaking problems this is likely to present, for example liquid in tanks, scrap in piles.

(v) Consider whether expert involvement is likely to be required as a result of any circumstances noted in (iv) above.

(vi) Obtain a full list of all locations at which stock is held, including an estimate of the amount and value of stock held at different locations.

(vii) Using the results of the above steps, plan for audit attendance by appropriately experienced audit staff at all locations where material stocks are held, subject to other factors (for example rotational auditing, reliance on internal controls).

(viii) Consider the impact of internal controls upon the nature and timing of the stocktaking attendance.

(ix) Ascertain whether stocks are held by third parties and if so make arrangements to obtain written confirmation of them or, if necessary, to attend the stocktake of them.

(b) Procedures to ensure a complete count and to prevent double-counting are particularly important in this case because stock movements will continue throughout the stocktake.

(i) Clear instructions should be given as to stocktaking procedures, and an official, preferably not someone normally responsible for stock, should be given responsibility for organising the count and dealing with queries.

(ii) Before the count, all locations should be tidied and stock should be laid out in an orderly manner.

(iii) All stock should be clearly identified and should be marked after being counted by a tag or indelible mark, so that it is evident that it has been counted.

(iv) Prenumbered stock sheets should be issued to counters and should be accounted for at the end of the stocktake.

(v) Counters should be given responsibility for specific areas of the warehouse. Each area should be subject to a recount.

(vi) A separate record should be kept of all goods received or issued during the day (for example by noting the GRN or despatch note numbers involved).

(vii) Goods received on the day should be physically segregated until the count has been completed.

(viii) Similarly, goods due to be despatched on the day should be identified in advance and moved to a special area or clearly marked so that they are not inadvertently counted in stock as well as being included in sales.

---

3 CUT-OFF

3.1 Cut-off is most critical to the accurate recording of transactions in a manufacturing enterprise at particular point in the accounting cycle as follows:

- The **point of purchase** and **receipt of goods and services**
- The **requisitioning of raw materials** for production
- The **transfer of completed work-in-progress** to finished goods stocks
- The **sale and despatch of finished goods**

3.2 The auditors should consider whether management has instituted adequate cut-off procedures: procedures intended to ensure that movements into, within and out of stocks are properly identified and reflected in the accounting records.

3.3 **Purchase invoices** should be recorded as liabilities only if the goods were received prior to the stock count. A schedule of 'goods received not invoiced' should be prepared, and items on the list should be accrued for in the accounts.

3.4 **Sales cut-off** is generally more straightforward to achieve correctly than purchases cut-off. Invoices for goods despatched after the stock count should not appear in the profit and loss accounts for the period.

3.5 Prior to the stock-take management should make arrangements for cut-off to be properly applied.

(a) Appropriate systems of recording of receipts and despatches of goods are in place, and also a system for documenting materials requisitions. Goods received notes (GRNs) and goods despatched notes (GDNs) should be sequentially pre-numbered.

(b) Final GRN and GDN and materials requisition numbers are noted. These numbers can then be used to check subsequently that purchases and sales have been recorded in the current period.

(c) Arrangements should be made to ensure that the cut-off arrangement for stock held by third parties are satisfactory.

3.6 There should ideally be no movement of stocks during the stock count. Preferably, receipts and despatches should be suspended for the full period of the count. It may not be practicable to suspend all deliveries, in which case any deliveries which are received during the count should be segregated from other stocks and carefully documented.

AUDIT PROGRAMME: CUT OFF

Stocktake

- Record **all movement notes** relating to the period, including:
  - All interdepartmental requisition numbers
  - The last goods received notes(s) and despatch note(s) prior to the count
  - The first goods received notes(s) and despatch note(s) after the count
- **Observe** whether **correct cut-off procedures** are being **followed** in the despatch and receiving areas
- **Discuss procedures** with **company staff** performing the count to ensure they are understood
- **Ensure** that **no goods finished** on the day of the count are **transferred** to the warehouse

Final audit

- **Match up** the **goods received notes** with **purchase invoices** and ensure the **liability** has been **recorded** in the **correct period** (only goods received before the year end should be recorded as purchases)
- **Match up** the **goods despatched notes** to **sales invoices** and ensure the **income** has been **recorded** in the **correct period** (only stocks despatched before the year end should be recorded as sales)
- **Match up** the **requisition notes** to the **work in progress** figures for the receiving department to ensure correctly recorded

Question: Cut off

Using the information in the last question, describe the audit procedures you would carry out at the time of the stocktake in order to ensure that cut-off is correct.

Answer

In order to ensure that stock cut-off is correct, the following procedures should be carried out.

(a) Make a record during the stocktaking attendance of all movement notes relating to the period, including:

- All interdepartmental requisition numbers
- The last goods received note and despatch note prior to the count
- The first goods received note and despatch note after the count. This information can be used for subsequent cut-off tests

(b) Observe whether correct cut-off procedures are being followed in the despatch and receiving areas. Discuss procedures with company staff performing the count to ensure they are understood.

(c) Ensure that no goods finished on the day of the count are transferred to the warehouse.

4 STOCK VALUATION **Pilot paper, 12/02**

Exam focus point

Valuation of stock has always been a very popular exam topic. You must know the audit work needed to confirm valuation of stock when overheads have been absorbed, and to confirm stock is stated at the lower of cost and net realisable value.

Knowledge of the requirements of SSAP 9 is essential when considering absorption of overheads, hence we have gone into detail about these provisions. You should refer back to your Paper 2.5 notes if you are still unsure about this area.

4.1 Auditors must understand how the company determines the cost of an item for stock valuation purposes. Cost should include an appropriate proportion of overheads, in accordance with SSAP 9.

4.2 There are several ways of determining cost. Auditors must ensure that the company is **applying** the method **consistently** and that each year the method used **gives** a **fair approximation** to cost. They may need to support this by additional procedures such as:

- **Reviewing price** changes near the year end
- **Ageing the stock** held
- **Checking gross profit** margins to reliable management accounts

Valuation of raw materials and brought in components

4.3 The auditors should check that the correct prices have been used to value raw materials and brought in components valued at actual costs by **referring to suppliers' invoices**. The stock valuation may include unrealised profit if stock is valued at the latest invoice price. Reference to suppliers' invoice will also provide the auditors with assurance as regards ownership.

4.4 If standard costs are used, auditors should **check the basis of the standards, compare standard costs** with **actual costs** and **confirm** that **variances** are being **treated appropriately.**

Valuation of work in progress and finished goods (other than long-term contract work in progress)

4.5 As we saw above, SSAP 9 defines 'cost' as comprising the cost of purchase plus the costs of conversion (production costs).

4.6 The audit procedures will depend on the methods used by the client to value work in progress and finished goods, and on the adequacy of the system of internal control.

4.7 The auditors should consider what tests they can carry out to check the reasonableness of the valuation of finished goods and work in progress. **Analytical procedures** may assist comparisons being made with stock items and stock categories from the previous year's stock summaries.

AUDIT PROGRAMME: STOCK PRODUCTION COSTS
• For materials: ◦ **Check** the **valuation** of raw materials to **invoices** and **price lists** ◦ **Confirm appropriate basis** of **valuation** (for example, FIFO) is being used ◦ **Confirm correct quantities** are being used when calculating raw material value in work in progress and finished goods • For labour costs: ◦ **Check labour costs** to **wage records** ◦ **Review standard labour costs** in the light of actual costs and production ◦ **Check labour hours** to **time summaries**

4.8 The auditors should ensure that the client includes a proportion of overheads **appropriate** to **bringing the stock to its present location and condition**. The basis of overhead allocation should be:

- **Consistent with prior years**
- **Calculated on the normal level of production activity**

4.9 Thus, overheads arising from **reduced levels** of **activity**, **idle time** or **inefficient production** should be written off to the profit and loss account, rather than being included in stock.

GUIDELINE: ALLOCATION OF OVERHEADS
(a) All **abnormal conversion** costs (such as idle capacity) must be **excluded**. (b) Where **firm sales contracts** have been entered into for the provision of goods or services to customer's specification, **design, marketing and selling costs** incurred before manufacture may be **included**. (c) Overheads are **classified by function** when being allocated (eg whether they are a function of production, marketing, selling or administration). (d) The **costs of general management**, as distinct from functional management, are not directly related to current production and are, therefore, **excluded**. (e) The allocation of costs of **central service departments** should depend on the function or functions that the department is serving. **Only** those costs that can reasonably be allocated to the **production function** should be **included**. (f) In determining what constitutes '**normal**' **activity** the following factors need to be considered: • The volume of production which the production facilities are **designed to achieve** • The **budgeted level** of **activity** for the year under review and for the ensuing year • The **level of activity achieved** both in the **year under review** and in **previous years** Although temporary changes in the level of activity may be ignored, persistent variation should lead to revision of the previous norm.

Question: Cost of stock

Give a brief list of general procedures the auditors might undertake to determine whether a company is operating at a normal level of activity.

Answer

The procedures, in brief, are likely to be as follows.

(a) Compare the level of production with previous years.

(b) Compare production/sales with budget.

(c) Investigate overtime levels of production staff, compared to previous years.

(d) Enquire of management about any changes in production during the year, and investigate:

(i) Board/management minutes
(ii) New machinery/production space

4.10 Difficulty may be experienced if the client operates a system of total overhead absorption. It will be necessary for those overheads that are of a general, non-productive nature to be identified and excluded from the stock valuation.

Cost vs NRV

4.11 Auditors should **compare cost and net realisable value** for each item of stock. Where this is impracticable, the comparison may be done by stock group or category.

4.12 Net realisable value is likely to be less than cost when there has been:

- An **increase in costs** or a fall in selling price
- **Physical deterioration** of stocks
- **Obsolescence** of products
- A **decision** as part of **marketing strategy** to manufacture and sell products at a loss
- **Errors in production or purchasing**

AUDIT PROGRAMME: STOCK – COST V NRV
• **Review and test the client's system** for **identifying slow-moving**, obsolete or damaged stock
• **Follow up** any such **items** that were **identified** at the **stocktaking**, ensuring that the client has made adequate provision to write down the items to net realisable value
• **Examine stock records** to identify slow-moving items (it may be possible to incorporate into a computer audit program certain tests and checks such as listing items whose value or quantity has not moved over the previous year)
• **Examine the prices** at which finished goods have been sold after the year-end and ascertain whether any finished goods items need to be reduced below cost
• **Review quantities of goods sold after the year end** to determine that year end stock has, or will be, realised
• If significant quantities of finished goods stock remain unsold for an unusual time after the year-end, **consider** the **need** to **make appropriate provision**

4.13 For work in progress, the **ultimate selling price** should be **compared** with the **carrying value** at the year end plus **costs** to be **incurred** after the year end to bring work in progress to a finished state.

Question: Cost v NRV

Your firm is the auditor of Arnold Electrical Ltd and you have been asked to audit the valuation of the company's stock at 31 May 20X1 in accordance with SSAP 9 *Stocks and long-term contracts*. Arnold Electrical Ltd operates from a single store and purchases domestic electrical equipment from wholesalers and manufacturers and sells them to the general public. These products include video and audio equipment, washing machines, refrigerators and freezers. In addition, it sells small items such as electrical plugs, magnetic tape for video and audio recorders, records and compact discs.

A full stocktake was carried out at the year end, and you are satisfied that the stock was counted accurately and there are no cut-off errors. Because of the limited time available between the year end and the completion of the audit, the company has valued the stock at cost by recording the selling price and deducting the normal gross profit margin. Stock which the company believes to be worth less than cost has been valued at net realisable value. The selling price used is that on the item in the store when it was counted.

The stock has been divided into three categories.

(a) Video and audio equipment: televisions, video recorders, video cameras and audio equipment
(b) Domestic equipment: washing machines, refrigerators and freezers
(c) Sundry stocks: electrical plugs, magnetic tapes and compact discs

The normal gross profit margin for each of these categories has been determined and this figure has been used to calculate the cost of the stock (by deducting the gross profit margin from the selling price). In answering the question you should assume there are no sales taxes (for example, value added tax in the UK).

Required

(a) List and describe the audit work you will carry out to check that the stock has been correctly valued at cost.

(b) List and describe the audit work you will carry out to:

  (i) To find stock which should be valued at net realisable value
  (ii) To check that net realisable value for this stock is correct

(c) List and describe the other work you will perform to check that the stock value is accurate.

Note. In answering the question you are only required to check that the price per unit of the stock is correct. You should assume that the stock quantities are accurate and there are no purchases or sales cut-off errors.

Answer

(a) This method of valuation at cost is permitted by SSAP 9, but it is usually applied to large retail concerns which stock thousands of low value items, for example supermarket chains. This method is only permitted when it can be shown that it gives a reasonable approximation of the actual cost.

The following tests should be performed to ensure that the stock is correctly valued at cost.

(i) Obtain a schedule of the client calculations of the gross profit margins. Check the mathematical accuracy and consider the reliability of all sources of information used in the calculation.

(ii) Where the normal overall gross margin has been used, check the reasonableness of the figure by comparing it to the monthly management accounts for the year and last year's published accounts.

Test a sample of items to make sure that gross profit does not vary too much across all items of stock (which is unlikely for Arnold Electrical). The test will compare selling price to purchase price.

(iii) If a weighted average gross margin has been used, check that the weighting is correct in terms of the proportion of each type of product in closing stock.

(iv) Select a sample of high value stock lines and check the reasonableness of the gross profit estimate by calculating the gross profit for each of those lines. Sales price will be compared to stock sheets and to sale prices in the shop at the year end. Cost will be checked by examining purchase invoices. The weighted average profit margin for the selected lines can then be calculated and compared to the gross margin applied to the whole stock. *(Note.* High value stock lines may consist of individual items with a high selling price, or a large number of low value items.)

(v) Overvaluation of slow moving stock is possible when the prices of those items are affected by inflation. To check this, examine the stock sheets for any slow moving items (or ask the management of the company or use my own observation). Compare the value of the stock at the end of the accounting period to cost according to purchase invoices. If an overvaluation has occurred it should be quantified.

(vi) Check whether any goods were being offered for sale at reduced prices at the year end. If the reduced price is greater than cost, the use of an average gross profit percentage will cause stock to be undervalued. This undervaluation must be quantified. If full selling price was used in the calculation then the problem will not arise. Check a sample of stock items to sales invoices issued around the year end to make sure that the correct price was used in the stock costing calculation.

(b) (i) Stock which may be worth less than cost will include:

(1) Slow moving stock
(2) Obsolete or superseded stock
(3) Seconds stock and items that have been damaged
(4) Stock which is being, or is soon likely to be, sold at reduced prices
(5) Discontinued stock lines

Finished goods where the selling price is less than cost will be valued at net realisable value. This is defined as the actual or estimated selling price less costs to completion and marketing, selling and distribution expenses.

To identify stock which may be worth less than cost the following work will be carried out.

(1) Examine the computerised stock control system and list items showing an unacceptably low turnover rate. An unacceptable rate of turnover may be different for different items, but stock representing more than six months' sales is likely to qualify.

(2) Check the stock printout for items already described as seconds or recorded as damaged.

(3) Discuss with management the current position regarding slow moving stock and their plans and expectations in respect of products that may be discontinued. The standard system must be carefully considered and estimates obtained of the likely selling price of existing stock. The most likely outcome regarding the use and value of discontinued components must be decided.

(4) At the stocktake, look for stock which is dusty, inaccessible and in general not moving and mark on the stock sheets.

(5) Find out whether any lines are unreliable and therefore frequently returned for repairs as these may be unpopular.

(6) Check with the trade press or other sources to see whether any of the equipment is out of date.

(ii) Determining the net realisable value of stock is a difficult task and involves management in judging how much stock can be sold and at what price, together with deciding whether to sell off raw materials and components separately or to assemble them into finished products. Each separate type of stock item should be considered separately in deciding on the level of prudent provision.

To determine the net realisable value of the stock the following tests should be carried out.

(1) Find the actual selling prices from the latest sales invoice. For items still selling, invoices will be very recent, but for slow moving and obsolete items the invoiced prices will be out of date and allowance will have to be made for this (probably a reduction in estimating the most likely sale price of the stock concerned).

(2) Estimate the value of marketing, selling and distribution expenses using past figures for the types of finished goods concerned as a base. I would update and check for reasonableness against the most recent accounting records.

(3) Discuss with management what selling prices are likely to be where there is little past evidence. Costs to completion will be questioned where these are difficult to estimate and where there are any unusual assembly, selling or distribution problems.

(c) The following procedures would also be performed to check the value of stock at the year end.

(i) Compare current results with prior year(s). This would include gross profit margins, sales and stock turnover. Marked variations from the current year's results should be investigated.

(ii) Consider the effects of new technology and new fashions. The electrical appliance business will be exposed to obsolescence problems. Quantify any necessary write down.

(iii) Compare selling prices to those charged elsewhere. If the prices elsewhere are lower, than the distortion in selling price might affect the value of the stock of Arnold Electrical.

Alternatively, if prices elsewhere are higher, then the company's prices may occasionally fall below cost. Again, any adjustment discovered to be necessary must be quantified.

(iv) Compare the valuation of stock this year to that at the end of last year. This will be particularly useful for lines held at both dates. If the values are comparable, taking account of inflation, then the current valuation is more likely to be correct.

(v) Sale prices should be checked as long after the year end as possible, to make sure that prices were not kept artificially high over the year end and then reduced at a later date. Stock turnover should also be examined on this same basis.

Chapter roundup

- The audit of stocks and work in progress is difficult and time consuming, but it is of primary importance.
- The **valuation** and **disclosure** rules for stock are laid down in SSAP 9 and CA 1985.
- An old APC guideline on the auditors' attendance at the stocktake still demonstrates best practice.
- Stocktake procedures are vital as they provide evidence which cannot be obtained elsewhere or at any other time about the quantities and conditions of stocks and work in progress.
  - Before the stocktake the auditors should ensure audit **coverage** of **stock-taking** is **appropriate**, and that the client's **stock-taking instructions** have been reviewed.
  - During the stocktake the auditors should **check stock count** is being carried out according to instructions, carry out **test counts**, and watch for **third party, slow moving stock, cut-off problems.**
  - After the stocktake the auditors should check that **final stock sheets** have been **properly compiled** from stock count records and that **book stock** has been appropriately adjusted.
- Auditors should check **cut-off** by noting the **serial numbers** of items received and despatched just before and after the year-end, and subsequently checking that they have been included in the correct period.
- Auditing the valuation of stock includes:
  - Checking the **allocation of overheads** is appropriate
  - Confirming stock is carried at the lower of **cost** and **net realisable value**

Quick quiz

1 Complete the definition, using the words given below.

…………………….. is defined by SSAP …… as that expenditure which ahs been incurred in the ………… …………………….. ……….. ……………………… in bringing the product or service to its present location and condition. This includes the ……………………….. ……………………… plus …………… …………….. (costs of conversion) appropriate to bringing the ………… to its present location and condition.

stock of business, normal price, purchase cost, cost, 9, course, production

2 Name three methods of stocktaking

1 …………………………………………………………………

2 …………………………………………………………………

3 …………………………………………………………………

3 When should the following stocktaking tests take place?

(a) Check client staff are following instructions
(b) Review previous year's stocktaking arrangements
(c) Assess method of accounting for stocks
(d) Trace counted items to final stock sheets
(e) Check replies from third parties about stock held for them
(f) Conclude as to whether stocktake has been properly carried out
(g) Gain an overall impression of levels and values of stocks
(h) Consider the need for expert help

BEFORE	DURING	AFTER

4 Name four points in the accounting cycle when cut off is critical.

1 ………………………………………………………

2 ………………………………………………………

3 ………………………………………………………

4 ………………………………………………………

5 Give four reasons for the net realisable value of stock to fall below cost.

1 ………………………………………………………

2 ………………………………………………………

3 ………………………………………………………

4 ………………………………………………………

Answers to quick quiz

1 cost, 9, normal course of business, purchase price, production cost, stock

2
- Year end
- Pre/post year end
- Continuous

3 (a) DURING (b) BEFORE (c) BEFORE (d) AFTER
(e) AFTER (f) DURING (g) DURING (h) BEFORE

4
- The **point of purchase** and **receipt of goods and services**
- The **requisitioning of raw materials** for production
- The **transfer of completed work-in-progress** to finished goods stocks
- The **sale and despatch of finished goods**

5
- An **increase in costs** or a fall in selling price
- **Physical deterioration** of stocks
- **Obsolescence** of products
- A **decision** as part of **marketing strategy** to manufacture and sell products at a loss
- **Errors in production or purchasing**

Now try the questions below from the Exam Question Bank

Number	Level	Marks	Time
14	Exam	20	36 mins

Chapter 15

DEBTORS AND PREPAYMENTS

Introduction

Debtors will generally be a material figure on a company's balance sheet, and must therefore be given due weight.

You should make sure that you are fully conversant with the 'standard' procedures such as the **debtors' circularisation**. The debtors' circularisation is primarily designed to test the client's entitlement to receive the debt, not the debtor's ability to pay that is, it tests **existence** and **rights**, not **valuation**. Auditors also need to consider **cut-off** for debtors.

Debtors were examined in conjunction with sales system controls in the pilot paper. In December 2001, the debtors' circularisation was examined.

1 DEBTORS

Debtors' listing and aged analysis

1.1 Much of the auditors' detailed work will be based on a selection of debtors' balances chosen from a listing of sales ledger balances, prepared by the client or auditors. Ideally the list should be aged, showing the period or periods of time money has been owed. The following substantive procedures to check the **completeness** and **accuracy** of a client-prepared list.

- **Check** the **balances** from the **individual sales ledger accounts** to the **list of balances** and vice versa
- **Check** the **total** of the **list** to the **sales ledger control account**
- **Cast** (that is, add up) the **list of balances** and the **sales ledger control account**
- **Confirm** whether **list of balances reconciles** with the **sales ledger control account**

The debtors' circularisation 12/01

Objectives of circularisation

1.2 The verification of trade debtors by direct circularisation is the normal means of providing audit evidence to satisfy the objective of checking whether debtors exist and owe *bona fide* amounts due to the company (**existence, rights** and **obligations**)

1.3 Circularisation will produce for the current audit file a written statement from each respondent debtor that the amount owed at the date of the circularisation is correct. This is, *prima facie*, reliable audit evidence, being from an independent source and in 'documentary' form.

Timing

1.4 Ideally the circularisation should take place immediately after the year-end and hence cover the year-end balances to be included in the balance sheet. However, time constraints may make it impossible to achieve this ideal.

1.5 In these circumstances it may be acceptable to carry out the circularisation **prior to the year-end** provided that circularisation is no more than three months before the year-end and internal controls are strong.

Client's mandate

1.6 Circularisation is essentially an act of the **client**, who alone can authorise third parties to divulge information to the auditors.

1.7 Should the client refuse to co-operate in the circularisation the auditors will inevitably consider whether they should **qualify** their **audit report**, as they may not be able to satisfy themselves, by means of other audit procedures, as to the validity and accuracy of the debtor balances.

Positive v negative circularisation

1.8 When circularisation is undertaken the method of requesting information from the debtor may be either 'positive' or 'negative'.

- Under the **positive** method the debtor is requested to confirm the accuracy of the balance shown or state in what respect he is in disagreement.

- Under the **negative** method the debtor is requested to reply if the amount stated is disputed.

1.9 The positive method is generally preferable as it is designed to encourage definite replies from those circularised.

1.10 The negative method may be used if the client has good internal control, with a large number of small accounts. In some circumstances, say where there is a small number of large accounts and a large number of small accounts, a combination of both methods, as noted above, may be appropriate.

1.11 A specimen 'positive' confirmation letter is shown below.

1.12 The statements will normally be prepared by the client's staff, from which point the auditors, as a safeguard against the possibility of fraudulent manipulation, must maintain strict control over the checking and despatch of the statements.

1.13 Precautions must also be taken to ensure that undelivered items are returned, not to the client, but to the auditors' own office for follow-up by them.

MANUFACTURING CO LIMITED
15 South Street
London

Date

Messrs (debtor)

In accordance with the request of our auditors, Messrs Arthur Daley & Co, we ask that you kindly confirm to them directly your indebtedness to us at (insert date) which, according to our records, amounted to £.......... as shown by the enclosed statement.

If the above amount is in agreement with your records, please sign in the space provided below and return this letter direct to our auditors in the enclosed stamped addressed envelope.

If the amount is not in agreement with your records, please notify our auditors directly of the amount shown by your records, and if possible detail on the reverse of this letter full particulars of the difference.

Yours faithfully,

For Manufacturing Co Limited

Reference No: ....

....

(Tear off slip)

The amount shown above is/is not * in agreement with our records as at

Account No	....	Signature	....
Date	....	Title or position	....

* The position according to our records is shown overleaf.

Note:

- The letter is on the client's paper, signed by the client.
- A copy of the statement is attached.
- The reply is sent directly to the auditor in a pre-paid envelope.

Sample selection

1.14 Auditors will normally only circularise a sample of debtors. If this sample is to yield a meaningful result it must be based upon a complete list of all debtor accounts. In addition, when constructing the sample, the following classes of account should receive special attention:

- **Old unpaid accounts**
- **Accounts written off** during the period under review
- **Accounts with credit balances**
- **Accounts settled by round sum payments**

Similarly, the following should not be overlooked:

- **Accounts with nil balances**
- **Accounts which** have been **paid** by the date of the examination

Follow up procedures

1.15 Auditors will have to carry out further work in relation to those debtors who:

- **Disagree** with the **balance stated** (positive and negative circularisation)
- **Do not respond** (positive circularisation only)

1.16 In the case of disagreements, the debtor response should have identified specific amounts which are disputed.

REASONS FOR DISAGREEMENTS
There is a **dispute** between the client and the customer. The reasons for the dispute would have to be identified, and provision made if appropriate against the debt.
Cut-off problems exist, because the client records the following year's sales in the current year or because goods returned by the customer in the current year are not recorded in the current year. Cut-off testing may have to be extended (see below).
The customer may have sent the **monies before** the year-end, but the monies were **not recorded** by the client as receipts until **after** the year-end. Detailed cut-off work may be required on receipts.
Monies received may have been posted to the **wrong account** or a cash-in-transit account. Auditors should check if there is evidence of other mis-posting. If the monies have been posted to a cash-in-transit account, auditors should ensure this account has been cleared promptly.
Customers who are also suppliers may **net off balances** owed and owing. Auditors should check that this is allowed.
Teeming and lading, stealing monies and **incorrectly posting** other receipts so that no particular debtor is seriously in debt is a fraud that can arise in this area. If auditors suspect teeming and lading has occurred, detailed testing will be required on cash receipts, particularly on prompt posting of cash receipts.

1.17 When the positive request method is used the auditors must follow up by all practicable means those debtors who **fail to respond**. Second requests should be sent out in the event of no reply being received within two or three weeks and if necessary this may be followed by telephoning the customer, with the client's permission.

1.18 After two, or even three, attempts to obtain confirmation, a list of the outstanding items will normally be passed to a responsible company official, preferably independent of the sales accounting department, who will arrange for them to be investigated.

1.19 If it proves impossible to get confirmations from individual debtors, alternative procedures may be carried out.

AUDIT PROGRAMME: DEBTORS – ALTERNATIVE PROCEDURES
• **Check receipt of cash** after date • **Verify valid purchase** orders if any • **Examine the account** to see if the balance outstanding represents specific invoices and **confirm** their **validity** • **Obtain explanations** for **invoices remaining unpaid** after subsequent ones have been paid • **Check** if the **balance** on the account is **growing**, and if so, why • **Test company's control** over the issue of **credit notes** and the **write-off of bad debts**

Non purchase ledger accounting

1.20 Certain companies, government departments and local authorities operate systems, often computerised, which make it impossible for them to confirm the balance on their account.

1.21 Typically in these circumstances their 'purchase ledger' is merely a list of unpaid invoices in date order.

1.22 However, given sufficient information the debtor will be able to confirm that any given invoice is outstanding. Hence the auditors can circularise such enterprises, but they will need to break down the total on the account into its constituent outstanding invoices.

1.23 Confirmation letters should nevertheless state the full balance so that the debtor has the option of confirming the balance and also has the opportunity to object if he thinks the total appears incorrect.

Additional procedures where circularisation is carried out before year-end

1.24 The auditors will need to carry out the following procedures where their circularisation is carried out before the year-end.

- **Review** and **reconcile entries** on the **sales ledger control account** for the intervening period
- **Verify sales entries** from the control account by checking sales day book entries, copy sales invoices and despatch notes
- **Check** that **appropriate credit entries** have been made for goods returned notes and other evidence of returns/allowances to the sales ledger control account
- Select a sample from the cash received records and **ensure** that **receipts** have been **credited** to the control account
- **Review** the **list of balances** at the **circularisation** date and year end and **investigate** any **unexpected movements** or lack of them (it may be prudent to send further confirmation requests at the year end to material debtors where review results are unsatisfactory)

- **Carry out analytical review** procedures, comparing debtors' ratios at the confirmation date and year-end
- **Carry out** year end **cut-off tests**, in addition to any performed at the date of the confirmation (see below)

Evaluation and conclusions

1.25 All circularisations, regardless of timing, must be properly recorded and evaluated. All **balance disagreements** and **non-replies** must be **followed up** and their effect on total debtors evaluated.

1.26 **Differences** arising that merely represent **invoices** or **cash in transit** (normal timing differences) generally do not require adjustment, but disputed amounts, and errors by the client, may indicate that further substantive work is necessary to determine whether material adjustments are required.

2 BAD DEBTS 12/01

2.1 A significant test of bad debts is reviewing the **cash received** after date. This will provide evidence of collectability of debts (and hence valuation). It also provides some evidence of correctness of title (rights and obligations), although ideally it should be carried out as well as a debtors' circularisation (which is the main test on rights and obligations).

AUDIT PROGRAMME: BAD DEBTS

- **Confirm necessity/adequacy** of provision against **write-off** of specific debts by review of correspondence, solicitors' debt collection, agencies' letters, liquidation statements
- **Examine customer files** on **overdue debts**, and **assess** whether **provision** is required in the circumstances
- **Consider** whether **amounts owed** may be **not recovered** where there has been:
  - Round sum payments on account
  - Invoices unpaid after subsequent invoices paid
- **Review customer files/correspondence** from solicitors and **debtors' circularisation results** for evidence of potential bad debts
- **Confirm general provisions** for bad debts considering:
  - How well previous year's provision predicted actual bad debts
  - Whether calculation correct
  - Whether formula used reasonable and consistent with previous years
  - Exclusion of debtors against whom specific provision is made
- **Examine credit notes** issued after the year-end for **provisions** that should be made against current period balances
- **Check accuracy** of **aged debtor analysis** by comparing analysis with dates on invoices and **matching cash receipts** against outstanding invoices
- **Investigate** and **consider need for provision against unusual features** on aged debtors analysis, such as:
  - Unapplied credits
  - Unallocated cash

- **Investigate** and **consider need for provision against unusual items** in the sales ledger, such as:
  - Journal entries transferring balances from one account to another
  - Journal entries that clear post year-end debtor balances
  - Balanccs not madc up of spccific invoices
  - Sales ledger accounts with significant adjustments or credit notes

2.2 Auditors should also consider the collectability of material debtor balances other than those contained in the sales ledger. Auditors should request certificates of loan balances from employees and others, and inspect the authority if necessary.

3 SALES

3.1 Debtors will often be tested in conjunction with sales. Auditors are seeking to obtain evidence that sales are **completely** and **accurately recorded**. This will involve carrying out certain procedures to test for **completeness** of sales and also testing **cut-off.**

Completeness and occurrence of sales

3.2 **Analytical review** is likely to be important when testing completeness. Auditors should consider the following.

- The **level of sales** over the year, compared on a month-by-month basis with the previous year
- The effect on sales value of **changes in quantities** sold
- The effect on sales value of **changes in products** or **prices**
- The level of **goods returned, sales allowances** and **discounts**
- The **efficiency of labour** as expressed in sales or profit per tax per employee

3.3 In addition auditors must record reasons for changes in the **gross profit margin** ($\frac{\text{Gross profit}}{\text{Turnover}} \times 100\%$). Analysis of the gross profit margin should be as detailed as possible, ideally broken down by **product area** and **month or quarter**.

3.4 As well as analytical review, auditors may feel that they need to test **completeness of recording** of individual sales in the accounting records. To do this, auditors should start with the documents that first record sales (**goods despatched notes** or **till rolls** for example), and trace sales recorded in these through intermediate documents such as sales summaries to the **sales ledger**.

3.5 Auditors must ensure that the population of documents from which the sample is originally taken is itself complete, by checking for example the **completeness** of the **sequence** of goods despatched notes.

> **Exam focus point**
>
> You must remember the direction of this test. Since we are checking the completeness of recording of sales in the sales ledger, we cannot take a sample from the ledger since the sample cannot include what has not been recorded.

3.6 If on the other hand, the auditors suspect that sales may have been **invalidly** recorded, and have not **occurred**, then the sample will be taken from the **sales ledger** and **confirmed** to **supporting documentation** (orders, despatch notes etc).

AUDIT PROGRAMME: SALES (MEASUREMENT)
• Check the **pricing calculations** and **additions** on invoices • Check whether **discounts** have been **properly calculated** • **Check** whether **VAT** has been **added appropriately**

3.7 Other tests that may be carried out on sales include:

- **Trace debits** in the **sales account** to credit notes
- **Check casting** of **sales ledger accounts** and **sales ledger control account**
- **Review reconciliations** of sales ledger control account and other relevant reconciliations (for example till rolls) and investigate unusual items

Sales cut-off

3.8 We can now turn to the requirement to confirm that sales cut-off is satisfactory and hence sales are completely recorded. During the stocktake the auditors will have obtained details of the last serial numbers of goods outward notes issued before the commencement of the stocktaking.

AUDIT PROGRAMME: SALES CUT OFF
• **Check goods despatched** and **returns inwards** notes around year-end to ensure: • **Invoices** and **credit notes** are **dated** in the **correct period** • **Invoices** and **credit notes** are **posted** to the **sales ledger** and **general ledger** in the correct period • **Reconcile entries** in the **sales ledger control account** around the **year-end** to daily batch invoice totals ensuring batches are posted in correct year • **Review sales ledger control account** around year-end for **unusual items** • **Review material after-date invoices, credit notes** and **adjustments** and ensure that they are properly treated as following year sales

Goods on sale or return

3.9 Care should be exercised to ensure that goods on sale or return are properly treated in the accounts. Except where the client has been notified of the sale of the goods they should be reflected in the accounts as **stock** at cost and not as debtors, otherwise profits may be incorrectly anticipated.

4 PREPAYMENTS

AUDIT PROGRAMME: PREPAYMENTS
• **Verify prepayments** by reference to the cash book, expense invoices, correspondence and so on • **Check calculations** of prepayments • **Review** the **detailed profit and loss account** to ensure that all likely prepayments have been provided for • **Review** the **prepayments** for **reasonableness** by comparing with prior years and using analytical procedures where applicable

Question: Debtors

Sherwood Textiles plc manufactures knitted clothes and dyes these clothes and other textiles. You are carrying out the audit of the accounts of the company for the year ended 30 September 20X6 which show a turnover of about £10 million, and a profit before tax of about £800,000.

You are attending the final audit in December 20X6 and are commencing the audit of trade debtors, which are shown in the draft accounts at £2,060,000.

The interim audit (tests of control) was carried out in July 20X6 and it showed that there was a good system of internal control in the sales system and no serious errors were found in the audit tests. The company's sales ledger is maintained on a computer, which produces at the end of each month:

(i) A list of transactions for the month

(ii) An aged list of balances

(iii) Open item statements which are sent to customers. (*Note.* Open item statements show all items which are outstanding on each account, irrespective of their age.)

Required

(a) List and briefly describe the audit tests you would carry out to verify trade debtors at the year end. You are not required to describe how you would carry out a debtors' circularisation.

(b) Describe the audit work you would carry out on the following replies to a debtors' circularisation:

  (i) Balance agreed by debtor

  (ii) Balance not agreed by debtor

  (iii) Debtor is unable to confirm the balance because of the form of records kept by the debtor

  (iv) Debtor does not reply to the circularisation

Answer

(a) The auditors will carry out the following tests on the list of balances.

  (i) Check the balances from the individual sales ledger accounts to the list of balances and vice versa.

  (ii) Check the total of the list to the sales ledger control account.

  (iii) Cast the list of balances and the sales ledger control account.

  Other general tests auditors will carry out will be:

  (i) Agree the opening balance on the sales ledger control account to last year's working papers to ensure that last year's audit adjustments were recorded.

  (ii) Scrutinise ledger balances for unusual entries.

  (iii) Carry out analytical procedures considering particularly changes in debtors' collection period and in age profile of debtors.

  The determination of whether the company has made reasonable provision for bad and doubtful debts, will be facilitated as the company produces an aged listing of balances.

Auditors will carry out the following procedures to check bad debts.

(i) Debts against which specific provision has been made (and debts written off) should be examined in conjunction with correspondence, solicitors'/debt collection agencies' letters, liquidators' statements and so on, and their necessity or adequacy confirmed.

(ii) A general review of relevant correspondence may reveal debts where a provision is warranted, but has not been made.

(iii) Where specific and/or general provisions have been determined using the aged analysis, the auditors should ensure that the analysis has been properly prepared by comparing analysis with dates on invoice and matching cash receipts against outstanding invoices. They should check the reasonableness and consistency of any formula used to calculate general provisions.

(iv) Additional tests that should be carried out on individual balances will include the ascertainment of the subsequent receipt of cash, paying particular attention to, round sum payments on account, examination of specific invoices and, where appropriate, goods received notes, and enquiry into any invoices that have not been paid when subsequent invoices have been paid.

(v) Excessive discounts should be examined, as should journal entries transferring balances from one account to another and journal entries that clear debtor balances after the year end.

(vi) Credit notes issued after the year end should be reviewed and provisions checked where they refer to current period sales.

In order to check cut-off and hence completeness, the auditors should, during the stocktake, have obtained details of the last serial numbers of goods outwards issued before the commencement of stocktaking. The following substantive procedures are designed to test that goods taken into stock are not also treated as sales in the year under review and, conversely, goods despatched are treated as sales in the year under review and not also treated as stock.

(i) Check goods outwards and returns inwards notes around year end to ensure that:

  (1) Invoices and credit notes are dated in the correct period.

  (2) Invoices and credit notes are posted to the sales ledger and nominal ledger in the correct period.

(ii) Reconcile entries in the sales ledger control around the year end to daily batch invoice totals ensuring batches are posted in correct year.

(iii) Review sales ledger control account around year end for unusual items.

(iv) Review material after date invoices and ensure that they are properly treated as following year sales.

(b) The verification of trade debtors by direct communication is the normal means of providing audit evidence to prove that debtors represent bona fide amounts due to the company (existence and rights and obligations).

The audit work required on the various replies to a debtors' circularisation would be as follows.

(i) *Balances agreed by debtor*

Where the balance has been agreed by the debtor all that is required would be to ensure that the debt does appear to be collectable. This would be achieved by reviewing cash received after date or considering the adequacy of any provision made for a long outstanding debt.

(ii) *Balances not agreed by debtor*

All balance disagreements must be followed up and their effect on total debtors evaluated. Differences arising that merely represent invoices or cash in transit (which are normal timing differences) generally do not require adjustment, but disputed amounts, and errors by the client, may indicate that further substantive work is necessary to determine whether material adjustments are required.

(iii) *Debtor is unable to confirm the balance because of the form of records he or she maintains*

Certain companies, often computerised, operate systems which make it impossible for them to confirm the balance on their account. Typically in these circumstances their purchase ledger is merely a list of unpaid invoices. However, given sufficient information the debtor will be able to confirm that any given invoice is outstanding. Hence the auditors can circularise such enterprises successfully, but they will need to break down the total on the account into its constituent outstanding invoices.

(iv) *Debtor does not reply to circularisation*

When the positive request method is used the auditors must follow up by all practicable means those debtors who fail to respond. Second requests should be sent out in the event of no reply being received within two or three weeks and if necessary this may be followed by telephoning the customer with the client's permission.

After two, or even three attempts to obtain confirmation, a list of the outstanding items will normally be passed to a responsible company official, preferably independent of the sales department, who will arrange for them to be investigated.

This does not, of course, absolve the auditors from satisfying themselves that the clearance procedure is properly carried out and from examining the results. Where there is any limitation in the follow-up procedure it is all the more important to apply other auditing tests to establish that there existed a valid debt from a genuine customer at the date of the verification. Alternative procedures might include the following.

(1) Check receipt of cash after date.
(2) Verify valid purchase orders, if any.
(3) Examine the account to see if the balance represents specific outstanding invoices.
(4) Obtain explanations for invoices remaining unpaid after subsequent ones have been paid.
(5) See if the balance on the account is growing, and if so, why.
(6) Test the company's control over the issue of credit notes and the write-off of bad debts.

Chapter roundup

- A **circularisation** of **trade debtors** is a major procedure. The **choice** and **performance** of the circularisation must be carefully thought out.
- Auditors must follow up **debtor disagreements** and **failure by debtors** to **respond**.
- The **recoverability** of **debts** can be tested by a combination of methods. The provision for bad debts can have a significant impact on profits.

Quick quiz

1 The negative method of debtors' circularisation should only be used if the client has a good internal control and a small number of large debtors accounts.

True ☐

False ☐

2 Name four types of account which should receive special attention when picking a sample for a debtors' circularisation.

1 ....

2 ....

3 ....

4 ....

3 Complete the following tests which aim to confirm the valuation of bad debts.

(a) Confirm adequacy of provision by reviewing correspondence with

(i) ....

(ii) ....

(b) Examine .... issued after the year end for provisions that should be made against current period balances.

4 Name three things that can be considered when undertaking analytical review on sales.

1 ……………………………………………………..

2 ……………………………………………………..

3 ……………………………………………………..

5 Give two examples of tests to verify prepayments

1 ……………………………………………………..

2 ……………………………………………………..

Answers to quick quiz

1 False

2 **Four** from:

- **Old unpaid accounts**
- **Accounts written off** during the period under review
- **Accounts with credit balances**
- **Accounts settled by round sum payments**
- **Accounts with nil balances**
- **Accounts which** have been **paid** by the date of the examination

3 (a) debtors, solicitors
(b) credit notes

4 1 level of sales, month by month
2 price
3 goods returned

5 1 Verify by reference to invoices, cash book correspondence
2 Check calculations

Now try the questions below from the Exam Question Bank

Number	Level	Marks	Time
15	Exam	20	36 mins

Chapter 16

BANK AND CASH

Topic list		Syllabus reference	Study guide
1	Bank	6	21
2	Cash	6	21

Introduction

Work on bank and cash will concentrate on **completeness** and accuracy of balances. The audit of cash book transactions has been considered in the chapters on sales, purchases and wages cycles, and fixed asset additions and disposals.

Bank reconciliation testing is often the most important in practice, and so may be where exam questions are focused.

1 BANK 6/02

1.1 The audit of bank balances will need to cover **completeness, existence, rights and obligations and valuation**. All of these elements can be audited directly through the device of obtaining third party confirmations from the client's banks and reconciling these with the accounting records, having regard to cut-off.

1.2 As preparation, the auditors should update details of bank accounts held, ensuring the client holds accounts with bona fide banks.

Bank reports

1.3 The Auditing Practices Board issued Practice Note 16 *Bank reports for audit purposes* in August 1998. The note sets out a revised process for auditors when requesting information from the banks. It draws a distinction between standard and supplementary information.

1.4 The standard request consists of information about account and balance details, facilities, securities, and additional banking relationships. The request for supplementary information is concerned with requests for trade finance information, and derivatives and commodity trading information.

1.5 **Bank confirmation request letter - illustration**

[XXXXXX Bank plc
25 XXX Street
Warrington
Cheshire
WA1 1XQ]

Dear Sirs,

In accordance with the agreed practice for provision of information to auditors, please forward information on our mutual client(s) as detailed below on behalf of the bank, its branches and subsidiaries. This request and your response will not create any contractual or other duty with us.

COMPANIES OR OTHER BUSINESS ENTITIES
(attach a separate listing if necessary)

[Parent Company Ltd
Subsidiary 1 Ltd
Subsidiary 2 Ltd]

AUDIT CONFIRMATION DATE (30 APRIL 2000)

Information required	Tick
Standard	
Trade finance	
Derivative and commodity trading	
Custodian arrangements	
Other information (see attached)	

> The authority to disclose information signed by your customer is attached / already held by you (delete as appropriate). Please advise us if this authority is insufficient for you to provide full disclosure of the information requested.
>
> The contract name is [John Caller] Telephone [01 234 5678]
>
> Yours faithfully,
> [XXX Accountants]

1.6 The procedure is simple but important.

(a) The banks will require **explicit written authority** from their client to disclose the information requested.

(b) The **auditors' request** must **refer** to the **client's letter** of authority and the date thereof. Alternatively it may be countersigned by the client or it may be accompanied by a specific letter of authority.

(c) In the case of joint accounts, **letters of authority** signed by all **parties** will be necessary.

(d) Such **letters of authority** may either **give permission** to the bank to disclose information for a specific request or grant permission for an indeterminate length of time.

(e) The request should **reach** the **branch manager** at least **two weeks in advance** of the client's **year-end** and should state both that year-end date and the previous year-end date.

(f) The **auditors** should themselves **check** that the bank response covers all the information in the standard and other responses.

Standard request for information

1.7 The following information should always be disclosed by banks upon receipt of a request for information for audit purposes. Responses should be given in the order below and if no information is available then this must be stated as 'None' in the response.

> 1 **Account and balance details**
>
> Give full titles of all bank accounts including loans, (whether in sterling or another currency) together with their account numbers and balances. For accounts closed during the 12 months up to the audit confirmation date give the account details and date of closure.
>
> Note. Also give details where your customer's name is joined with that of other parties and where the account is in a trade name.
>
> State if any account or balances are subject to any restriction(s) whatsoever. Indicate the nature and extent of the restriction, eg garnishee order.
>
> 2 **Facilities**
>
> Give the following details of all loans, overdrafts and associated guarantees and indemnities:
>
> - Term
> - Repayment frequency and/or review date
> - Details of period of availability of agreed finance, ie finance remaining undrawn
> - Detail the facility limit

3 **Securities**

With reference to the facilities detailed in (2) above give the following details:

- Any security formally charged (date, ownership and type of charge). State whether the security supports facilities granted by the bank to the customer or to another party.

  Note. Give details if a security is limited in amount or to a specific borrowing or if to your knowledge there is a prior, equal or subordinate charge.

- Where there are any arrangements for set-off of balances or compensating balances, eg back to back loans, give particulars (ie date, type of document and accounts covered) of any acknowledgement of set-off, whether given by specific letter of set-off or incorporated in some other document.

4 **Additional banking relationship**

State if you are aware of the customer(s) having any additional relationships with branches or subsidiaries of the bank not covered by the response. Supply a list of branches etc.

Request for supplementary information

1.8 The Practice Note also gives example letters if information about **trade finance**, **derivatives** and **custodian arrangements** is required.

Cut-off

1.9 Care must be taken to ensure that there is no **window dressing**, by checking cut-off carefully. Window dressing in this context is usually manifested as an attempt to overstate the liquidity of the company by:

(a) Keeping the cash book open to take credit for **remittances actually received** after the year end, thus enhancing the balance at bank and reducing debtors

(b) **Recording cheques paid in** the period under review which are not actually despatched until after the year end, thus decreasing the balance at bank and reducing creditors

A combination of (a) and (b) can contrive to present an artificially healthy looking current ratio.

1.10 With the possibility of (a) above in mind, where lodgements have not been cleared by the bank until the new period the auditors should **examine the paying-in slip** to ensure that the amounts were actually paid into the bank on or before the balance sheet date.

1.11 As regards (b) above, where there appears to be a particularly **large number of outstanding cheques** at the year-end, the auditors should check whether these were **cleared** within a **reasonable time** in the new period. If not, this may indicate that despatch occurred after the year-end.

AUDIT PROGRAMME: BANK
• **Obtain standard bank confirmations** from each bank with which the client conducted business during the audit period • **Check arithmetic** of bank reconciliation • **Trace cheques shown as outstanding** from the bank reconciliation to the cash book prior to the year-end and to the **after date bank statements** and **obtain explanations** for any **large or unusual items** not cleared at the time of the audit • **Compare cash book(s)** and **bank statements** in detail for the last month of the year, and **check items outstanding** at the reconciliation date to bank reconciliations • **Review bank reconciliation** previous to the year-end bank reconciliation and check that **all items** are **cleared** in the last period or **taken forward** to the year-end bank reconciliation • **Obtain satisfactory explanations** for **all items** in the **cash book** for which there are **no corresponding entries** in the **bank statement** and vice versa • **Verify contra items** appearing in the cash books or bank statements with original entry • **Verify** by checking pay-in slips that **uncleared bankings** are **paid in** prior to the year end • **Examine all lodgements** in respect of which payment has been refused by the bank; ensure that they are cleared on representation or that other appropriate steps have been taken to effect recovery of the amount due • **Verify balances** per the **cash book** according to the **bank reconciliation** with **cash book, bank statements and general ledger** • **Verify** the **bank balances** with reply to **standard bank letter** and with the **bank statements** • **Scrutinise** the cash book and bank statements before and after the balance sheet date for **exceptional entries** or **transfers** which have a material effect on the balance shown to be in hand • **Identify** whether any **accounts** are **secured** on the **assets** of the company • **Consider** whether there is a **legal right** of **set-off** of overdrafts against positive bank balances • **Determine** whether the **bank accounts** are **subject** to any **restrictions**

Note. Auditors should ensure that all cheques are despatched immediately after signature and entry in the cash book. Examine the interval between dates of certain of the larger cheques in the cash book and payment by the bank since this may indicate that cheques were despatched after the year-end (window dressing).

Exam focus point

Remember that the bank letter contains the balance held by the client at the bank **per the bank's records**. This must be reconciled to the balance held with the bank **per the client's records.**

2 CASH

2.1 Cash balances/floats are often individually immaterial but they may require some audit emphasis because of the opportunities for fraud that could exist where internal control is weak and because in total they may be material.

2.2 However in enterprises such as hotels, the amount of cash in hand at the balance sheet date could be considerable; the same goes for retail organisations. Cash counts may be important for internal auditors, who have a role in **fraud prevention**.

2.3 Where the auditors determine that cash balances are potentially material they may conduct a cash count, ideally at the balance sheet date. Rather like attendance at stocktaking, the conduct of the count falls into three phases: planning, the count itself and follow up procedures.

Planning

2.4 Planning is an essential element, for it is an important principle that all cash balances are counted at the same time as far as possible. Cash in this context may include unbanked cheques received, IOUs and credit card slips, in addition to notes and coins.

2.5 As part of their planning procedures the auditors will hence need to determine the **locations** where cash is held and which of these locations warrant a count.

2.6 Planning decisions will need to be recorded on the current audit file including:

- The **precise time** of the count(s) and location(s)
- The **names** of the **audit staff** conducting the counts
- The **names** of the **client staff** intending to be present at each location

Where a location is not visited it may be expedient to obtain a letter from the client confirming the balance.

Cash count

2.7 The following matters apply to the count itself.

- All cash/petty **cash books** should be **written up** to date in ink (or other permanent form at the time of the count.
- All **balances** must be **counted** at the **same time.**
- All **negotiable securities** must be **available** and **counted** at the time the cash balances are counted.
- At **no time** should the **auditors** be left **alone** with the cash and negotiable securities.
- **All cash** and securities **counted** must be **recorded** on working papers subsequently filed on the current audit file. Reconciliations should be prepared where applicable (for example imprest petty cash float).

AUDIT PROGRAMME: CASH COUNT

- **Count cash balances** held and agree to petty cash book or other record:
  - Count all balances simultaneously
  - All counting to be done in the presence of the individuals responsible
  - Enquire into any IOUs or cashed cheques outstanding for unreasonable periods of time
- **Obtain certificates** of cash in hand from responsible officials
- **Confirm** that bank and cash **balances** as reconciled above are **correctly stated** in the accounts

Follow up procedures

- Ensure **certificates of cash-in-hand** are **obtained** as appropriate.
- Check **unbanked cheques/cash receipts** have subsequently been **paid in** and agree to the bank reconciliation.
- Check **IOUs** and cheques cashed for employees have been **reimbursed.**
- Ensure **IOUs or cashed cheques outstanding** for **unreasonable periods** of time have been provided for.
- Verify that the **balances** as **counted** are **reflected** in the **accounts** (subject to any agreed amendments because of shortages and so on).

Question: Bank

(a) Explain the importance of the bank letter and describe the procedures used to obtain confirmations from the bank.

(b) Describe how you would check a client's bank reconciliation.

Answer

(a) The bank letter is important because it is independent confirmation of a number of important matters in the client's financial statements. It confirms cash and bank balances which may well be a significant asset. It also provides confirmation of customer's assets held as security, customers' other assets held (as custodian) and contingent liabilities. Auditors also ask the bank to give details of other banks and branches that the respondent bank is aware have a relationship with the client.

Audit procedures

(i) Obtain written authority from the client to the bank to disclose the necessary information.

(ii) Send a bank letter in standard form to the bank in sufficient time for it to arrive at least two weeks before the year-end. The letter should state both the year-end date and the previous year-end date, and should refer to the client's granting of authority.

(iii) If additional information over and above what is in the standard letter is requested, send a separate letter requesting that information.

(iv) When confirmation is received from the bank, check that the bank have answered all the questions in the letter.

(v) Follow up all points disclosed in the bank letter.

(b) **Bank reconciliation procedures**

(i) Obtain standard bank confirmations from each bank with which the client conducted business during the period.

(ii) Check arithmetic of bank reconciliation.

(iii) Trace cheques shown as outstanding from the bank reconciliation to the cash book prior to the year-end and to the after date bank statements and obtain explanations for any large or unusual items not cleared at the time of the audit.

(iv) Verify by checking pay-in slips that uncleared bankings are paid in prior to the year end, and check uncleared bankings are cleared quickly after the year-end.

(v) Verify balances per cash book according to the reconciliation with cash book and general ledger.

(vi) Verify the bank balances with reply to standard bank letter and with the bank statements.

(vii) Scrutinise the cash book and bank statements before and after the balance sheet date for exceptional entries or transfers which have a material effect on the balance shown to be in hand.

(viii) Identify whether any accounts are secured on the assets of the company.

(ix) Consider whether there is a legal right of set-off of overdrafts against positive bank balances.

(x) Determine whether the bank accounts are subject to any restrictions.

Chapter roundup

- **Bank balances** are usually **confirmed directly with the bank** in question. The bank letter can be used to ask a variety of questions, including queries about outstanding interests, contingent liabilities and guarantees.
- **Cash balances** should be **checked** if irregularities are suspected.

Quick quiz

1 Summarise the procedure for obtaining confirmation from a client's bank.

1 ....

2 ....

3 ....

4 ....

5 ....

6 ....

2 Complete these two of the audit tests performed to verify the bank reconciliation.

(a) Trace cheques shown as outstanding on the .... to the .... prior to the year end and ....

(b) Obtain satisfactory explanations for all items in the .... for which there is no corresponding entry in the .... and ....

3 Give two examples of business where cash floats could be considerable.

1 ....

2 ....

4 What planning matters relating to a cash count should be recorded in the current audit file?

1 ....

2 ....

3 ....

Answers to quick quiz

1 (1) The banks will require **explicit written authority** from their client to disclose the information requested.

(2) The **auditors' request** must **refer** to the **client's letter** of authority and the date thereof. Alternatively it may be countersigned by the client or it may be accompanied by a specific letter of authority.

(3) In the case of joint accounts, **letters of authority** signed by all **parties** will be necessary.

(4) Such **letters** of **authority** may either **give permission** to the bank to disclose information for a specific request or grant permission for an indeterminate length of time.

(5) The request should **reach** the **branch manager** at least **two weeks in advance** of the client's **year-end** and should state both that year-end date and the previous year-end date.

(6) The **auditors** should themselves **check** that the bank response covers all the information in the standard and other responses.

2 bank reconciliation, cash book, after date bank statements

3 hotels
retail operations

4 Time of count
Names of client staff attending
Names of audit staff attending

Now try the questions below from the Exam Question Bank

Number	Level	Marks	Time
16	Exam	20	36 mins

Chapter 17

LIABILITIES AND CAPITAL

Topic list		Syllabus reference	Study guide
1	Trade creditors and purchases	6	20
2	Accruals	6	20
3	Long-term liabilities	6	22
4	Provisions and contingencies	6	22
5	Capital and other issues	6	22

Introduction

Some of the liability components of the balance sheet are technically quite difficult in that they are regulated by company law. This mainly applies to share capital and reserves which we examine in part 5. We will try to avoid the more complex legalistic aspects of these items and concentrate on the fundamental auditing procedures involved.

In the case of other liabilities, circularisation for verification purposes is quite rare and other procedures are normally used. This can be one of the most sensitive areas of the audit as it affects the company's liquidity and gearing ratios and these may be closely related to bank borrowing covenants or debenture agreements. Testing for **understatement** and **completeness** is particularly important.

Auditing provisions can be complex due to the complexity of the accounting for them.

As long term liabilities are often used to finance fixed assets, these could be examined jointly. Trade creditors could be examined in conjunction with purchase controls.

1 TRADE CREDITORS AND PURCHASES 12/02

1.1 As with debtors, creditors are likely to be a material figure in the balance sheet of most enterprises. The purchases cycle tests of controls will have provided the auditors with some assurance as to the completeness of liabilities.

1.2 Auditors should however be particularly aware, when conducting their balance sheet work, of the possibility of **understatement** of **liabilities** to improve liquidity and profits (by understating the corresponding purchases). The primary objective of their balance sheet work will be to ascertain whether **liabilities** existing at the year-end have been **completely** and **accurately recorded**.

1.3 As regards **trade creditors**, this primary objective can be subdivided into two detailed objectives.

- Is there a **satisfactory cut-off** between goods received and invoices received, so that purchases and trade creditors are recognised in the correct year?
- Do trade creditors represent the **bona fide** amounts due by the company?

1.4 Before we ascertain how the auditors design and conduct their tests with these objectives in mind, we need to establish the importance, as with trade debtors, of the list of balances.

Trade creditors listing and accruals listing

1.5 The list of balances will be one of the principal sources from which the auditors will select their samples for testing. The listing should be extracted from the purchase ledger by the client. The auditors will carry out the following substantive tests to verify that the extraction has been properly performed.

- **Check** from the **purchase ledger accounts** to the **list of balances** and *vice versa*
- **Reconcile** the **total** of the list with the **purchase ledger control account**
- **Cast** the **list** of balances and the purchase ledger control account

The client should also prepare a detailed schedule of trade and sundry accrued expenses.

Completeness, rights and obligations and existence of trade creditors

1.6 The most important test when considering **trade creditors** is comparison of suppliers' statements with purchase ledger balances.

1.7 When selecting a sample of creditors to test, auditors must be careful not just to select creditors with large year-end balances. Remember, it is errors of **understatement** that auditors are primarily interested in when reviewing creditors, and errors of understatement could occur equally in creditors with low or nil balances as with high.

1.8 When comparing **supplier statements** with **year-end purchase ledger balances**, auditors should include within their sample creditors with nil or negative purchase ledger balances. Auditors should be particularly wary of low balances with major suppliers. Remember the client has no incentive to record liabilities before being invoiced.

1.9 You may be wondering why if as we normally carry out a debtors' circularisation whether we would also circularise creditors. The answer is generally no.

1.10 The principal reason for this lies in the nature of the purchases cycle: third party evidence in the form of suppliers' invoices and even more significantly, **suppliers' statements,** are part of the standard documentation of the cycle. The auditors will hence concentrate on these documents when designing and conducting their tests.

1.11 In the following circumstances the auditors may, however, determine that a circularisation is necessary. In these cases confirmation requests should be sent out and processed in a similar way to debtors' confirmation requests. 'Positive' replies will be required where:

- **Suppliers' statements** are, for whatever reason, **unavailable** or **incomplete**.
- **Weaknesses in internal** control or the nature of the client's business make possible a material misstatement of liabilities that would not otherwise be picked up.
- It is thought that the **client** is **deliberately** trying to **understate creditors**.
- The **accounts** appear to be **irregular** or if the nature or size of balances or transactions is abnormal.

Exam focus point

Testing suppliers' statements is frequently examined in auditing exams.

Purchases and expenses

1.12 When testing purchases and expenses, auditors are testing whether they are for **valid** reasons, that goods and services purchased have provided benefits to the company. They are also checking for **accuracy of recording** so again **cut-off** procedures will be important.

1.13 As with sales, **analytical procedures** will be important. Auditors should consider:

- The **level of purchases and expenses** over the year, compared on a month-by-month basis with the previous year
- The effect on value of purchases of **changes in quantities purchased**
- The effect on purchases value of changes in **products** purchased (for example a change in ingredients), or **prices of products**
- How the **ratio of trade creditors to purchases** compares with previous figures
- How the **ratio of trade creditors to stock** compares with previous years' figures

AUDIT PROGRAMME: PURCHASES – COMPLETENESS AND OCCURRENCE

- Check **purchases and other expenses recorded** in the **purchase or general ledger or cash book** to supporting documentation (books of prime entry, invoices, delivery notes) considering whether:
  - **Purchases and expenses are valid** (invoices addressed to the client, for goods and services ordered by the client, for the purposes of the business)
  - **Purchases** and expenses have been **allocated** to the correct **purchase or general ledger** account

- Consider **reasonableness of deductions** from purchases or expenses by reference to subsequent events
- Check whether **valid debts** are **recorded** in **purchase ledger** by checking **credit notes**

1.14 One important expense is obviously wages and salaries which we consider below.

Purchases cut-off (completeness)

1.15 The procedures applied by the auditors will be designed to ascertain whether:

- **Goods received** for which **no invoice** has been **received** are **accrued**
- **Goods received** which have been **invoiced** but **not yet posted** are **accrued.**
- **Goods returned** to suppliers **prior** to the **year-end** are **excluded** from **stock** and **trade creditors**

1.16 At the year-end stocktaking the auditors will have made a note of the last serial numbers of goods received notes.

AUDIT PROGRAMME: PURCHASES CUT OFF

- **Check from goods received notes** with serial numbers before the year-end to ensure that invoices are either:
  - Posted to purchase ledger prior to the year-end, or
  - Included on the schedule of accruals
- **Review the schedule of accruals** to ensure that goods received after the year-end are not accrued
- **Check from goods returned notes prior to year-end** to ensure that **credit notes** have been **posted** to the purchase ledger prior to the year-end or accrued
- **Review large invoices** and **credit notes** included after the year-end to ensure that they refer to the following year
- **Review outstanding purchase orders** for indications of any purchases completed but not invoiced
- **Reconcile daily batch invoice totals** around the year-end to purchase ledger control ensuring batches are posted in the correct year
- **Review** the **control account** around the year-end for **any unusual items**

Purchase of goods subject to reservation of title clauses

1.17 Under certain transactions, the seller may retain legal ownership of goods passed to a 'purchaser'. The requirements are known as 'reservation of title'.

1.18 The cases of *Borden (UK) Limited v Scottish Timber Products, Re Bond Worth* and the *Romalpa* case, suggest that a reservation of title clause will only be upheld if it states that the seller has a charge over the goods and the goods, any products made from them and any sale proceeds are kept separately and are readily identifiable.

AUDIT PROGRAMME: PURCHASES (RESERVATION OF TITLE)
• **Ascertain** how the **client identifies suppliers selling** on terms which **reserve title** by enquiry of those responsible for purchasing and the board • **Review** and test the **procedures** for **quantifying** or **estimating** the **liabilities** • **Consider** whether **disclosure** is **sufficient** by itself if the directors have decided quantification is impractical • **Consider** the adequacy of the **disclosures** in the accounts • **Review the terms of sale** of **major suppliers** to confirm that liabilities not provided for do not exist or are immaterial

2 ACCRUALS

2.1 Checking the completeness and valuation of sundry accruals is an area that lends itself to **analytical procedures** and reconciliation techniques.

2.2 A variety of sources can indicate possible accruals. These include **last year's accruals, expense items** where an accrual would be expected, and **invoices received** and **cash paid** after the year-end.

2.3 Auditors should also use their **knowledge of the business** to consider whether there are accruals which they would expect to be there, but which may not be invoiced or paid until long after the year-end.

AUDIT PROGRAMME: ACCRUALS
• Check that **accruals** are **fairly calculated** and **verify** by reference to **subsequent payments** and **supporting documentation** • **Review the profit and loss account** and **prior years' figures** and consider liabilities inherent in the trade to **ensure** that all **likely accruals have been provided** • **Scrutinise payments** made **after year-end** to ascertain whether any payments made should be accrued • **Consider basis** for **round sum accruals** and ensure it is consistent with prior years • **Ascertain** why any **payments on account** are being **made** and **ensure** that the **full liability is provided** • **PAYE**. Normally this should represent one month's deductions. Check amount paid to Revenue by inspecting receipted annual declaration of tax paid over, or returned cheque • **VAT**. Check reasonableness to next VAT return. **Verify last amount paid in year** per cash book to VAT return

Wages and salaries

2.4 Although auditors may test other expenses solely by analytical review, they may carry out more detailed testing on wages and salaries, partly because of the consequences of failure to deduct PAYE and NIC correctly.

2.5 Analytical procedures will nonetheless be used to give some assurance on wages and salaries. Auditors should consider:

- **Wages and salaries levels** month-by-month with **previous years**
- **Effect on wages and salaries of rate changes** during the year
- **Average wage** per month **over the year**
- **Sales/profits** per **employee**
- **Payroll proof in total** (Pay rise × staff changes × staff mix)

AUDIT PROGRAMME: WAGES AND SALARY CREDITOR

Occurrence

- **Check individual remuneration** per payroll to **personnel records, records of hours** worked, **salary agreements** etc
- **Confirm existence** of **employees** on payroll by meeting them, attending wages payout, inspecting personnel and tax records, and confirmation from managers
- **Check benefits** (pensions) on payroll to **supporting documentation**

Measurement

- **Check accuracy of calculation of remuneration**
- **Check** whether **calculation** of **statutory deductions** (PAYE, NIC) is **correct**
- Check **validity** of **other deductions** (pension contributions, share save etc) by agreement to supporting documentation (personnel files, conditions of pension scheme) and **check accuracy** of **calculation** of other deductions

Completeness

- **Check casts** of **payroll records**
- **Confirm** payment of **net pay** per payroll records to **cheque** or **bank transfer** summary
- **Agree net pay** per cash book to **payroll**
- **Scrutinise payroll** and **investigate unusual items**

Question: Creditors

You have been assigned to the audit of Carter Brandon Ltd, and you are drafting the audit programme for creditors, accruals and provisions for the year ended 31 December 20X7.

The company operates from a site in West London. All raw materials are received in the stores and all deliveries are checked to the delivery note and purchase order. The stores supervisor raises a goods received note and is also responsible for raising credit requests if there are any problems with the raw materials delivered.

When the bought ledger department staff receive the purchase invoices, they match them to the relevant goods received notes and purchase orders, and post them to the computerised purchase ledger. Suppliers are paid on the last day of each month.

Other creditors and accruals consist of VAT, wages and statutory deductions (PAYE and NI) accruals and time-apportioned expenses such as electricity and telephone.

The company has two significant provisions in its accounts. The first is a new provision in 20X7 for £100,000 that relates to a legal action brought by a competitor who claims their manufacturing process has been illegally copied.

The second provision was set up in the accounts of 20X6 and relates to sums required to be spent on urgent repairs to the factory foundations. The provision in the 20X6 accounts was £60,000. Although

£51,000 was spent on repairs to the foundations during 20X7, the directors are proposing that the provision in the balance sheet of the 20X7 accounts should increase to £75,000.

Required

Describe the audit work you will carry out:

(a) To compare suppliers' statements with balances recorded on the purchase ledger

(b) To check that purchases cut-off has been applied correctly

(c) To confirm that other creditors and accruals have been accurately stated.

Answer

(a) **Audit work to check suppliers' statements to the purchase ledger**

Select a sample of creditors and **compare suppliers' statements with purchase ledger balances**. The extent of the sample will depend on the results of tests of controls and assessment of the effectiveness of controls within the purchases system (ie if the system of control is strong I will check fewer items).

Select the **sample on a random basis**. Selection of only large balances or those with many transactions will not yield an appropriate sample as I am looking for understatement of liabilities. Nil and negative balances will also need to be included in the sample.

If **no statement** was **available** for the supplier, I would ask for **confirmation** of the balance **from the supplier**.

If the balance **agrees exactly**, no further work needs to be carried out.

Where differences arise these need to be categorised as either in-transit items or other (including disputed) items.

In transit items

In-transit items will be either goods or cash.

If the difference relates to goods in transit, I would **ascertain** whether the **goods** were **received** before the year end by reference to the GRN and that they are included in year end stock and purchase accruals. If not, a cut-off error has occurred and should be investigated.

If the goods were received after the year end, the difference with the suppliers' accounts is correct.

Similarly, cash in transit would arise where the payment to the supplier was made by cheque before the year end but was not received by him until after the year end. The **date** the **cheque** was **raised** and its subsequent **clearing** through the bank account after the year end should be **verified by checking the cash book** and the post year end bank statements.

However, if the cheque clears after the year end date, it may indicate that the cheque, though raised before the year end was not sent to the supplier until after the year end. The relevant amount should be added back to year end creditors and to the end of year bank balance.

Other items

Differences which do not arise from in-transit items need to be investigated and **appropriate adjustments** made where necessary.

These differences may have arisen due to **disputed invoices**, where for example the client is demanding credit against an invoice which the supplier is not willing to agree. The client may decide not to post the invoice to the supplier account as he does not consider it to be a liability of the company. However, differences may also arise because **invoices** have been **held back** in order to reduce the level of year-end creditors.

If significant unexplained differences are discovered it may be necessary to **extend** my **testing**. There may also be a problem if sufficient suppliers' statements are not available. Alternative procedures, eg a circularisation may then be required.

(b) **Purchases cut-off**

(i) From my notes taken at the stocktake I will have the **number** of the **last GRN** that was issued before the year end.

(ii) **Select a sample** of **GRNs** issued in the period immediately before and immediately after the year end. The period to be covered would be at least two weeks either side of the year end.

(iii) **Concentrate** my sample on **high value items**, and more on those GRNs from before the year end as these represent the greatest risk of cut-off error.

(iv) **Check** that the **GRNs** have a **correct number**, according to the last GRN issued in the year and whether the **goods** were **received before or after the year end**.

(v) For **GRNs** issued **before the year end**, check whether the **stock** has been included in the year end stock total. In addition, I will check whether that the **creditor** is either **included** in **trade creditors** or **purchase accruals**.

(vi) For **GRNs** issued **after the year end**, to ensure that the **stock** is **included** in the stock records **after the year end**. In addition, I will need to **check** to the **purchase ledger** to ensure that the relevant **invoice** has been **posted** to the supplier account after the year end.

(c) **Other creditors and accruals**

(i) **Assess the system of control** instituted by management to identify and quantify accruals and creditors.

(ii) From the client's sundry creditors and accruals listing, **check** that **accruals** are **calculated correctly** and verify them by reference to subsequent payments. **Check** that **all time apportionments** have been made correctly (for example, for electricity).

(iii) **PAYE and VAT balance**

(1) **Check** the **amount paid to the Inland Revenue** for PAYE and NI. The balance at the year end would normally represent one month's deductions and can be verified to the payroll records. The payment should be traced from the cash book to the PAYE payment book (if used) and subsequent bank statements.

(2) For the VAT balance, **review** for **reasonableness** to the **next VAT return**. I would also **ensure** that the **payment** for the **previous return** was for the **correct** amount and had cleared through the bank.

(iv) **Review the profit and loss account** and **prior year figures** (for any accruals which have not appeared this year or which did not appear last year) and consider liabilities inherent in the trade (eg weekly wages) to ensure that all likely accruals have been provided.

(v) **Scrutinise payments** made after the year end to ascertain whether any payments made should be accrued. This will include consideration of any payments relating to the current year which are made a long time after the year-end.

(vi) **Consider and document** the basis for **round sum accruals** and ensure it is consistent with prior years.

(vii) **Ascertain** why any **payments on account** are being made and **ensure** that the full **liability** is **provided**.

(viii) **Accrued interest** and basic **charges on loans** or overdrafts can be **agreed** to the **bank letter** received for audit purposes.

3 LONG-TERM LIABILITIES

3.1 We are concerned here with long-term liabilities comprising debentures, loan stock and other loans **repayable** at a date **more than one year after the year-end.**

3.2 Auditors will primarily try and determine:

- **Completeness:** whether all long-term liabilities have been disclosed
- **Measurement:** whether interest payable has been calculated correctly and included in the correct accounting period
- **Disclosure:** whether long-term loans and interest have been correctly disclosed in the financial statements

3.3 The major complication for the auditors is that debenture and loan agreements frequently contain conditions with which the company must comply, including restrictions on the company's total borrowings and adherence to specific borrowing ratios.

AUDIT PROGRAMME: LONG-TERM LIABILITIES

• **Obtain/prepare schedule of loans** outstanding at the balance sheet date showing, for each loan: name of lender, date of loan, maturity date, interest date, interest rate, balance at the end of the period and security
• **Compare opening balances** to previous year's papers
• **Test the clerical accuracy** of the analysis
• **Compare balances** to the **general ledger**
• **Check name** of **lender** etc, to **register** of **debenture holders** or equivalent (if kept)
• **Trace additions** and **repayments** to **entries** in the **cash book**
• **Confirm repayments** are in accordance with **loan agreement**
• **Examine cancelled cheques** and **memoranda of satisfaction** for **loans repaid**
• **Verify** that **borrowing limits** imposed either by Articles or by other agreements are **not exceeded**
• **Examine signed Board minutes** relating to **new borrowings/repayments**
• **Obtain direct confirmation** from **lenders** of the amounts outstanding, accrued interest and what security they hold
• **Verify interest charged** for the period and the adequacy of accrued interest
• **Confirm assets charged** have been **entered** in the **register of charges** and **notified** to the **Registrar**
• **Review restrictive covenants** and provisions relating to default:
    ◦ **Review** any **correspondence** relating to the loan
    ◦ **Review confirmation** replies for non-compliance
    ◦ If a **default appears** to exist, **determine** its **effect**, and schedule findings
• **Review minutes, cash book** to **check** if all **loans have been recorded**

4 PROVISIONS AND CONTINGENCIES 12/02, 6/03

4.1 When considering the audit of these two issues, it is important to revise the accounting requirements here first.

FRS 12 *Provisions, contingent liabilities and contingent assets*

KEY TERMS

A **provision** is a liability that is of uncertain timing or amount, to be settled by the transfer of economic benefits.

A **contingent liability** is either

(a) a possible obligation arising from past events whose existence will be confirmed only by the occurrence of one or more uncertain future events not wholly within the entity's control, or

(b) a present obligation that arises from past events but is not recognised because it is not probable that a transfer of economic benefits will be required to settle the obligation or because the amount of the obligation cannot be measured with sufficient reliability.

A **contingent asset** is a possible asset arising from past events whose existence will be confirmed only by the occurrence of one or more uncertain future events not wholly within the entity's control.

4.2 The key distinction in FRS 12 therefore is between provisions which are accrued in the accounts, and contingent assets and liabilities, which are not accrued but which may be disclosed.

ACCOUNTING REQUIREMENTS	
Recognition	A provision should be recognised when an entity has a **present obligation** as a result of a past event, it is **probable** that a **transfer** of **economic benefits** will be **required** to settle the obligation, and a **reasonable estimate** can be made of the amount of the obligation. Unless these conditions are met, no provision should be recognised.
Measurement	The amount recognised as a provision should be the **best estimate** of the expenditure required to settle the present obligation at the balance sheet date.
Reimbursements	Where some or all of the expenditure required to settle a provision is expected to be reimbursed by another party, the reimbursement should be recognised only when it is **virtually certain** that the reimbursement will be received if the entity settles the obligation. The reimbursement should be treated as a separate asset.
Changes in provisions	Provisions should be reviewed at each balance sheet date and adjusted to reflect the current best estimate.

Contingent assets and liabilities

CONTINGENT LIABILITIES		
Where, as a result of past events, there may be a transfer of future economic benefits in settlement of (a) a present obligation or (b) a possible obligation whose existence will be confirmed by the occurrence of one or more uncertain future events not wholly within the entity's control, and		
there is a present obligation that probably requires a transfer of economic benefits in settlement,	there is a possible obligation or a present obligation that may, but probably will not, require a transfer of economic benefits in settlement,	there is a possible obligation or a present obligation where the likelihood of a transfer of economic benefits in settlement is remote,
a provision is recognised and disclosures are required for the provision.	no provision is recognised but disclosures are required for the contingent liability.	no provision is recognised and no disclosure is required.

4.3 A contingent liability also arises in the extremely rare case **where there is a liability** that cannot be recognised because it cannot be **measured reliably**. Disclosures are required for the contingent liability.

CONTINGENT ASSETS		
Where, as a result of past events, there is a possible asset whose existence will be confirmed by the occurrence of one or more uncertain future events not wholly within the entity's control, and		
the inflow of economic benefits is virtually certain,	the inflow of economic benefits is probable but not virtually certain,	the inflow is not probable,
the asset is not contingent.	no asset is recognised but disclosures are required.	no asset is recognised and no disclosure is required.

AUDIT PROGRAMME: PROVISIONS/CONTINGENCIES

- **Obtain details** of all **provisions** which have been included in the **accounts** and all **contingencies** that have been disclosed
- **Obtain** a **detailed analysis** of all **provisions** showing opening balances, movements and closing balances
- **Determine** for each material provision **whether** the **company** has a **present obligation** as a result of past events by:
  - **Review** of **correspondence** relating to the item
  - **Discussion** with the **directors.** Have they created a valid expectation in other parties that they will discharge the obligation?
- **Determine** for each material provision **whether** it is **probable** that a **transfer of economic benefits** will be required to settle the obligation by the following tests.
  - **Check** whether any **payments** have been **made** in the post balance sheet period in respect of the item

- ○ **Review correspondence** with solicitors, banks, customers, insurance company and suppliers both pre and post year end
- ○ **Send** a **letter** to the **solicitor** to obtain their views (where relevant)
- ○ **Discuss** the **position** of similar **past provisions** with the directors. Were these provisions eventually settled?
- ○ **Consider** the **likelihood** of **reimbursement**

- **Recalculate** all **provisions** made
- **Compare** the **amount provided** with any post year end payments and with any amount paid in the past for similar items
- In the event that it is not possible to estimate the amount of the **provision**, check that this **contingent liability** is **disclosed** in the accounts
- **Consider** the **nature** of the **client's business**. Would you expect to see any other provisions for example, warranties?

Exam focus point

You should appreciate that the problems of accounting for contingencies makes their audit difficult.

5 CAPITAL AND OTHER ISSUES

Share capital

5.1 The issued share capital as stated in the accounts must be **agreed** in total with the **share register**. An examination of transfers on a test basis should be made in those cases where a company handles its own registration work. Where the registration work is dealt with by independent registrars, auditors will normally examine the reports submitted by them to the company, and obtain from them at the year-end a certificate of the share capital in issue.

5.2 Company law prescribe that the directors must:

(a) Have the general powers of management to be able to allot shares.

(b) Not exercise that power without **authority** from the **members**. That authority may either be given by the company's **articles** or by **resolution** passed in **general meeting** (s 80 of the Companies Act).

(c) Respect the **pre-emption rights** of **existing members**. Under s 89 of the Companies Act directors must first offer shares to holders of similar shares in proportion to their holdings. A private company can permanently exclude these rules in its memorandum and articles. Any company can decide by special resolution that the rules should not apply on a specific occasion.

5.3 Auditors should take particular care if there are any movements in reserves that cannot be distributed, and should **confirm** that these movements are **valid**.

AUDIT PROGRAMME: CAPITAL AND RELATED ISSUES

Share capital
• **Agree** the **authorised share capital** with the **memorandum** and **articles of association**
• **Agree changes** to **authorised share capital** with **properly authorised resolutions**
Issue of shares
• **Verify any issue** of share capital or other changes during the year with general and board **minutes**
• **Ensure issue or change** is within the **terms** of the **memorandum** and **articles** of association, and directors possess appropriate authority to issue shares
• **Confirm** that **cash** or **other consideration** has been **received** or **debtor(s) is included** as called up share capital not paid
• **Confirm** that any **premium** on issue of shares has been **credited** to the **share premium** account
• Where a public company has issued shares for **non-cash consideration,** check fair **value** has been **received for** the shares, and that valuation reports have been obtained
• For **redeemable shares** issued, check their **terms provide** for payment on **redemption**
Transfer of shares
• **Verify transfers of shares** by reference to:
  ◦ Correspondence
  ◦ Completed and stamped transfer forms
  ◦ Cancelled share certificates
  ◦ Minutes of directors' meeting
• **Check the balances** on **shareholders' accounts** in the register of members and the total list with the amount of issued share capital in the general ledger
Dividends
• **Agree dividends** paid and proposed to **authority** in minute books and **check calculation** with **total share capital** issued to ascertain whether there are any outstanding or unclaimed dividends
• **Check dividend payments** with **documentary evidence** (say, the returned dividend warrants)
• **Check** that **dividends do not contravene** the distribution provisions of the **Companies Act 1985**
Reserves
• **Check movements on reserves** to **supporting authority**
• **Ensure that movements on reserves do not contravene** the **Companies Act 1985** and the memorandum and articles of association
• **Confirm** that the **company** can **distinguish** those reserves at the balance sheet date that are **distributable** from those that are **non-distributable**
• **Ensure appropriate disclosures** of movements on reserves are made in the company's accounts

AUDIT PROGRAMME: STATUTORY BOOKS

Register of directors and secretaries

- **Update permanent file** giving details of directors and secretary
- **Verify** any **changes** with the **minutes** and ensure that the necessary details have been filed at Companies House
- **Verify** that the **number of directors complies** with the **Articles**

Register of directors' interests in shares and debentures

- **Ensure** that **directors' interests** are **noted** on the permanent file for cross-referencing to directors' reports
- **Ensure** that **directors' shareholdings comply** with the **Articles**

Minute books of directors and general meetings

- **Obtain photocopies** or **prepare extracts** from the **minute books** of meetings concerning financial matters, cross-referencing them to appropriate working papers
- **Ensure** that **extracts** of **agreements** referred to in the minutes are **prepared** for the permanent file
- **Check agreements** with the company's seal book where one is kept
- **Note the date** of the last **minute reviewed**
- **Check** that **meetings** have been **properly convened** and that quorums attended them

Register of interests in shares (if applicable)

- **Scrutinise register** and verify that *prima facie* it appears to be in order
- **Ensure** that **significant interests** are **noted on** the permanent file

Register of charges

- **Update permanent file schedule** from the register
- **Ensure** that **any assets** which are **charged** as security for loans from third parties are **disclosed** in the **accounts**
- **Obtain confirmation** that there are **no charges** to be recorded if no entries are recorded in the register
- **Consider carrying out company search** at Companies House to verify the accuracy of the register

Accounting records

- Consider whether the accounting records are adequate to:
  - **Show** and **explain** the **company's transactions**
  - **Disclose** with **reasonable accuracy**, at any time, the **financial position** of the **company**
  - **Comply** with the **Act** by recording money received and expended, assets and liabilities, year-end stock and stock-taking, sales and purchases
  - **Enable** the **directors** to **ensure** that the **accounts give** a **true and fair view**

General ledger and journals

- **Check opening balances** in general ledger to **previous year's audited accounts**
- **Check additions** of general ledger accounts
- **Review general ledger accounts** and ensure significant transfers and unusual items are *bona fide*
- **Review the journal** and ensure that **significant entries** are **authorised** and **properly recorded**
- **Check extraction** and **addition** of **trial balance** (if prepared by the client)

Returns

- **Check** that the **following returns** have been filed properly:
  - Annual return and previous year's accounts
  - Notices of change in directors or secretary
  - Memoranda of charges or mortgages created during the period
  - VAT returns
  - Other tax returns

Directors' service contracts

- **Inspect copies** of directors' service contracts or memoranda.
- **Ensure** that they are **kept** at
  - The **registered office**, or
  - The **principal place of business**, or
  - The place where the register of members is kept, if not the registered office
- Verify that long-term service contracts (lasting more than five years) have been approved in general meeting.

Directors' emoluments

5.4 The auditors have a duty to include in their report the required disclosure particulars of directors' emoluments and transactions with directors, if these requirements have not been complied with in the accounts (s 237).

5.5 The auditors will have carried out an evaluation of salaries payroll procedures, including the system in operation for directors' salaries, earlier in the audit. At the year end, they can probably concentrate on limited substantive work designed to ensure that the final **figures** in the **accounting records** are **complete** and the disclosure requirements in respect of directors have been complied with.

AUDIT PROGRAMME: DIRECTORS' EMOLUMENTS
• **Ascertain** whether **monies payable or benefits** in kind provided have been **properly approved** in accordance with the company's memorandum and articles of association and that they are not prohibited by the Act • **Confirm** that all **monies payable** and **benefits receivable** in relation to the current accounting period have been **properly accounted for**, unless the right to any of these has been waived by inspecting: ◦ Salary records ◦ Service contracts ◦ Board minutes ◦ Other relevant records • **Consider** whether the **most common types of benefit** (company cars or cheap loans) may have been **omitted** • **Review directors' service contracts** • **Review** the **company's procedures** to ensure that **all directors advise** the board of all disclosable **emoluments** • **Review** the **procedures** for ensuring that any **payments made to former directors** of the company are **identified** and **properly disclosed** • **Consider** the **need** for any **amounts** included in directors' remuneration to be **further disclosed** in accordance with the Companies Act 1985 (for example property rented by directors from a company at below market rental)

Valuation of benefits in kind

5.6 In accordance with the Companies Act 1985 the amount to be disclosed for a benefit in kind is its **estimated money value**.

Golden hellos

5.7 Under the Companies Act 1985 rules emoluments in respect of a person's accepting office as director shall be treated as emoluments in respect of his services as director.

Chapter roundup

- The largest figure in current liabilities will normally be trade creditors generally checked by comparison of suppliers' statements with purchase ledger accounts.
- A creditors' circularisation might be appropriate, although they are relatively rare in practice.
- Accruals can be significant in total. Expense accruals will tend to repeat from one year to the next. Auditors should review after-date invoices and payments, and consider whether anything else that would have been expected has not been accrued.
- Long-term liabilities are usually authorised by the board and should be well documented.
- The accounting provisions for provisions and contingencies are complex and that can make them difficult to audit.
- The main concern with share capital and reserves (including distributions) will be that all transactions comply with the Companies Act.
- When auditing statutory books auditors should consider whether:
  - The company has complied with the Companies Act.
  - The records contain information that affects other areas of the audit.
- Auditors should ensure that directors' emoluments have been completely recorded in the accounts.

Quick quiz

1 What are the two primary objectives of balance sheet work on liabilities?

1 ....

2 ....

2 Nil balances should not be included in a supplier statement test.

True ☐

False ☐

3 Give two instances where creditors' circularisation is required.

1 ....

2 ....

4 Give four things auditors should consider when carrying out analytical review on wages and salaries.

1 ....

2 ....

3 ....

4 ....

5 Complete the definition

Long term liabilities comprise ...., ...-.......................... and other loans .... at a date .... a year .... the year end.

Answers to quick quiz

1 To ensure (1) completely and (2) accurately recorded

2 False

3 1 Supplier statements are unavailable
  2 Weak internal controls

4 1 Salary rate changes
  2 Average wage by month over the year
  3 Sale/employee
  4 Payroll proof in total

5 debentures, loan-stock, repayable, more than, after.

Now try the questions below from the Exam Question Bank

Number	Level	Marks	Time
17	Exam	20	36 mins

Chapter 18

AUDIT REVIEWS AND FINALISATION

Introduction

In this chapter will consider the reviews that take place to complete the audit and the procedures carried out before the audit conclusion is drawn and the opinion reached.

Firstly we consider two key reviews

- Going concern
- Subsequent events

These are both important disclosure issues in the financial statements. If the disclosures are not correct, this will impact on the auditors' report, which is discussed in Chapter 19.

In Chapter 12, in the context of accounting estimates, we discussed how there are some items in financial statements where facts or knowledge is confined to management. In the final stages of the audit, the auditor must consider this evidence, and obtain written representations from directors where necessary.

The remaining reviews are linked by their common aim of giving assurance as to the company's **stability** and the **validity** of the financial statements. The results of analytical procedures will be applied when considering the going concern situation and so on.

Accountancy knowledge is particularly important in this chapter. Auditors need to be able to interpret accounts understand the requirements of specific accounting standards.

These procedures are extremely important; failure to carry them out can lead to the gravest consequences for the auditors. Given this fact, they tend to be fairly standard in most audit approaches. A useful summary of these procedures is given in the checklist at the end of the chapter and you should refer to the checklist throughout this chapter.

All the reviews are very important to the audit, but particularly going concern. This is highly examinable. Letters of representation were examined in December 2002.

1 GOING CONCERN 12/03

1.1 SAS 130 *Going concern basis in financial statements* was developed separately from the bulk of the other auditing standards because of its importance. This arises from the exposure of the auditors should they miss the going concern problems of a client and the difficulties surrounding the determination of going concern status in any given situation.

Going concern as an accounting concept

KEY TERM

The **going concern** concept: the enterprise will continue in operational existence for the foreseeable future. This means in particular that the profit and loss account and balance sheet assume no intention or necessity to liquidate or curtail significantly the scale of operation.

1.2 There are also legal requirements concerning going concern. Under these requirements, the financial statements of an entity are assumed to be prepared on a going concern basis.

1.3 Where the going concern basis is **not** appropriate:

- The entity may not be able to recover the amounts recorded in respect of assets.
- There may be changes in the amounts and dates of maturities of liabilities.

Therefore, if material, the amounts and classification of assets and liabilities would need to be adjusted.

1.4 Consequently, the **directors** must satisfy themselves that the going concern basis is appropriate. Even where it is, further disclosure may be required to give a true and fair view.

The applicability and scope of this SAS

1.5 The SAS gives guidance to auditors in the context of the going concern basis in financial statements which are required to be properly prepared under CA 1985 and to show a true and fair view. The SAS does **not** give guidance relating to the going concern in any other context, for example, *Cadbury Report* matters. Auditors are required to consider the entity's ability to continue as a going concern and any disclosures about going concern in the financial statements.

Foreseeable future

1.6 FRS 18 uses the term 'foreseeable future' but does not define it. The SAS recognises that any consideration of foreseeable future involves 'making a judgement, at a particular point in time, about future events which are inherently uncertain'.

1.7 The SAS suggests that the degree of **uncertainty increases significantly** the **further into the future** the consideration is taken and the 'foreseeable future' depends on the specific circumstances at a point in time.

1.8 As a consequence there can never be any certainty in relation to going concern. The auditors' judgement is only valid at that time and can be 'overturned by subsequent events'.

Consideration of going concern by the directors

1.9 The directors must assess going concern by looking at a period into the future and considering all available and relevant information. The SAS states that a minimum length for this period cannot be specified; it would be 'artificial and arbitrary' as there is no 'cut off point' after which the directors would change their approach.

1.10 FRS 18 requires the directors to make disclosures about the period they have determined to be the 'foreseeable future' if that period is less than one year.

Procedures

1.11 The audit procedures will be based on the directors' deliberations and the information they used. The auditors must assess whether the audit evidence is sufficient and appropriate and whether they agree with the directors' judgement. They should consider:

- The nature of the entity (its size and the complexity of its circumstances, for instance)
- Whether the information relates to future events, and if so how far into the future those events lie

A lengthy appendix to the SAS gives examples of how auditors might apply the SAS in different circumstances.

Audit evidence

1.12 The SAS states 'the auditors should assess the adequacy of the means by which the directors have satisfied themselves that:

(a) It is appropriate for them to adopt the going concern basis in preparing the financial statements; and

(b) The financial statements include such disclosures, if any, relating to going concern as are necessary for them to give a true and fair view.

For this purpose:

(i) The auditors should make enquiries of the directors and examine appropriate available financial information; and

(ii) Having regard to the future period to which the directors have paid particular attention in assessing going concern, the auditors should plan and perform procedures specifically designed to identify any material matters which could indicate concern about the entity's ability to continue as a going concern'.

Preliminary assessment

1.13 The auditors' approach includes a preliminary assessment, when the overall audit plan is being developed, of the risk that the entity may be unable to continue as a going concern. The auditors should consider:

(a) **Whether the period** to which the directors have paid particular attention in assessing going concern is **reasonable** in the client's circumstances

(b) The **systems,** or other means (formal or informal), **for timely identification of warnings of future risks** and uncertainties the entity might face

(c) **Budget and/or forecast information** (cash flow information in particular) produced by the entity, and the quality of the systems (or other means, formal or informal) in place for producing this information and keeping it up to date

(d) Whether the **key assumptions** underlying the budgets and/or forecasts appear appropriate in the circumstances, including consideration of:

- Projected profit
- Forecast levels of working capital
- The completeness of forecast expenditure
- Whether the client will have sufficient cash at periods of maximum need
- The financing of capital expenditure and long-term plans

(e) The **sensitivity of budgets and/or forecasts** to variable factors both within the control of the directors and outside their control

(f) Any **obligations, undertakings or guarantees** arranged with other entities (in particular, lenders, suppliers and group companies)

(g) The **existence, adequacy and terms of borrowing facilities**, and supplier credit

(h) The **directors' plans** for resolving any matters giving rise to the concern (if any) about the appropriateness of the going concern basis. In particular, the auditors may need to consider whether:

- The plans are realistic
- There is a reasonable expectation that the plans are likely to resolve any problems foreseen
- The directors are likely to put the plans into practice effectively

1.14 The auditors' and directors' procedures can be very simple in some cases, particularly in the case of smaller companies, where budgets and forecasts are not normally prepared and no specific systems are in place to monitor going concern matters.

The auditors' examination of borrowing facilities

1.15 The auditors will usually:

- Obtain confirmations of the existence and terms of bank facilities
- Make their own assessment of the intentions of the bankers relating thereto

1.16 These procedures will become more important if (for example) there is a **low margin** of **financial resources** available to the entity, correspondence between the bankers and the entity reveals that the **last renewal** of facilities was **agreed with difficulty** and a **significant deterioration in cash flow** is projected.

1.17 If the auditors cannot satisfy themselves then, in accordance with the audit reporting standard (SAS 600), they should consider whether the relevant matters need to be:

- **Disclosed in the financial statements** in order that they give a true and fair view
- **Referred to in the auditors' report** (by explanatory paragraph or qualified opinion)

Determining and documenting the auditors' concerns

1.18 The SAS states 'the auditors should determine and document the extent of their concern (if any) about the entity's ability to continue as a going concern. In determining the extent of their concern, the auditors should take account of all relevant information of which they have become aware during their audit'. The following are given in the SAS as examples of indicators of an entity's inability to continue as a going concern.

Going concern	
Financial	An excess of liabilities over assets
	Net current liabilities
	Necessary borrowing facilities have not been agreed
	Default on terms of loan agreements, and potential breaches of covenant
	Significant liquidity or cash flow problems
	Major losses or cash flow problems which have arisen since the balance sheet date and which threaten the entity's continued existence
	Substantial sales of fixed assets not intended to be replaced
	Major restructuring of debts
	Denial of (or reduction in) normal terms of trade credit by suppliers
	Major debt repayment falling due where refinancing is necessary to the entity's continued existence
	Inability to pay debts as they fall due
Operational	Fundamental changes to the market or technology to which the entity is unable to adapt adequately
	Externally forced reductions in operations (for example, as a result of legislation or regulatory action)
	Loss of key management or staff, labour difficulties or excessive dependence on a few product lines where the market is depressed
	Loss of key suppliers or customers or technical developments which render a key product obsolete
Other	Major litigation in which an adverse judgement would imperil the entity's continued existence
	Issues which involve a range of possible outcomes so wide that an unfavourable result could affect the appropriateness of the going concern basis

Exam focus point

Any question on going concern is likely to ask you to identify signs that a particular client may not be a going concern.

1.19 Auditors may still obtain sufficient appropriate audit evidence in such situations to conclude that the going concern basis is still appropriate. Further procedures such as discussions with the directors and further work on forecasts may be required.

1.20 Where auditors consider that there is a significant level of concern about the going concern basis, they might write to the directors suggesting the need to take suitable advice.

Written confirmations of representations from the directors

1.21 Representations may be critical in terms of audit evidence. The SAS requires auditors to consider whether they need the directors to provide written representation concerning going concern. If they do **not** receive such representations the auditors should consider whether:

- There is a limitation of scope in their work and a qualified opinion is required in 'except for' or 'disclaimer' terms.
- The failure of the directors to provide written confirmation could indicate concern.

Assessing disclosures in the financial statements

1.22 The auditors must also consider whether the disclosures concerning going concern in the financial statements are sufficient to give a true and fair view. The main concern here is **sufficiency** of disclosure where:

- There are going concern worries.
- The future period the directors have considered is less than one year.

1.23 The auditors must assess whether the statements show a true and fair view and hence whether their opinion should be qualified, as well as whether all matters have been satisfactorily disclosed.

Reporting on the financial statements

1.24 The SAS summarises, in flowchart form, how auditors formulate their opinion as to whether the financial statements give a true and fair view and this is shown on a following page.

Going concern and reporting on the financial statements

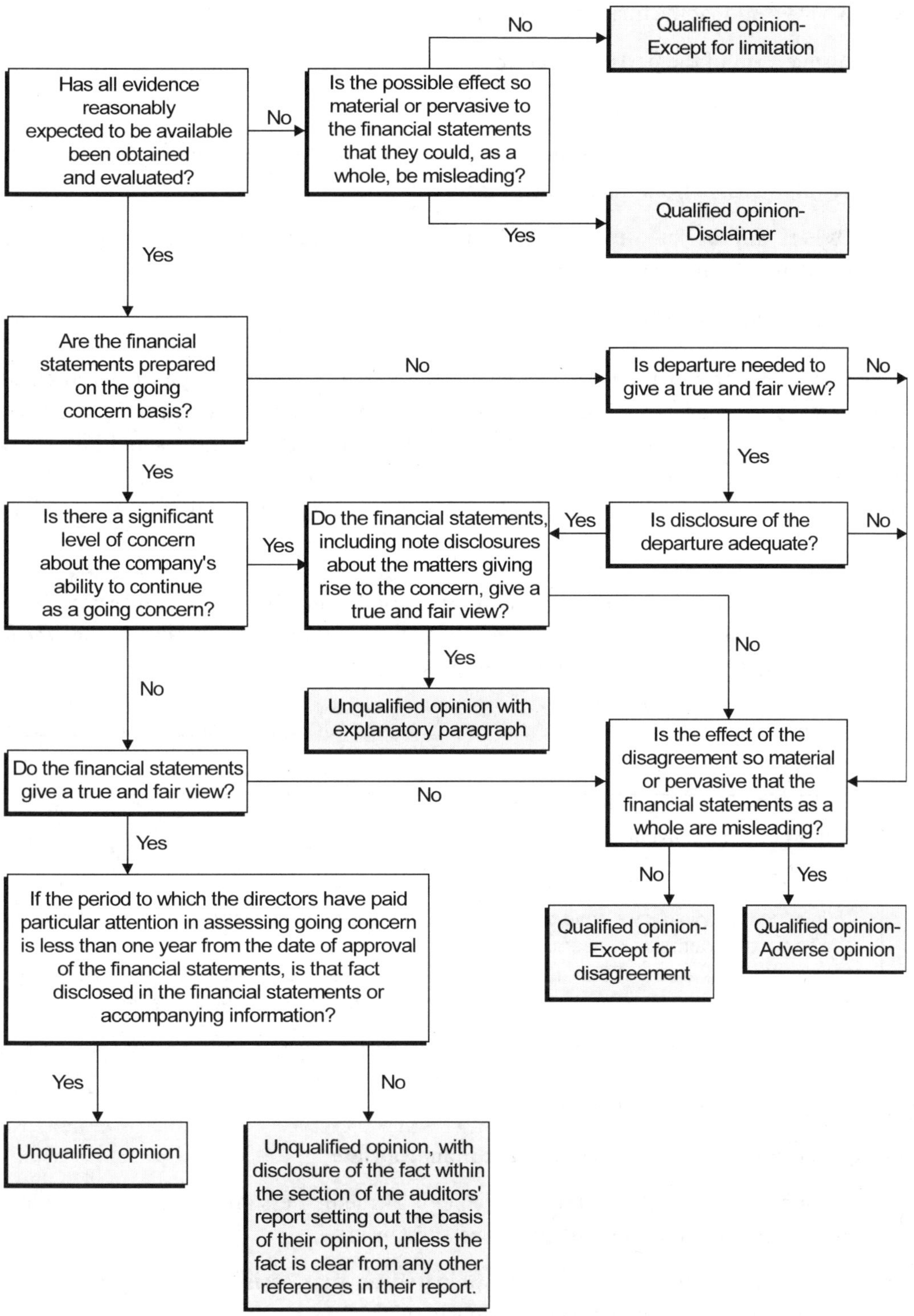

1.25 The SAS states 'where the auditors consider that there is a significant level of concern about the entity's ability to continue as a going concern, but do not disagree with the preparation of the financial statements on the going concern basis, they should include an explanatory paragraph when setting out the basis of their opinion. They should not quality their opinion on these grounds alone, provided the disclosures in the financial statements of the matters giving rise to the concern are adequate for the financial statements to give a true and fair view'.

1.26 The following matters must be included in the financial statements for disclosure to be regarded as adequate.

- A statement that the financial statements have been prepared on the **going concern basis**
- A statement of the **pertinent factors**
- The **nature** of the concern
- A statement of the **assumptions** adopted by the directors, which should be clearly distinguishable from the pertinent facts
- (Where appropriate and practicable) a statement regarding the directors' **plans for resolving the matters** giving rise to the concern
- Details of any **relevant actions** by the directors

1.27 The SAS also states 'if the period to which the directors have paid particular attention in assessing going concern is less than one year from the date of approval of the financial statements, and the directors have not disclosed that fact, the auditors should do so within the section of their report setting out the basis of their opinion, unless the fact is clear from any other references in their report. They should not qualify their opinion on the financial statements on these grounds alone'.

1.28 The auditors will also qualify their opinion if they consider that the directors have not taken adequate steps to satisfy themselves that it is appropriate for them to adopt the going concern basis. This will be a limitation in the scope of the auditors' work'.

1.29 The audit report will contain the following paragraph if disclosure is considered to be inadequate.

Basis of opinion: excerpt

Going concern

In forming our opinion, we have considered the adequacy of the disclosures made in note 1 of the financial statements concerning the uncertainty as to the continuation and renewal of the company's bank overdraft facility. In view of the significance of this uncertainty we consider that it should be drawn to your attention but our opinion is not qualified in this respect.

Going concern presumption is inappropriate

1.30 Where the going concern presumption is **inappropriate**:

- Even disclosure in the financial statements of the matters giving rise to this conclusion is **not** sufficient for them to give a true and fair view.
- The effect on financial statements prepared on that basis is so material or pervasive that the financial statements are seriously misleading.

Accordingly, the auditors must give an **adverse opinion**.

Financial statements not prepared on the going concern basis

1.31 In rare circumstances, the accounts may be prepared on a basis that reflects the fact that assets may need to be realised other than in the ordinary course of operations. The auditors may wish to refer to the basis on which the financial statements are prepared. However, they will not have to qualify their opinion if the financial statements give a true and fair view.

1.32 Section summary

- Director and auditor assessment of the going concern basis should take place over the **foreseeable future.**
- Auditors should make a **preliminary assessment** of going concern and be alert during the audit for **signs** of **going concern problems.**
- Specific audit procedures include **assessment** of **client forecasts,** examination of **borrowing facilities** and obtaining **representations** from the directors.
- Auditors may **qualify** the audit report because they disagree with the use of the **going concern basis** or **extent of disclosure.**
- Alternatively auditors may consider it appropriate to give an unqualified opinion with a **fundamental uncertainty** paragraph.

2 SUBSEQUENT EVENTS

2.1 Before describing the steps taken by the auditors to obtain reasonable assurance in respect of subsequent events (also called post balance sheet events - the terms are interchangeable) we need to revise the accounting requirements of the relevant accounting standard SSAP 17 *Accounting for post balance sheet events.*

SSAP 17 **12/03**

KEY TERMS

Post balance sheet events are those events, both favourable and unfavourable, which occur between the balance sheet date and the date on which the financial statements are approved by the board of directors.

Adjusting events are post balance sheet events which provide additional evidence of conditions existing at the balance sheet date. They include events which because of statutory conventional requirements are reflected in financial statements.

Non-adjusting events are post balance sheet events which concern conditions which did not exist at the balance sheet date.

2.2 Standard practice in respect of the disclosure of post balance sheet events is as follows.

'Financial statements should be prepared on the basis of conditions existing at the balance sheet date.

A material post balance sheet event requires changes in the amounts to be included in financial statements where:

(a) It is an adjusting event; or

(b) It indicates that application of the going concern concept to the whole or a material part of the company is not appropriate.

A material post balance sheet event should be disclosed where:

(a) It is a non-adjusting event of such materiality that its non-disclosure would affect the ability of the users of financial statements to reach a proper understanding of the financial position; or

(b) It is the reversal or maturity after the year end of a transaction entered into before the year end, the substance of which was primarily to alter the appearance of the company's balance sheet.'

2.3 In respect of each disclosable post balance sheet event, the notes to the financial statements should state:

- The **nature** of the event
- An **estimate** of the financial effect, or a statement that it is not practicable to make such an estimate

Exam focus point

Knowledge of the relevant accounting requirements is particularly important when dealing with post balance sheet events.

SAS 150 *Subsequent events*

KEY TERMS

Subsequent events are those relevant events (favourable or unfavourable) which occur and those facts which are discovered between the period end and the laying of the financial statements before the members or equivalent.

Relevant events are those which:

- Provide additional evidence relating to conditions existing at the balance sheet date, or
- Concern conditions which did not exist at the balance sheet date, but which may be of such materiality that their disclosure is required to ensure the financial statements are not misleading.

2.4 The SAS requires auditors to consider the effect of subsequent events on the financial statements and carry out procedures to ensure all relevant events requiring adjustments of or disclosure in the financial statements have been dealt with.

Procedures

PROCEDURES TESTING SUBSEQUENT EVENTS	
Enquiries of management	Status of items involving **subjective judgement**/ accounted for using preliminary data New **commitments**, borrowings or guarantees **Sales** or destruction of **assets** **Issues** of **shares/debentures** or changes in business structure **Developments** involving **risk areas, provisions** and **contingencies** **Unusual accounting adjustments** **Major events** (eg going concern problems) affecting appropriateness of accounting policies for estimates
Other procedures	**Consider procedures** of management for identifying subsequent events **Read minutes** of general board/committee meetings **Review latest accounting records** and financial information

2.5 These procedures should be performed as near as possible to the date of the auditors' report. Reviews and updates of these procedures may be required, depending on the length of the time between the procedures and the signing of the auditors' report and the susceptibility of the items to change over time.

Subsequent events discovered after the date of the auditors' report but before the financial statements are issued

2.6 The financial statements are the directors' responsibility. The directors should therefore inform the auditors of any material subsequent events between the date of the auditors' report and the date the financial statements are issued. The auditors do **not** have any obligation to perform procedures, or make enquires regarding the financial statements **after** the date of their report.

2.7 The SAS states 'when, after the date of their report but before the financial statements are issued, auditors become aware of subsequent events which may materially affect the financial statements, they should establish whether the financial statements need amendment, should discuss the matter with the directors and should consider the implications for their report, taking additional action as appropriate'.

2.8 When the financial statements are amended, the auditors should extend the subsequent events procedures discussed above to the date of their new report, carry out any other appropriate procedures and issue a new audit report dated the day it is signed.

2.9 The situation where the statements are not amended but the auditors feel that they should be is discussed below.

Subsequent events discovered after the financial statements have been issued but before their laying before the members, or equivalent

2.10 Auditors have no obligations to perform procedures or make enquiries regarding the financial statements **after** they have been issued.

2.11 The SAS says 'when, after the financial statements have been issued, but before they have been laid before the members or equivalent, auditors become aware of subsequent events which, had they occurred and been known of at the date of their report, might have caused them to issue a different report, they should consider whether the financial statements need amendment, should discuss the matter with the directors, and should consider the implications for their report, taking additional action as appropriate'.

2.12 The SAS gives the appropriate procedures which the auditors should undertake when the directors revise the financial statements.

- **Carry out the audit procedures** necessary in the circumstances
- **Consider**, where appropriate, whether Stock Exchange or financial services regulations require the **revision to be publicised** or a regulator informed
- **Review the steps taken by the directors** to ensure that anyone in receipt of the previously issued financial statements together with the auditors' report thereon is informed of the situation
- **Issue a new report** on the revised financial statements

2.13 When the auditors issue a **new report** they:

- **Refer in their report to the note to the financial statements** which more extensively discusses the reason for the revision of the accounts
- **Refer to the earlier report** issued by them on the financial statements
- **Date** their new report **not earlier** than the date the revised financial statements are approved
- **Have regard** to the **guidance** relating to reports on revised annual financial statements and directors' reports as set out in APB's Practice Note 8 *Reports by auditors under company legislation in the United Kingdom*

2.14 Where the directors do **not** revise the financial statements but the auditors feel they should be revised, and where the statements have been issued but not yet laid before the members; or if the directors do not intend to make an appropriate statement at the AGM, then the auditors should consider steps to take, on a timely basis, to prevent reliance on their report for example, a statement at the AGM. The auditors have **no** right to communicate to the members directly in writing.

3 MANAGEMENT REPRESENTATIONS 12/02

3.1 The auditors receive many representations during the audit and some may be critical to obtaining sufficient appropriate audit evidence. Representations may also be required for general matters, for example, full availability of accounting records.

3.2 Written confirmation of oral representations avoids confusion and disagreement. The written confirmation may take the form of:

- A **representation letter** from **management** (see example below)
- A **letter from the auditors** outlining their understanding of management's representations, duly acknowledged and confirmed in writing by management
- **Minutes of meetings of the board** or directors, or similar body, at which such representations are approved

3.3 SAS 440 *Management representations* states 'auditors should obtain written confirmation of appropriate representations from management before their report is issued.

Acknowledgement by directors of their responsibility for the financial statements

3.4 Auditors must obtain evidence that directors acknowledge responsibility for the financial statements and have approved them. They usually do this when they receive a signed copy of the financial statements which incorporate a relevant statement of the directors' responsibilities.

Representations by management as audit evidence

3.5 In addition to representations relating to responsibility for the financial statements, the auditors may wish to rely on management representations as audit evidence which the SAS allows them to do when they are critical to obtaining sufficient audit evidence.

3.6 Such matters should be discussed with those responsible for giving the written confirmation, to ensure that they understand what they are confirming. Written confirmations are normally required of appropriately senior management.

3.7 Only matters which are material to the financial statements should be included in a letter of representation.

3.8 When the auditors receive such representations they should:

(a) Seek **corroborative audit evidence**

(b) Evaluate whether the representations made by management appear **reasonable and are consistent** with other audit evidence obtained, including other representations

(c) Consider whether the individuals making the representations can be expected to be **well-informed** on the particular matters

3.9 There are two instances given in the SAS where management representations **may** be the only audit evidence available.

- **Knowledge of the facts is confined to management**, for example, the facts are a matter of management intention.
- **The matter is principally one of judgement or opinion**, for example, the trading position of a particular customer.

3.10 There may be occasions when the representations received do not agree with other audit evidence obtained. In such cases, the auditors must investigate and consider whether this casts doubt on other representations they have obtained.

Basic elements of a management representation letter

3.11 A management representation letter should:

- Be **addressed** to the **auditors**
- **Contain specified information**
- Be **appropriately dated**
- Be **approved by those with specific knowledge** of the relevant matters

3.12 The auditors will normally request that the letter is:

- Discussed and agreed by the board of directors (or equivalent)
- Signed on its behalf by the chairman and secretary before the auditors approve the financial statements.

3.13 The letter will usually be **dated on** the day the financial statements are **approved**, but if there is any significant delay between the representation letter and the date of the auditors' report, then the auditors should consider the need to obtain further representations.

Action if management refuses to provide written confirmation of representations

3.14 The SAS states 'if management refuses to provide written confirmation of a representation that the auditors consider necessary, the auditors should consider the implications of this scope limitation for their report'. In these circumstances, the auditors should consider whether it is appropriate to rely on other representations made by management during the audit.

Example of a management representation letter

3.15 An **example** of a management representation letter is provided in an appendix to the SAS. It is **not** a standard letter, and representations do not have to be confirmed in letter form.

(Company letterhead)

(To the auditors) (Date)

We confirm to the best of our knowledge and belief, and having made appropriate enquiries of other directors and officials of the company, the following representations given to you in connection with your audit of the financial statements for the period ended 31 December 20...

(1) We acknowledge as directors our responsibilities under the Companies Act 1985 for preparing financial statements which give a true and fair view and for making accurate representations to you. All the accounting records have been made available to you for the purpose of your audit and all the transactions undertaken by the company have been properly reflected and recorded in the accounting records. All other records and related information, including minutes of all management and shareholders' meetings, have been made available to you.

(2) The legal claim by ABC Limited has been settled out of court by a payment of £258,000. No further amounts are expected to be paid, and no similar claims have been received.

(3) In connection with deferred tax not provided, the following assumptions reflect the intentions and expectations of the company:

(a) capital investment of £450,000 is planned over the next three years;

(b) there are no plans to sell revalued properties; and

(c) we are not aware of any indications that the situation is likely to change so as to necessitate the inclusion of a provision for tax payable in the financial statements.

(4) The company has not had, or entered into, at any time during the period any arrangement, transaction or agreement to provide credit facilities (including loans, quasi-loans or credit transactions) for directors or to guarantee or provide security for such matters.

(5) There have been no events since the balance sheet date which necessitate revision of the figures included in the financial statements or inclusion of a note thereto.

As minuted by the board of directors at its meeting on .... (date)

....

Chairman Secretary

3.16 The following notes are provided by the SAS on the example.

- Other signatories may include those with specific knowledge of the relevant matters, for example the chief financial officer.
- Examples of other issues which may be the subject of representations from management include:
- The extent of the purchase of goods on terms which include reservation of title by suppliers
- The absence of knowledge of circumstances which could result in losses on long-term contracts
- The reasons for concluding that an overdue debt from a related party is fully recoverable
- Confirmation of the extent of guarantees, warranties or other financial commitments relating to subsidiary undertakings or related parties

Exam focus point

The most important points to remember about a letter of representation are:

- The circumstances in which it can be used
- The auditors' response if the client fails to agree to it

You should also be able to draft appropriate representations if asked.

Question: Management representations

Management representations are an important source of audit evidence. These representations may be oral or written, and may be obtained either on an informal or formal basis. The auditors will include information obtained in this manner in their audit working papers where it forms part of their total audit evidence.

Required

(a) Explain the nature and role of the letter of representation.

(b) Explain why it is important for the auditors to discuss the contents of the letter of representation at an early stage of the audit.

(c) Explain why standard letters of representation are becoming less frequently used by the auditing profession.

Answer

(a) The letter of representation is a letter normally signed by appropriate directors normally on behalf of the whole board. Such a letter contains representations relating to matters which are material to the financial statements but concerning which knowledge of the facts is confined to management, or where the directors have used judgement or opinion in the preparation of the financial statements.

The precise scope and content of the letter of representation should be appropriate to the particular audit. An example of a typical situation in which representations may be required would be a case in which an employee's legal claim is settled out of court and the directors are asked to set out in writing their view that no further similar claims are expected to be paid. An absence of independent corroborative evidence and the fact that judgement on the part of directors is involved indicates the need for written evidence of the judgement in the letter of representation.

Representations are not a substitute for other necessary audit work, and they do not relieve the auditors of any of their responsibilities. Even where written representations are obtained, the auditors need to decide whether in the circumstances these representations, together with other audit evidence obtained, are sufficient to justify an unqualified opinion on the financial statements.

However, written representations by the directors do form part of the total audit evidence, and form part of the auditors' working papers. Their status as evidence is given weight by the fact that s 389 of the Companies Act 1985 makes it a criminal offence for directors knowingly or recklessly to make false statements to the auditors in the course of their duty.

One function which the letter of representation may also serve, although it is subsidiary to its central purposes, is that such a letter may act as a reminder to the directors of their responsibilities. For example, the letter will remind them of their responsibilities with regard to the truth and fairness of the accounts, and of their responsibility for statements made orally to the auditors but only recorded in writing in the letter of representation.

(b) The letter of representation should not be seen as an afterthought in the audit process, even though the letter should be finally approved and signed on a date as close as possible to the date of the audit report and after all other audit work has been completed.

Discussion of the contents of the letter early in the audit is an important part of the audit planning process. It makes the auditors aware at an early stage of the areas in which representations may be required. It also acts as prior warning to management of errors. This may usefully give management a chance to think carefully about the nature of any representations which are likely to be required in writing, and may encourage directors to become more fully aware of their responsibilities in relation to such written confirmations.

If discussion of the contents of the representation letter are left until the last stages of the audit, senior management may justifiably object that, the matters covered by the letter ought to have been raised earlier by the auditors. Management might object that if this had been done there would have been an opportunity to assemble appropriate corroborative evidence and thus avoid the need for written representations by the directors. Such objections may be made especially where audit deadlines are tight, which is often the case for companies which are part of a group. Lengthy discussions of judgemental matters on which representations are being sought may, if left until the end of the audit process, detract from a good working relationship between the auditors and client management, and in extreme cases management may become reluctant to comply with the auditors' requests.

(c) Some audit firms make use of a standard form of letter of representation. The principal merit of using a standard letter is that, by using a standard for all audit work in the firm, the firm has more assurance that staff on each audit will have considered all of the typical kinds of matter on which written representations are normally sought from clients. Audit staff may benefit from using such a standard letter as a checklist of possible matters to include in a draft letter to discuss with management. However, in all cases there will be a need to 'tailor' the standard letter to suit the needs of the particular audit engagement. This may involve adapting paragraphs of a standard letter, or adding new paragraphs to cover matters special to the assignment.

Instead of using a full standardised letter, some firms make use of 'specimen paragraphs' to be included in draft letters of representation. Such specimen paragraphs offer the advantage of suggesting appropriate wording dealing with common matters on which representations are required. Given the judgmental nature of many such matters, careful wording is important.

As with all standardised audit documentation, there remains the danger that standardisation may encourage a 'mechanical' approach to audit work and this probably explains why many firms are becoming reluctant to use standard forms of letter. Where audit staff fail to use their initiative and imagination, the standard letter may be followed too closely, and important matters may be missed. However, it could be argued that the problem in such cases lies more with a lack of adequate training of audit staff than with the fact that standardised documentation is available.

In presenting a letter of representation to the directors, it is important that the letter is not treated as merely a standard formality. Even if the letter for a particular assignment contains only similar material to that included generally in such letters, and is little different from last year's letter for the same client, each point should be discussed with management in order to encourage the signatories to consider its contents fully.

4 UNAUDITED PUBLISHED INFORMATION

4.1 The APB's SAS 160 *Other information in documents containing audited financial statements* provides guidance for auditors in this area.

4.2 The SAS uses the term 'other information' by which it means financial and non-financial information **other than** the audited financial statements and the auditors' report, which an entity may include in its annual report, either by custom or statute. Examples are:

- A directors' report (required by statute)
- A chairman's statement
- An operating and financial review
- Financial summaries

4.3 Auditors have no responsibility to report that other information is properly stated because an audit is only an expression of opinion on the truth and fairness of the financial statements.

4.4 However, they may be engaged separately, or required by statute, to report on elements of other information, for example, review the directors' statement of compliance with the Cadbury Code. This would be an example of a non-statutory review.

4.5 The SAS then moves on to the auditors' general responsibilities towards 'other information'. It says 'auditors should read the other information. If as a result they become aware of any apparent misstatements therein, or identify any material inconsistencies with the audited financial statements, they should seek to resolve them'.

Auditors' consideration of other information

4.6 The SAS goes on to say 'if auditors identify an inconsistency between the financial statements and the other information, or a misstatement within the other information, they should consider whether an amendment is required to the financial statements or to the other information and should seek to resolve the matter through discussion with the directors'.

4.7 A **misstatement** within other information exists when it is stated incorrectly or presented in a misleading manner. An **inconsistency** exists when the other information contradicts, or appears to contradict information contained in the financial statements. This could lead to doubts about audit evidence or even the auditors' opinion.

4.8 Such matters will have implications for the report. The SAS says 'if, after discussion with the directors, the auditors conclude

(a) That the financial statements require amendment and no such amendment is made, they should consider the implications for their report

(b) That the other information requires amendment and no such amendment is made, they should consider appropriate actions including the implications for their report'.

4.9 The auditors have a statutory duty to consider a company's directors' report. S 235 Companies Act 1985 states that:

> 'the auditors shall consider whether the information given in the directors' report for the financial year for which the accounts are prepared is consistent with those accounts; and if they are of opinion that it is not they shall state that fact in their report.'

4.10 Matters which may require resolution or reference in an explanatory paragraph within the auditors' report include:

(a) An **inconsistency between amounts or narrative** appearing in the financial statements and the directors' report

(b) An **inconsistency between the bases of preparation** of related items appearing in the financial statements and the directors' report, where the figures themselves are not directly comparable and the different bases are not disclosed

(c) An **inconsistency between figures** contained in the financial statements **and a narrative interpretation** of the effect of those figures in the directors' report

4.11 Other information may contain misstatements or inconsistencies with the financial statements and the auditors may be unable to resolve them by discussion with the directors. They may need to use an **explanatory paragraph** within the auditors' report to describe the apparent misstatement or material misconsistency.

Timing considerations

4.12 SAS 600 *Auditors' reports on financial statements* (see Chapter 19) requires all other information to be approved by the entity, and the auditors to consider all necessary evidence, before the audit opinion is expressed.

Question: Subsequent events

You are auditing the financial statements of Hope Engineering Ltd for the year ending 31 March 20X8. The partner in charge of the audit instructs you to carry out a review of the company's activities since the financial year end. Mr Smith, the managing director of Hope Engineering Ltd, overhears the conversation with the partner and is surprised that you are examining accounting information which relates to the next accounting period.

Mr Smith had been appointed on 1 March 20X8 as a result of which the contract of the previous managing director, Mr Jones, was terminated. Compensation of £500,000 had been paid to Mr Jones on 2 March 20X8.

As a result of your investigations you find that the company is going to bring an action against Mr Jones for the recovery of the compensation paid to him, as it had come to light that two months prior to his dismissal, he had contractually agreed to join the board of directors of a rival company. The company's solicitor had informed Hope Engineering Ltd that Mr Jones' actions constituted a breach of his contract with them, and that an action could be brought against the former managing director for the recovery of the moneys paid to him.

Required

(a) Explain the nature and purpose of a review of the period after the balance sheet date.

(b) List the audit procedures which would be carried out in order to identify any material subsequent events.

(c) Discuss the audit implications of the company's decision to sue Mr Jones for the recovery of the compensation paid to him.

Answer

(a) The auditors' active responsibility extends to the date on which they sign their audit report. As this date is inevitably after the year end, it follows that in order to discharge their responsibilities, the auditors must extend their audit work to cover the post balance sheet period.

The objective of the audit of the post balance sheet period is to ascertain whether the directors have dealt correctly with any events, both favourable and unfavourable, which occurred after the year end and which need to be reflected in the financial statements, if those statements are to show a true and fair view and comply with the Companies Act.

The general rule is that, in the preparation of year end financial statements, no account should be taken of subsequent events unless to do so is required by statute or to give effect to retrospective legislation, or to take account of an adjusting event. In accordance with SSAP 17, a material subsequent event may be an *adjusting event* where it provides information about a condition existing at the balance sheet date, for example realisable values of stock, or indicates that the going concern concept is no longer applicable. Additionally, *non-adjusting events* may have such a material effect on the company's financial condition, for example a merger, that disclosure is essential to give a true and fair view.

(b) The audit procedures which should be carried out in order to identify any material subsequent events consist of discussions with management, and may also include consideration of the following.

   (i) Procedures should be implemented by management to ensure that all events after the balance sheet date have been identified, considered and properly evaluated as to their effect on the financial statements.

   (ii) Relevant accounting records should be reviewed, specifically to identify subsequent cash received from debtors, to check items uncleared at the year end on the bank reconciliation, to check NRV of stocks from sales invoices, and so on. However, window dressing also may be identified.

   (iii) Budgets, profit forecasts, cash flow projections and management accounts for the new period should be reviewed to assess the company's trading position.

   (iv) Known 'risk' areas and contingencies, whether inherent in the nature of the business or revealed by previous audit experience, or by solicitors' letters, should be considered.

   (v) Minutes of shareholders', directors' and management meetings and correspondence and memoranda relating to items included in the minutes should be reviewed.

   (vi) Relevant information which has come to the auditors' attention from sources outside the enterprise, including public knowledge of competitors, suppliers and customers, should be taken into account.

The subsequent events review should be carried out to a date as near as practicable to that of the audit report by making enquiries of management and considering the need to carry out further tests. It should be fully documented and, where appropriate, a letter of representation should be obtained from management.

(c) The compensation paid to Mr Smith would be disclosed as part of directors' emoluments for the year ended 31 March 20X8. However, the question then arises as to whether or not the financial statements need to take any account of the possible recovery of the compensation payment.

The auditors should first ascertain from the board minutes that the directors intend to proceed with the lawsuit and should then attempt to assess the outcome by consulting the directors, the company's legal advisors and perhaps by taking Counsel's opinion. Only if it seems probable that the compensation will be recovered should a contingent asset be disclosed in the notes to the accounts, along with a summary of the facts of the case. A prudent estimate of legal costs should be deducted.

It could be argued that Mr Smith's breach of contract existed at the balance sheet date and that the compensation should therefore be treated as a current asset, net of recovery costs. However, this would not be prudent, given the uncertainties over the court case.

---

5 OVERALL REVIEW OF FINANCIAL STATEMENTS 12/03

5.1 Once the bulk of the substantive procedures have been carried out, the auditors will have a draft set of financial statements which should be supported by appropriate and sufficient audit evidence.

5.2 SAS 470 *Overall review of financial statements* covers the beginning of the end of the audit process. It says 'auditors should carry out such a review of the financial statements as is sufficient, in conjunction with the conclusions drawn from the other audit evidence obtained, to give them a reasonable basis for their opinion on the financial statements'.

5.3 This review requires appropriate skill and experience on the part of the auditors.

Compliance with accounting regulations

5.4 The SAS says 'auditors should consider whether the information presented in the financial statements is in accordance with statutory requirements and that the accounting policies employed are in accordance with accounting standards, properly disclosed, consistently applied and appropriate to the entity'.

5.5 The SAS goes on to list the factors which the auditors should consider when examining the **accounting policies.**

- Policies **commonly adopted** in **particular industries**
- Policies for which there is substantial **authoritative support**
- Whether any **departures from applicable accounting standards are necessary** for the financial statements to give a true and fair view
- Whether the **financial statements reflect** the **substance** of the underlying transactions and not merely their form

5.6 The SAS suggests that, when compliance with statutory requirements and accounting standards is considered, the auditors may find it useful to use a **checklist**.

Review for consistency and reasonableness

5.7 The SAS 'auditors should consider whether the financial statements as a whole and the assertions contained therein are consistent with their knowledge of the entity's business and with the results of other audit procedures, and the manner of disclosure is fair' and lists the principal considerations:

(a) Whether the financial statements adequately reflect the **information** and **explanations** previously obtained and conclusions previously reached during the course of the audit

(b) Whether it reveals any **new factors** which may affect the presentation of, or disclosure in, the financial statements

(c) Whether **analytical procedures** applied when completing the audit, such as comparing the information in the financial statements with other pertinent data, **produce results** which assist in arriving at the overall conclusion as to whether the financial statements as a whole are consistent with their knowledge of the entity's business (see Section 3)

(d) Whether the **presentation** adopted in the financial statements may have been **unduly influenced by the directors' desire** to present matters in a favourable or unfavourable light

(e) The potential impact on the financial statements of the **aggregate of uncorrected misstatements** (including those arising from bias in making accounting estimates) identified during the course of the audit and the preceding period's audit, if any

6 PROBLEMS OF ACCOUNTING TREATMENT

6.1 As noted in the previous section, SAS 470 requires that auditors review the financial statements. One of the things that they are required to assess is whether the **accounting policies are consistently applied.**

FRS 18

6.2 You should be aware of the details of FRS 18 from your 2.5 paper, but we shall revise the pertinent details here.

> **FRS 18 revision**
>
> FRS 18 prescribes the regular consideration of the entity's accounting policies. The **best** accounting policies should be adopted at all times.
>
> This is a move away from the position of SSAP 2 which was that **consistency** was a fundamental accounting concept.
>
> FRS 18 also required that the entity considers how a change in accounting policy will affect the **comparability** of the financial statements and strike a **balance** between selecting the most appropriate policies and presenting coherent an useful policies.

6.3 In light of FRS 18, therefore, the auditor will have to consider the reasonableness of all accounting polices, and when accounting policies have been changed whether

- The new policy is the best policy for the purposes of providing a true and fair view, and
- The financial statements provide a true and fair view as a whole, given the change in policy.

Alternative treatments

6.4 From your accounting studies, you should also be aware that there are some accounting standards which allow a choice of treatments.

6.5 As always, when reviewing the accounting treatment used, the auditors should consider whether they provide a true and fair view. Given that the options in treatment could be:

- Capitalise, or
- Write off

The difference between the two choices of treatment is likely to be **material** to the financial statements.

7 ANALYTICAL PROCEDURES

7.1 In Chapter 12 we discussed how analytical review procedures are used as part of the overall review procedures at the end of an audit.

7.2 Remember the areas that the analytical review at the final stage must cover:

- Important accounting ratios
- Related items
- Changes in products; customers
- Price and mix changes
- Wages changes
- Variances
- Trends in production and sales
- Changes in material and labour content of production
- Other profit and loss account expenditure
- Variations caused by industry or economy factors

7.3 As at other stages, significant fluctuations and unexpected relationships must be investigated and documented.

8 COMPLETION OF THE AUDIT

Summarising errors

8.1 Auditors are required to consider the materiality of the aggregate of uncorrected misstatements. The aggregate of uncorrected misstatements comprises:

(a) **Specific misstatements** identified by the auditors, including uncorrected misstatements identified during the audit of the previous period if they affect the current period's financial statements

(b) Their **best estimate** of **other misstatements** which cannot be quantified specifically

8.2 If the auditors consider that the aggregate of misstatements may be material, they must consider reducing audit risk by extending audit procedures or requesting the directors to adjust the financial statements (which the directors may wish to do anyway).

8.3 The auditors should consider the implications for their audit report if:

- The directors refuse to adjust.

- The extended audit procedures do not enable the auditors to conclude that the aggregate of uncorrected misstatements is not material.

8.4 The summary of errors will not only list errors from the current year, but also those in the previous year(s). This will allow errors to be highlighted which are reversals of errors in the previous year, such as in the valuation of closing/opening stock. Cumulative errors may also be shown, which have increased from year to year.

SCHEDULE OF UNADJUSTED ERRORS

	20X2				*20X1*			
	P & L account		*Balance sheet*		*P & L account*		*Balance sheet*	
	Dr	*Cr*	*Dr*	*Cr*	*Dr*	*Cr*	*Dr*	*Cr*
	£	£	£	£	£	£	£	£
(a) ABC Ltd debt unprovided	10,470			10,470	4,523			4,523
(b) Opening/ closing stock under-valued*	21,540			21,540		21,540	21,540	
(c) Closing stock undervalued		34,105	34,105					
(d) Opening unaccrued expense								
Telephone*		453	453		453			453
Electricity*		905	905		905			905
(e) Closing unaccrued expenses								
Telephone	427			427				
Electricity	1,128			1,128				
(f) Obsolete stock write off	2,528			2,528	3,211			3,211
Total	36,093	35,463	35,463	36,093	9,092	21,540	21,540	9,092
*Cancelling items	21,540			21,540				
		453	453					
		905	905					
	14,553	34,105	34,105	14,553				

8.5 The schedule will be used by the audit manager and partner to decide whether the client should be requested to make adjustments to the financial statements to correct the errors.

Completion checklists

8.6 Audit firms frequently use checklists which must be signed off to ensure that all final procedures have been carried out, all material amounts are supported by sufficient appropriate evidence, etc.

Chapter roundup

- Evaluation of going concern is most important. Auditors should consider the **future plans** of directors and any signs of **going concern problems** which may be noted throughout the audit. **Bank facilities** may have to be confirmed.
- When reporting on the accounts, auditors should consider whether the going concern basis is **appropriate,** and whether **disclosure** of going concern problems is **sufficient**.
- Auditors should consider the effect of **subsequent events** (after the balance sheet date) on the accounts.
- Auditors have a responsibility to **review subsequent events** before they sign their audit report, and may have to take action if they become aware of subsequent events between the date they sign their audit report and the date the financial statements are laid before members.
- **Representations from management** should generally be restricted to matters that cannot be verified by other audit procedures.
- Any representations should be **compared** with other evidence and their **sufficiency** assessed.
- **Unaudited published information** includes the **directors' report,** and other statements such as the **chairman's statement** and an **operating and financial review.** Auditors have a statutory responsibility to report inconsistencies between the directors' report and accounts.
- The auditors must perform and document an **overall review** of the financial statements before they can reach an opinion, covering:
  - Compliance with statute and accounting standards
  - Consistency with audit evidence
  - Overall reasonableness
- **Analytical procedures** should be used at the final stage of audit. The review should cover:
  - Key business ratios
  - Related items in accounts
  - The effect of known changes on the accounts
- As part of their completion procedures, auditors should consider whether the **aggregate of uncorrected misstatements** is material.

Quick quiz

1 Complete the definition, using the words given below.

The .... concept: the enterprise will .... in operational .... for the ....

future, existence, going, continue, foreseeable, concern

2 Name two instances where the going concern basis is not appropriate.

1 ....

2 ....

3 Complete the table putting the indicators of an entity's inability to continue as a going concern under the correct headings.

Financial	Operational	Other

(a) Litigation
(b) Inability to pay due debts
(c) Fundamental changes to market
(d) Loss of key customers
(e) Denial of trade credit by suppliers
(f) Loss of key management

4 The directors must satisfy themselves that the going concern basis in the financial statements is appropriate.

True ☐

False ☐

5 Complete the definition, using the words given in the box below.

………………… ………………. are those which provide ………………… evidence relating to the conditions …………………….. and the balance sheet date, or concern ……………. which …………… …………… ……………… at the balance sheet, but which may be of such ………………….. that their ………………….. is required to ensure the financial statements are not misleading.

events, existing, relevant, not, conditions, exist, additional, did, disclosure, materiality

6 Name three enquires that should be made of management to test subsequent events.

1 ……………………………………………………

2 ……………………………………………………

3 ……………………………………………………

7 When should auditors issues a new report?

8 Name two instances given in SAS 440 of when management representation may be the only audit evidence available.

1 ……………………………………………………

2 ……………………………………………………

9 Give five examples of what areas analytical review at the final stage should cover.

1 ……………………………………………………

2 ……………………………………………………

3 ……………………………………………………

4 ……………………………………………………

5 ……………………………………………………

10 In which three instances might unaudited published information be referred to in the audit report?

1 ……………………………………………………

2 ……………………………………………………

3 ……………………………………………………

Answers to quick quiz

1 going concern, continue, existence, foreseeable future

2 (1) The entity may not be able to recover the amount recorded in respect of assets
(2) There may be changes in the amounts and dates of maturities or assets.

3

Financial	Operational	Other
(b)	(c)	(a)
(e)	(d)	
	(f)	

4 True

5 relevant events, additions, existing, conditions, did not exist, materiality, disclosure

6 (From)

- What the status is of items involving subjective judgement.
- Whether there are any new commitments, borrowings or guarantees.
- Whether any assets have been sold or destroyed.
- Whether any new shares/debentures have been issued.
- Whether there have been any developments in risk areas.
- Any unusual accounting adjustments.
- Any major events.

7 When the directors revise the financial statements before they have been issued, but after the date of the auditors' report.

8 (1) When the knowledge of facts confined to management
(2) When the matter is judgement/opinion

9 (1) Important accounting ratios
(2) Related items
(3) Changes in products/ customers
(4) Price/mix changes
(5) Wage changes
(for others see paragraph 7.2)

10 (1) Inconsistency between amounts/narrative in financial statements/directors reports.

(2) Inconsistency between bases of preparation in financial statements/directors reports

(3) Inconsistency between figures in financial statements and narrative interpretation in the directors report.

Now try the question below from the Exam Question Bank

Number	Level	Marks	Time
18	Exam	20	36 mins

Part E
Reporting

Chapter 19

PUBLIC REPORTING

Topic list		Syllabus reference	Study guide
1	**SAS 600 *Auditors' report on financial statements***	7	26
2	**Qualifications in audit reports**	7	26
3	**Reporting inherent uncertainty**	7	26
4	**The audit report as a means of communication**	7	26

Introduction

The **audit report** is the means by which the external auditors express their opinion on the **truth and fairness** of a company's financial statements. This is for the benefit principally of the shareholders, but also for other users as the audit report is usually kept on public record, with the filed financial statements.

As we saw in chapter 2, many of the contents of the auditor's report are prescribed by the statute. They are also subject to the professional requirements in the form of SAS 600 *Auditors' reports on financial statements.* This makes it extremely different to the private reports auditors produce which we will look at in more detail in Chapter 20.

The difference between this public report and the private report is not an issue of formality. Although other reports do not go on the public record, they are no less formal than the statutory audit report. There are two key differences, however:

- Purpose
- Understandability

The **purpose** of the publicised audit report is, as you know, to report on whether the accounts show a **true and fair view** to the **shareholders.** The private reports are for the purposes of directors and management.

The second issue is that of **understandability**, how the purpose and conclusion of the public report is **communicated** to shareholders. Directors and management work in the business, the report submitted to them may well be more meaningful to them than the audit report is to more isolated shareholders. We discuss communication and the **expectations gap** briefly in Section 4.

You need to be comfortable with all the terms of the audit report (qualified and unqualified) and to be able to describe and analyse them.

You will not be required to reproduce a full audit report in the exam; however you may be required to describe:

- How the audit report in a specific situation differs from an unqualified audit report, or
- Give extracts from an audit report dealing with uncertainties or disagreements

In December 2001, the requirement was to compare and contrast the audit report and the review report.

1 SAS 600 AUDITORS' REPORT ON FINANCIAL STATEMENTS 12/01

1.1 Remember that the Companies Act 1985 requires the auditors to state **explicitly** (s 235) whether in their opinion the annual accounts have been properly prepared in accordance with the Act and in particular whether a **true and fair view** is given. In addition certain requirements are reported on by exception.

1.2 SAS 600 *Auditors' report on financial statements* states that 'auditors' reports on financial statements should contain a clear expression of opinion, based on review and assessment of the conclusions drawn from evidence obtained in the course of the audit'.

1.3 The auditors' report should be placed before the financial statements. The directors' responsibilities statement (see Paragraph 1.7) should be placed before the auditors' report.

Basic elements of the auditors' report

1.4 The example of an unqualified audit report from an appendix to the SAS, as amended by Bulletin 2001/02, is given here. Certain elements are items the SAS requires to be present, as indicated by the notes:

(1) The title, showing to whom the financial statements are addressed

(2) An introductory paragraph, which sets out the financial statements being audited.

(3) Separate sections, headed 'respective responsibilities of directors and auditors', 'basis of opinion', 'opinion'.

(4) The auditors' signature

(5) The date of signature.

Notes

Independent auditors' report to the shareholders of XYZ Limited (1)

We have audited the financial statements of (name of entity) for the year ended ... which comprise (state the primary financial statements such as the profit and loss account, the balance sheet, the cash flow statement, the statements of total recognised gains and losses) and the related notes. These financial statements have been prepared under the historical cost convention (as modified by the revaluation of certain fixed assets) and the accounting policies set out therein.

Respective responsibilities of directors and auditors

The director's responsibilities for preparing the annual report and the financial statements in accordance with applicable law and United Kingdom Accounting Standards are set out in the statement of director's responsibilities. (2)

Our responsibility is to audit the financial statements in accordance with relevant legal and regulatory requirements and United Kingdom Auditing Standards.

We report to you our opinion as to whether the financial statements give a true and fair view and are properly prepared in accordance with the (Companies Act 1985). We also report to you if, in our opinion, the director's report is not consistent with the financial statements, if the company has not kept proper accounting records, if we have not received all the information and explanations we required for our audit, or if information specified by law regarding directors remuneration and transactions with the company is not disclosed.

We read other information contained in the annual report and consider whether it is consistent with the audited financial statements. This other information comprises only (the Director's Report, the Chairman's Statement, the Operating and Financial Review). We consider the implications for our report if we become aware of any apparent misstatements or material inconsistencies with the financial statements. Our responsibilities do not extend to any other information.

Notes

Basis of audit opinion

We conducted our audit in accordance with United Kingdom Auditing Standards issued by the Auditing Practices Board. An audit includes examination, on a test basis, of evidence relevant to the amounts and disclosures in the financial statements. It also includes an assessment of the significant estimates and judgements made by the directors in the preparation of the financial statements, and of whether the accounting polices are appropriate to the company's circumstances, consistently applied and adequately disclosed. (3)

We planned and performed our audit so as to obtain all the information and explanations which we considered necessary in order to provide us with sufficient evidence to give reasonable assurance that the financial statements are free from material misstatement, whether caused by fraud or other irregularity or error. In forming our opinion we also evaluated the overall adequacy of the presentation of information in the financial statements.

Opinion

In our opinion the financial statements give a true and fair view of the state of the company's affairs as at ... and of its profit (loss) for the year then ended and have been properly prepared in accordance with the (Companies Act 1985).

Registered auditors *Address* (4)

Date (5)

1.5 The report recommended for a **listed company** is also reproduced here. The significant differences from the standard report are highlighted in grey.

ILLUSTRATIVE AUDITORS' REPORT FOR A QUOTED COMPANY INCOPOARATED IN GREAT BRITIAN

INDEPENDENT AUDITORS' REPORT TO THE SHAREHOLDERS OF XYZ PLC

We have audited the financial statements of (name of entity) for the year ended ... which comprise (state the primary financial statements such as the Profit and Loss Account, the Balance Sheet, the Cash Flow Statement, the Statement of Total Recognised Gains and Losses) and the related notes. These financial statements have been prepared under the historical cost convention (as modified by the revaluation of certain fixed assets) and the accounting policies set out therein. We have also audited the information in the Directors' Remuneration Report that is described as having been audited.

Respective responsibilities of directors and auditors

The directors' responsibilities for preparing the Annual Report, the Directors' Remuneration Report and the financial statements in accordance with applicable law and United Kingdom Accounting Standards are set out in the Statement of Directors' Responsibilities.

Our responsibility is to audit the financial statements and the part of the Directors' Remuneration Report to be audited in accordance with relevant legal and regulatory requirements and United Kingdom Auditing Standards.

We report to you our opinion as to whether the financial statements give a true and fair view and whether the financial statements and the part of the Directors' Remuneration Report to be audited have been properly prepared in accordance with the Companies Act 1985. We also report to you if, in our opinion, the Directors' Report is not consistent with the financial statements, if the company has not kept proper accounting records, if we have not received all the information and explanations we require for our audit, or if information specified by law regarding directors' remuneration and transactions with the company (and other members of the group) is not disclosed.

We review whether the Corporate Governance Statement reflects the company's compliance with the seven provisions of the Combined Code specified for our review by the Listing Rules of the Financial Services Authority, and we report if it does not. We are not required to consider whether the board's statements on internal control cover all risks and controls, or form an opinion on the effectiveness of the (company's) (group's) corporate governance procedures or its risks and control procedures.

We read other information contained in the Annual Report and consider whether it is consistent with the audited financial statements. The other information comprises only (the Directors' Report, the unaudited part of the Directors' Remuneration Report, the Chairman's Statement, the Operating and Financial Review and the Corporate Governance Statement). We consider the implications for our report if we become aware of any apparent misstatements or material inconsistencies with the financial statements. Our responsibilities do not extend to any other information.

Basis of audit opinion

We conducted our audit in accordance with United Kingdom Auditing Standards issued by the Auditing Practices Board. An audit includes examination, on a test basis, of evidence relevant to the amounts and disclosures in the financial statements and the part of the Directors' Remuneration Report to be audited. It also includes an assessment of the significant estimates and judgements made by the directors in the preparation of the financial statements, and of whether the accounting policies are appropriate in the company's circumstances, consistently applied and adequately disclosed.

We planned and performed our audit so as to obtain all the information and explanations which we considered necessary in order to provide us with sufficient evidence to give reasonable assurance that the financial statements and the part of the Directors' Remuneration Report to be audited are free from material misstatement, whether caused by fraud or other irregularity or error. In forming our opinion we also evaluated the overall adequacy of the presentation of information in the financial statements and the part of the Directors' Remuneration Report to be audited.

Opinion

In our opinion:

- The financial statements give a true and fair view of the state of the (group's and the) company's affairs as at ... and of (the group's) (its) profit (loss) for the year then ended; and
- The financial statements and the part of the Directors' Remuneration Report to be audited have been properly prepared in accordance with the Companies Act 1985.

Registered auditors *Address*

Date

1.6 The SAS recommends the use of standard format as an aid to the reader, including headings for each section, for example 'Qualified opinion'. The title and addressee and the introductory paragraph are fairly self explanatory.

Statements of responsibility and basic opinion

1.7 The SAS requires auditors to distinguish between auditor and director responsibilities in their report by including:

'(i) A statement that the financial statements are the responsibility of the reporting entity's directors

(ii) A reference to a description of those responsibilities when set out elsewhere in the financial statements or accompanying information and

(iii) A statement that the auditors' responsibility is to express an opinion on the financial statements.'

If the financial statements/other information in the annual report do not include an adequate description of directors' relevant responsibilities, 'the auditors' report should include a description of those responsibilities'.

1.8 A description of the directors' responsibilities is given in an example in an appendix. It can be produced by the directors or included by the auditors in their report.

> Company law requires the directors to prepare financial statements for each financial year which give a true and fair view of the state of affairs of the company and of the profit or loss of the company for that period. In preparing those financial statements, the directors are required to:
>
> (a) select suitable accounting policies and then apply them consistently;
>
> (b) make judgements and estimates that are reasonable and prudent;
>
> (c) state whether applicable accounting standards have been followed, subject to any material departures disclosed and explained in the financial statements (large companies only);
>
> (d) prepare the financial statements on the going concern basis unless it is inappropriate to presume that the company will continue in business (if no separate statement on going concern is made by the directors).
>
> The directors are responsible for keeping proper accounting records which disclose with reasonable accuracy at any time the financial position of the company and to enable them to ensure that the financial statements comply with the Companies Act 1985. They are also responsible for safeguarding the assets of the company and hence for taking reasonable steps for the prevention and detection of fraud and other irregularities.

This wording can be adapted to suit the specific situation.

Explanation of auditors' opinion

1.9 The SAS goes on to say 'auditors should explain the basis of their opinion by including in their report:

(a) A statement as to their compliance or otherwise with Auditing Standards, together with the reasons for any departure therefrom;

(b) A statement that the audit process includes:

(i) Examining, on a test basis, evidence relevant to the amounts and disclosures in the financial statements

(ii) Assessing the significant estimates and judgements made by the reporting entity's directors in preparing the financial statements

(iii) Considering whether the accounting policies are appropriate to the reporting entity's circumstances, consistently applied and adequately disclosed

(c) A statement that they planned and performed the audit so as to obtain reasonable assurance that the financial statements are free from material misstatement, whether caused by fraud or other irregularity or error, and that they have evaluated the overall presentation of the financial statements.'

Expression of opinion

1.10 The SAS requires auditors to give a clear expression of opinion. An unqualified opinion on financial statements is expressed when in the auditors' judgement they give a true and fair view (where relevant) and have been prepared in accordance with relevant accounting or other requirements. This judgement entails concluding whether:

(a) The financial statements have been prepared using **appropriate consistently applied accounting policies.**

(b) The financial statements have been **prepared** in accordance with **relevant legislation, regulations** or **applicable accounting standards** (and that any departures are justified and adequately explained in the financial statements).

(c) There is **adequate disclosure** of all information relevant to the proper understanding of the financial statements.

Date and signature of the auditors' report

1.11 The date on the auditor's report is the date the auditors express their opinion and sign their report. This should not be until after the directors have approved the financial statements and the auditors have reviewed all the necessary evidence.

1.12 If the date on which the auditors sign the report is later than that on which the directors approve the financial statements, then the auditors must check that the post balance sheet event review has been carried out up to the date they sign their report and that the directors would also have approved the financial statements on that date.

Forming an opinion on financial statements

1.13 Appendix 1 of the SAS considers the process of forming an audit opinion using the flowchart shown on the next page. The flowchart is drawn up on the basis that the directors make no further amendments to the financial statements following the audit.

1.14 The principal matters which auditors consider in forming an opinion may be expressed in three questions.

- Have they **completed all procedures necessary** to meet auditing standards and to obtain all the information and explanations necessary for their audit?
- Have the financial statements been **prepared in accordance** with the **applicable accounting requirements**?
- Do the financial statements, as prepared by the directors, give **a true and fair view**?

FORMING AN OPINION ON FINANCIAL STATEMENTS

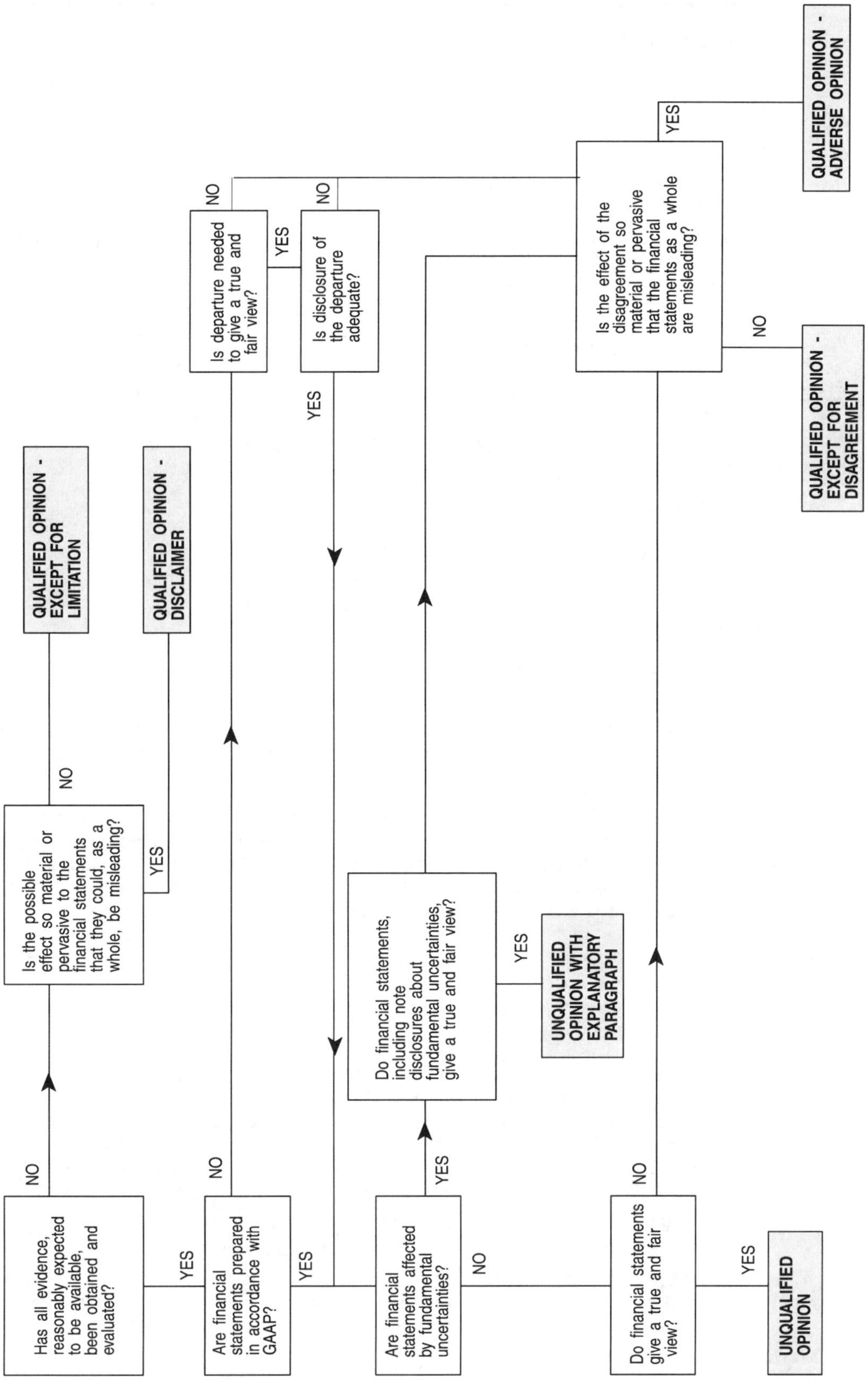

Question: Auditors' report

The following is a series of extracts from an unqualified audit report which has been signed by the auditors of Kiln Ltd.

AUDITORS' REPORT TO THE SHAREHOLDERS OF KILN LIMITED

We have audited *the financial statements on pages .... to ....* which have been prepared under the historical cost convention.

We have conducted our audit *in accordance with Auditing Standards* issued by the Auditing Practices Board. An audit includes examination on a test basis of evidence relevant to the amounts and disclosures in the financial statements.

In our opinion the financial statements give a true and fair view of the state of the company's affairs as at 31 December 20X3 and of its profit for the year then ended and have been properly prepared in accordance with the Companies Act 1985.

Required

Explain the purpose and meaning of the following phrases taken from the above extracts of an unqualified audit report.

(a) '... the financial statements on pages .... to ....'
(b) '... in accordance with Auditing Standards.'
(c) 'In our opinion ...'

Answer

(a) *'...the financial statements on pages 8 to 20...'*

Purpose

The purpose of this phrase is to make it clear to the reader of an audit report the part of a company's annual report upon which the auditors are reporting their opinion.

Meaning

An annual report may include documents such as a chairman's report, employee report, five year summary and other voluntary information. However, under the Companies Act, only the profit and loss account, balance sheet and associated notes are required to be audited in true and fair terms. FRS 1 requires a cash flow statement and FRS 3 requires a statement of total recognised gains and losses which, under auditing standards, are audited in true and fair terms. Thus the page references (for instance, 8 to 20) cover only the profit and loss account, balance sheet, notes to the accounts, cash flow statement and statement of total recognised gains and losses. The directors' report, although examined and reported on by exception if it contains inconsistencies, is not included in these page references.

(b) *'...in accordance with Auditing Standards...'*

Purpose

This phrase is included in order to confirm to the reader that best practice, as laid down in Auditing Standards, has been adopted by the auditors in both carrying out their audit and in drafting their audit opinion. This means that the reader can be assured that the audit has been properly conducted, and that should he or she wish to discover what such standards are, or what certain key phrases mean, he or she can have recourse to Auditing Standards to explain such matters.

Meaning

Auditing Standards are those auditing standards prepared by the Auditing Practices Board.

These prescribe the principles and practices to be followed by auditors in the planning, designing and carrying out various aspects of their audit work, the content of audit reports, both qualified and unqualified and so on. Members are expected to follow all of these standards.

(c) *'In our opinion ...'*

Purpose

Under the Companies Act, auditors are required to report on every balance sheet, profit and loss account or group accounts laid before members. In reporting, they are required to state their *opinion* on those accounts. Thus, the purpose of this phrase is to comply with the statutory requirement to report an opinion.

Meaning

An audit report is an expression of opinion by suitably qualified auditors as to whether the financial statements give a true and fair view, and have been properly prepared in accordance with the Companies Act. *It is not a certificate*; rather it is a statement of whether or not, in the professional judgement of the auditors, the financial statements give a true and fair view.

2 QUALIFICATIONS IN AUDIT REPORTS 12/03

2.1 Qualified audit reports arise when auditors do not believe that they can state without reservation that the accounts give a true and fair view.

The qualification 'matrix'

2.2 SAS 600 gives the circumstances in which each sort of qualification would be appropriate. Where the auditors are unable to report affirmatively on the matters contained in the paragraphs about which they have reservations, they should give:

- A **full explanation** of the reasons for the qualification
- Whenever possible, a **quantification** of its effect on the financial statements
- Where appropriate, reference should be made to **non-compliance** with relevant **legislation** and **other requirements**

2.3 The standard stresses the fact that **a qualified audit report should leave the reader in no doubt as to its meaning and its implications for an understanding of the financial statements.**

2.4 The APB takes the view that the nature of the circumstances giving rise to a qualification of the auditor's opinion will generally fall into one of two categories:

- Where there is a **limitation in the scope of work** which prevents the auditors from forming an opinion on a matter (uncertainty), or
- Where the auditors are able to form an opinion on a matter but this **conflicts** with the view given by the financial statements (disagreement)

2.5 Either case, uncertainty or disagreement, may give rise to alternative forms of qualification. This is because the uncertainty or disagreement can be:

- Material but not pervasive
- Pervasive to the overall true and fair view

The standard requires that the following forms of qualification should be used in the different circumstances outlined below.

QUALIFICATION MATRIX

Nature of circumstances	*Material but not pervasive*	*Pervasive*
Limitation in scope	Except for .. might	Disclaimer of opinion
Disagreement	Except for ...	Adverse opinion

Except for . . . might	Auditors disclaim an opinion on a particular aspect of the accounts which is not considered pervasive.
Disclaimer of opinion	Auditors state they are unable to form an opinion on truth and fairness.
Except for	Auditors express an adverse opinion on a particular aspect of the accounts which is not considered pervasive.
Adverse opinion	Auditors state the accounts do not give a true and fair view.

Limitations on the scope of an audit

2.6 One source of uncertainties is **limitations in the scope of the audit**. Scope limitations will arise where the auditor is unable for any reason to obtain all the information and explanations which he considers necessary for the purpose of his audit, arising from:

(a) Absence of proper accounting records

(b) An inability to carry out audit procedures considered necessary as, for example, where the auditor is unable to obtain satisfactory evidence of the existence or ownership of material assets

2.7 In this situation, the SAS requires that:

'(a) The auditors' report should include a description of the factors leading to the limitation in the opinion section of their report

(b) The auditors should issue a disclaimer of opinion when the possible effect of a limitation on scope is so material or pervasive that they are unable to express an opinion on the financial statements

(c) A qualified opinion should be issued when the effect of the limitation is not as material or pervasive as to require a disclaimer, and the wording of the opinion should indicate that it is qualified as to the possible adjustments to the financial statements that might have been determined to be necessary had the limitation not existed'.

2.8 When giving this type of qualified opinion, auditors should assess:

- The **quantity and type of evidence** which may reasonably be expected to be available to support the figure or disclosure in the financial statements
- The **possible effect** on the financial statements of the matter for which insufficient evidence is available

2.9 SAS 600 gives the following examples.

Example 8. Qualified opinion: limitation on the auditors' work

(Basis of opinion: excerpt)

.... or error. However, the evidence available to us was limited because £... of the company's recorded turnover comprises cash sales, over which there was no system of control on which we could rely for the purposes of our audit. There were no other satisfactory audit procedures that we could adopt to confirm that cash sales were properly recorded.

In forming our opinion we also evaluated the overall adequacy of the presentation of information in the financial statements.

Qualified opinion arising from limitation in audit scope

Except for any adjustments that might have been found to be necessary had we been able to obtain sufficient evidence concerning cash sales, in our opinion the financial statements give a true and fair view of the state of the company's affairs as at 31 December 20.. and of its profit (loss) for the year then ended and have been properly prepared in accordance with the Companies Act 1985.

In respect alone of the limitation on our work relating to cash sales:

(a) we have not obtained all the information and explanations that we considered necessary for the purpose of our audit; and

(b) we were unable to determine whether proper accounting records had been maintained.

Example 9. Disclaimer of opinion

(Basis of opinion: excerpt)

.... or error. However, the evidence available to us was limited because we were appointed auditors on (date) and in consequence we were unable to carry out auditing procedures necessary to obtain adequate assurance regarding the quantities and condition of stock and work in progress, appearing in the balance sheet at £... . Any adjustment to this figure would have a consequential significant effect on the profit for the year.

In forming our opinion we also evaluated the overall adequacy of the presentation of information in the financial statements.

Opinion: disclaimer on view given by financial statements

Because of the possible effect of the limitation in evidence available to us, we are unable to form an opinion as to whether the financial statements give a true and fair view of the state of the company's affairs as at 31 December 20.. or of its profit (loss) for the year then ended. In all other respects, in our opinion the financial statements have been properly prepared in accordance with the Companies Act 1985.

In respect of the limitation on our work relating to stock and work-in-progress:

(a) we have not obtained all the information and explanations that we considered necessary for the purpose of our audit; and

(b) we were unable to determine whether proper accounting records had been maintained.

Note. Because of the length of the audit report, we have only shown those parts of each qualified report which differ from the unqualified report shown in Section 1.

2.10 In March 1999 the APB published SAS 601 *Imposed limitation of audit scope* which provides guidance for auditors when the directors or those who appoint the auditors place limitations upon the scope of the audit.

2.11 The SAS points out that agreeing to such a limitation would **threaten** the **independence** of auditors and make it impossible for them to meet the requirements of auditing standards. Auditors should therefore not accept such appointments (unless the law requires them to).

2.12 The APB also believes that in accepting such a limited engagement, the auditors are **complicit** in the client evading the **spirit** of the **legal requirement to be audited**. The SAS points out that even if there is a requirement for an entity to appoint auditors, this does not automatically mean that there is a requirement on the auditors to accept appointment.

2.13 If the auditors become aware of such an imposed limitation after they have been engaged as auditors, they should ask the directors to remove the limitation. If it is not removed, they should consider whether they need to resign as auditors.

2.14 If the auditors do not consider it necessary to resign but do issue a disclaimer, the audit report should give full details of why the disclaimer was given.

Circumstances giving rise to disagreements

2.15 The explanatory notes suggest that circumstances giving rise to disagreement include:

- **Inappropriate accounting policies**
- **Disagreement** as to the **facts or amounts** included in the financial statements
- **Disagreement** as to the **manner or extent of disclosure** of facts or amounts in the financial statements
- **Failure to comply** with **relevant legislation** or other **requirements**

2.16 SAS 110 suggests also that the auditors conclude that a suspected or actual fraud has a material effect on financial statements and the auditors disagree with the disclosure (or lack of) in relation to it, they may qualify.

2.17 The SAS states 'where the auditors disagree with the accounting treatment or disclosure of a matter in the financial statements, and in the auditors' opinion the effect of that disagreement is material to the financial statements:

(a) The auditors should include in the opinion section of their report:

 (i) A description of all substantive factors giving rise to the disagreement;
 (ii) Their implications for the financial statements;
 (iii) Whenever practicable, a quantification of the effect on the financial statements;

(b) When the auditors conclude that the effect of the matter giving rise to disagreement is so material or pervasive that the financial statements are seriously misleading, they should issue an adverse opinion;

(c) In the case of other material disagreements, the auditors should issue a qualified opinion indicating that it is expressed except for the effects of the matter giving rise to the disagreement'.

Example 7. Qualified opinion: disagreement

Qualified opinion arising from disagreement about accounting treatment

Included in the debtors shown on the balance sheet is an amount of £Y due from a company which has ceased trading. XYZ plc has no security for this debt. In our opinion the company is unlikely to receive any payment and full provision of £Y should have been made, reducing profit before tax and net assets by that amount.

Except for the absence of this provision, in our opinion the financial statements give a true and fair view of the state of the company's affairs as at 31 December 20.. and of its profit (loss) for the year then ended and have been properly prepared in accordance with the Companies Act 1985.

Example 10. Adverse opinion

Adverse opinion

As more fully explained in note ... no provision has been made for losses expected to arise on certain long-term contracts currently in progress, as the directors consider that such losses should be off-set against amounts recoverable on other long-term contracts. In our opinion, provision should be made for foreseeable losses on individual contracts as required by Statement of Standard Accounting Practice 9. If losses had been so recognised the effect would have been to reduce the profit before and after tax for the year and the contract work in progress at 31 December 20.. by £.. .

In view of the effect of the failure to provide for the losses referred to above, in our opinion the financial statements do not give a true and fair view of the state of the company's affairs as at 31 December 20.. and of its profit (loss) for the year then ended. In all other respects, in our opinion the financial statements have been properly prepared in accordance with the Companies Act 1985.

3 REPORTING INHERENT UNCERTAINTY 12/03

Inherent and fundamental uncertainty

KEY TERMS

An **inherent uncertainty** is an uncertainty whose resolution is dependent upon uncertain future events outside the control of the reporting entity's directors at the date the financial statements are approved.

A **fundamental uncertainty** is an inherent uncertainty where the magnitude of its potential impact is so great that, without clear disclosure of the nature and implications of the uncertainty, the view given by the financial statements would be seriously misleading.

3.1 Inherent uncertainties about the outcome of future events frequently affect, to some degree, a wide range of components of the financial statements at the date they are approved. In forming an opinion, auditors take into account:

- The **appropriateness of the accounting policies**
- The **adequacy of the accounting treatment**
- **Estimates and disclosures of inherent uncertainties** in the light of evidence available at the date they express their opinion

3.2 Inherent uncertainties are regarded as **fundamental** when they involve a **significant level of doubt** about the validity of the **going concern basis** or other matters whose potential effect on the fundamental statements is unusually great. A common example of a fundamental uncertainty is the outcome of major litigation. There may also be a fundamental uncertainty over a suspected or actual fraud.

3.3 The SAS states:

'(a) In forming their opinion on financial statements, auditors should consider whether the view given by the financial statements could be affected by inherent uncertainties which, in their opinion, are fundamental.

(b) When an inherent uncertainty exists which:

(i) in the auditors' opinion is fundamental; and

(ii) is adequately accounted for and disclosed in the financial statements;

the auditors should include an explanatory paragraph referring to the fundamental uncertainty in the section of their report setting out the basis of their opinion.

(c) When adding an explanatory paragraph, auditors should use words which clearly indicate that their opinion on the financial statements is not qualified in respect of its concepts'.

3.4 The auditor will need to consider:

- The possibility that the **estimate** included in the accounts may be **subject to change**
- The **possible range of values** it may take
- The **consequences** of that range of potential values on the view shown in the financial statements

Example 4. Unqualified opinion with explanatory paragraph describing a fundamental uncertainty.

Fundamental uncertainty (insert just before opinion paragraph)

In forming our opinion, we have considered the adequacy of the disclosures made in the financial statements concerning the possible outcome to litigation against B Limited, a subsidiary undertaking of the company, for an alleged breach of environmental regulations. The future settlement of this litigation could result in additional liabilities and the closure of B Limited's business, whose net assets included in the consolidated balance sheet total £... and whose profit before tax for the year is £... . Details of the circumstances relating to this fundamental uncertainty are described in note .... . Our opinion is not qualified in this respect.

Question: Qualifications

During the course of your audit of the fixed assets of Eastern Engineering plc at 31 March 20X4 two problems have arisen.

(a) The calculations of the cost of direct labour incurred on assets in course of construction by the company's employees have been accidentally destroyed for the early part of the year. The direct labour cost involved is £10,000.

(b) The company has upwardly revalued a previously unrevalued asset by £25,000 The revaluation has been credited in full to the profit and loss account as exceptional income.

(c) Other relevant financial information is as follows.

	£
Profit before tax	100,000
Fixed asset additions	133,000
Assets constructed by company	34,000
Fixed asset at net book value	666,667

Required

(a) List the general forms of qualification available to auditors in drafting their report and state the circumstances in which each is appropriate.

(b) State whether you feel that a qualified audit report would be necessary for each of the two circumstances outlined above, giving reasons in each case.

(c) On the assumption that you decide that a qualified audit report is necessary with respect to the treatment of the government grant, draft the section of the report describing the matter (the whole report is not required).

(d) Outline the auditors' general responsibility with regard to the statement in the directors' report concerning the valuation of land and buildings.

Answer

(a) SAS 600 *Auditors' report on financial statements* suggests that the auditors may need to qualify their audit opinion under one of two main circumstances:

(i) Limitation in scope of the auditors' examination; and

(ii) Disagreement with the treatment or disclosure of a matter in the financial statements (including inherent uncertainties).

For both circumstances there can be two 'levels' of qualified opinion:

(i) *Material but not pervasive,* where the circumstances prompting the uncertainty or disagreement is material but confined to one particular aspect of the financial statements, so that it does not affect their overall value to any potential user;

(ii) The more serious qualification where the extent of the uncertainty or disagreement is such that it will be *pervasive* to the overall view shown by the financial statements, ie the financial statements are or could be misleading.

The general form of qualification appropriate to each potential situation may be seen by the following table.

Circumstance	*Material but not pervasive*	*Pervasive*
Limitation of scope	Except for ... might	Disclaimer of opinion
Disagreement	Except for ...	Adverse opinion

(b) Whether a qualification of the audit opinion would be required in relation to either of the two circumstances described in the question would depend on whether or not the auditors considered either of them to be material. An item is likely to be considered as material in the context of a company's financial statements if its omission, misstatement or non-disclosure would prevent a proper understanding of those statements on the part of a potential user. Whilst for some audit purposes materiality will be considered in absolute terms, more often than not it will be considered as a relative term.

(i) *Loss of records relating to direct labour costs for assets in the course of construction*

The loss of records supporting one of the asset figures in the balance sheet would cause a limitation in scope of the auditors' work. The £10,000, which is the value covered by the lost records, represents 29.4% of the expenditure incurred during the year on assets in course of construction but only 6% of total additions to fixed assets during the year and 1.5% of the year end net book value for fixed assets. The total amount of £10,000 represents 10% of pre-tax profit but, as in relation to asset values, the real consideration by the auditors should be the materiality of any over- or under-statement of assets resulting from error in arriving at the £10,000 rather than the total figure itself.

Provided there are no suspicious circumstances surrounding the loss of these records and the total figure for additions to assets in the course of construction seems reasonable in the light of other audit evidence obtained, then it is unlikely that this matter would be seen as sufficiently material to merit any qualification of the audit opinion. If other records have been lost as well, however, it may be necessary for the auditors to comment on the directors' failure to maintain proper books and records.

(ii) *Upwards revaluation credited in total to profit and loss account*

The situation here is one of disagreement, since best accounting practice, as laid down by FRS 15, requires that revaluations should be credited to the statement of recognised gains and losses.

This departure from FRS 15 does not seem to be justifiable and would be material to the reported pre-tax profits for the year, representing as it does 22.5% of that figure.

Whilst this overstatement of profit (and corresponding understatement of undistributable reserves) would be material to the financial statements, it is not likely to be seen as pervasive and therefore an 'except for' qualified opinion would be appropriate.

(c) *Qualified audit report extract*

'As explained in note ... a revaluation of fixed assets of £25,000 has been credited in full to profits instead of being recognised in the statement of total recognised gains and losses as required by FRS 15; the effect of so doing has been to increase profits before and after tax for the year by £25,000.

Except for ...'

(d) The auditors' general responsibility with regard to the statement in the directors' report concerning the valuation of land and buildings is to satisfy themselves that this is consistent with the treatment and disclosure of this item in the audited financial statements. If the auditors are not satisfied on the question of consistency then an appropriate opinion will be required following their audit report.

4 THE AUDIT REPORT AS A MEANS OF COMMUNICATION

4.1 Unqualified audit reports may not appear to give a great deal of information. The report says a lot, however, by implication. The real problem here is that, unfortunately, **most users do not know** that this is what an unqualified audit report tells them.

4.2 This difference between the actual and the public perception is part of what is called the 'expectation gap'. The question remains: how can we make the **meaning** of an unqualified audit report clear to the user? The Auditing Practices Board (APB) came up with the audit report in SAS 600, as an answer to this problem.

4.3 The APB made it clear that the new audit report was to be seen as a step towards closing the 'expectation gap' which was defined in an earlier consultative paper as 'the difference between the apparent public perceptions of the responsibilities of auditors on the one hand (and hence the assurance that their involvement provides) and the legal and professional reality on the other'.

4.4 The APB stressed that the above definition is not definitive and that the expectations gap is not a 'static phenomenon'. However, the Board has addressed specific issues.

(a) **Misunderstandings of the nature of audited financial statements**, for example that:

- The balance sheet provides a fair valuation of the reporting entity.
- The amounts in the financial statement are stated precisely.
- The audited financial statement will guarantee that the entity concerned will continue to exist.

(b) **Misunderstanding as to the type and extent of work undertaken by auditors.**

(c) **Misunderstanding about the level of assurance provided by auditors**, for example that:

- An unqualified auditors' report means that no frauds have occurred in the period.
- The auditors provide absolute assurance that the figures in the financial statements are correct (ignoring the concept of materiality and the problems of estimation).

4.5 Note that the Cadbury Report also recommends many of the suggestions made in SAS, particularly the statement of both directors' and auditors' responsibilities.

Exam focus point

Questions about audit reports could be about possible qualifications in specific situations.

Chapter roundup

- The Companies Act requires **specific reference** in the audit report to:
  - The truth and fairness of the state of the company's affairs at the period-end
  - The truth and fairness of the profit or loss
  - Whether the accounts have been properly prepared in accordance with the Companies Act
- The Companies Act requires certain matters to be reported on by **exception**.
- The main elements of an **unqualified audit report** under SAS 600 are:
  - A **title** identifying the addressee
  - An **introductory paragraph** identifying the **financial statements audited**
  - Sections dealing with:
    - **Responsibilities** of **directors** and **auditors**
    - **Basis** of the **auditors' opinion**
    - A **clear statement of opinion**
- Auditors may qualify their audit opinion on the grounds of **disagreement or limitation of scope**; these may be **material** or **fundamental.**
- Auditors are principally concerned with the correct **treatment** and **disclosure** of **inherent** and **fundamental uncertainties**, which relate to uncertain future events.
- Auditors should include an **explanatory paragraph** in their audit report if **fundamental uncertainties** exist.

Quick quiz

1 What are the three explicit opinions and the five implied opinions of the audit report?

1	1 ....
2	2 ....
3	3 ....
	4 ....
	5 ....

2 Complete the standard opinion paragraph.

In our opinion the .... give a .... of the state of the company's affairs as at 31.XX.XX and of its .... (............) for .... and have been .... in accordance with the Companies Act 1985.

3 The statement of directors' responsibilities is always included in the auditors' report.

True ☐

False ☐

4 Complete the diagram by filling in the type of report that would be issued in each situation.

FORMING AN OPINION ON FINANCIAL STATEMENTS

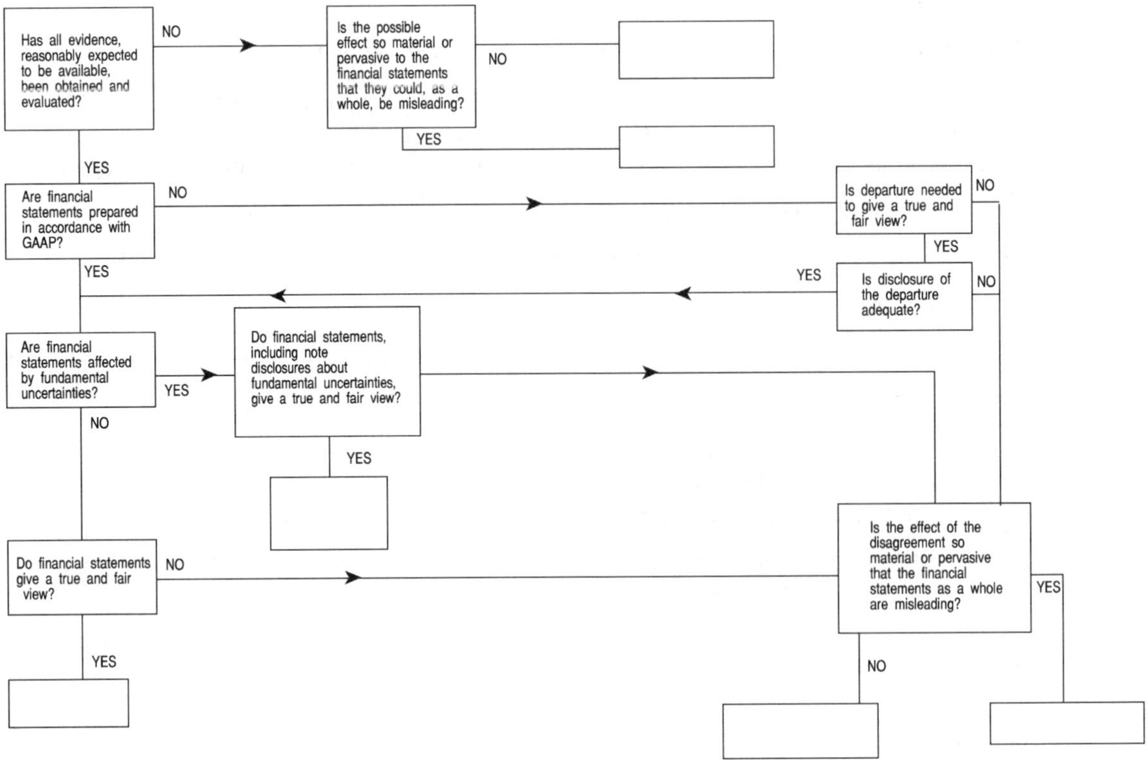

5 Draw the qualification matrix

6 Complete the definition

An .... uncertainty is an uncertainty whose resolution is dependent upon .... outside the control of the reporting entity's directors at .... the financial statements are ....

Answers to quick quiz

1 **Expressly**
State of the company's affairs
Company's profit and loss
Consolidation (if applicable)

By implication
Proper accounting records
Accounts in agreement with records
Information and explanations received
Directors' emoluments disclosed right
Directors' report consistent with accounts

2 financial statements, true and fair view, profit (loss) the year then ended, properly prepared

3 False

4

FORMING AN OPINION ON FINANCIAL STATEMENTS

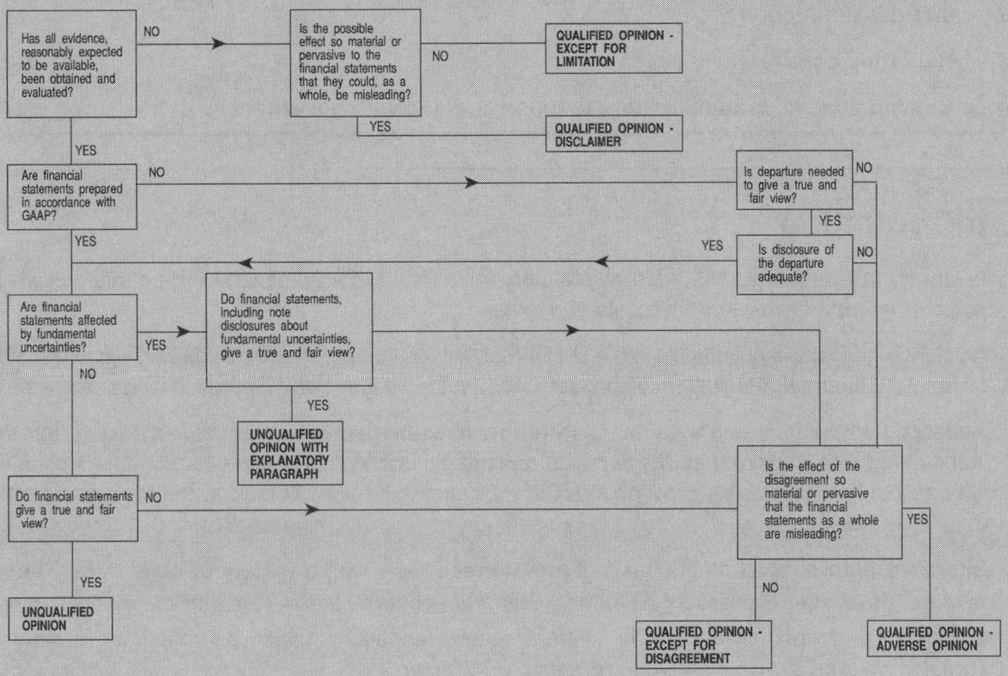

5 QUALIFICATION MATRIX

Nature of circumstances	*Material but not pervasive*	*Pervasive*
Disagreement	Except for .. might	Disclaimer of opinion
Limitation in scope	Except for ...	Adverse opinion

Except for . . . might	Auditors disclaim an opinion on a particular aspect of the accounts which is not considered pervasive.
Disclaimer of opinion	Auditors state they are unable to form an opinion on truth and fairness.
Except for	Auditors express an adverse opinion on a particular aspect of the accounts which is not considered pervasive.
Adverse opinion	Auditors state the accounts do not give a true and fair view.

6 inherent, uncertain future events, the date, approved

Now try the question below from the Exam Question Bank

Number	Level	Marks	Time
19	Exam	20	36 mins

Chapter 20

PRIVATE REPORTING

Topic list		Syllabus reference	Study guide
1	External review reports	7	27
2	Internal audit reports	7	27
3	Reporting control weaknesses	7	13 - 16
4	Communication of audit matters to those charged with governance	7	27

Introduction

In Chapter 19 we looked at the formal statutory audit report to members. In this chapter we will look at the other reports arising from audits and reviews.

As there is no formal requirements in the UK for reporting on the results of **external reviews**, we shall look briefly at the **international guidance**, found in ISRE 2400, *Engagement to Review Financial Statements.*

Auditors, both internal and external, also **report to management** about issues arising from audit work undertaken. **External auditors** report on controls and systems issues, and matters connected with accounting policies as a **by-product** of their audit and we will look at the form these reports take in Section 3.

Internal auditors report on the basis of **pre-planned work** with a **variety of objectives.** The work may be '**risk-based**' assessing whether systems an controls are in line with the objectives of the entity, or '**performance-enhancing**' where recommendations might be made in a wider risk context. We discussed these types of audits in Chapter 3. Here, in Section 2, we will look at the reporting process.

Lastly, **external auditors** are **required** by auditing standards to report to **those charged with governance**. We shall investigate what SAS 610 requires in this regard in Section 4.

You are unlikely to be asked to draft a report, but might have to outline what points should be included in a report given a particular scenario, or discuss the level of assurance given in such a report. In December 2001, the external review report was contrasted with the audit report, and in the controls question, the candidate was asked to set out control weaknesses in report format.

1 EXTERNAL REVIEW REPORTS 12/01

1.1 The concept of an **external review** was introduced in Chapter 1. It is an exercise, similar to an audit, which is designed to give a reduced degree of assurance concerning the proper preparation of a set of financial statements.

1.2 There is no current UK guidance on review engagements, so here we shall consider the international guidance, ISRE 2400, *Engagements to Review Financial Statements*. Remember that, as discussed in Chapter 1, negative assurance is given on review assignments.

No matters have come to the attention of the auditor

1.3 In this case, the auditor should give a clear expression of negative assurance in his report. An example of an unqualified review report is given in the appendix to the ISA, and it is reproduced here.

> **Form of Unqualified Review Report**
>
> REVIEW REPORT TO...
>
> We have reviewed the accompanying balance sheet of ABC Company at December 31, 20XX, and the related statements of income and cash flows for the year then ended. These financial statements are the responsibility of the Company's management. Our responsibility is to issue a report on these financial statements based on our review.
>
> We conducted our review in accordance with the International Standard on Auditing (or refer to relevant national standards or practices) applicable to review engagements. This Standard requires that we plan and perform the review to obtain moderate assurance as to whether the financial statements are free of material misstatement. A review is limited primarily to inquiries of company personnel and analytical procedures applied to financial data and thus provides less assurance than an audit. We have not performed an audit and, accordingly, we do not express an audit opinion.
>
> Based on our review, nothing has come to our attention that causes us to believe that the accompanying financial statements do not give a true and fair view (or 'are not presented fairly, in all material respects,') in accordance with International Accounting Standards.
>
> *Date* *AUDITOR*
>
> *Address*

Matters have come to the attention of the auditor

1.4 If matters have come to the attention of the auditor, he should **describe those matters**. The matters may have the following effects.

Impact	Effect on report
Material	Express a **qualified** opinion of negative assurance
Pervasive	Express an **adverse** opinion that the financial statements do not give a true and fair view

1.5 The auditor may feel there has been a limitation in the scope of the work he intended to carry out for the review. If so, he should **describe the limitation.** The limitation may have the following effects.

Impact	Effect on report
Material to one area	Express a **qualified** opinion of negative assurance due to amendments which might required if the limitation did not exist
Pervasive	Do not provide any assurance

2 INTERNAL AUDIT REPORTS 6/03

2.1 Internal audit make reports to directors and management as a result of work performed. These reports are internal to the business and are unlikely to be shared with third parties other than the external auditors.

2.2 We looked in detail at the types of assignment internal audit will carry out in Chapter 3. These may be summarised as '**risk-based**', where the internal auditors consider internal and external risks and discuss company operations and systems in place in respect of them or '**performance enhancement**' where internal audit consider risk and strategy on a higher level.

2.3 For the most part, as seen in Chapter 3, work is likely to be **risk-based**. Regardless of the nature of the assignment, however, all internal audits are likely to result in a formal report.

Reporting on internal review assignment

2.4 There are **no formal requirements** for such reports in the UK as there are for the statutory audit. The statutory audit report is a highly stylised document which is substantially the same for any audit. A report from the internal auditors in relation to an assignment can take essentially any form. However, some points should be borne in mind.

2.5 There is a generally accepted format for reports in business, which is laid out below. This format makes reports useful to readers as it highlights the conclusions drawn and gives easy reference to the user.

Standard report format

TERMS OF REFERENCE

EXECUTIVE SUMMARY – summarising conclusions drawn from assignment

BODY OF THE REPORT

APPENDICES FOR ANY ADDITIONAL INFORMATION

2.6 The report is likely also to be dated, designated as to whether it is draft or final and have a 'distribution list' of directors and management who should read it attached.

2.7 Some internal audit reports will be modified as responses are made to it may various members of staff. If this is the case, the report should clearly state which version it is. The distribution list may also be annotated to show who has commented on the report at any time.

Contents of the report

2.8 The **executive summary** of an internal audit report should give the following information.

- Background to the assignment
- Objectives of the assignment
- Major outcomes of the work
- Key risks identified
- Key action points
- Summary of the work left to do

2.9 The **main body** of the report will contain the detail; for example the audit tests carried out and their findings, full lists of action points, including details of who has responsibility for carrying them out, the future time-scale and costs.

3 REPORTING CONTROL WEAKNESS 12/01, 6/03

3.1 One of the matters which the external auditor is required to report on by SAS 610 is the area of weaknesses in control systems. Many external auditors produce a report to management as a by-product of an external audit, listing any weaknesses they have found in systems and making recommendations for improvements.

Report to management Pilot paper

3.2 External auditors should report any weaknesses discovered in the system of internal control to the management of the company as part of their audit communications. This report usually takes the form of a **letter**, but other types of report are acceptable.

3.3 Such a report to management is **not** a substitute for a qualified audit report (see Chapter 19), when such a qualification is required. Inconsistencies between reports to management and the auditors' report should be avoided.

Material weaknesses in the accounting and internal control systems

3.4 When material weaknesses in the accounting and internal control systems are identified during the audit, auditors are required to report them to those charged with governance (see Section 4) and may also **report them in writing** to management on a **timely basis.**

3.5 A **material weakness** is one which may result in a **material misstatement** in the financial statements. If it is corrected by management, it need not be reported, but the discovery and correction should be documented

3.6 To be effective, the report should be made **as soon as possible** after **completion** of the audit procedures. A written report is usual, but some matters may be raised orally with a file note to record the auditors' observation and the directors' response.

3.7 Where no report is felt to be necessary, the auditors should inform the directors that no material weaknesses have been found.

3.8 Where the audit work is performed on more than one visit, the auditors will **normally report** to management **after the interim audit work** has been completed as well as after the final visit.

Other matters

3.9 If the auditors choose not to send a formal letter or report but consider it preferable to discuss any weaknesses with management, the discussion should be **minuted** or otherwise recorded in writing. Management should be provided with a copy of the note.

3.10 The auditors should explain in their report that it **only** includes those matters which **came to their attention** as a result of the audit procedures, and that it **should not be regarded as a comprehensive statement of all weaknesses** that exist or all improvements that might be made.

3.11 The auditors should request a **reply** to all the points raised, indicating what action management intends to take as a result of the comments made in the report.

3.12 If **previous points** have **not been dealt with effectively** and they are still considered significant, the auditors should enquire why action has not been taken.

3.13 The report may contain matters of varying levels of significance and thus make it difficult for senior management to identify points of significance. The auditors can deal with this by giving the report a '**tiered**' **structure** so that major points are dealt with by the directors or the audit committee and minor points are considered by less senior personnel.

Specimen letter

3.14 A specimen letter is provided below which demonstrates how the principles described in the previous paragraphs are put into practice. This could form part of a more extensive communication to those charged with governance as discussed in Section 4.

Exam focus point

You may be asked to draft paragraphs for such a report in the exam. You should follow the format we have used. The pilot paper contained 6 marks on items to be included in a report to management.

SPECIMEN MANAGEMENT LETTER

AB & Co
Certified Accountants
29 High Street
London, N10 4KB

The Board of Directors,
Manufacturing Co Limited,
15 South Street
London, S20 1CX

1 April 20X8

Members of the board,

Financial statements for the year ended 31 May 20X8

In accordance with our normal practice we set out in this letter certain matters which arose as a result of our review of the accounting systems and procedures operated by your company during our recent interim audit.

We would point out that the matters dealt with in this letter came to our notice during the conduct of our normal audit procedures which are designed primarily for the purpose of expressing our opinion on the financial statements of your company. In consequence our work did not encompass a detailed review of all aspects of the system and cannot be relied on necessarily to disclose defalcations or other irregularities or to include all possible improvements in internal control.

1 *Purchases: ordering procedures*

Present system

During the course of our work we discovered that it was the practice of the stores to order certain goods from X Ltd orally without preparing either a purchase requisition or purchase order.

Implications

There is therefore the possibility of liabilities being set up for unauthorised items and at a non-competitive price.

Recommendations

We recommend that the buying department should be responsible for such orders and, if they are placed orally, an official order should be raised as confirmation.

2 *Purchase ledger reconciliation*

Present system

Although your procedures require that the purchase ledger is reconciled against the control account on the nominal ledger at the end of every month, this was not done in December or January.

Implications

The balance on the purchase ledger was short by some £2,120 of the nominal ledger control account at 31 January 20X8 for which no explanation could be offered. This implies a serious breakdown in the purchase invoice and/or cash payment batching and posting procedures.

Recommendations

It is important in future that this reconciliation is performed regularly by a responsible official independent of the day to day purchase ledger, cashier and nominal ledger functions.

3 *Sales ledger: credit control*

Present system

As at 28 February 20X8 debtors account for approximately 12 weeks' sales, although your standard credit terms are cash within 30 days of statement, equivalent to an average of about 40 days (6 weeks) of sales.

Implications

This has resulted in increased overdraft usage and difficulty in settling some key suppliers accounts on time.

Recommendations

We recommend that a more structured system of debt collection be considered using standard letters and that statements should be sent out a week earlier if possible.

4 *Preparation of payroll and maintenance of personnel records*

Present system

Under your present system, just two members of staff are entirely and equally responsible for the maintenance of personnel records and preparation of the payroll. Furthermore, the only independent check of any nature on the payroll is that the chief accountant confirms that the amount of the wages cheque presented to him for signature agrees with the total of the net wages column in the payroll. This latter check does not involve any consideration of the reasonableness of the amount of the total net wages cheque or the monies being shown as due to individual employees.

Implications

It is a serious weakness of your present system, that so much responsibility is vested in the hands of just two people. This situation is made worse by the fact that there is no clearly defined division of duties as between the two of them. In our opinion, it would be far too easy for fraud to take place in this area (eg by inserting the names of 'dummy workmen' into the personnel records and hence on to the payroll) and/or for clerical errors to go undetected.

Recommendations

(i) Some person other than the two wages clerks be made responsible for maintaining the personnel records and for periodically (but on a surprise basis) checking them against the details on the payroll;

(ii) The two wages clerks be allocated specific duties in relation to the preparation of the payroll, with each clerk independently reviewing the work of the other;

(iii) When the payroll is presented in support of the cheque for signature to the chief accountant, that he should be responsible for assessing the reasonableness of the overall charge for wages that week.

Our comments have been discussed with your finance director and the chief accountant and these matters will be considered by us again during future audits. We look forward to receiving your comments on the points made. Should you require any further information or explanations do not hesitate to contact us.

This letter has been produced for the sole use of your company. It must not be disclosed to a third party, or quoted or referred to, without our written consent. No responsibility is assumed by us to any other person.

We should like to take this opportunity of thanking your staff for their co-operation and assistance during the course of our audit.

Yours faithfully

ABC & Co

Question: Management letter

During the post-audit meeting at Auckland Limited, one of the directors has asked why auditors produce a management letter, as he thought that the auditors only produced an audit report.

Write a letter to the director, Mr Venkataraghavan, indicating why auditors produce a management letter, and describe briefly its advantages and disadvantages.

Answer

Mr A Venkataraghavan
Auckland Limited
51 Central Street
Westnorth, Southshire
WN2 1SW

21 July 20X0

Dear Mr Venkataraghavan

I am writing to answer your queries about the purposes of a management letter.

Purposes

Auditors are required by auditing guidance to communicate audit matters with those charged with governance. The main purposes of a management letter are for us as auditors to communicate information and suggestions:

(a) On the design and operation of internal control systems and to make suggestions for their improvement

(b) For improvements in the economy and efficiency of the use of the company's resources

(c) On adjusted or unadjusted errors in the accounts or on specific accounting policies

(d) Of problems during the audit which may have prolonged the audit and resulted in increased costs

(e) Of significant differences between the financial accounts and management accounts which may limit the usefulness of the management accounts

(f) Of any results of our analytical procedures which we believe will be of use to management

These matters would not necessarily lead to the audit report being qualified, but we believe our suggestions in these areas will benefit management.

Advantages and disadvantages

The main advantages of a management letter are:

(a) The letter shows that we have been doing during the audit and what we have found. It is thus a very important means of communication between ourselves and yourselves.

(b) The letter contains suggestions we make having used our experience and knowledge of the business environment.

(c) As indicated above, the suggestions we make cover matters other than those which are mentioned in our audit report.

Yours faithfully

ABC & Co

4 COMMUNICATION OF AUDIT MATTERS TO THOSE CHARGED WITH GOVERNANCE

KEY TERMS

Those charged with governance are those persons entrusted with the supervision, control and direction of an entity. Those charged with governance include the directors of a company or other body, the partners, proprietors, committee of management or trustees or other forms of entity, or equivalent persons responsible for directing the entity's affairs and preparing its financial statements.

Management is those persons who have executive responsibility for the conduct of the entity's operations and the preparation of its financial statements.

4.1 **External auditors** are required by auditing standards to communicated matters arising from the audit with those charged with governance. Guidance is given in SAS 610 *Communication of audit matters to those charged with governance* which states that auditors must communicate relevant matters on a timely basis.

4.2 In Chapter 5 we discussed the importance of ensuring mutual understanding between client and auditor concerning the terms of the engagement. This SAS points to the need for **mutual understanding** of the **scope of the audit** and the **respective responsibilities** of the auditors and those charged with governance in the entity.

4.3 It is also important to the audit process that the two parties **share available information**, and that the auditors can make **constructive observations** to the entity.

The communication process

4.4 Many of the factors in the communication process, such as, 'to whom?' 'when?' 'how often?', will depend on the size of the entity and the environment in which it operates.

4.5 The SAS requires auditors to 'plan with those charged with governance the form and timing of communications to them and determine whether there are particular persons to whim they should communicate certain matters'.

4.6 The **addressees** of such a communication might be the **board of directors**, or the **audit committee**. The SAS states that, **ordinarily**, before discussing matters with those charged with governance, the auditors are likely to **discuss them with management**.

4.7 Similarly, the **form** of the communication will depend upon circumstances. It may be **written** or **oral**. Matters to consider are:

- The size, structure, and communication process of the entity
- The nature, sensitivity and significance of the matters arising
- Statutory or regulatory requirements
- Arrangements made by the parties, as outlined above

Relevant matters

Matters of independence and objectivity

4.8 The SAS also requires that 'at least annually, for all audit engagements where the audited company is a listed company, auditors should:

(a) Disclose in writing to the audit committee, and discuss as appropriate:

- All relationships between the audit firm and its related entities and the client entity and its related entities that may reasonable be thought to bear on the firm's independence and the objectivity of the audit engagement partner and the audit staff and

- The related safeguards that are in place and

(b) Where this is the case, confirm in writing to the audit committee that, in their professional judgement, the firm is independent within the meaning of the regulatory and professional requirements and the objectivity of the audit engagement partner and audit staff is not impaired'.

Planning matters

4.9 The SAS requires auditors to outline the scope of the audit work and reports. Such matters might include materiality, material misstatements, approach to internal controls, extent to which external auditors intend to rely on internal auditors and any work to be undertaken by other auditors.

Audit findings

4.10 The SAS requires the following matters to be discussed with those charged with governance:

- Expected modifications to the auditors' report

- Unadjusted misstatements

- Material weaknesses in the accounting and internal control systems identified during the audit

- Their views about the qualitative aspects of the entity's accounting practices and financial reporting

- Matters specifically required by other Auditing Standards to be communicated to those charged with governance and

- Any other relevant matters relating to the audit.

4.11 The auditors should discuss significant misstatements with those charged with governance. It might be that the auditors want the financial statements amended, while the directors do not want to make amendments. If this is the case, the SAS advises that the auditors seek written confirmation of their reasons.

Third parties

4.12 There may be occasion when third parties are interested in the report to those charged with governance. The auditor should ensure that the recipients of the letter understand that it is not intended for third parties.

4.13 It might be appropriate to include a **disclaimer** in the letter, stating that it is for the sole use of the addressee and must not be quoted or referred to without the written consent of the auditor.

Chapter roundup

- In the UK, there is no guidance on reporting on external review assignments. There is international guidance, however.
- Assurance is given in the form of negative assurance. Apart from this, the internationally accepted format is very similar to the statutory audit opinions.
- Both internal and external auditors will produce formal reports on systems addressed to management and directors.
- The internal auditors' report may take any form, but is likely to contain the following elements.
  - Executive summary (background, major outcomes, key risks, key action points, summary of work to do)
  - Main body (full details of work carried out and still required, also responsibilities, time-scale and cost
  - Appendices
- Such reports are also likely to have a circularisation list. Reports should clearly state whether they are draft or final and whether they should be modified.
- External auditors will report to management about systems weaknesses they have observed during the course of their audit.
- Auditing standards require auditors to report certain matters relating to the audit with these charged with governance.

Quick quiz

1 Complete the definition.

.... is moderate assurance given by auditors when no matters have come to their attention to indicate .... do not give a .... and .... view.

2 List the main contents of a typical internal audit report.

3 There are formal reporting requirements in the UK for internal review reports.

True ☐

False ☐

4 What are the six matters which a report under SAS 610 should contain?

1 ....

2 ....

3 ....

4 ....

5 ....

6 ....

5 Auditors can never be liable to third parties on the basis of information contained within the report communicating audit matters to those charged with governance.

True ☐

False ☐

Answers to quick quiz

1 Negative assurance, financial statements, true, fair

2
- Executive summary (background, major outcomes, key risks, key action points, summary of work to do)
- Main body (full details of work carried out and still required, also responsibilities time-scale and cost
- Appendices

3 False

4 Unexpected modifications to the audit report
Unadjusted misstatements
Material weaknesses in accounting and internal control systems
Qualitative aspects of accounting policies and financial reporting
Other matters required to be communicated by other auditing standards
Other relevant matters

5 False - so they are advised to insert disclaimers and limitations on their liability in the report

Now try the question below from the Exam Question Bank

Number	Level	Marks	Time
20	Exam	20	36 mins

Part F

Not for profit organisations

Chapter 21

NOT FOR PROFIT ORGANISATIONS

Introduction

This chapter looks at the audit of two not for profit organisations. Remember, that such entities may or may not be required to have a **statutory audit** under legislation. They may choose to have a **non statutory audit** under the terms of a charitable deed, or as part of good practice.

Once thing an auditor should do when conducting a non statutory audit is confirm that a statutory opinion is not required.

The points made in this chapter about the issues inherent in these entities are **relevant for any kind of assurance work in not for profit organisations**, that is, internal auditors and external auditors undertaking audits or reviews. These entities will have inherent features, the most obvious being the difference in **objective** of the entity, which will **affect the way the work is carried out**.

The study guide refers to questions being about small not-for-profit organisations, so it seems reasonable to expect one.

1 OBJECTIVES

1.1 In Chapter 1, we looked at some of the objectives of directors of companies, the key of which was to manage well the shareholders' investments. In a large majority of cases, 'manage the shareholders' investment' means 'create a profit', as this will create returns to the shareholders in the terms of dividends or growth in the capital value of the share.

1.2 Also in Chapter 1, we made reference to the fact that some companies and other entities who do not operate for the purpose of making profit will require an audit, either statutory or otherwise.

Not for profit organisations

1.3 Before considering what a not for profit organisation's audit will entail, it will be helpful to consider what sort of entities might exist with objectives other than to make a profit and what their objectives are, as these will impact on the way that they report and the audit that is carried out.

Question: Not for profit organisations

List as many types of not for profit organisations as you can.

1.4 The following diagram shows a number of organisations you might have come up with in your answer to question 1.

1.5 You may be thinking that some of the associations above might aim to operate at a profit, and you are correct, not for profit organisations may (conversely it may seem) operate at a profit, however, this may not be their key aim.

1.6 EXAMPLE

A hospital could operate at a profit by not spending all the money it receives in its budget. However, the key objective of a hospital is to provide health services to the public, not to make a profit. As its income is wholly fixed, it is more likely to focus on **cost-saving** so that it can operate within its budget.

Question: Objectives

Identify the key objectives and focus of the types of association listed above.

Answer

Charities and friendly societies	To meet the 'raison d'etre' of the charity, that is, to carry out the charitable purpose. May involve fund-raising, receiving donations, managing invested funds, controlling costs.
Schools	To provide education. Likely to involve managing a tight budget (either from fees or government funds).
Clubs, associations, societies, unions	To further the aims of the club, provide a service to members. May include managing subscriptions paid and keeping costs of running the club down.
Housing association	Managing the related houses and providing facilities for residents. May involve rent collection and maintenance costs or even building costs of future developments.
Local councils, public services	To provide local services to a budget based on public money. Likely to be focused on value for money as they are in the public eye.

Reporting

1.7 We noted in Chapter 1 that many of these organisations are legislated for (for example, Housing Associations Act 1985) and the Acts which relate to them may specify how they are to report their results.

1.8 Many of the organisations mentioned above may be companies (often companies limited by guarantee) and so are required to prepare financial statements and have them audited under Companies Act 1985.

1.9 Some of the entities will have statements of recommended accounting practice. For example, there is a charities SORP outlining what a charity's accounts should comprise. It suggests:

(a) A **statement of financial activities** (SOFA) that shows all resources made available to the charity and all expenditure incurred and reconciles all changes in its funds

(b) Where the charity is required to prepare accounts in accordance with the 1985 Companies Act, or similar legislation, or where the governing instrument so requires, a **summary income and expenditure account** (in addition to the SOFA) in certain circumstances

(c) A **balance sheet** that shows the assets, liabilities and funds of the charity. The balance sheet (or its notes, see (e) below) should also explain, in general terms, how the funds may or, because of restrictions imposed by donors, must be utilised

(d) A **cash flow statement**, where required by FRS 1

(e) **Notes**

Audit

1.10 Where a statutory audit is required, the auditors will be required to produce the statutory audit opinion concerning the truth and fairness of financial statements.

1.11 Where a statutory audit is not required, it is possible that the organisation might have one anyway for the benefit of interested stakeholders, such as the public or people who give to a charity.

1.12 It is also possible that such entities will have special, additional requirements of an audit. These may be required by a Regulator, or by the constitution of the organisation. For example, a charity's constitution may require an audit of whether the charity is operating in accordance with its charitable purpose.

Conclusion

1.13 An audit of a not for profit organisation may vary from a 'for profit audit' due to:

- Its objectives and the impact on operations and reporting
- The purpose an audit is required

1.14 When carrying out an audit of a not for profit organisation, it is vital that the auditor establishes:

- Whether a statutory audit is required
- If not, what the objectives of the engagement are
- What the engagement is to report on, and
- To whom the report should be addressed, and
- What form the report should take

1.15 As we have seen, there are many types of not for profit organisation and their audits could all be different depending on the purpose the audit is required and correspondingly, the objectives of the organisation. The study guide specifically focuses on small not for profit organisations, so for the rest of this chapter we shall focus on the following scenarios.

Exam focus point

You should think around the issues raised for the audit in relation to all the following entities, and be able to apply similar facts and reasoning to any not for profit organisation which comes up in the exam. Remember, the issues relating to small companies that we have discussed throughout this Study Text may also apply to small not for profit organisations as well.

Small charity scenario

Headington Hospice Ltd is a small, local charity which operates a small children's hospice and two charity shops which raise money for the ongoing work of the hospice. The hospice receives grants from the health authority, sponsorship from some local businesses, receives income from the charity shop which is entirely voluntarily operated and receives donations from individuals. It employs three nurses, a part-time hospice manager and an accountant donates his time to keep the books and produce the annual accounts. As the company's turnover falls below the exemption limit, it is not required to have an audit by law, but the terms of its constitution require that an audit of the accounts is required for the benefit of the trustees that gives an opinion as to whether the financial statements give a true and fair view and to whether the charity is meeting its objects, as set out in the constitutional document.

Small association scenario

The Midvale League is a small association. It runs several local football leagues for various ages and stages. It employs a general administrator and some casual bar staff. Any player who appears in more than 30% of a team's games for the season is required to pay a subscription to the association. The subs pay for the administrator's wages, the referee's fees, team coaches' expenses and a lease on a sport's club comprising a clubhouse and changing facilities and three football pitches. The administrator also acts as groundsman. There is a bar in the clubhouse which is run for the benefit of members at a profit which covers bar staff wages and contributes to other expenses of the club. The association pays a local firm of accountants to prepare management accounts every quarter and to produce annual financial statements which it then audits for the benefit of members of the club.

2 PLANNING 12/03

Small charity

2.1 When planning the audit of a charity, the auditors should particularly consider the following:

- The **scope** of the audit
- Recent **recommendations** of the **Charity Commissioners** or the other regulatory bodies
- The **acceptability of accounting policies** adopted
- **Changes in circumstances** in the sector in which the charity operates
- **Past experience** of the effectiveness of the charity's accounting system
- **Key audit areas**
- The **amount of detail included** in the financial statements on which the auditors are required to report

2.2 In the case of Headington Hospice, the scope of the audit is two-fold. The auditors are to report on the truth and fairness of the financial statement for the benefit of the trustees and also on whether the charity is meeting its objectives. The auditors should therefore establish what the objectives are, and consider how they are to identify whether the objectives are being met.

2.3 The auditors should consider whether any recommendations of the Charity Commissioners apply to Headington Hospice. It is unlikely that there have been any substantial changes in the sector in which it works.

2.4 In order to identify the key audit areas, the auditors will have to consider audit risk.

Audit risk

2.5 There are certain risks applicable to charities that might not necessarily be applicable to other small companies. The auditors should consider the following:

Inherent risk

Key factors include:

- The complexity and extent of regulation
- The significance of donations and cash receipts
- Difficulties of the charity in establishing ownership and timing of voluntary income where funds are raised by non-controlled bodies
- Lack of predictable income or precisely identifiable relationship between expenditure and income
- Uncertainty of future income
- Restrictions imposed by the objectives and powers given by charities' governing documents
- The importance of restricted funds
- The extent and nature of trading activities must be compatible with the entity's charitable status
- The complexity of tax rules (whether Income, Capital, Value Added or local rates) relating to charities
- The sensitivity of certain key statistics, such as the proportion of resources used in administration
- The need to maintain adequate resources for future expenditure while avoiding the build up of reserves which could appear excessive

Control risk

Key factors include:

- The amount of time committed by trustees to the charity's affairs
- The skills and qualifications of individual trustees
- The frequency and regularity of trustee meetings
- The form and content of trustee meetings
- The independence of trustees from each other
- The division of duties between trustees
- The degree of involvement in, or supervision of, the charity's transactions on the part of individual trustees

Control environment

Key elements are:

- A recognised plan of the charity's structure showing clearly the areas of responsibility and lines of authority and reporting
- Segregation of duties
- Supervision by trustees of activities of staff where segregation of duties is not practical
- Competence, training and qualification of paid staff and any volunteers appropriate to the tasks they have to perform
- Involvement of the trustees in the recruitment, appointment and supervision of senior executives
- Access of trustees to independent professional advice where necessary
- Budgetary controls in the form of estimates of income and expenditure for each financial year and comparison of actual results with the estimates on a regular basis
- Communication of results of such reviews to the trustees on a regular basis

2.6 In the case of Headington Hospice, the auditor will need to devote attention to cash receipts and income, as the Hospice receives donations from the public and also receives cash income from the charity shop.

2.7 It will also be necessary to consider fixed assets, to determine whether the premises the hospice and the charity shop should be included on the balance sheet of the charity. The auditor will also need to assess the nature of the grants received from the health authority to determine how they should be accounted for. These things should all be considered as part of the accounting policy review. The auditor should also be aware of issues such as depreciation during this review, as the hospice may own specialised medical equipment which makes such issues complex.

2.8 Another matter which the auditor must consider is the issue of going concern. This will include an assessment of the sponsorship deals which the charity has in place and any consideration of future sponsorship. The grant position must also be considered, as must the likelihood of future donations. The auditors should also consider matters such as personnel, for example, whether any existing arrangements with doctors' practices will continue in existence.

Internal controls

2.9 Small charities will generally suffer from internal control weaknesses common to small enterprises, such as **lack of segregation of duties** and use of **unqualified staff**. Shortcomings may arise from the staff's lack of training and also, if they are volunteers, from their attitude, in that they may resent formal procedures.

2.10 The auditors will have to consider particularly carefully whether they will be able to obtain adequate assurance that the accounting records do reflect all the transactions of the enterprise and bear in mind whether there are any related statutory reporting requirements.

2.11 The following sorts of internal control might be typical of a number of charities.

Cash donations

Source	*Examples of controls*
Collecting boxes and tins	Numerical control over boxes and tins
	Satisfactory sealing of boxes and tins so that any opening prior to recording cash is apparent
	Regular collection and recording of proceeds from collecting boxes
	Dual control over counting and recording of proceeds
Postal receipts	Unopened mail kept securely
	Dual control over the opening of mail
	Immediate recording of donations on opening of mail or receipt
	Agreement of bank paying-in slips to record of receipts by an independent person

Other donations	
Source	*Examples of controls*
Deeds of covenant	Regular checks and follow-up procedures to ensure due amounts are received Regular checks to ensure all tax repayments have been obtained
Legacies	Comprehensive correspondence files maintained in respect of each legacy, Regular reports and follow-up procedures undertaken in respect of outstanding legacies
Donations in kind	In case of charity shops, separation of recording, storage and sale of stock

Other income	
Source	*Examples of controls*
Fund-raising activities	Records maintained for each fund-raising event Other appropriate controls maintained over receipts Controls maintained over expenses as for administrative expenses
Central and local government grants and loans	Regular checks that all sources of income or funds are fully utilised and appropriate claims made Ensuring income or funds are correctly applied

Use of resources	
Resource	*Examples of controls*
Restricted funds	Separate records maintained of relevant revenue, expenditure and assets Terms controlling application of fund Oversight of application of fund money's by independent personnel or trustees
Grants to beneficiaries	Records maintained, as appropriate, of requests for material grants received and their treatment Appropriate checks made on applications and applicants for grants, and that amounts paid are intra vires Records maintained of all grant decisions, checking that proper authority exists, that adequate documentation is presented to decision-making meetings, and that any conflicts of interest are recorded Control to ensure grants made are properly spent by the recipient for the specified purpose, for example requirements for returns with supporting documentation or auditors' reports concerning expenditure, or monitoring visits

2.12 For Headington Hospice, the issues relating to cash donations and grants will be particularly relevant.

Small association

2.13 The Midvale League (ML) requires an audit for the benefit of its members. This makes the audit of ML similar to any small company audit such as those which we have considered throughout this Study Text.

2.14 However, the nature of the association may give rise to some particular audit risks and control issues.

Question: Audit risks

Identify any audit risks arising from The Midvale League.

Answer

Inherent risks

The classification of the sport's club **lease** may be problematic. It is certainly likely to be their biggest financial commitment. The auditor will need to determine whether the terms of the lease mean that it should be included on the balance sheet as an asset, showing the corresponding liability or whether it does not so qualify. If the terms of the lease agreement imply that the lease is merely an operating lease, the auditors should consider whether this has implications for the **going concern** of the association, as if it obtains no long-term benefit from the lease, it might be faced with the situation where it has nowhere to operate in the foreseeable future, in which case, the purpose of the association is gone.

The auditors will also have to consider the role of the general administrator, who fulfils a number of roles. He is clearly a **key man** to the association, and it might find that it had difficulties if he was incapacitated, not least perhaps in affording a replacement and any sickness benefit they were required to pay by law.

It is unclear what degree of financial record keeping the administrator takes on. The audit firm are hired to produce quarterly management **accounts**. They will gain some assurance from the fact that they prepare the accounts themselves, but there is also a risk that day to day transactions are not **properly recorded**, as there appears to be no one with financial expertise 'at the coal face'. Given that the administrator will record or maintain the relevant records to be passed on to the accountancy firm, there is also an issue of **segregation of duties** here.

The auditors should also be aware of any legal issues relating to the bearing of a license for the bar, particularly perhaps the danger that the license might be jeopardised by the sale of liquor to underage drinkers. The loss of the license to serve alcohol could severely diminish the income of the club to the point where it could no longer function.

The auditors will also need to pay attention to the membership of the association from the point of view of completeness of income.

3 EVIDENCE

Small charity

3.1 When designing substantive procedures for charities the auditors should give special attention to the possibility of:

- **Understatement or incompleteness** of the **recording of all income** including gifts in kind, cash donations, and legacies
- **Overstatement of cash grants or expenses**

- **Misanalysis** or misuse in the application of funds
- **Misstatement** or omission of **assets** including donated properties and investments
- The existence of **restricted or uncontrollable funds** in foreign or independent branches

3.2 Completeness of income can be a particularly problematic area. Areas auditors may check:

- Loss of income through fraud
- Recognition of income from professional fund raisers
- Recognition of income from branches, associates or subsidiaries
- Income from informal fundraising groups
- Income from grants

3.3 Particular matters which might be an issue at Headington Hospice are:

- Completeness of cash income from various sources
- Accounting for the grants from the local authority

Overall review of financial statements

3.4 The auditors must consider carefully whether the **accounting policies** adopted are **appropriate** to the activities, constitution and objectives of the charity, and are consistently applied, and whether the financial statements adequately disclose these policies and fairly present the state of affairs and the results for the accounting period.

3.5 In particular the auditors should consider the basis of disclosing income from fund-raising activities (for example net or gross), accounting for income and expenses (accruals or cash), the capitalising of expenditure on fixed assets, apportioning administrative expenditure, and recognising income from donations and legacies.

3.6 Charities without significant endowments or accumulated funds will often be dependent upon future income from voluntary sources. In these circumstances auditors may question whether a going concern basis of accounting is appropriate.

Small association

3.7 In the case of the Midvale League, establishing the **number of members** might prove to be difficult. Once the number of members has been established, there should be good analytical evidence available about the income from subscriptions. It would also be sensible for the auditor to encourage the association to foster subscription by bank transfer, as this would reduce the problems associated with any subscriptions which are made by cash and would provide a record of subscriptions being made (the bank records).

3.8 The problem of the **maintenance** and **retention of relevant accounting records** for the association has already been mentioned. It is possible that the auditors might find that their audit suffers a **limitation in scope** if sufficient records have not been kept.

3.9 In the absence of the association employing qualified accountancy staff, the audit firm will also need to consider whether the association have accounted correctly for **income tax** on wages, as it is possible that significant **tax liabilities** could ensue if they have not.

Accounting policies

3.10 As has already been mentioned in connection with risk, the lease is likely to pose the biggest issue for the auditor in terms of accounting policies.

4 REPORTING

4.1 On not for profit audits where a statutory audit report is required, the auditors should issue the same report as we have considered in Chapter 19. They should also consider whether any additional statutory requirements fall on the audit report.

4.2 Where an association or charity is having an audit for the benefit of its members or trustees, the standard audit report may not be required or appropriate. The auditor should bear in mind the objectives of the audit and make suitable references in the audit report. However, the SAS 600 format will still be relevant. The auditor should ensure that he makes the following matters clear:

- The addressees of the report
- What the report relates to
- The scope of the engagement
- The respective responsibilities of auditors and management/trustees/directors
- The work done
- The opinion drawn

4.3 EXAMPLE: AUDIT REPORT FOR A CHARITY

REPORT OF THE AUDITORS TO THE TRUSTEES OF XYZ CHARITY

We have audited the financial statements on pages ... to ... which have been prepared under the historical cost convention [as modified by the revaluation of certain fixed assets] and the accounting policies set out on page ...

Respective responsibilities of trustees and auditors

As described on page ... you are responsible as trustees for the preparation of the financial statements. It is our responsibility to form an independent opinion, based on our audit, on those statements and to report our opinion to you. We have been appointed as auditors under section 43 of the Charities Act 1993 and report in accordance with regulations made under section 44 of that Act.

Basis of opinion

We conducted our audit in accordance with Auditing Standards issued by the Auditing Practices Board. An audit includes examination, on a test basis, of evidence relevant to the amounts and disclosures in the financial statements. It also includes an assessment of the significant estimates and judgements made in the preparation of the financial statements, and of whether the accounting policies are appropriate to the charity's circumstances, consistently applied and adequately disclosed.

We planned and performed our audit so as to obtain all the information and explanations which we considered necessary in order to provide us with sufficient evidence to give reasonable assurance that the financial statements are free from material misstatement, whether caused by fraud or other irregularity or error. In forming an opinion we also evaluated the overall adequacy of the presentation of information in the financial statements.

Opinion

In our opinion the financial statements give a true and fair view of the charity's state of affairs as at 31 December 20.. and of its incoming resources and application of resources in the year then ended and have been properly prepared in accordance with the Charities Act 1993.

Registered auditors *Address*

Date

Exam focus point

The points made above are general points, the remember that not all clubs and charities will be the same. If you have a question in the exam relating to a charity, apply this general knowledge to the specifics given in the question and the **logical** when formulating your answer.

Question: Charity audit

You have recently been appointed audit of Links Famine Relief, a small registered charity which receives donations from individuals to provide food in famine areas in the world.

The charity is run by a voluntary management committee, which has monthly meetings, and it employs the following full-time staff:

(a) A director, Mr Roberts, who suggests fund raising activities and payments for relief of famine, and implements the policies adopted by the management committee

(b) A secretary (and bookkeeper), Mrs Beech, who deals with correspondence and keeps the accounting records

You are planning the audit of income of the charity for the year ended 5 April 20X7 and are considering the controls which should be exercised over income.

The previous year's accounts, to 5 April 20X6 (which have been audited by another firm) show the following income.

	£	£
Deeds of covenant by bankers order		14,745
Tax reclaimed on covenants (1/3 of net income)		4,915
		19,660
Donations through the post		63,452
Autumn Fair		2,671
Other income		
Legacies	7,538	
Bank deposit account interest	2,774	
		10,312
		96,095

Notes

(a) Income from deeds of covenant is stated net. Each person who pays by deed of covenant has filled in a deed of covenant form, which is kept by the secretary, Mrs Beech.

(b) All deeds of covenant are paid by banker's order - they are credited directly to the charity's bank account from the donor's bank. Donors make their payments by deed of covenant either monthly or annually.

(c) The tax reclaimed on deeds of covenant is 1/3 of the net value of the covenants, and relates to covenant income received during the year - as the tax is received after the year-end, an appropriate debtor is included in the balance sheet. The covenant treasurer, who is a voluntary (unpaid) member of the management committee, completes the form for reclaiming the income tax, using the deed of covenant forms (in (a) above) and he checks to the full-time secretary's records that each donor has made the full payment in the year required by the deed of covenant.

(d) Donations received through the post are dealt with by Mrs Beech, the full-time secretary. These donations are either cheques or cash (bank notes and coins). Mrs Beech prepares a daily list of donations received, which lists the cheques received and total cash (divided between the different denominations of bank note and coin). The total on this form is recorded in the cash book. She then prepares a paying-in slip and banks these donations daily. When there is a special fund-raising campaign, Mrs Beech receives help in dealing with these donations from voluntary members of the management committee.

(e) The Autumn Fair takes place every year on a Saturday in October - members of the management committee and other supporters of the charity give items to sell (for example food, garden plants, clothing) - a charge is made for entrance to the fair and coffee and biscuits are available at a small charge. At the end of the fair, Mrs Beech collects the takings from each of the stalls, and she banks them the following Monday.

(f) Legacies are received irregularly, and are usually sent direct to the director of the charity, who gives them to Mrs Beech for banking - they are stated separately on the daily bankings form (in (d) above).

(g) Bank deposit account interest is paid gross by the bank, as the Links Famine Relief is a charity.

Required

List and briefly describe the work you would carry out on the audit of income of the charity, the controls you would expect to see in operation and the problems you may experience for the following sources of income, as detailed in the income statement above.

(a) Deeds of covenant by bankers order
(b) Tax reclaimed on covenants
(c) Donations received through the post
(d) Autumn Fair
(e) Other income

Answer

The audit consideration in relation to the various sources of income of the Links Famine Relief charity would be as follows.

(a) *Deeds of covenant*

This type of income should not present any particular audit problem as the donations are made by banker's order direct to the charity's bank account and so it would be difficult for such income to be 'intercepted' and misappropriated.

Specific tests required would be as follows.

(i) Check a sample of receipts from the bank statements to the cash book to ensure that the income has been properly recorded.

(ii) Check a sample of the receipts to the deed of covenant forms to ensure that the full amount due has been received.

Any discrepancies revealed by either of the above tests should be followed up with Mrs Beech.

(b) *Tax reclaimed on covenants*

Once again this income should not pose any particular audit problems. The auditors should check the claim form submitted to the Inland Revenue and ensure that the amount of the claim represents $^{1}/_{3}$ of the net value of the covenants recorded as having been received.

(c) *Donations received through the post*

There is a serious problem here as the nature of this income is not predictable and also because of the lack of internal check with Mrs Beech being almost entirely responsible for the receipt of these monies, the recording of the income and the banking of the cash and cheques received. The auditors may ultimately have to express a qualified opinion relating to the uncertainty surrounding the completeness of income of this type.

Notwithstanding the above reservations, specific audit tests required would be as follows.

(i) Check the details on the daily listings of donations received to the cash book, bank statements and paying-in slips, ensuring that the details agree in all respects and that there is no evidence of any delay in the banking of this income.

(ii) Check the donations received by reference to any correspondence which may have been received with the cheques or cash.

(iii) Consider whether the level of income appears reasonable in comparison with previous years and in the light of any special appeals that the charity is known to have made during the course of the year.

(iv) Carry out, with permission of the management committee, surprise checks to vouch the completeness and accuracy of the procedures relating to this source of income.

(d) *Autumn fair*

Once again there is a potential problem here because of the level of responsibility vested in one person, namely Mrs Beech.

Specific work required would be as follows.

(i) Attend the event to observe the proper application of laid down procedures and count the cash at the end of the day.

(ii) Check any records maintained by individual stallholders to the summary prepared by Mrs Beech.

(iii) Check the vouchers supporting any expenditure deducted from the proceeds in order to arrive at the net bankings.

(iv) Agree the summary prepared by Mrs Beech to the entry in the cash book and on the bank statement.

(e) *Other income*

The unpredictable nature of legacies means that as with donations, it will be difficult to check the completeness of this source of income. There should be no particular problem relating to bank deposit interest.

Specific work required would be as follows.

(i) Check legacies received to entries in the cash book, paying-in slips, bank statements and any other supporting evidence, such as correspondence with the executors of the donor's estate.

(ii) Check bank deposit interest to the bank statement and obtain direct confirmation of the amount involved from the charity's bankers.

Question: Safe Haven

You have been appointed the auditor of Safe Haven which has a year end of 31 May. Safe Haven is a small registered charity based in Leamington Spa, Warwickshire. The organisation provides shelter for abandoned dogs and puppies with the aim of finding new homes for as many as possible.

The charity is managed by a voluntary committee, including a Chairman (Alun Jenkins) a Treasurer (Gordon Brand) and a Secretary (Amanda Jones). Appointment is by annual election by the committee each year however Alun, Gordon and Amanda have held their posts for a number of years as other committee members feel unable to give the required time commitment.

Safe Haven also employs a number of paid employees. The shelter is managed by John and Jane Sheldon, who are husband and wife. There is a kennel maid and a part time bookkeeper. In addition a number of unpaid volunteers help out at the shelter as and when they are needed depending on the number of animals at the centre at a particular point in time.

The main sources of income are as follows:

(a) **Charity shop**

This is run by a full time manager, assisted by a team of volunteers. Members of the public make donations (primarily clothes and toys) which are then sold in the shop. All transactions are in cash. The shop does not accept cheques or credit cards. The transactions are recorded by the till, with completed till rolls being passed on to the bookkeeper.

(b) **Collections**

Volunteers make house to house calls on a regular basis. In addition, on Saturday mornings volunteers make collections in the town centres of Leamington, Warwick and Kenilworth. All cash is counted by the volunteers, and returned to the bookkeeper with a receipt confirming the amount.

(c) **Dog Show**

Each year on 1st June, a Peace Festival is held in Leamington. As part of this event Safe Haven organise a dog show. Any member of the public can enter their dog by completing an entry form which can be obtained from the shop.

Tickets to see the show can be purchased up to two weeks in advance from the shop or can be purchased on the day at the Festival. In recent years the show has been a great success although two years ago it had to be cancelled due to bad weather.

T shirts can also be purchased from a stall manned by volunteers.

(d) **Sponsorship**

Safe Haven is sponsored by a local pet supplies company. The company makes an annual donation and provides prizes for the winners of the dog show. In return for this their services are advertised in the event programme and their logo is printed on the T shirts.

The main expenses are as follows:

(a) **Rent, rates, heat and light**

Both the shelter and the shop are rented properties. These expenses are all paid by monthly direct debit.

(b) **Employee costs**

John and Jane Sheldon and the shop manager are salaried. They are paid directly into their bank accounts on a monthly basis. The kennel maid and the bookkeeper are paid by the hour. They are paid by cheque on a weekly basis.

(c) **Vet bills**

The local vet provides his time free but any medicines etc do need to be paid for. Payments are made by cheque on receipt of the invoice.

(d) **Printing costs**

Leaflets are produced to support fund raising campaigns The most significant element of this cost is the dog show programme which outlines the timetable of events. The programmes are printed and delivered to Safe Haven in May. The printer invoices at the time of delivery.

The accounts are maintained by the bookkeeper on a computerised spreadsheet. Occasionally, the treasurer may also assist with the preparation of accounting information at particularly busy times in the year, for example, immediately after the dog show.

Required

(a) List the factors specific to the audit of a charity which would affect inherent and control risk.

(b) As the auditor of Safe Haven discuss the key planning issues based on the above scenario.

(c) Outline the audit work you would plan to perform in respect of the following expenses:

(i) Rent, rates, light and heat
(ii) Employee costs
(iii) Vet bills
(iv) Printing costs.

Answer

(a) The following factors would be relevant:

Inherent risk

- The extent of regulation depending on the specific nature of the charity
- The significance of donations and cash receipts
- The extent of credit card and internet donations
- The valuation of gifts of assets
- Lack of predictable income
- Lack of direct relationship between income and expenditure
- The sensitivity of issues including the proportion of resources used in admin and fund raising

Control risk

- The time committed by trustees to the charity's affairs
- The skills and qualifications of the individual trustees
- The frequency, form and content of trustee meetings
- The division of duties between trustees
- The supervision by the trustees of volunteers

(b) Planning issues for Safe Haven would be as follows:

Completeness of income

Overall this risk is high due to the following factors: the majority of the income is generated in cash, there are numerous different sources of income, and a wide range of people have access to the asset itself due to the use of volunteers.

Looking at each source of income in turn the following points are relevant:

Charity shop

Whilst till receipts can be agreed to cash received this does not guarantee that all sales have been put through the till. The main problem here is that it may be difficult to establish an expected relationship between 'sales' and 'cost of sales'. Items sold are donated by the public so much will depend on how these items are valued by the charity.

Street collections

Reconciliations can be performed between cash collected and the receipts submitted by the volunteers to determine accurate recording. Completeness of income, however, will depend largely on the integrity of the volunteers and the overall controls put in place by the charity. In this instance risk is increased by the unpredictable nature of this source of income and the fact that the collection boxes are not sealed. Those responsible for collecting the cash are also responsible for opening the boxes and counting the cash before handing it over to the bookkeeper. This increases the risk of misappropriation.

Dog show tickets and T shirts sales

Completeness of income in respect of these sources of revenue is still a concern due to the cash nature of these transactions but more reliable evidence should be available. Revenue generated from ticket sales can be reconciled to the number of tickets sold. This assumes that the charity exercises some control over the issue of tickets for example, tickets are numbered so that it is possible to determine the number sold.

For the T shirt sales it should be possible to validate the income by comparing the number of items sold with the revenue generated. This depends on the charity adopting very simple stock control.

Sponsorship

Completeness should not be an issue here as the amount involved is predetermined and is likely to be paid by cheque or by bank transfer.

Controls

In addition to the specific control issue mentioned above the assessment of the overall control environment will be essential at the planning stage of the audit. As there are concerns about the completeness of income the control environment will provide key evidence about the integrity of the revenue balance.

The auditor will need to consider the ability of the committee to run the organisation effectively. The information suggests that the three main committee members are responsible for the majority of the management so it will be important to determine their respective skills and whether they are able to devote sufficient time.

The ability of the bookkeeper will also need to be established in particular the possible lack of segregation of duties and the fact that the job is currently only done on a part time basis. It may be that records are not being maintained as they should be due to the limited number of hours being worked by that individual. This is emphasised by the fact that the Treasurer is sometimes required to help out.

Accounting Treatment

At the planning stage the accounting policies of the charity will need to be reviewed to ensure that they are appropriate and consistent. In particular the point at which income is recognised will need to be established together with any related costs. This is relevant to the income generated from the sale of tickets for the annual dog show. Tickets are available in the last two weeks in May, that is, the last two weeks before the year end and the main cost involved in the show, being the printing of the show programme is also incurred and invoiced in May. The show itself takes place in June.

In respect of the ticket sales made in May it could be argued that this income should not be recognised until the show takes place as it is only earned at this point. However, if the proceeds are non-returnable irrespective of whether the show takes place or not it could be argued that it represents a donation which can be recognised on receipt.

In respect of the programme costs the treatment is a little clearer. These should be provided for at the end of the year even though they relate to an activity which will take place after the year end. Per FRS 12 there is an obligation to pay for the programmes as a result of a past event that is, the printing company have produced and delivered the programmes.

Evidence

At the planning stage the overall strategy to adopt will need to be determined. In this case it is likely that a controls based approach will be adopted (as completeness of income is one of the key risks) supported by substantive testing, the extent of which will depend on the results of the tests of controls. The use of analytical review will be more limited due to the lack of predictive patterns in relation to many aspects of the organisation and the lack of relationships between account balances.

(c) The audit plan would include the following:

Rent, rates, light and heat

- Agree total rent/rates for the year to the lease/annual bill
- Check direct debit amounts in the cash book/bank statement
- Compare the cost of heat and light for this year and the previous year and follow up if there are any major differences
- Look at the date on the last utility bill to determine the need for any prepayment or accrual adjustment.

Employee costs

- For salaried staff check annual salary to personnel details/contract of employment.
- For the bookkeeper and the kennel maid review the controls over the recording of hours worked and check the hourly rates applied to personnel details/contracts of employment.
- Check a sample of standing data used to process the payroll for example, NI rates
- Recalculate a sample of monthly calculations to ensure that deductions are being made correctly.
- Review controls over the weekly authorisation of pay checks and monthly bank transfers.

Vet bills

- Confirm with the vet that he has given his time for free.
- Compare the total vet bill for this year and last year and calculate a 'cost per animal rescued' if possible.
- Trace a sample of entries made in the cash book in respect of vet fees back to the original invoice to confirm that the cost is in respect of this.
- Review invoices received after the year end to ensure that any necessary accruals have been recognised.

Printing costs

- Obtain the printers' invoice and check that a provision has been included in the accounts at the year end for an amount matching that on the invoice.
- Confirm that the programmes have been received.

---

5 PUBLIC SECTOR

5.1 Another type of organisation which might operate as not-for-profit organisations are public sector organisations. We will consider these briefly here also.

5.2 The public sector in the UK comprises a great variety of organisations. They all **must have their accounts audited by an independent external auditor**, in order to provide external accountability to the community at large.

5.3 In the public sector there is a **tendency for an external audit to cover a much wider scope than in the private sector**. The scope of public sector audit includes not only auditing of

financial records and auditing to check **compliance with regulations** but also auditing the **achievement of economy, efficiency and effectiveness.**

5.4 The audit is an important part of public accountability and it provides an independent check on how **public funds** have been raised and spent. More specifically audit is needed to ensure that:

- **Public funds** have been **spent** on **proper, authorised purposes** and **legally within statutory powers.**
- Organisations **install and operate controls** to limit the possibility of corrupt practice, fraud and poor administration.
- Arrangements are in place to secure **economy, efficiency and effectiveness** in the use of resources.

External auditors in the public sector

5.5 The table below summarises the position on who acts as auditor in the various parts of the public sector.

	National Audit Office	*Audit Commission*	*Monopolies and Mergers Commission*	*Private sector firms*
Central departments	All	-	-	-
Non-departmental public bodies	Most	-	-	A few
Nationalised industries	-	-	VFM	All
Local authorities	-	Most	-	Some
Health authorities	Rights of access and inspection	Most	-	Some
Universities	Rights of access and inspection	-	-	All

The regulatory framework

5.6 The public sector is subject to a **high degree of regulation** including statutory regulations and detailed administrative requirements. For most public sector audits, the scope and objectives of the audit are affected by the **interests and requirements of certain third party organisations** such as audit **supervisory bodies** and **government sponsoring departments** which have specific regulatory responsibilities.

Exam focus point

Public sector organisations are likely to be too large to come within the 'small not for profit organisations' focus of the Study Guide. However, given that you have considered best value (a local authority issue) from the point of view of internal auditors, you should be prepared in case a question set in the public sector comes up. Remember to think what they **key factors** and objectives for that organisation are likely to be. In the public sector, **cost control** is always likely to be an issue.

Chapter roundup

- Various types of organisations which do not exist for the purpose of maximising shareholder wealth.
- If such organisations are set up as companies, they are likely to require a statutory audit. If not, the organisation may choose to have an audit anyway.
- If such an organisation chooses to have an audit, the nature of the audit will be subject to the requirements of the entity and/or by statutory restrictions relating to the organisation.
- The audit risks associated with not for profit organisations may well be different from other entities.
    - Cash may be significant in small not for profit organisations and controls are likely to be limited.
    - Income may well be a risk area, particularly where money is donated or raised informally.
- Obtaining audit evidence may be problem, particularly where associations have informal arrangements and there might be limitations on the scope of the audit.
- It will be necessary to ensure accounting policies used are appropriate.
- The nature of the report will depend on statutory and entity requirements, but it should conform to SAS 600 criteria.
- The public sector comprises a large number of different not for profit organisations.
- Internal audit may provide a key role in assessing matters such as 'value for money' and 'best value.
- There are various 'official' auditors, such as the National Audit Office, involved in the public sector and other external auditors are less likely to be brought in.

Quick quiz

1 Explain why income can be a problem when auditing charities.

2 Complete the table, giving two examples of controls in each area.

Cash donations	Other donations	Other income

3 All limited companies must have a statutory audit.

True ☐

False ☐

Answers to quick quiz

1
- Loss of income through fraud
- Recognition of income from professional fund raisers
- Recognition of income from branches, associates or subsidiaries
- Income from informal fundraising groups
- Income from grants

2

Cash donations	Other donations	Other income
Numerical control over boxes and tins	Regular checks and follow-up procedures to ensure due amounts are received	Records maintained for each fund-raising event Other appropriate controls maintained over receipts
Satisfactory sealing of boxes and tins so that any opening prior to recording cash is apparent	Regular checks to ensure all tax repayments have been obtained	Controls maintained over expenses as for administrative expenses
Regular collection and recording of proceeds from collecting boxes	Comprehensive correspondence files maintained in respect of each legacy	Regular checks that all sources of income or funds are fully utilised and appropriate claims made
Dual control over counting and recording of proceeds	Regular reports and follow-up procedures undertaken in respect of outstanding legacies	Ensuring income or funds are correctly applied
Unopened mail kept securely	In case of charity shops, separation of recording, storage and sale of stock	
Dual control over the opening of mail		
Immediate recording of donations on opening of mail or receipt		
Agreement of bank paying-in slips to record of receipts by an independent person		

3 False

Now try the question below from the Exam Question Bank

Number	Level	Marks	Time
21	Exam	20	36 mins

The scenario and requirement of this question have been analysed in some detail in the Exam Question Bank because as well as being a question on a not for profit organisation, it is an example of a question where you are asked to identify **audit risks**, which is a key skill for the exam.

Exam question bank

Examination standard questions are indicated by mark and time allocations.

1 PRINCETOWN AND YALE *15 mins*

Princetown and Yale are in partnership. Previously accounts have been prepared by their bookkeeper but as their business is growing they are considering asking your firm to act as auditors to the partnership.

Required

(a) State how a non-statutory audit could assist the partnership.

(b) Identify the major difficulty you could potentially face in a non-statutory audit, and state how you would try to overcome it.

2 STANDARDS *30 mins*

You are required to discuss the advantages and disadvantages of accounting and auditing standards to auditors and the consequences of such standards being enforceable by statute.

3 ROLE OF INTERNAL AUDIT (20 marks) *36 mins*

(a) You are a member of the internal audit team at Golden Holdings plc, a listed company. The board of directors wants to raise the profile of the internal audit department in the company. They have asked the internal audit department to give a series of seminars on the corporate governance and the role of internal audit in achieving corporate objectives to other members of staff.

The head of internal audit has asked you to prepare some notes on this subject.

Required

Prepare the notes which the head of internal audit wants. (12 marks)

You should cover the following matters:

(i) The Board of Directors
(ii) Accountability
(iii) The meaning of risk management

(b) After the seminars, the various departments of Golden Holdings have been asked to carry out risk management brainstorming sessions to identify risks in each of their departments and to design internal control systems to reduce those risks. The sales director, Wayne, has asked you if you will attend the brainstorming session in the sales department and whether you will assist them in the risk identification and management process.

Required

Draft a memorandum to the Sales Director, answering his questions. (8 marks)

You should cover the following matters

(i) Whether you will attend the meeting, and in what capacity.

(ii) Whether you attend the meeting or not, what involvement you, as a member of the internal audit team, will have in the risk management exercise.

4 OBJECTIVITY (20 marks) *36 mins*

(a) Explain the concept of objectivity, with reference to

(i) External auditors
(ii) Internal auditors, who are members of ACCA,

outlining any general threats to objectivity that exist. (8 marks)

(b) *Scenario 1*

Bakers Ltd is an audit client of Hinkley Innes, a firm of Chartered Certified Accountants. The firm has had the audit of Bakers for 17 years and the fee represents 7% of firm income. Bakers is considering a major new project and has asked the firm if it would be happy to undertake some one off consultancy work for the firm. It is possible that the fee income for this contract would represent 10% of that year's income for Hinkley Innes. The new business services partner, who heads up a new division of the firm, is keen to take on the work, as this would represent his best contract yet.

Scenario 2

Peter works in the purchasing department of Murphy Manufacturing plc. He has been instrumental in setting up control systems in the purchasing department as part of a recent risk management exercise. He has a poor relationship with his immediate supervisor, the Purchasing Director. Murphy Manufacturing has just advertised the post of trainee internal auditor. Peter is interested in the work that internal audit do, having liased substantially with the department during the recent controls exercise. No formal accountancy qualifications are required for the post, because the successful candidate will be put through accountancy training. Peter has had a chat with the head of internal audit concerning the post and is seriously considering making an application.

Required

Discuss the threats and the safeguards to objectivity that could be implemented in the two situations given above. (12 marks)

5 NEW ENGAGEMENT *30 mins*

Effective audit planning is essential to ensure both quality of service to the client and the minimising of risk to the practitioner.

Required

(a) What general points should auditors consider before accepting a new audit client?
(b) What is the purpose of the letter of engagement; what major matters should it refer to?

6 GLO (20 marks) *36 mins*

Glo-Warm Ltd is a company which manufactures various heating products which it sells to both High Street and catalogue retailers.

The balance sheets for the years ended 2003 and 2004 are set out below. Last year, materiality was set at £10,000.

	2004		*2003*	
	£'000	£'000	£'000	£'000
Fixed Assets				
Tangible Fixed Assets		20		21
Investments		2		2
Current Assets				
Stock	52		179	
Debtors	78		136	
Cash at bank	12		34	
Cash in hand	1		1	
	143		350	
Creditors: amounts falling due within one year				
Trade creditor	121		133	
Bank loan	5		5	
	126		138	
Net current assets		17		212
Creditors: amounts falling due after more than one year				
Bank loan		(20)		(25)
Provision*		(20)		-
Total (liabilities)/assets		(1)		210
Capital and reserves				
Share capital		2		2
Profit and loss account		(3)		208
		(1)		210

*The provision of £20,000 consists entirely of a warranty provision.

Required

(a) Without carrying out any calculations, discuss whether the materiality level used in 2001 will be appropriate for this year's audit, giving reasons for your answer. (3 marks)

(b) Explain audit risk. (3 marks)

(c) Review the balance sheet given above and set out the areas on which audit work should be concentrated, giving reasons in each case. (14 marks)

7 USING THE WORK OF AN EXPERT (20 marks) *36 mins*

An auditing standard has been issued, SAS 520 *Using the work of an expert.*

You are carrying out the audit of Ravenshead Construction plc. The company's business includes large civil engineering contracts (the construction of buildings and roads). It also owns investment properties which are let to third parties and these comprise offices and industrial buildings.

During the year ended 31 October 20X6 the company received a substantial claim for damages from Netherfield Manufacturing plc for faults in a building it had constructed. This claim includes the cost of repairs and damages, as the customer alleges that the building cannot be used because of the faults, so alternative accommodation has had to be found. The company has obtained advice on the likely outcome of this claim from a local solicitor.

In the year end accounts the investment properties had been revalued by an independent valuer and the long-term contract work in progress has been valued by an employee of the company who is a qualified valuer.

Required

Describe the matters you would consider and the other evidence you would obtain to enable you to assess the reliability of the work of experts in the following cases:

(a) Legal advice obtained from the local solicitor on the outcome of the claim by Netherfield Manufacturing (7 marks)

(b) Valuation of the investment properties by the independent valuer (7 marks)

(c) Valuation of the long-term contract work in progress by the internal valuer (6 marks)

8 AUDIT EVIDENCE (20 marks) *36 mins*

(a) For each of the following substantive tests you are required to state, together with any limitations, whether they provide strong or weak evidence of the completeness, existence, accuracy and valuation and (where applicable) ownership of the asset or liability at the financial year end.

(i) Inspecting inventories and testing perpetual records by making test counts and noting damaged, obsolete and slow moving items (6 marks)

(ii) Vouching fixed assets additions to supporting documentation (3 marks)

(iii) Verification of bank balances by bank confirmation request (4 marks)

(b) Explain why it is important that audit evidence is fully documented and list the details relating to the audit tests which should be recorded in the working papers. (7 marks)

9 INTERNAL CONTROLS (20 marks) *36 mins*

(a) State four objectives of an internal control system. (4 marks)

(b) Internal and external auditors may review internal control systems. Explain the reason for their reviews, distinguishing between them. (6 marks)

(c) Suggest the work an internal auditor could carry out to check procedures in a purchase system to minimise the risk of fraud and error. (5 marks)

(d) If the risk of fraud and error is assessed as higher than normal, how would that affect the work of an external auditor and an internal auditor? (5 marks)

10 FENTON DISTRIBUTORS (20 marks) *36 mins*

Fenton Distributors Ltd is a small company which maintains its sales, purchase and nominal ledgers on a small PC, using a standard computerised accounting package. The company buys products from large manufacturers and sells them to shops which either sell or hire them to the general public. The products include drain clearing machines, portable generators, garden cultivators and wallpaper strippers.

You have been asked to carry out an audit of the nominal ledger system to verify that items are accurately recorded in the year. At the end of the year, the nominal ledger produces a trial balance, which is used to prepare the annual accounts.

The company employs a bookkeeper, who is responsible for posting the sales and purchase ledgers, and maintaining the nominal ledger. Data is posted to the nominal ledger as follows.

(a) At the start of the financial year, all the balances on the nominal ledger accounts are set to zero (using the standard year-end procedure of the computer package).

(b) The following procedures relate to purchase transactions.

  (i) When invoices are posted to the purchase ledger, the purchase analysis code (for the nominal ledger), the purchases value and the VAT value are entered. The total invoice value is posted to the purchase ledger.

  (ii) At the end of the month, the computer posts the following items to the nominal ledger.

    (1) The total of each category of invoice expense and VAT for purchase invoices and credit notes posted in the month (at the same time the computer prints details of the individual invoices making up the total of each invoice expense and VAT for the month).

    (2) The total of purchase ledger cash payments, discount received and adjustments posted to the purchase ledger in the month (the computer prints details of the individual items comprising the total cash discount and adjustments for the month).

    (3) Where there is no account in the nominal ledger relating to the items being posted, the computer posts the items to a creditors suspense account. Also, all adjustments are posted to the suspense account.

(c) Sales ledger data is posted to the nominal ledger in a similar way to purchase ledger data.

(d) Journals are posted manually to the nominal ledger for:

  (i) The opening balances at the start of the year
  (ii) Other cash book items (other than sales and purchase ledger cash)
  (iii) Petty cash payments
  (iv) Wages analysis (details are obtained from the computerised payroll system)
  (v) Adjustments, which include:

    (1) Correction of errors

    (2) Dealing with items in the sale and purchase ledger suspense accounts (adjustments posted to the ledger, and items where there is no account in the nominal ledger)

  All these journals are written manually in an accounts journal book, and they must be authorised by the managing director before posting. The opening balances are posted to the nominal ledger when the previous year's accounts have been approved by the auditors. Although the employee wages are calculated using another computer package, the total wages expense is posted to the nominal ledger manually. The wages expense is calculated from the payroll's monthly summary, using a spreadsheet package, and the wages expense is analysed into directors, sales, warehouse and office wages (or salaries).

Your are required to list and describe the audit work you would perform on the computerised nominal ledger system, and in particular:

(a) The checks you would perform to verify the accuracy of purchases transactions which are posted to the nominal ledger. (5 marks)

(b) The checks you would perform to verify the validity and accuracy of journals posted to the nominal ledger. Also, you should briefly describe any other checks you would perform to verify the accuracy of the year end balances on the nominal ledger. (15 marks)

Note. You should assume that sales transactions are accurately recorded and correctly posted to the nominal ledger.

11 CHEQUE PAYMENTS AND PETTY CASH (20 marks) *36 mins*

Mr A Black has recently acquired the controlling interest in Quicksand Ltd, who are importers of sportswear. In his review of the organisational structure of the company Mr Black became aware of weaknesses in the procedures for the signing of cheques and the operation of the petty cash system. Mr Black engages you as the company's auditor and requests that you review the controls over cheque payments and petty cash. He does not wish to be a cheque signatory himself because he feels that such a procedure is an inefficient use of his time. In addition to Mr Black, who is the managing director, the company employs 20 personnel including four other directors, and approximately three hundred cheques are drawn each month. The petty cash account normally has a working balance of about £300, and £600 is expended from the fund each month. Mr Black has again indicated that he is unwilling to participate in any internal control procedures which would ensure the efficient operation of the petty cash fund.

Required

(a) Prepare a letter to Mr Black containing your recommendations for good internal control procedures for:

(i) Cheque payments (9 marks)
(ii) Petty cash (7 marks)

(Marks will be awarded for the style and layout of the answer.)

(b) Discuss the audit implications, if any, of the unwillingness of Mr Black to participate in the cheque signing procedures and petty cash function. (4 marks)

12 ANALYTICAL REVIEW *30 mins*

(a) Explain the purpose of analytical review and at what stages of the audit it should be carried out.
(b) Explain the importance of analytical review in a review assignment.

13 BOSTON MANUFACTURING (20 marks) *36 mins*

You are the audit assistant assigned to the audit of Boston Manufacturing. The audit senior has asked you to plan the audit of fixed assets. He has provisionally assessed materiality at £72,000.

Boston Manufacturing maintain a register of fixed assets. The management accountant reconciles a sample of entries to physical assets and vice versa on a three-monthly basis. Authorisation is required for all capital purchases. Items valued less than £10,000 can be authorised by the production manager, item costing more than £10,000 must be authorised by the Managing Director. The purchasing department will not place an order for capital goods unless it has been duly signed.

The company has invested in a large amount of new plant this year in connection with an 8 year project for a government department.

The management accountant has provided you with the following schedule of fixed assets:

	Land and buildings	*Plant and equipment*	*Computers*	*Motor vehicles*	*Total*
	£	£	£	£	£
Cost	*				
At 31 March 2003	500,000	75,034	30,207	54,723	659,964
Additions		250,729	1,154		251,883
At 31 March 2004	500,000	325,763	31,361	54,723	911,847
Accumulated depreciation					
At 31 March 2003	128,000	45,354	21,893	25,937	221,184
Charge for the year	8,000	28,340	2,367	13,081	51,788
At 31 March 2004	136,000	73,694	24,260	39,018	272,972
Net realisable value					
At 31 March 2004	364,000	252,069	7,101	15,705	638,875
At 31 March 2003	372,000	29,680	8,314	28,786	438,780

*Of which, £100,000 relates to land.

Required

(a) Without undertaking any calculations, assess the risk of the tangible fixed assets audit, drawing reasoned conclusions. (6 marks)

(b) Outline the audit procedures you would undertake on fixed assets in respect of the following assertions:

(i) Existence (3 marks)
(ii) Valuation (excluding depreciation) (4 marks)
(iii) Completeness (3 marks)

(c) Describe how you would assess the appropriateness of the depreciation rates. (4 marks)

14 SITTING PRETTY (20 marks) *36 mins*

Sitting Pretty Ltd is a small, family run company that makes plastic chairs in a variety of shapes and colours for children and 'fun at heart' adults. It buys in sheets of plastic which can be cut and bent into the correct shape and a plastic leg that is custom made by another company to Sitting Pretty's requirements. All off-cut plastic is sent back to the supplier who melts it down and re-uses it, for which Sitting Pretty receive a 10% discount off their purchase price.

For the stocktake, the factory manager ensures that no work in progress is outstanding and closes down production for the day. The factory workers come in early on the day of the stocktake to count the stock, and they are entitled to go home as soon as stock is counted. Good controls have always been maintained over the stocktake in previous years. There are no perpetual stock records. Raw materials are all kept in the stores and are only taken out when they are required for production. Finished goods are kept in the end of the factory, near the delivery exit.

You are the audit assistant assigned to attend the stocktake. You have just rung the factory manager and he has mentioned that on the day of the stocktake a large consignment of plastic is going to be delivered. It is the only day that his supplier can make the delivery, and he needs the material to continue with production on the day after the stocktake.

The audit engagement partner has told you that he is aware that Sitting Pretty changed the specification of their customised leg recently, after a series of complaints over the stability of their chairs. Last year's stock was valued at £200,000 in the balance sheet, of which £30,000 related to raw material stocks.

Finished goods are all carried at the same valuation as each other as there is very little difference between the stock ranges. Planning materiality for this year has been set at £5,000 on the grounds, at this stage, that the figures are expected to be similar to last years.

Required

(a) Explain the importance of the stocktake in this situation. (3 marks)

(b) Prepare notes for your audit supervisor detailing the procedures you propose to undertake in relation to your stocktake attendance. (7 marks)

(c) Outline the procedures which should be taken in relation to cut off at the final audit. (5 marks)

(d) List the audit procedures you would carry out on the valuation of stock at the final audit. (5 marks)

15 BRIGHT SPARKS (20 marks) *36 mins*

Bright Sparks Ltd distributes domestic electrical equipment from one warehouse. Customers are mainly installers of such equipment, but there is a 'cash and carry' counter in the warehouse for retail customers. The warehousemen are responsible for raising invoices and credit notes relating to credit sales as well as handling cash sales.

You have carried out your interim audit in respect of the year ending 31 December 20X0 which included a circularisation of 80 debtors as at 30 September 20X0 selected from a total credit customer list of 1,000. Replies were received from all debtors circularised. The interim audit work disclosed the following.

(a) Of the 80 customers accounts circularised, 8 disagreed but could be reconciled by bringing into account payments stated by the customers concerned to have been made before 30 September 20X0 but which in each case were recorded in Bright Sparks Ltd's books between 14 and 18 days after the dates stated by the customers as the date of payment.

(b) Your tests suggested that some 25% of credit customers were allowed settlement discounts of 2½% although payments were consistently received after the latest date eligible for discount.

(c) A large number of credit notes were raised representing approximately 12% of the total number of invoices raised. A review of the copy credit notes indicated that they usually arose from arithmetical and pricing errors on invoices raised.

You are required to set out the conclusions you would draw as a result of the interim audit and the work you would plan to carry out at the final audit on debtors at 31 December 20X0 based upon those conclusions.

16 NEWPIECE (20 marks) *36 mins*

Your firm is the auditor of Newpiece Textiles Limited and you are auditing the financial statements for the year ended 31 October 19X7. The company has a turnover of £2.5 million and a profit before tax of £150,000.

(a) The company has supplied you with the following bank reconciliation at the year end. You have entered the 'date cleared' on the bank reconciliation, which is the date the cheques and deposits appeared on the November's bank statement.

				£	£
Balance per bank statement at 31 October 19X7					(9,865)
Add: deposits not credited					
CB date		*Type*	*Date cleared*		
31 Oct		SL	3 Nov	11,364	
24 Oct		CS	3 Nov	653	
27 Oct		CS	4 Nov	235	
28 Oct		CS	5 Nov	315	
29 Oct		CS	6 Nov	426	
30 Oct		CS	7 Nov	714	
31 Oct		CS	10 Nov	362	
					14,069
Less: uncleared cheques					
CB date	*Cheque no*	*Type*	*Date cleared*		
30 Oct	2163	CP	3 Nov	1,216	
31 Oct	2164	PL	18 Nov	10,312	
31 Oct	2165	PL	19 Nov	11,264	
31 Oct	2166	PL	18 Nov	9,732	
31 Oct	2167	PL	20 Nov	15,311	
31 Oct	2168	PL	21 Nov	8,671	
31 Oct	2169	PL	19 Nov	12,869	
31 Oct	2170	PL	21 Nov	9,342	
31 Oct	2171	CP	3 Nov	964	
					(79,681)
Balance per cash book at 31 October 19X7					(75,477)

Notes

1 'CB date' is the date the transaction was entered in the cash book

2 Type of transaction

SL sales ledger receipt
CS receipt from cash sales
PL purchase ledger payment
CP cheque payment (for other expenses)

3 All cheques for purchase ledger payments are written out at the end of the month.

Required

(i) Describe the matters which cause you concern from your scrutiny of the bank reconciliation.

(ii) Describe the investigations you will carry out on the items in the bank reconciliation which cause you concern.

(iii) Describe the adjustments you will probably require to be made to the financial statements if your investigations confirm the problems you have highlighted in (i) above. (10 marks)

(b) The manager in charge of the audit has asked you to consider the petty cash system and recommend what audit work may be necessary. You have found that petty cash is recorded in a hand written analysed petty cash book and it is not kept on an imprest system. From the petty cash book you have recorded the petty cash expenditure for each month.

	£
1996	
November	855
December	6,243
1997	
January	972
February	796
March	893
April	751
May	986
June	695
July	749
August	8,634
September	948
October	849
Total	23,371

Required

(i) Advise the audit manager as to the desirability of performing further substantive procedures on petty cash. You should consider materiality and audit risk in relation to the petty cash system. (4 marks)

(ii) Assuming the audit manager decides that further audit work is necessary, describe the detailed substantive tests of transactions and balances you should carry out on the petty cash system. (6 marks)

17 TRURO ELECTRONICS (20 marks) *36 mins*

You are the audit senior in charge of the audit of Truro Electronics plc.

Required

State the audit procedures you would carry out to verify the following items appearing in the balance sheet at 31 March 20X8.

(a)	Trade creditors	£3,200,000
(b)	Bank overdraft	£2,100,000
(c)	Corporation tax creditor	£5,200,000
(d)	Accruals	£2,300,000
(e)	Value Added Tax creditor	£1,700,000

18 GOING CONCERN (20 marks) *36 mins*

Carrington Joinery Ltd is a private company, owned by its directors, which manufactures wooden window frames, doors and staircases for domestic houses. It has prepared draft accounts for the year ended 30 September 20X6 and you are concerned that they indicate serious going concern problems. The profit and loss accounts and balance sheets for the last five years (each ended 30 September) are given below.

PROFIT AND LOSS ACCOUNTS

	20X2	20X3	20X4	20X5	20X6
	£'000	£'000	£'000	£'000	£'000
Sales	625	787	1,121	1,661	1,881
Cost of sales	(478)	(701)	(962)	(1,326)	(1,510)
Gross profit	147	86	159	335	371
Other expenses	(88)	(86)	(161)	(240)	(288)
Interest	(6)	(9)	(58)	(90)	(117)
Net profit/(loss)	53	(9)	(60)	5	(34)

BALANCE SHEETS

	20X2	20X3	20X4	20X5	20X6
	£'000	£'000	£'000	£'000	£'000
Fixed assets	89	161	544	600	587
Current assets					
Stock	67	133	181	307	449
Debtors	91	240	303	313	364
	158	373	484	620	813
Current liabilities					
Creditors	90	317	355	490	641
Bank overdraft	10	65	211	269	365
Hire purchase creditor	14	28	98	92	59
	114	410	664	851	1,065
Net assets	133	124	364	369	335
Capital and reserves					
Share capital	17	17	17	17	17
Reserves	116	107	47	52	18
	133	124	64	69	35
Long term loan	-	-	300	300	300
	133	124	364	369	335

The company has been in business for about fifteen years. In January 20X3 it decided to build a new factory on a site leased from the local authority which would allow a major increase in sales. This new factory with new machinery was completed a year later. The factory was financed by a long-term loan of £300,000 from a merchant bank and an increase in the bank overdraft.

The loan from the merchant bank is secured by a fixed charge on the leasehold factory and the bank overdraft is secured by a second charge on the leasehold factory, a fixed charge on the other fixed assets and a floating charge on the current assets.

The company purchases its main raw material, wood, from timber wholesalers. It sells about 75% of its production to about twelve local and national builders of new domestic houses. The remaining sales are mainly to smaller builders with a very few sales to local builders merchants.

Required

(a) In relation to the accounts above, list and briefly describe the factors which indicate that the company may not be a going concern. You should also highlight certain figures and calculate relevant ratios in the accounts. (13 marks)

Note. You will only be given credit for going concern problems which can be determined from the accounts above.

(b) Describe the investigations and checks you would carry out, in addition to those described in part (a) above, to determine whether the company is a going concern. (7 marks)

19 THE STANDARD EXTERNAL AUDIT REPORT (20 marks) *36 mins*

(a) What are the main elements of the audit report prescribed by SAS 600? (4 marks)

(b) You are an audit partner and are reviewing the audit files of four clients, on each of which there is a significant matter arising.

(i) The audit team were not informed about the year-end stock take until after it had taken place. Stock is material in the financial statements. (4 marks)

(ii) No provision has been made against a material amount owed by a debtor who is now in liquidation. (4 marks)

(iii) The accounts of a plc client do not contain a cash flow statement. (4 marks)

(iv) A substantial claim has been lodged against the company by a major customer. The matter is fully explained in the notes to the accounts, but no provision has been made for legal costs or compensation payable as it is not possible to determine with reasonable accuracy the amounts, if any, which may become payable. The directors have received legal advice which appears to be reliable that the claim can be successfully defended. (4 marks)

Required

Explain what impact each of these matters would have on the audit report.

20 INTERNAL AUDIT REPORTING (20 marks) *36 mins*

You have been appointed manager of internal audit in a large organisation and asked to set up an appropriate department.

Required

You are required to produce a formal memorandum for the Board of Directors, briefing them on the following matters.

(a) Brief comparison of the role of external audit with internal audit. (5 marks)

(b) Explain the role of the internal audit function at the design stage of a new accounting system. (7 marks)

(c) Explain the format and nature of reporting that the internal audit department will carry out. (8 marks)

21 'TAP!' (20 marks) *36 mins*

You are an audit assistant in the firm Rogers and Smith. You have been asked to plan the audit of 'Tap!' for the year ended 30 June 2004. It is the first time your audit firm has audited the charity, which has not been audited previously. The trustees have expressed interest in receiving a 'value added' audit and are particularly interested in business advice, especially in the area of systems controls.

'Tap!' is a registered charity that raises money for projects building wells in Africa through musical entertainment in the UK. The group consists of volunteers who travel around the country, putting on variety shows of music and dance, the proceeds of which are put towards building the wells. The main show is an tap dance production, acting out the difficulties many people face when they are not near a clean water supply.

The administrative offices of 'Tap!' are located in Leicester. It owns a house, donated by legacy in the past, where the administration is carried out and where the volunteers stay during off periods.

A large proportion of 'Tap!''s income comes from box office receipts which are taken by the theatre at which they are performing. The theatres usually waive their standard terms for use of the premises and merely take a 10% commission on ticket receipts to cover light and heat and other such expenses. Income usually comes in after every booking in the form of a lump sum cheque from the theatre, together with a break down of takings and commission.

Tap also receives donations towards the work. These come from a variety of sources:

- Cash donations from buckets passed around at the interval of each performance
- Cash donations on the (rare) occasion that the team do street performances
- Cash donations made over the phone or by post by interested donors

The troupe consists largely of volunteers so they are only paid expenses for their work. The cost of housing the group while they are on the road is borne by the charity. The charity employs an administrator who organises bookings, handles publicity and co-ordinates all the finances.

Required

(a) Discuss the risks arising for the audit of the year ending 30 June 2004. (8 marks)

(b) Outline the audit procedures you would undertake in respect of cash income in the financial statements. (6 marks)

(c) Outline some controls over cash which the charity should implement. (6 marks)

Approaching the answer

You should read through the requirement before working through and annotating the question as we have so that you are aware what things you are looking for.

> First time audit for firm so little CAKE knowledge and experience.

> Impact on opening balances and comparatives.

You are an audit assistant in the firm Rogers and Smith. You have been asked to plan the audit of 'Tap!' for the year ended 30 June 2004. It is the first time your audit firm has audited the charity, which has not been audited previously. The trustees have expressed interest in receiving a 'value added' audit and are particularly interested in business advice, especially in the area of systems controls.

> Not just a simple audit. This may make the engagement too risky – given the potential bad publicity that could result if there were problems with the audit.

Where is the audit evidence? Also, is expenditure in line with the Trust Deed.

High degree of regulation. Do we have any experience in this field?

'Tap!' is a registered charity that raises money for projects building wells in Africa through musical entertainment in the UK. The group consists of volunteers who travel around the country, putting on variety shows of music and dance, the proceeds of which are put towards building the wells. The main show is an tap dance production, acting out the difficulties many people face when they are not near a clean water supply.

Is this common? Are there restrictions on expenditure? Also ensure accounts are correct for disclosures.

The administrative offices of 'Tap!' are located in Leicester. It owns a house, donated by legacy in the past, where the administration is carried out and where the volunteers stay during off periods.

How accounted?

Trust?

A large proportion of 'Tap!''s income comes from box office receipts which are taken by the theatre at which they are performing. The theatres usually waive their standard terms for use of the premises and merely take a 10% commission on ticket receipts to cover light and heat and other such expenses. Income usually comes in after every booking in the form of a lump sum cheque from the theatre, together with a break down of takings and commission.

Cash income - risky

Trust for completeness

Again cash. Also, poor in future years for analytical evidence. Lack of good evidence available.

Tap also receive donations towards the work. These come from a variety of sources:

- Cash donations from buckets passed around at the interval of each performance
- Cash donations on the (rare) occasion that the team do street performances
- Cash donations made over the phone or by post by interested donors

Again cash. Also, what are the controls here? Completeness has to be a problem.

No salaries

Expenditure issues again.

The troupe consists largely of volunteers so they are only paid expenses for their work. The cost of housing the group while they are on the road is borne by the charity. The charity employs an administrator who organises bookings, handles publicity and co-ordinates all the finances.

Not a specialist? But drafting complex accounts.

You should have been noticing and annotating risks as you have worked through the scenario. Try and categorise them in your mind (Inherent Control , Detection)

Required

Note you are looking specifically for **audit** risks.

(a) Discuss the risks arising for the audit of the year ending 30 June 2004 (8 marks)

(b) Outline the audit procedures you would undertake in respect of cash income in the financial statements. (6 marks)

Only cash income!!

(c) Outline some controls over cash which the charity should implement. (6 marks)

A standard requirement, but you must **tailor** your answer to the scenario.

Think of control objectives and then design reasonable controls that meet the objective. There are more control problems in the scenario than you need to identify/solve for the marks.

Answer plan

Then organise the things you have noticed and your points arising into a coherent answer plan. Not all the points you have noticed will have to go into your answer – you should spend a few minutes thinking them through and prioritising them.

(a) **Audit risks**

Overall risk of being auditor to a charity in terms of potential bad publicity in the event of problems arising on the audit.

Inherent risk	*Control risk*	*Detection risk*
Cash – susceptible to loss or theft.	Appears to be very little control over cash.	First year audit – lack of detailed knowledge of the business on the part of the auditor.
Charity – high degree of regulation		First ever audit of the charity – need to take extra care over audit of opening balances, implications for comparatives, audit report.
Lack of an accounting specialist drafting the accounts		Whereabouts of audit evidence – some may be posted to Leicester – is it all retained there?
Completeness of income appears to be a problem		
Disclosure of income – net or gross of commission		
Expenditure – substantiating, in accordance with Trust Deed?		

(b) **Audit procedures**

Income from box office takings

Verified to bank records/statement from the theatre. Possible to circularise the theatres to get them to verify numbers of seats sold so as to gain a little more assurance about the completeness of income?

Income from buckets

Are there any original records of cash counts? Verify from them to the banking documentation if so.

Income from other donations

Original documents such as letters/forms or original records of cash received should be traced to banking documentation and bank records.

(c) **Controls over cash**

Box office

The theatre should try and get more assurance re completeness of income. Is it possible to get a schedule of seats sold from the theatres – this should be available on their system.

Buckets

Two people should collect and count to avoid loss, misappropriation and/or error.

The money should be made more secure both during collection and between banking: use collecting tins, have a transportable safe and bank frequently.

An initial record of the cash count should be kept, signed by both the counters.

Other income

Other income should be recorded on pre-numbered forms to help ensure completeness.

The Trustees should carry out a periodic review of the work of the administrator to protect both the charity and the administrator.

Exam answer bank

1 PRINCETOWN AND YALE

> *Tutorial note*. This is not an exam standard question but it includes the simple benefits of an audit which you must understand and be able to outline. However remember that in a small company, these same benefits could also be provided by an alternative assurance service, perhaps a review. You need to be able to evaluate the difference between the levels of assurance given.

(a) A non-statutory audit could assist the partnership of Princetown and Yale in the following ways.

   (i) It would highlight any weaknesses in the partnership's systems, and should provide constructive suggestions for improvements.

   (ii) It would help to substantiate the partnership accounts in case of any disagreement between the partners or any query arising as to the results shown in the accounts.

   (iii) Audited accounts carry more weight with interested third parties such as the Inland Revenue, Customs and Excise and bankers or other potential sources of loan finance or credit.

(b) There is a risk that, in the absence of statutory guidance, auditors and clients have different expectations of the non-statutory audit. For instance, as discussed in (b) above, the client may expect the audit to be aimed at detecting fraud. A letter of engagement should be sent by the client to the auditors, having been discussed and agreed by both parties, setting out the areas to be covered by the audit. This should help to ensure that the client understands what degree of comfort the audit will give, and that the auditors are aware of the client's requirements.

2 STANDARDS

> *Tutorial note*. Although not exam style, this is a useful discussion about important issues which could be examined. The examiner has stated that an understanding of the overall regulatory environment is essential. Auditing standards were specifically examined in December 2001.

The major *advantages* of accounting standards and auditing standards can be summarised as follows.

(a) *Accounting standards*

   (i) They reduce the areas of uncertainty and subjectivity in accounts.

   (ii) They narrow the areas where different accounting policies can be adopted.

   (iii) They increase the comparability of financial statements.

   (iv) They codify what is considered in most circumstances to be best accounting practice.

   (v) They give an indication of the interpretation of the concept 'true and fair' in many circumstances.

(b) *Auditing standards*

   (i) They give a framework for all audits around which a particular audit can be developed.

   (ii) They help to standardise the approach of all auditors to the common objective of producing an opinion.

   (iii) They assist the court in interpretation of the concept of 'due professional care' and may assist auditors when defending their work.

   (iv) They increase public awareness of what an audit comprises and the work behind the production of an audit report.

   (v) They provide support for auditors in a dispute with clients regarding the audit work necessary.

The possible *disadvantages* include the following.

(a) *Accounting standards*

   (i) They are considered to be too rigid in some areas and too general in others, making their application difficult in some circumstances.

   (ii) They can be onerous for small companies to adopt.

(iii) Their proliferation could be said to increase proportionately the number of qualified audit reports thereby reducing the impact of such qualifications.

(iv) They can create divisions within the profession of those who agree and those who disagree with a particular standard.

(v) They would be difficult to change once they become statutory as alterations to company law can take years rather than months to enact.

(b) *Auditing standards*

(i) It may appear that they impinge on, rather than assist, professional judgement.

(ii) They are considered by some to stifle initiative and developments of new auditing methods.

(iii) They may create additional and unnecessary work and thus raise fees, particularly on the audit of small companies.

If either type of standard were to be enforceable by statue it would mean that there would be government intervention in areas currently controlled solely by the profession itself. This might ultimately lead to a diminished role in self-regulation. To be enforceable by statute the standards would have to be applicable to all circumstances and thus need to be very general and broad in their instructions. This might reduce their usefulness to the auditors. Auditors might spend unnecessary time ensuring that they have complied with the law rather than considering the quality of their service to their clients.

Finally, it should be considered whether full statutory backing for standards would force auditors into narrow views and approaches which might gradually impair the quality of accounting and auditing practices.

Note. A legal opinion on truth and fairness, accounting standards and the law in the *Foreword to Accounting Standards* strengthens the legal backing for accounting standards and UITF pronouncements.

3 ROLE OF INTERNAL AUDIT

Tutorial note. The examiner has recently written an article on the role of internal audit in risk management, and has stated that it is an important area both in practice and in this syllabus. It is important that you get to grips with the all the issues relating to internal audit and risk management.

Part (a) of this question requires you to state what you know about the background corporate governance issues and any requirements which companies must meet. Note that Golden Holdings is a listed company, so things such as the Combined Code are mandatory.

Part (b) requires you to apply the role of internal audit in a practical situation. It demands that you draw some conclusions about what your role will be. You should provide reasoning for the conclusions you draw, so that the marker can credit you both for your conclusions and your thought-processes. As internal auditor you have been asked to educate the senior management about the role of internal audit, so in practice it would be appropriate for you to appraise the director of your reasoning.

(a) **Notes on the role of internal audit**

(i) *Requirements in relation to the Board of Directors*

As a listed company, Golden Holdings is bound by the requirements of the Combined Code. This contains the following requirements:

- Board must meet regularly
- There should be a clearly accepted division of responsibilities
- Positions of Chief Executive and Chairman should be distinct
- A formal schedule of matters for referral to the Board should exist
- There should be a balance of executive and non-executive directors on the board

Companies should also set up remuneration committees comprised of non-executive directors to determine executive remuneration. Committee should report annually to the shareholders setting out the company's policy to remuneration and making disclosures about director's remuneration packages.

These recommendations specifically relate to listed companies, and if listed companies do not comply with the recommendations, they must explain themselves. However, they also represent good practice for other companies.

(ii) *Requirements in relation to accountability*

The Combined Code contains the following matters in relation to accountability:

- Directors must explain their responsibility for preparing accounts
- Directors must report on the going concern status of the company
- The Board should establish an audit committee

In addition, the financial statements must be audited by an independent auditor who qualifies for the position under legislation. The company is required as part of the annual report to include a narrative statement of how it has applied the principles of the combined code.

(iii) *Risk management*

The Combined Code requires that the directors review the effectiveness of internal control systems at least annually.

Internal control systems are maintained to enable the business to operate efficiently, to ensure that assets are safeguarded and that reliable records are maintained. An internal control system reduces risk to a company.

As such, an internal control system is part of a company's risk management. Directors are required to review the system as part of their risk management exercise, to ensure that the system is still reducing risks, and that all risks have been considered.

The directors are also required to appraise the need for an internal audit department annually. Internal audit have a role in monitoring the risk management of an entity.

(b) **Sales department brainstorming session**

MEMORANDUM

To: Sales director

(i) I should be able to come along to your brainstorming session in July. However, it is probably best that I attend in an **advisory and interested capacity** only.

As we shall be involved in monitoring the systems which the sales department put into place to mitigate risks in the business, it is i**nappropriate** for me to get **too involved** in the initial systems **design stage**, as this will **impair my future objectivity** when **monitoring** how the system is operating and achieving its objectives.

(ii) In terms of **assessing risks**, I am not best qualified to undertake this role. You guys work in the department everyday, **you are the specialists** and should be able to identify the major risks arising in the department.

Just to give you a better idea of what my role can be, I can say that internal audit are able to provide three things:

- **Objective assurance** on the operation of systems once you have them up and running

- Assistance in **setting up a process to help you identify risks**

- Assistance in **strengthening the control process** once you have identified risks.

In other words, if you are struggling to identify risks at the meeting, I can give you some pointers on how to go about it, but after that my job will be looking at the systems you come up with, and helping you improve them continually.

See you at the meeting, if not before,

Internal auditor

4 OBJECTIVITY

Tutorial note. It is important to be able to discuss ethical issues from the point of view of both external and internal auditors. This question focuses on your ability to do that.

Part (c) of this question breaks down into four parts: the two situations, and the two requirements (threats and safeguards). Do not spend so much time on the first scenario that you lose the chance to obtain any of the marks available for the second one.

As you read through both the scenarios, highlight or underline key words and scribble notes in the margin (we have bracketed notes which you could have scribbled in the margins). The following approach may have been helpful:

'Bakers Ltd is an audit client of Hinkley Innes, a firm of Chartered Certified Accountants. The firm has had the audit of Bakers for **17 years** [LONG ASSOCIATION]and the fee represents **7% of firm income**[WITHIN ACCA FEE RULES]. Bakers is considering a major new project at the present time and has asked the firm if it would be happy to undertake some once off **consultancy** [OTHER SERVICE] work for the firm. It is possible that the fee income for this contract would represent **10%** of that year's income [NOT RECURRING FEES] for Hinkley Innes. The **new business services partner**, who heads up a **new division** [NEW DEPARTMENT – SEGREGATED] of the firm, is keen to take on the work, as this would represent his best contract yet.'

'Peter works in the purchasing department of Murphy Manufacturing plc. He has been **instrumental in setting up control systems** [RISK OF REVIEWING HIS OWN WORK] in the purchasing department as part of a recent risk management exercise. He has a **poor relationship** [IA NEED OBJECTIVITY IN RELATIONSHIPS] with his immediate supervisor, the Purchasing Director. Murphy Manufacturing has just advertised the post of trainee internal auditor. Peter is interested in the work that internal audit do, having liased substantially with the department during the recent controls exercise. No formal accountancy qualifications are required for the post, because the successful candidate will be put through accountancy training. Peter has had a **chat with the head of internal audit** [NEED OBJECTIVITY IN RECRUITMENT PROCESS]concerning the post and is seriously considering making an application.'

There are fewer pointers in scenario 2, so you are required to notice the relevant issues contained amongst the other information and apply this to the other issues you know exist for internal auditors. Any internal auditor could not review systems he has designed, so this will be an issue for Peter. Given the importance of objectivity to internal auditors, how will the recruitment process be handled, now that Peter and the head of internal audit have had an informal chat about the post? Use details in the scenario to remind you of the key issues in such a situation.

(a) **Objectivity**

Objectivity is defined by the ACCA as being 'a state of mind which has regard to all considerations relevant to the task in hand but no other. It pre-supposes intellectual honesty.'

(i) **External auditors**. Objectivity is usually hallmarked by '**independence**' in the case of external auditors. The auditor must 'be, and be seen to be, independent'. ACCA provides a number of guidelines as to how an auditor should maintain his independence.

(ii) **Internal auditors**. Internal auditors are usually employees of the people they report to, so independence is a more difficult issue to understand here. However, it is vital that they maintain objectivity towards their tasks within a company, so they must **avoid conflicts of interest** and maintain **integrity in their relationships** with other staff members.

In particular, as an ACCA member, an internal auditor is bound by the ACCA's Fundamental Principles and Rules of Professional Conduct. Objectivity is a fundamental principle.

Threats to objectivity

The following are all threats to objectivity:

- **Personal interest** (for example, fear of losing fees or a good relationship with a client/fellow staff member)

- **Review of own work** (for example, if an auditor audits financial statements he has compiled, or an internal auditor monitors systems he has designed)
- **Disputes** (for example, with a client, or where an audit firm advocates for its client, or where an internal auditor has a personal issue with a staff member)
- **Long association or undue sympathy** (for example, through close personal relationships)
- **Intimidation** (this is linked to self-interest. For example, fear of losing a client or an internal auditor losing his job)

(b) **Two situations**

Scenario 1

(i) **Threats**

The situation raises three potential threats to objectivity.

The first is the issue that the firm has had a **long association** with the audit client. It is unclear whether the same engagement staff have been associated with the entity in that time.

The second is that the firm has been offered the opportunity to carry out work other than audit for the firm. ACCA guidance states that **provision of other services** can affect objectivity.

Connected to the previous point is the fact that a **self-interest threat** arises through the **substantial fee income** that this client may generate in the current year. ACCA's guideline in respect to recurring income is that 15% of office income from one client is likely to adversely affect objectivity (for a Ltd company). The income in this year is likely to be 17%, but much of that is not recurring. However, the firm should consider that the result of the consultancy might be that the business expands and the audit fee might rise in the future. They should lay down contingency plans.

(ii) **Safeguards**

In relation to the other services, the key inherent safeguard is that it is a **one off project**, as stated above. It appears that it will also be carried out by a **department other than the audit department**, which will help to maintain objectivity.

In terms of the audit, as the client has been associated with the audit firm for a number of years, the firm should consider laying out procedures for **rotation of the engagement partner** in relation to the client, so that the relationship cannot become too close over time.

If this is considered inappropriate, it might consider instituting a **second partner review** as another measure to maintain objectivity.

Scenario 2

(i) **Threats**

If Peter was to get the job in the internal audit department, there would be considerable threat of **self-review**, as he would have to monitor the systems which he has set up in the purchasing department.

As Peter is a current employee of the company, there is also a risk that his objectivity towards an internal audit role would be affected by his **relationships with fellow employees**.

This is particularly the case with regard to his relationship with his current boss, the **Purchasing Director**, as he has a **poor relationship** with him. As a member of the internal audit department, Peter would in all likelihood have to report directly on matters relating to this director.

(ii) **Safeguards**

If Peter gets the job, an important safeguard would be that he **did not work on matters relating to the purchasing department for a period of time**, or perhaps until the systems have been reviewed again and/or the Purchasing Director moves on.

It would also be important to address the issue of objectivity as part of the recruitment process. The issue of **relationships with staff** would have to be **discussed** and **understood**.

Lastly, it would is important to have **objectivity in the recruitment process**. As Peter has had an informal discussion with the head of Internal Audit, the head of Internal Audit should ensure that other staff members are included in the recruitment process.

5 NEW ENGAGEMENT

> *Tutorial note.* This question is not exam standard but the considerations it covers could form part of a larger, scenario question on accepting audit and ethical considerations, for example.

(a) Prospective auditors should consider the following before accepting a new audit appointment.

(i) Do I have the technical competence to carry out the assignment?

(ii) Will I have the time and resources (including staff) to carry out the work?

(iii) Could there be a conflict of interest involved?

(iv) Do there appear to be any professional reasons why I should not take up the appointment?

(b) The auditing standard SAS 140 *Engagement letters* states that: 'The auditors and the client should agree on the terms of the engagement, which should be recorded in writing'. This will help to avoid misunderstandings between the client and the auditors.

The engagement letter also provides written confirmation of the auditors' acceptance of their appointment, of the scope of the audit and of the form of the audit report.

The following important items should be included in the letter of engagement.

(i) A statement of management's responsibilities to keep proper accounting records and to prepare the financial statements

(ii) A statement of management's responsibility for the detection of fraud

(iii) A description of the auditors' responsibilities in forming their opinion on the financial statements

(iv) An explanation of the scope of the audit, stating that it will be carried out in accordance with auditing standards

(v) An explanation that weaknesses in internal controls will be reported to management in a letter

(vi) An explanation of the need to obtain written management representations in certain circumstances

(vii) Details of the basis for charging and paying for fees

(viii) Applicable law governing the letter (usually CA 1985) and a statement that neither party has the right to object to any action in the courts

(ix) A request that the directors agree the terms of the letter

6 GLO

> *Tutorial note.* In part (a) you must discuss the issues raised by the question. It is not appropriate to answer a 3 mark question by saying 'no, it will not be appropriate.' The question asks you to discuss, so you must explain your reasoning and come to a conclusion.
>
> Part (b) should represent easy marks. However, remember to explain what you know swiftly to bank those marks and then move on to section (c) where a large number of marks are available for identifying risk areas in practice.
>
> In part (c) you need to identify what looks odd in the balance sheet because this will indicate that it is potentially a risk area requiring a higher level of audit work. However, you should not just read through the balance sheet and compile an answer which lists the balance sheet areas in balance sheet order, explaining they are risky because 'stock has fallen' etc.

> You should explain **why things may be risky** for the audit, in other words, **explain what the balance sheet movement may indicate**. Stock may have fallen because a large amount of stock held at a third parties wasn't included in the stocktake, or because of a tremendous recent marketing push. The first explanation shows the risk that the financial statements are materially misstated in terms of stock completeness.
>
> You should **structure your answer** in terms of what you feel is the **greatest risk**. This may involve **making links between the various lines of the balance sheet** and pulling together an **overview of the situation**. In our answer below, we highlight the issue of going concern. There is no point in auditing the balance sheet in its current form if the going concern basis is inappropriate, therefore going concern is a key risk in this audit. There are various indicators that the going concern assumption may be inappropriate: fall in value in the whole balance sheet, retained loss, fall in cash position, suggestion of fall in activity.

(a) **Materiality**

It is **never appropriate** to apply the prior year's materiality figure to the current year figures. Materiality should be assessed in each year.

If the financial position has not changed much, and the results are very comparable with the prior year, it is possible that the materiality assessed year on year is very similar, but this does not mean that the auditors should not assess it for each audit. When assessing materiality, the auditor must consider **all known factors at the current date**. In this case, the position has changed considerably, increasing the risk of the audit, which may lower materiality in itself.

As the **balance sheet position** has **changed considerably**, so when materiality is assessed, it is unlikely that it will be similar to the prior year. Using the information available, **materiality is likely to be assessed extremely low** in monetary terms, due to the overall decrease in assets and the loss that appears to have been made in the year. It is also possible that given the current balance sheet position, the balance sheet figures will not be used to assess materiality in this year.

(b) **Audit risk**

Audit risk is the risk that the auditor will give an inappropriate opinion on financial statements. It is made up of three different elements of risk:

- **Inherent risk**: the risks arising naturally in the business and specific accounts/transactions
- **Control risk**: the risk that the accounting system will fail to detect and prevent errors
- **Detection risk**: the risk that the auditors will not detect material misstatements

Detection risk is comprised of **sampling risk** (the risk that the auditors' conclusion drawn from a sample is different to what it would have been, had the whole population been tested) and **non-sampling risk** (the risk that auditors may use the inappropriate procedures or misinterpret evidence).

Inherent and control risk are assessed by the auditors. Detection risk is then set at a level which makes overall audit risk acceptable to them.

(c) **Specific audit areas of risk**

A review of this balance sheet suggests that audit work should be directed in the following areas:

Going concern

The **balance sheet has reduced considerably in value** since the previous year. Net current assets has fallen from £212,000 to £17,000, and the total position in 2002 is **net liabilities**, albeit this is only marginal. Although the profit and loss account has not been reviewed, the balance sheet shows a **retained loss** for the year of £211,000.

Net assets shows a **reduction in both stock and debtors**, which **suggest a decrease in activity**, although trade creditors does not seem to have fallen so considerably. However, this could be accounted for by Glo-Warm not paying its suppliers in a similar fashion to the previous year. It will be **necessary to review** the **profit and loss account** to substantiate whether activity has reduced.

The **cash position has also worsened**, with cash falling by £22,000. The cash flow statement should reveal more detail about this fall. However, the company has paid of £5,000 of its bank loan, reducing over all net debt.

In summary, audit work should be directed at going concern as **several indicators of going concern problems** exist in the balance sheet. This will be further amplified when the profit and loss account is available.

Stock

Stock has been mentioned above in the context of going concern. Audit work should be directed at stock specifically as this **balance has fallen significantly** from the previous year, which seems **odd in a manufacturing company**. There is no suggestion on the balance sheet for why this should be so (for example, debtors are not correspondingly high, suggesting high pre-year end sales, and creditors are not correspondingly low, suggested low pre-year end purchases). It may be that the stocktake did not include every item of stock. Alternatively it could simply point to a fall in activity (discussed above).

Warranty provision

A provision of £20,000 has been included in 2004 for warranties. The reasons for this must be investigated and the auditors must check that it has been accounted for correctly in accordance with FRS 12.

It seems **odd that a warranty provision should suddenly appear in a balance sheet**. It suggests a change in the terms of contracts given to customers, or a change in the customers themselves (with different terms then applying). Alternatively it suggests that **FRS 12** has been **wrongly applied in the current year, or should have been applied in the previous year**, and was not.

Other material items

As stated above, given the indications of loss and the reduction in total asset value, it is likely that materiality will be assessed low in monetary terms. In this case, most balances on the balance sheet are likely to be material (excluding investments and cash in hand which appear to be very low risk).

However, as the bank loan is likely to have good audit evidence available, the most risky of the other balances are **trade debtors** and **trade creditors**, for reasons discussed above in going concern. More detail is required to make a judgement about the risk of tangible fixed assets.

7 USING THE WORK OF AN EXPERT

> *Tutorial note.* Note that as well as considering the independence and qualifications of experts, auditors should consider the scope of the expert's work and carry out *some* confirmation work on the expert's opinion. You do not need (and would not expected to have) a detailed knowledge of valuation of long-term contracts to be able to answer Part (c)

(a) In assessing the reliability of the legal advice obtained from a local solicitor on the outcome of the claim by Netherfield Manufacturing plc, the auditors should consider the following.

(i) The materiality of the claim is important as the significance to the company of the amount involved would clearly affect the extent of the audit work required.

(ii) The qualification, experience, reputation and standing of the local solicitor would be relevant. Presumably the solicitor would be qualified, but it would also be necessary to consider his suitability to advise on this type of claim. The experience of the solicitor and his firm and their reputation in this field of litigation would be an important factor in determining the extent of reliance to be placed on the solicitor's advice. In particular, consideration should be given as to whether the solicitor had advised the company in respect of similar litigation in the past and how reliable his advice had proved to be on those earlier occasions.

(iii) The independence of the solicitor must be checked as any suggestion that the solicitor or his firm had any direct connection with the company or its management would tend to reduce somewhat the reliability of the evidence provided.

(iv) The nature and extent of the evidence provided by the company to the solicitor, and on which he has based his opinion, should be carefully reviewed to ensure that the solicitor's decision appears to have been based upon all relevant facts available to the company.

(v) The solicitor's opinion should be examined and its reasonableness assessed, in the light of the auditor's knowledge and experience of similar cases against both Ravenshead and other clients engaged in similar activities.

(vi) If the auditors consider the amount of the claim to be material, and there is uncertainty in relation to the outcome of the claim and/or the solicitor's evidence, the auditors should consider recommending to the client that a second opinion from an independent specialist in the field be obtained. If the client was not agreeable to this action or if the auditors still considered there to be material uncertainty, then a qualification of the audit report would probably be required.

(b) The factors to be considered by the auditors in assessing the reliability of the valuation of investment properties by an independent valuer would be as follows.

(i) The independence of the valuer should be considered in a similar way to that of the local solicitor, and for the same reasons.

(ii) The qualification, reputation and experience of the valuer should be considered. The valuer should be a qualified member of a professional valuation body with experience of valuing similar properties within the same geographical area as the properties owned by Ravenshead. If the valuer does not have experience of the type of properties held by the company or of the areas in which they are located, then the value of his evidence is likely to be considerably reduced. The reputation of the valuer or his firm would also affect the reliability of his evidence so far as the auditors are concerned, with the likelihood that more reliance could be placed on a valuation made by a large firm with a good reputation, than one obtained from a little-known small firm.

(iii) The actual valuation of the properties by the valuer should be carefully examined. The auditors would need to satisfy themselves that a reasonable basis for the valuation had been adopted. Typically, an open market value based upon existing usage would be expected. The valuation of leasehold properties should be assessed in the light of the remaining length of the leases and the value of freehold properties would be affected by whether or not they are leased and, if they are, the remaining period of the leases, the amount of the rental income and the frequency of rent reviews.

(iv) Any change in the valuation of the properties since the time of the previous valuation should be assessed. The validity of any significant changes in the valuation of the properties should be considered in the light of any statistical or other evidence available for similar properties.

(v) The reasonableness of the valuations should be considered against any profits or losses made on any properties disposed of in recent times, as this could be a good indication of any tendency to over or under value the properties to a material extent, either over or under valuation being likely to distort the truth and fairness of the financial statements.

(vi) The reasonableness of the valuations could also be considered by the auditors comparing the valuations with those used by other clients holding similar properties in the same locations.

(c) The matters to be considered when assessing the valuation of the long-term contract work in progress by an internal valuer would be as follows.

(i) How material is this asset in the financial statements: as it is likely to be highly material, it needs to be valued accurately.

(ii) The basis of the valuation should be carefully checked to consider the extent to which it appears to comply with the requirements of SSAP 9.

(iii) Recognition of the fact that, as the valuer is an employee of Ravenshead, this will reduce the reliability of the evidence provided. However this may be countered to a certain extent by the fact that the valuer should have a more detailed knowledge of the work in progress than it would perhaps ever be possible for an independent valuer to obtain.

(iv) Confirmation should be sought that the valuer had actually visited all of the contract sites, or otherwise obtained satisfactory evidence as to the stage of completion of the contracts in order to provide himself with a reliable basis for their valuation.

(v) The valuer's basis of determining costs to date should be ascertained and the auditor would need to be satisfied as to the reliability of the company's records in this respect and, in particular, that a consistently applied satisfactory basis of overhead recognition had been employed.

(vi) The valuer's estimates of the further costs to completion of the contracts should be carefully reviewed and confirmation obtained that reasonable allowance had been made for increases in the costs of material and labour having regard to the current and projected rates of inflation.

8 AUDIT EVIDENCE

> *Tutorial note.* Each of the numbered sections in this question could form part of a question on auditing a specific balance sheet area. In such a question, you could be asked to set out the audit procedures you would undertake (what evidence would you seek) and ask for an assessment of the quality and quantity of that evidence, (that is, how much evidence do you need and why).

(a) (i) Inspecting inventories and testing perpetual records by making test counts provides:

(1) Strong evidence of completeness with the limitation that items not physically in stock or on the perpetual records will not be identified. This may apply to goods in the receiving area at the time of the stocktake

(2) Strong evidence of existence

(3) Strong evidence of accuracy

(4) Weak evidence of valuation, and

(5) Weak evidence of ownership as stock items may be on consignment or help under Romalpa conditions.

(ii) Vouching fixed asset additions to supporting documentation provides:

(1) Weak evidence of completeness as such a test will not highlight omissions only overstatement

(2) Weak evidence of existence as, although the additions were purchased by the company, there is no evidence that they are physically held by the company at the year end

(3) Strong evidence of accuracy

(4) Strong evidence of valuation in respect of cost but not for any subsequent fall in value, and

(5) Strong evidence of ownership as the purchases will be invoiced in the company name. However, this assumes no subsequent sales or transfers.

(iii) Verification of bank balances by bank confirmation request provides strong evidence for existence, accuracy, valuation and ownership for balances at the particular bank circularised. However, only weak evidence is given of completeness, because undetectable balances may be held at other banks. The same applies to liens.

(b) Audit evidence should be fully documented so that the auditor has a written record of the work and conclusions thereon on which he has based his audit opinion.

Documentation also acts as a means of quality control on the work done providing evidence for the reviewer. It is particularly important in litigation situations.

The details relating to the audit tests which should be regarded are as follows.

(i) Detailed audit tests carried out, the reasons for the timing and level of the tests and the objectives of the tests

(ii) Notes of errors or exceptions found and action taken

(iii) Conclusions drawn by staff who performed the tests

9 INTERNAL CONTROLS

> *Tutorial note*. Parts (a) and (b) to this question should be reasonably straight-forward. Part (c) requires you to set out the work that the internal audit department would routinely do to reduce the risk of fraud and error. Remember that one of the risks facing the purchases department is that fraud may be perpetrated: internal controls have been put in place to ensure that this risk is reduced. Therefore, on a routine basis, this would fall within the role of the internal audit department checking that controls are operating effectively. In your answer to part (c) then, you should identify what controls would exist to mitigate against fraud and set out the procedures that internal audit would carry out to test their effectiveness.
>
> In part (d), you are asked how a risk assessment would affect the work of both internal and external auditors. You are not asked specifically for procedures that would be carried out. You should therefore note that as a higher than normal risk has been identified, more work would be carried out than usual. For the external auditor this would mean a higher number of the same procedures, for the internal auditor, it might mean a special investigation. However, you could also note that internal audit might disguise their special operations as normal operations so as not to alert the suspected party that they are investigating him. If fraud was expected to have a material impact on the financial statements, the external auditors would carry out some procedures that they might not have otherwise carried out (for example, a creditors' circularisation). You should note these in your answer.

(a) **Four objectives of an internal control system**

SAS 300 outlines the following objectives of internal control systems:

- To enable management to carry on the business of the company in an orderly and efficient manner
- To satisfy management that their policies are being adhered to
- To ensure that the assets of the company are safeguarded
- To ensure, as far as possible, that the enterprise maintains complete and accurate records

(b) **Review of internal control systems**

External auditor

As part of his audit, the external auditor is required to **ascertain the system and controls**. Once the system has been ascertained, the external auditor will walkthrough the systems to ensure that they operate as he has been led to believe that they do.

The auditor will then determine his **audit approach**. If he is planning to rely on the controls in the system, he has to evaluate the controls in the accounting system to assess whether they are **reliable enough to produce financial records which are free of material misstatement**. In other words, he is assessing whether the systems achieve the fourth objective given above.

He will conduct tests of controls to ensure that the controls have operated properly in the year. If these tests produce good results, the auditor can rely on the systems and undertake reduced substantive testing on the financial statements.

The auditor will decide not to undertake tests of controls if the controls do not appear effective, or it is more cost effective to undertake high substantive procedures.

Internal auditor

Internal audit is an appraisal or monitoring activity established by the directors. It functions, amongst other things, by **examining and evaluating the adequacy and effectiveness of components of the accounting and internal control systems**.

Internal audit therefore review and test internal control systems to assess whether the systems are **achieving the four objectives** stated above.

Conclusion

The external auditor is interested in the internal control systems which help to produce the financial statements which he is auditing. Internal auditors are interested more generally in internal controls to ensure that they meet their objectives of helping the business to operate effectively and reduce risks.

(c) **Internal auditor work**

The sort of frauds which could be carried out in a purchases system are: processing non-businesses expenses as business expenses or paying fictional suppliers inflated prices.

The work an internal auditor could carry out to check procedures in the purchase system and to lessen the risk of fraud and error is as follows:

(i) Check Individual purchases to the invoice, agreeing the details to the purchase order and delivery note. If these items are not available this should be noted.

(ii) Review individual purchases to ensure that they are related to **business expenses**. If an item appears questionable, it should be investigated further.

(iii) Review the **prices paid** for purchases and ensure that alternative supply options have been considered (either on an individual basis, or on a yearly basis)

(iv) Test **cheque payments** to ensure that they **related to approved invoices**

(v) Perform **reconciliations to supplier statements** to ensure that payments have been made to the **correct suppliers for genuine invoices**

(vi) Check reconciliations made between the purchase ledger and the purchase control account to ensure that **all differences have been investigated and reconciled**.

(vii) Review the purchase ledger on a regular basis to ensure that there are **no unusual or unexplained balances or debits**.

(d) **Risk of fraud and error**

The auditors should consider the reasons that the risk of fraud and error has been assessed as high, as this will affect the work that they do. The factors that cause each set of auditors to assess risk as high may be different.

External auditors' work

SAS 110 *Fraud and error* states that 'auditors should plan and perform their audit procedures and evaluate and report the results thereof, recognising that fraud or error may materially affect the financial statements...when planning the audit the auditors should assess the risk that fraud or error may cause the financial statements to contain material misstatements'.

In this case, the risk has been assessed and it appears to be higher than normal. This means that the external auditor will have to perform **additional procedures** to **reduce the risk that the financial statements are materially misstated** as a result of fraud. The additional risk would mean that materiality was assessed lower. This would result in a greater proportion of transactions and balances being subject to evidence gathering.

If a purchase ledger fraud was suspected, the external auditors would **circularise creditors**, to obtain third party evidence as to the value of creditors at the year end. If a sales ledger fraud was suspected, they would conduct a debtors' circularisation, or extend the sample from previous years.

They would scrutinise the ledgers for indications of suppliers or customers who may be connected to management.

The external auditors might also carry out detailed transactions tests such as have been outlined above in part (c) to be carried out by internal audit.

Internal auditors' work

Internal auditors might assess the risk of fraud or error as high if they had **specific suspicions** about a particular member of staff. This would direct their additional work.

Investigating fraud would be a special project for the internal audit department, outside of the scope of their normal work. However, it is possible that they would want the operation to be covert, so as to ensure that the person suspected would not be alerted to their suspicions. The special project would involve scrutinising past records, looking for **evidence of controls having been bypassed**, particularly evidence of authorisation not being sought. This would be done by scrutinising documents for evidence of controls being kept, for example, authorising initials, or 'paid' stamps. They would interview staff to assess whether if controls are maintained as they should be. They would also observe the system operating at the current time.

They might also run company searches on all the suppliers on their central suppliers' register to ensure that they did not appear to be connected to members of staff.

If the suspicions of fraud were strong, the company might hire specialist forensic practitioners to assist the internal audit department's investigations.

10 FENTON DISTRIBUTORS

> *Tutorial note.* In (b) significant emphasis is placed on testing unusual or suspicious items (particularly the adjustment journals). Note also the importance of accounting controls at the year-end. Correct categorisation of expenses is important from the viewpoint of the statutory accounts (directors' emoluments), and in ensuring the quality of management information, which the auditors may use for analytical procedures.

(a) To verify the accuracy of the purchases transactions posted to the nominal ledger I would perform the following checks.

(i) I would check that the bookkeeper was up to date with the monthly posting of all purchases transactions to the nominal ledger.

(ii) Specific checks on purchase transactions will include the following.

(1) Purchase transactions will be traced from the invoice to the nominal ledger and the analysis and analysis code will be checked.

(2) The total invoice value will be traced to the nominal ledger.

(3) The category of invoice expense and the expense amount will be checked to confirm that it appears correctly on the detailed computer list for the month concerned.

(4) The total of the items on the detailed list will be checked to the nominal ledger.

(5) Transactions will also be traced backwards from the entries in the nominal ledger making up the monthly total posted to the purchase ledger back to both the detailed analysis and the individual invoice.

(6) The amount of the invoice expense will be agreed with the amount posted to the nominal ledger.

The tests above check accounting entries forwards and backwards within the system and any errors would be fully investigated as to their type, cause, materiality and pattern.

(iii) The test checks on the detailed list and total postings of cash payments, discounts received and adjustments will follow the same procedure as for invoices and credit notes. The monthly cash book total will be checked to the total posted from the purchase ledger to the nominal ledger.

(iv) A check on the analysis and coding of purchase invoices will be carried out to establish the level of accuracy achieved. Particular care will be taken to see that the expense category 'purchases' is correctly identified and coded from invoices and is not confused with other categories, for example stationery, rates, gas and telephone. Incorrect analysis and/or coding may be indicated where the expense category is high or low in comparison with its budget to date.

Large variations between actual and budget on expense categories should be test checked to verify that they are not due to errors in analysis, coding or posting.

(b) To verify the validity and accuracy of the journals posted to the nominal ledger I would carry out the following checks.

(i) Firstly, I would check the opening balances at the start of the financial year. To do this I would check the value of each trial balance item on the opening trial balance back to the closing entries on the previous year's accounts. After this, each item would be checked to the nominal ledger ensuring that both the value and analysis are correct. These opening postings should be the first entries in the new year as all nominal ledger balances should have been set to zero, and this should be confirmed.

(ii) Other cash book items would be test checked to the nominal ledger to confirm that postings are correct as to value and expense category. Large items would require a larger sample size and large, unusual or suspicious items should all be checked and evidenced by supporting documentation or Board approval.

(iii) The year-end balances of cash and bank on the nominal ledger should be agreed with the year-end balances in the cash book. This would require the last month to be checked as the closing balances at all previous month-ends will have been checked already.

(iv) The checks on petty cash payments transactions would include the following.

(1) Check that transactions are supported by vouchers and correctly posted to the right nominal ledger account. This would include checking that transactions are valid and coded to the correct expense category.

(2) Check that petty cash transactions are within any limits, regarding the type of expenditure or maximum value, established by management.

(3) Check that the petty cash balance in the nominal ledger at the end of each month and at the financial year-end agrees with the balance in the petty cash book.

(v) The wages expense is posted manually to the nominal ledger from the monthly payroll summaries by means of a journal. To verify that the journals are correctly posted I would select several journals and check the following matters.

(1) The totals of the analysis columns on the monthly summary shown on the spreadsheet should be posted to the journal, and forward to the nominal ledger.

(2) The breakdown of wages expense into directors and the several departmental categories will be checked. The correct identification of directors' pay is important as this requires statutory disclosure. I would obtain the current list of directors. I would add up the totals in the analysis columns to confirm the summary total, and consider its reasonableness.

(3) Amounts owing at the year-end for PAYE, NI, accrued pay, superannuation and other deductions will be verified and any reconciliation drawn up by the bookkeeper agreed.

(4) Any additions to, or amendments of, weekly wages records posted to the nominal ledger through the adjustments journal will be fully investigated and their validity established.

(5) The analysis of wages expense for the year will be compared with the budget and an explanation will be sought for any significant variances.

(vi) Adjustment journals are potentially a high-risk area and any checks would include the following.

(1) Check that all the manually written adjustment journals were authorised by the managing director and supported by documentation and proper narratives.

(2) Check journals are posted in numerical order and there should be no missing numbers gaps in the postings.

(3) Examine all large adjustments and the reasons given for the errors. These will be traced to the nominal ledger to ensure that postings do correct the errors.

(4) Investigate closely recurring errors to establish their cause and whether these can be avoided in future by management action.

(5) Examine the purchase ledger suspense account (creditors suspense) and trace all postings in and out.

(6) Where there was no account in the nominal ledger, check back to the purchase invoice, establish the account number and verify that the item has been posted from the suspense account to the correct account.

(7) Where the adjustment is due to the wrong account number being used, check that the journal correctly transfers the item to the right account.

(8) Where the bookkeeper has created contra entries between the purchase ledger and the sales ledger, check that the creditor/debtor company concerned is posted with a purchase ledger and sales ledger contra of the same value.

(9) All other adjustments will be checked for validity and supporting documentation.

Reasons will be established for postings that increase or reduce purchase ledger balances.

(vii) Year-end balances on the nominal ledger would be further checked as follows.

(1) Any balances remaining on the purchase ledger and sales ledger suspense accounts should be itemised on a supporting schedule and the existence of each item justified.

(2) Nominal ledger balances for the cash book, petty cash book, sales ledger and purchase ledger should agree to, or be reconciled to, the cash book, petty cash book, total sales ledger and total purchase ledger balances at the year end. I will check that any difference is reconciled and explained. It may be that further adjustments are required to reduce or eliminate a difference.

(3) All fixed asset movements should be checked, including purchases, sales, revaluations and depreciation.

(4) All outstanding liabilities should be verified and their size reviewed for reasonableness.

(5) The bank reconciliation should establish the correctness of balances on all types of bank account, ie loan, current, deposit, special transactions and so on.

(6) A review of the financial statements would be carried out to ensure that material changes in assets, expenses, revenues, liabilities and share capital are justified and explained. Justification would be sought in both relative and absolute terms.

11 CHEQUE PAYMENTS AND PETTY CASH

Tutorial note. This question asks you to asses the controls over a particular area of a business. As such, it could have been posed to either an internal or an external auditor – remember that either would be possible in the exam. Notice that the answer refers to the objectives of the suggested controls as well as the controls themselves. Thinking through the control objectives in any given area will help you to suggest relevant controls. In another situation, it might help you to explain why current controls are weak.

(a) A Black Esq
Managing Director
Quicksand Limited
12 Kelvin Street
Anytown

MNO & Co
3 Green Street
Anytown

Date

Dear Mr Black

You recently requested that we should advise you on good internal controls over cheque payments and petty cash. We should like to make the following recommendations.

The main objectives of control over payments are to ensure that payments are made only in respect of valid transactions and that they are suitably authorised.

The following control procedures will contribute toward attaining these objectives.

Cheque payments

(i) Cheques should be raised only on the basis of authorisation, for example a purchase invoice which has been suitably authorised.

(ii) Cheques should be signed by people other than those who approve invoices.

(iii) There should be two independent signatories for each cheque, for instance, two directors might act as signatories. Signatories should inspect the documents supporting the cheque to ensure that the details agree. They should also mark the document so that it cannot be reused.

(iv) Cheques should be restrictively crossed.

(v) Unused cheques should be kept in a secure place. Cheques should never be signed in blank.

(vi) Cheques should be under sequential control and all numbers should be accounted for. Spoilt cheques should therefore be retained.

(vii) When cheques have been signed, they should be despatched immediately.

Petty cash

(i) Petty cash payments should be made only on the basis of suitably authorised vouchers, which should be under sequential control. Vouchers should be retained for subsequent references. Where independent evidence is also available, for example invoices and receipts, this should be retained.

(ii) An imprest system should be used to control petty cash. This means that the petty cash float is maintained at a specific amount and is reimbursed at regular intervals on the basis of vouchers showing the payments which have been made. It is suggested that the float should be kept at a level of £300 and be reimbursed on a weekly basis.

(iii) The petty cash float should be subject to a periodic surprise counts by a responsible person not involved with the petty cash system. The balance on hand should be reconciled to the imprest account by reference to the vouchers not yet reimbursed.

(iv) The size of individual payments out of petty cash should be subject to a maximum to be agreed by the directors.

(v) Staff should not be allowed to cash personal cheques or borrow from petty cash.

I hope that the above information is useful to you in designing your systems of internal control. If you require any more information, please let me know.

Yours sincerely,

A Smith

(b) Mr Black presumably feels that involvement in cash and cheque controls will be time-consuming, and that he is too busy to be involved in it. He may feel that he does not want to play a direct part in the petty cash function. Because of the small amounts involved, he may wish to delegate this function to another director. He should appreciate, however, that involvement at least in the authorisation of cheque payments would help to ensure that he is aware of major transactions in his business. He might consider the possibility of authorising cheques in excess of a given amount; this would minimise the demands on his time, while exercising control and keeping him informed of significant outgoings from the business.

Auditors may wish to consider whether Mr Black's lack of involvement may be symptomatic of insufficient attention being given to financial matters by the board.

12 ANALYTICAL REVIEW

> *Tutorial note.* This is not an exam standard question, but it is a useful look at what analytical procedures are and when they should be used. It is easy to fall into a trap of thinking that analytical procedures are only relevant at the start and end of the audit. This is not the case. They are valid procedures to use in the audit of every balance sheet area, and so might fall into an answer setting out procedures for the audit of any area. Analytical procedures are very important as part of a review.

(a) Analytical review involves studying **significant ratios**, **trends** and other **statistics** and investigating any unusual or expected variations. The precise nature of these procedures and the manner in which they are documented will depend on the circumstances of each audit.

What determines comparisons made

The comparisons which can be made will depend on the **nature, accessibility** and **relevance** of the data available. Once the auditors have decided on the comparisons which they intend to make in performing analytical procedures, they should determine what **variations** they expect to be disclosed by them.

Investigation and evaluation of results

Unusual or **unexpected variations**, and expected variations which fail to occur, should be **investigated**. **Explanations** obtained should be **verified** and **evaluated** by the auditor to determine whether they are consistent with his understanding of the business and his general knowledge. Explanations may indicate a change in the business of which the auditors were previously unaware in which case they should reconsider the adequacy of their audit approach. Alternatively, they may indicate the possibility of misstatements in the financial statements; in these circumstances the auditors will need to **extend** their **testing** to determine whether the financial statements do contain **material misstatements**.

Analytical review at different stages of the audit

Auditors use analytical review in **audit planning** to help them **understand** the **client's business** and to identify **areas** of particular **audit risk**. Analytical procedures help auditors decide on the **nature, timing** and **extent** of **audit procedures**. Auditors can use various sources of information at the planning stage, including **budgets**, **management accounts** and **bank** and **cash records**.

Auditors may use analytical procedures as substantive tests. Various factors determine how much they will do so. These include the **level** of **detail** available, the **predictability** of the **data** being studied, and the **objectives** of the **audit tests**.

At the final stage of the audit auditors will use analytical procedures (such as ratio analysis and comparisons with previous years) to help them draw a **conclusion** about the accounts. Auditors will carefully review the results of the procedures undertaken to see whether they are **consistent** with the **results** of **other audit procedures** and the auditors' **knowledge** of the **business**.

(b) Analytical procedures are likely to be used heavily as part of a review exercise. A review exercise will consist largely of observation and enquiry. Analytical procedures will be the key substantive procedure used.

13 BOSTON MANUFACTURING

Tutorial note. In part (a), where you are required to assess the risk of the tangible fixed assets section of the audit, you should assess each of the components of audit risk in relation to the information given to you and then draw a conclusion about overall audit risk. However, this does not mean you should give detailed definitions of each component of audit risk. That will not gain you any marks in this question. The requirement clearly asks you to assess audit risk in this situation. You need to understand what each component is in order to be able to assess the risk here, but this question requires application of your understanding, not explanation.

Part (b) is a very typical auditing question at this level. You should expect a question requiring you to set out appropriate procedures relating to any of the balance sheet areas you have studied. You should have a good knowledge of the sort of tests you are likely to carry out in respect of each balance sheet assertions, however, remember also to use information given to you in the question to direct you in the specific case.

For example, in this situation, there has been a heavy investment in plant in the year. A high proportion of the total fixed assets figure relates to this new plant. Information given to you about these assets should affect your answer to part (c) when you consider how the depreciation rate should be set and assessed. However, it is also clearly relevant to part (b). Knowing that depreciation on the new plant should in the region of £25K should point you towards the fact that there may be plant which is fully written down in the financial statements. This may in fact be plant which has been replaced by the new plant. If the plant is not in use, it should not be included in the balance sheet.

(a) **Risk in the tangible fixed asset audit**

Control risk

The controls over fixed assets at Boston Manufacturing appear to be strong. The company maintains and reconciles a fixed asset register and there are authorisation procedures in operation. These controls should be tested, and if they prove effective, control risk could be assessed low.

Inherent risk

The tangible fixed assets are material on the basis of the proposed materiality level. There has been a substantial movement on the plant and equipment account this year, but this appears to be supported by the information given by the management accountant. There appear to be no disposals in the year, which may indicate that they have been omitted, or that obsolete items are included in the register. It is also unclear whether land is being depreciated. It would be inappropriate if it was being depreciated. Overall, the inherent risk seems to be medium.

Detection risk

Given that inherent risk has been assessed as moderate and control risk has been assessed as low, detection risk will be assessed as higher. However, there is usually good evidence in relation to existence and valuation of fixed assets and these are the key assertions which the auditors are interested in. There will also be scope to carry out good analytical procedures, such as proof in total of depreciation.

Conclusion

The audit of fixed assets appears to be medium to low risk.

(b) **Audit procedures**

(i) **Existence**

In many cases it is self-evident that land and buildings exist. However, it is important for the auditors to verify all components of land and buildings contained within the balance sheet, if they are on a site different to the one which the auditors are primarily attending, for example. Land and buildings should also be verified to **title deeds** to ensure that they **not only exist**, but that **they are owned** by the client.

The other classes of asset should be **inspected**. A sample of assets from the **register should be agreed to the physical asset**. There may be scope to rely on the work that the management accountant has undertaken here. The auditor should check a reconciliation which the accountant has undertaken. The auditors should make use of any identification marks on assets recorded in the register, for example, security tages or bar codes which are kept on assets to distinguish them. The auditor should inspect the **condition** of the assets and ensure that they are **in use**.

The motor vehicles should be **reconciled in terms of number of vehicles existing at the opening and closing positions**. Again, to ensure that they not only exist, but are owned by the company, the auditors should check the **registration documents** to ensure that the company is the registered owner.

For all the above assets, the external auditor should also review the insurance provision for the assets. This gives **third party evidence** of the existence of assets as the insurer would not insure a non-existing asset.

(ii) **Valuation (excluding depreciation)**

Land and buildings appear to be stated at historic **cost** as the schedule does not contain the words 'or valuation'. The auditors should **confirm** that this is the case with the management accountant. The cost can then be **agreed to brought forward figures** as there have been no additions in the year. These figures will have been audited in the previous year. If the assets are held at valuation, the auditors must ensure that the requirements of FRS 15 in relation to revaluations are being complied with.

Similarly, as there have been no movements in the year, **motor vehicles** can be agreed to the **opening position**.

To audit the valuation of **plant and computers**, the auditors should **agree the opening position**. They should then **obtain a schedule of additions** to fixed assets, which can be **agreed to purchase invoices** to verify valuation.

Lastly, the auditors should investigate whether the cost figures include any **fully-written down assets**. This is implied by the fact that the depreciation charge on plant excluding additions is low. If so, the auditor should find out whether these assets **are still in use**, and if not, consider whether they **should be excluded** from the cost and accumulated depreciation figures contained within the notes to the accounts. Excluding them would have a net effect on the reported figure of £0.

(iii) **Completeness**

The schedule of fixed assets prepared should be reconciled to:

- The **opening position** (that is, the previous balance sheet)
- The **closing position** (what is disclosed in the financial statements)
- The **underlying records** (the nominal ledger)

If the fixed asset register contains details of the cost and accumulated depreciation of each asset, the **register should also be reconciled to the schedule**. Explanations should be sought for any differences.

The additions of the schedule should also be checked to ensure that the opening and closing positions reconcile within the schedule.

The auditors should also carry out a test on some of the **individual additions**, tracing the transaction through the system, from purchase orders to delivery notes and invoices and through the ledgers to the financial statements to ensure that additions have been included completely.

(c) **Depreciation**

(i) **Appropriateness**

The appropriateness of the rates should be considered and discussed with management. **Relevant factors** to consider are matters such as;

- The **replacement policy** for the asset
- The pattern of **usage** in the business
- The **purpose of the asset** being owned

In this instance, the auditors should establish the rationale behind the depreciation rates applied, particularly in the case of plant. In the case of the plant purchased this year, the depreciation rate applied is 10%. However, the assets have been purchased in relation to an 8 year project, so 12.5% might be a more appropriate rate.

(ii) **Audit procedures**

Depreciation on **buildings** can be verified by agreeing the purchase date of the buildings to last year's file or historic invoices/purchase documents and the valuation applied to the building portion.

For the other classes of asset, depreciation should be agreed for individual assets, as it is not possible to agree them in total. The auditors should obtain a **breakdown of the charges** for the year. They should be able to **recalculate the depreciation** from details in the fixed asset register and compare the results.

14 SITTING PRETTY

Tutorial note. This question covers all the important aspects of stock; existence, valuation and cut off. Part (b), which is for the most marks, requires you to plan the stocktake attendance. As you are planning, you should look for risk areas given to you in the question, just as you would in a more standard planning question.

In part (a) don't just give a standard answer about the importance of a stocktake (although this should form part of your answer). The question asks you to be specific about this situation.

The Study Text gives three useful steps in planning a stocktake attendance (on page 250) so you should bear these in mind, although not all the matters it mentions there are important in this case. You must practice being able to use standard lists of matters to consider but to *apply* them to a given scenario.

Similarly in parts (c) and (d), do not just write down everything you know about auditing cut off and valuation of stock. You must tailor your answer to the facts given in the question. In part (d), therefore, you will have to make a comment about the 10% discount, for example.

(a) **Importance of the stocktake**

The stocktake provides important **audit evidence** as to the **existence** and **completeness** of stock included in the financial statements.

In this case, the stocktake is particularly important because the **company does not maintain perpetual stock records**. As no perpetual records are maintained, the only basis for the stock entries in the financial statements is the results of this stocktake.

Stocks are **generally material** to the balance sheet of a manufacturing company and they are also one of the **higher risk areas** on the balance sheet. The stocktake provides important audit evidence reducing the risk of a material misstatement in relation to stock.

(b) **Planning for attendance**

Gain knowledge: I must review the notes of last year's stocktake and I must contact the factory manager to obtain details of this year's. I must review this year's details to ensure that the stocktake appears to be planned efficiently and effectively.

> *Tutorial note*. It is possible you assumed that this part of planning was already completed as the question tells you that you have just rung the factory manager. If so, you should have stated that assumption, or to cover yourself as we have, noted that this is a requirement. However, you should not have spent long on this aspect of the question.

Assess key factors: There are various key factors given in the scenario:

(i) **Nature and volume of the stocks**. There should be no WIP, so I will count raw materials (approximately 10% of the stock) and finished goods. However, raw material plastic should be low because a delivery is required to continue with production.

(ii) **Possible obsolescence**. I must make a note of the number of old chair legs maintained in raw materials as these are no obsolete, a new specification having been agreed.

(iii) **Cut off issues**. I need to ensure that the delivery on the day is isolated and that I obtain details of the delivery made during the stocktake. I need to determine whether this should be included as deliveries for the year, but most of all ensure that it does not get counted twice (as it arrives, and if it is put into stores). I should also obtain copies of the relevant documents, for example, the last invoices in the year and the last goods received and despatched notes.

(iv) **Off-cuts**. I need to consider whether any off cuts are maintained on site and whether these are being included in the stocktake. As the company receives a discount relating to them, they are unlikely to legally be considered Sitting Pretty's and so should not be included.

(v) **Staff issues**. It appears that the stocktake is undertaken by the people who work in the factory and handle the stock on a daily basis. This is not best practice, although in practical terms it is difficult to avoid. However, I should discuss this with the factory manager to assess whether staff can be allocated to counting stock they have not produced. Also, as the staff are allowed to go home as soon as the stocktake is completed, there is a risk that the stocktake will be rushed and mistakes will be made. The manager should ensure that it is made clear that the stocktake should be thorough and that no one will leave before checks on the thoroughness of the counts have been made.

Plan procedures: I need to determine my sample sizes and whether there is a need for expert assistance at this stocktake.

(i) **Procedures**. I will carry out test counts, checking from a sample of items to the count sheets and a sample of items from the count sheets to the physical items.

(ii) **Samples**. There are no higher value items that I should concentrate particularly on. Materiality for the year has been set at £5,000 currently. Dividing last year's figures for stock by this materiality level would give a sample size of 6 items for raw materials and 34 items for finished goods. I need to determine the batches in which stock is valued to ensure that I count the correct items. I need to assess the levels of stock when I arrive to ascertain whether this remains appropriate.

(c) **Cut off at final audit**

General procedures

The audit team should take a **sample of delivery notes** for sales and purchases on either side of the year end and **trace** these to **invoices** and **ledgers** and **stock** records to ensure that **sales and purchases have been included in the correct period** and that **stock is accounted for where appropriate**. (That is, sales have not be counted twice and purchases have been included in stock.) As the factory has been shut down, there is a lower risk that sale cut off is inappropriate than purchase cut off.

Stocktake delivery

Once it is determined whether this delivery should count as this year's stock (which it should if the stocktake was the year end date), the delivery information should be traced to purchase invoices and ledgers to ensure that the purchase is recorded in the year and that the creditor is accounted for in the year. The stock should then be included also.

Other matters

If **stock returns** are material, the stock returns after the year end should be reviewed to ensure that items are not included as sales in the year and that the stock is added to the stock figure unless it is now obsolete, whereupon it should be written off.

(d) **Valuation of stock**

The auditors should obtain the client's working papers relating to the valuation of stock. Items which the auditor sampled at the stocktale should already have been verified to the stocktake records as part of the verification of existence.

Cost

The auditors should then **trace a sample of items to purchase invoices** to ensure that **cost has been correctly applied**. Cost of purchase (per SSAP 9) excludes trade discounts and rebates, so the auditors should ensure that the valuation **cost excludes the 10% discount** received for returning the off-cuts of plastic.

The auditors should then ensure that for a sample of finished goods items, **costs of conversion** (comprising costs of labour and overheads) have been included. This should be on a comparable basis to the previous year and therefore can be audited by analytical review.

Net realisable value

The auditors should ensure that **cost is lower than net realisable value** by tracing their sample to **after date sales**. If no invoices are yet available, the auditors can make confirmations by reviewing sales orders and price lists.

Obsolete

Lastly, the auditors should ensure by review and by discussion with management that stock which has been identified as **obsolete** at the stocktake has **not been attributed value** and has been **scrapped**.

Analytical procedures

The auditors will undertake general analytical procedures to ensure that the stock figure stacks up. This could include calculating ratios such as stock turnover and ensuring that they stack up with the facts that have been presented them in the course of the stock audit.

15 BRIGHT SPARKS

Tutorial note. This question looks at the issue of control problems arising from an interim audit and then it asks you to draw conclusions for the final audit. The second part of this question is in effect a planning exercise. It requires you to look at specific procedures as a result of what has been done at the interim stage, however, you also need to include some more general procedures in your answer. This question is slightly unusual in that an interim audit has already been done. In an exam you are more likely to have to set out procedures from scratch. However, this question is also good practice in evaluating the results of procedures performed. This could also be examined, perhaps in the context of drawing conclusions for the audit report.

(a) *Conclusions to be drawn as a result of the interim audit*

The following weaknesses exist in the company's systems.

(i) In any system of internal control, one person should not be able to process a whole transaction:

(1) Authorisation
(2) Execution
(3) Recording

The most serious deficiency in the company's system is that warehousemen can:

(1) Sell goods
(2) Receive cash from cash sales
(3) Raise sales invoices for credit sales
(4) Raise credit notes

Moreover, there appears to be no procedure for checking any of their work. Since the accounting records are written up on the evidence of these invoices and credit notes, any errors made by the warehousemen will be carried into the records. It may also be the case that the issue of credit notes is not authorised by a senior member of staff.

Possible consequences

(1) Errors on invoices may not be detected except by customers

(2) Risk of unauthorised or fraudulent invoices or credit notes being raised without detection

(3) Risk of goods leaving the premises without being invoiced, whether through error or fraud (this is particularly dangerous in a business such as this, with a variety of high-value items)

(4) Time wasted by needless disagreements with customers about amounts owing

(ii) There appears to be a weakness in the recording of cash received by the company. The dates recorded in the books are presumably the dates when the entries were written up. If so, there is clearly an excessive delay in recording cash received, and possibly also in banking it. There may also be no record of cash received made when incoming mail is opened.

Possible consequences

(1) Errors and defalcations can arise where a cash received system is weak.

(2) The longer the gap between receipt and recording, the more likely it is that discrepancies can occur.

(3) Specific possibilities:

- Falsification of records leading to misappropriation of cash (teeming and lading)
- Mislaying of cheques if not banked promptly
- Errors in the records, especially concerning dates

(iii) Stricter control is needed over the granting of cash discounts (assuming that it is the actual receipt of cash which is later than the due date, not merely the late recording of same).

Possible consequence

Discounts given to a standard list of customers who may be friends of staff or regular customers, not necessarily prompt payers.

(b) *Audit work on debtors at the final audit*

(i) *Second circularisation*

(1) Consider circularising all debtors, or at least a larger sample than before of debtors not circularised at 30 September.

(2) Circularise, and investigate disagreeing replies. Discover if reasons are similar to those given at 30 September circularisation.

(ii) To gain further evidence about the rights and obligations and existence of debtors

(1) Check the sales invoices which make up the balances with backing documentation, for example purchase orders and despatch notes (if the latter exist).

(2) Ascertain extent of cash received from debtors after the year-end; reconcile the individual invoices to ensure that no discrepancies exist.

(3) Obtain explanations for invoices remaining unpaid after subsequent invoices have been paid.

To gain evidence about the valuation of debtors, I would review the cash received after date and would also carry out the following tests.

(1) Check calculation of outstanding invoices.

(2) Carry out further tests on settlement discounts and ascertain whether the position has improved or deteriorated since the time of the interim audit.

(3) Confirm necessity/adequacy of provision against write-off of specific debts by review of correspondence, solicitors' debt collection, agencies' letters, liquidation statements.

(4) Consider whether amounts owed may be not recovered where there have been round sum payments on account or invoices unpaid after subsequent invoices paid.

(5) Review customer files/correspondence from solicitors and debtors' circularisation results for evidence of potential bad debts.

(6) Confirm any general provisions for bad debts, considering how well previous year's provision considering predicted actual bad debts and whether the formula used is reasonable and consistent with previous years.

I would check the completeness of debtors by carrying out cut-off tests at 31 December to ensure that all goods leaving the premises by that date (and only those) have been included in sales. I would also check that all returns of goods after the year-end relating to 20X0 sales have been correctly recorded.

Other general tests include:

(1) Agree the opening balance on the sales ledger control account with the previous year's working papers to ensure all the necessary adjustments were put through last year.

(2) Scrutinise sales ledger control for unusual entries.

(3) Check list of debtor balances to and from sales ledger, and reconcile with sales ledger control account.

(4) Carry out analytical procedures, particularly reviewing changes in the debtor turnover period, and changes in the age profile of debtors.

(5) Check that trade debtors have been separately disclosed in the notes to the accounts.

16 NEWPIECE

> *Tutorial note.* The bank reconciliation is extremely important when auditing bank. It links the good, third party evidence of a bank letter to the client's actual position after timing differences. If a question on auditing bank comes up, it is likely to involve procedures relating to auditing a bank reconciliation, so this is good practice. Part (b) looks at some audit considerations in relation to petty cash.
>
> Always remember to consider (and write down that you have) materiality with regard to petty cash. It is often immaterial, and this should affect the audit approach you take.

(a) (i) The matters that are of concern in the bank reconciliation are as follows

(1) **Delay in banking cash sales**. Cash received does not appear to have been banked until a week after the cash was received. A **teeming** and **lading fraud** could have occurred, where an embezzlement of receipts is covered up by an apparent delay in banking subsequent receipts.

(2) **Delay in presentation of cheques by suppliers.** Most suppliers would bank cheques within seven to ten days. However payments to the majority of suppliers entered on October 31 have not been cleared for over two weeks. Cheques, although entered prior to the year-end, may not therefore have been sent to suppliers until some time after the year-end. The reason for doing this would be to **improve** the appearance of the company's **liquidity** in its accounts, by decreasing cash and creditors, and hence improving the company's current and acid test ratios.

(ii) **Cash sales**

The following tests should be carried out.

(1) **Compare** the **date** on the **bank statement** with the **date** stamped on the **paying-in slip**. If the dates are the same or a day apart, then that is strong evidence of when the cheques were actually banked.

(2) **Compare amounts banked** with **cash records** for the day (invoices or the till roll).

(3) **Compare sales ledger cash received** per **cash book** with **daily listing** of cash received.

(4) Carry out **further investigations** if there does appear to be a **significant delay** between **collecting** and **banking cash**. Investigations should cover other periods of the year and the situation at the date of the audit.

(5) If there is **unbanked cash** at the date of the **audit**, **inspect** this **cash**. Failure to produce this cash would be strong evidence of fraud.

Uncleared payments

The following tests should be carried out.

(1) **Ask cashiers** and others involved in sending cheques out **when** the **cheques** were **actually sent.**

(2) **Obtain suppliers' statements** after the year-end, and **check** the **date** the **cash** is **shown as received.** If this date is similar to the date shown on the bank statement, the cheques would probably have been sent out after the year-end.

(iii) (1) If the **cash receipts** represent monies that have been **embezzled,** these **receipts** should be **excluded** from the **cash balances** at the year-end (£2,705). If the **money** is **irrecoverable,** it should be charged as an **expense** in the profit and loss account; if it appears to be **recoverable,** it should be charged as an **amount owing.**

(2) **Cash** and **creditors** should be **increased** as it appears that the true date of the cheques, the date that the cheques were sent to suppliers, was after the year-end. Thus the bank balance and creditors due within one year should be increased by £77,501, the total of cheques 2164 to 2170.

Thus the true cash book balance will be £681 overdrawn.

(b) (i) **Materiality**

Two commonly used measures of materiality are **1% of turnover** and **5% of profit** before tax. For Newpiece these two measures would suggest materiality levels of £25,000 and £7,500 respectively. Total petty cash expenditure is well over the profit measure and slightly under the turnover measure, and this indicates that on balance it should be audited. However about £15,000 of total expenditure occurred in two months. This suggests that testing should be concentrated on these months, with a briefer review taking place of other months, since material fraud and error is unlikely to occur during those months.

Audit risk

Petty cash is a high risk audit area for the following reasons.

(1) Cash is the **most liquid asset**, and hence there is a high risk of defalcation.

(2) **Supporting documentation** for payments may be **limited.**

(3) The failure to keep petty cash on an imprest system means that it may **not** be **subject** to **regular management review.**

(4) Risk would be increased by a **large petty cash balance** (say over £1,000), as this would offer greater opportunity for fraud.

(ii) The audit tests that will be carried out are as follows.

Initial procedures

(1) **Agree opening balances** to working papers for last year.

(2) **Check additions** in **petty cash book**.

(3) **Check** that **petty cash book totals** have been **posted** to the **general ledger**.

(4) **Check** that **payments** in the **main cash book** shown as payments to **petty cash** have been shown as receipts in the **petty cash book**.

Review of unusual items and analytical review

(1) **Review cash payments** in the **general ledger** and **investigate unusual transactions**.

(2) **Carry out analytical procedures** on **balances** by **comparing amounts** with **cash flow forecasts**.

Transactions (to test existence, completeness and rights and obligations)

(1) **Verify individual payments** in petty cash book (concentrating on the larger items) to **supporting documentation** and check that employee has acknowledged receipt of cash.

(2) **Check cash cut-off** procedures have been performed by **reviewing reconciliation** at the year-end, and checking that all reconciling items can be satisfactorily **explained** and have **subsequently been cleared**.

Cash counts (to verify existence, completeness, rights and obligations and valuation)

(1) **Count all balances simultaneously** and **agree** to **petty cash book** or other record.

(2) **All counting** should be **done** in the **presence** of the **individuals responsible**. They should sign at the end of the count to acknowledge funds returned are complete.

(3) **Enquire** into any **IOUs** or **cashed cheques** outstanding for unreasonable periods of time.

(4) **Obtain certificates** of **cash in hand** from responsible officials.

(5) **Confirm** that bank and cash **balances** as reconciled above are **correctly stated** in the **accounts**.

Follow-up procedures should include the following tests.

(1) **Obtain certificates** of **cash-in-hand** as appropriate.

(2) **Check unbanked cheques/cash receipts** have subsequently been **paid in** and **agree** to the **bank reconciliation**.

(3) **Check IOUs** and **cheques cashed** for **employees** have been **reimbursed.**

(4) **Check IOUs** or **cashed cheques outstanding** for **unreasonable periods** of time have been **provided for**.

(5) **Check** the **balances** as **counted** are **reflected** in the **accounts** (subject to any agreed amendments because of shortages and so on).

Presentation and disclosure

Check presentation of cash balances in the accounts is **correct.**

17 TRURO ELECTRONICS

> *Tutorial note.* Again we have focused our answer round the financial statement assertions. This answer is longer than you would be expected to produce in an exam. The question is not really exam style – in the exam you might be asked a similar requirement, but probably in the context of a fuller audit scenario.

The substantive procedures that might be performed to verify the specified balance sheet items are as follows.

(a) *Trade creditors: £3,200,000*

We should carry out the following general tests on trade creditors

(i) Agree the opening balance on the purchase ledger control account with the previous year's working papers to ensure all the necessary adjustments were put through last year.

(ii) Obtain a list of purchase ledger balances in respect of the year-end and:

(1) Test check to and from purchase ledger accounts to list of balances.

(2) Check total of list with control account balance at year-end (obtain explanations if any reconciliation necessary).

(3) Cast list of balances and control account.

(iii) Carry out analytical review of statistics such as ratio of trade creditors to purchases and gross profit ratio; compare to previous periods and obtain explanations for major variances.

(iv) Scrutinise ledger balances for unusual entries especially items that are large and occur around the year-end.

Reconciliation of suppliers' statements with purchase ledger balances will be a key test of rights and obligations, valuation and existence. A creditors' circularisation should be carried out if suppliers' statements for significant creditors are not available.

The following tests should be carried out to check creditors are completely recorded.

(i) Check purchases cut-off.

(1) Check from goods received notes with serial numbers before the year-end to ensure that invoices are either:

- Posted to purchase ledger prior to the year-end; or
- Included on the schedule of accruals.

(2) Review the schedule of accruals to ensure that goods received after the year-end are not accrued.

(3) Check from goods returned notes prior to year-end to ensure that credit notes have been posted to the purchase ledger prior to the year-end or accrued.

(4) Review large invoices and credit notes included after the year-end to ensure that they refer to the following year.

(5) Reconcile daily batch invoice totals around the year-end to purchase ledger control account ensuring batches are posted in the correct year.

(6) Review purchase ledger control account around the year-end for any unusual items.

(ii) Compare current listing of creditors with that of the previous year and note any significant changes, for example changes in major suppliers, proportion of debit balances.

We should also check that trade creditors are disclosed separately in the notes to the accounts, and other necessary disclosures (for example amounts payable by instalments) made.

(b) *Bank overdraft: £2,100,000*

The bank letter will provide vital evidence concerning the financial statement assertions that relate to the bank overdraft We should carry out the following tests that relate to the bank letter and the year-end bank reconciliation.

(i) Check arithmetic of bank reconciliation.

(ii) Trace cheques shown as outstanding from the bank reconciliation to the cash book prior to the year-end and to the after date bank statements and obtain explanations for any large or unusual items not cleared at the time of the audit.

(iii) Verify by checking pay-in slips that uncleared bankings are paid in prior to the year end, and check uncleared bankings are cleared quickly after the year-end.

(iv) Verify balances per cash book according to the reconciliation with cash book and general ledger.

(v) Verify the bank balances with reply to standard bank letter and with the bank statements.

(vi) Scrutinise the cash book and bank statements before and after the balance sheet date for exceptional entries or transfers which have a material effect on the balance shown to be in hand.

(vii) Obtain explanations for all items in the cash book for which there are no corresponding entries in the bank statement and vice versa.

The following tests relate specifically to rights and obligations.

(i) Ensure that bank overdraft is within company's agreed limit with the bank.

(ii) Consider balance in terms of:

(1) Right of set-off with other balances

(2) Any security granted for the borrowing (if there is a charge over the assets it should be registered)

(3) The company's borrowing limits per its articles and authorisation in the directors' minutes

We should consider the classification of the overdraft in the accounts as current or longer term, and check that it has been disclosed separately in the notes to the accounts.

(c) *Corporation tax creditor: £5,200,000*

The main emphasis will be checking the calculation and reasonableness of the provision. The auditors will carry out the following tests:

(i) Obtain and recompute corporation tax computation for the current year, check that current year's provision has been computed at the correct rate, and reconcile the tax charge in the profit and loss account with tax at current rate applied to the profit before tax.

(ii) Check position regarding computations for previous years; note agreed computations and verify that provisions for computations not yet agreed appear reasonable. (*Note*. The provision of £5,200,000 may be in respect of more than one accounting period.).

(iii) Confirm tax paid to receipts from Inland Revenue.

The following tests should be carried out to check the completeness of the provision and also rights and obligations:

(i) Ensure that all disallowable items have been identified and added back by reviewing the financial and management accounts in conjunction with our own detailed working papers.

(ii) Review correspondence with the Inland Revenue for unusual items.

We should also check that the taxation provision is separately disclosed in the accounts, ensuring that the balance is properly identified as tax currently payable (within one year).

(d) *Accruals: £2,300,000*

We should obtain the list of accruals and check the list to the accounting records to confirm its accuracy.

We should check the valuation of accruals by carrying out the following tests:

(i) Verify the amounts of accruals by reference to subsequent payments and supporting documentation (this also provides evidence of rights and obligations).

(ii) Consider basis for any round sum accruals and ensure it is consistent with prior years.

(iii) Carry out analytical review of accruals.

The main emphasis on testing accruals will be on testing that accruals have been completely provided. We shall carry out the following tests.

(i) Scrutinise payments made and invoices received after year-end to ascertain whether any further accruals are necessary.

(ii) Compare with prior year's list of accruals. Investigate any items brought forward and items normally paid in arrears not included on current year's list.

(iii) Ascertain why any payments on account are being made and ensure full liability has been provided.

(iv) Consider whether there are any items which might not be invoiced until a long time after the year-end.

We should also check that accruals are disclosed separately in the notes to the accounts.

(e) *VAT creditor: £1,700,000*

The following tests should be carried out on the valuation of the creditor:

(i) Check that VAT accrual is correct amount outstanding by checking to returns/accounting records.

(ii) Ensure that no non-deductible tax is reclaimed.

(iii) Vouch payments or refunds of VAT to cash book from VAT returns.

We should perform the following tests to confirm the completeness of the creditor, also to confirm rights and obligations:

(i) Obtain VAT returns for the period, and check returns have been properly prepared and filed promptly (attention should be paid to the default surcharge provisions for late submission of returns or late payment of VAT due).

(ii) Test VAT totals from prime records to monthly/quarterly summaries and test cast summaries and scrutinise for unusual items.

(iii) Review correspondence with HM Customs & Excise and results of any recent control visits.

18 GOING CONCERN

> *Tutorial note.* Part (a) demonstrates what can be deduced from the calculations for example short-term funds used to purchase fixed assets and delayed payments to creditors. It is vital when you approach questions like this that you do not spend so long calculating ratios that you fail to make comments and draw conclusions from your work. Equally, having been asked in the question to undertake some calculations, it would be wrong not to do so. You must apply judgement in the balance between calculations and analysis in your answer, remembering that you will score better marks for analysis. Of course, to get those marks, you must have something to analyse ...

Workings

The following significant accounting ratios are based on the accounts provided in the question.

	20X2	*20X3*	*20X4*	*20X5*	*20X6*
Gross profit (%)	23.50	10.90	14.20	20.20	19.70
Other expenses: sales (%)	14.10	10.90	14.40	14.40	15.30
Interest: sales (%)	0.90	1.10	5.20	5.50	6.20
Net profit (%)	8.50	(1.10)	(5.40)	0.30	(1.80)
Current ratio	1.39	0.91	0.73	0.73	0.76
Liquidity ratio	0.80	0.59	0.46	0.37	0.34
Gearing	0.18	0.75	9.52	9.58	20.69
Stock (months)	1.68	2.28	2.26	2.77	3.57
Debtors (months)	1.75	3.66	3.24	2.26	2.32
Creditors (months)	1.73	4.83	3.80	3.54	4.09

Notes

Stock age $= \dfrac{\text{Year end stock}}{\text{Cost of sales}} \times 12$

Debtors age $= \dfrac{\text{Year end debtor}}{\text{Sales}} \times 12$

Creditors age $= \dfrac{\text{Year end creditor}}{\text{Sales}} \times 12$

Gearing $= \dfrac{\text{Long - term loans} + \text{Bank overdraft} + \text{Hire purchase}}{\text{Shareholders' funds}}$

(a) The various factors in the accounts which may be indicative of going concern problems are as follows.

(i) Only losses or low profits are being made; the company is not generating sufficient funds to finance the expansion required.

(ii) There has been a dramatic increase in the level of overdraft over the last year, there seems little prospect of the borrowing being reduced and the security is threatened.

(iii) There are signs of overtrading as the expansion has been financed by borrowings and the increase in current assets is being financed by creditors.

(iv) The gearing is high and increasing, with very little security being available for the loans.

(v) There is a low current ratio; short term funds are being used to finance long term assets.

(vi) The liquidity ratio is low and decreasing and the company's ability to meet its liabilities on demand must be very questionable.

(vii) Stock levels are increasing, suggesting that one or more of the following problems may exist: deteriorating sales, poor stock control, obsolete or slow moving stocks.

(viii) The value and age of creditors is increasing: some creditors must be having to wait a considerable time before being paid and it can only be a matter of time before pressure is put on the company by one or more of its creditors.

(ix) High and increasing interest charges make the company very vulnerable, especially in a period of recession and high interest rates.

(x) The fluctuating gross profit would suggest that the company's profit margins are under pressure. The present level of gross profit does not seem sufficient given the company's high level of expenses.

(b) The other important steps to be taken by the auditors in determining whether or not the company may be properly regarded as a going concern at the year end would include:

(i) Review carefully the cash and profit forecasts for the next year to see if they suggested any improvement in the company's position; consider the basis of preparation of these forecasts and whether they appear comprehensive.

(ii) Seek some evidence that the company's bank is prepared to continue supporting the company.

(iii) Review the level of post balance sheet trading to see if this supports the forecasts and show any signs of improvement in the company's position.

(iv) Examine correspondence files for any evidence that creditors might be putting pressure on the company for repayment of monies owing.

(v) Consider how the company's position compares with similar companies in the same business.

(vi) Discuss generally the situation with management and review any recovery plans which they may have in mind.

19 THE STANDARD EXTERNAL AUDIT REPORT

Tutorial note. The study guide states that you are required to be able to describe the unqualified audit report. Part (a) is a simple test of your knowledge in this area. Part (b) looks at some situations which have arisen in audits and asks you to assess the impact that each will have on the audit report. This is a higher skill. Think 'what impact will this have on my audit work?' – if it causes a limitation and there is no good alternative evidence available, the audit report will be affected by that. Think 'what is the best accounting practice?' – if it is not being followed and there is no good reason for non-compliance, the audit report will be affected by that.

(a) **Elements of the audit report**

(i) A title identifying the addressee of the report

(ii) An introductory paragraph identifying the financial statements audited

(iii) Separate sections dealing with:

The respective responsibilities of directors and auditors
The basis of the auditors' opinion
The auditors' opinion on the financial statements

(iv) The signature of the auditors

(v) The date of the auditors' report

(b) **Situations**

(i) *Stock take*

It is good practice for auditors to attend the stock take where stocks are material in the company's financial statements and the auditor is placing reliance on management's stock take in order to provide evidence of existence of stock.

There therefore appears to have been a material limitation on the scope of this audit.

The implications of this for the audit report would be that:

The basis of opinion section of the report should state

(1) The evidence available to us was limited because we could not attend the stock take

(2) We were unable to carry out alternative procedures necessary to give sufficient assurance as to the existence of stock (presumed)

(3) The amount of the stock involved

The opinion section of the report should be headed up as 'Qualified opinion due to limitation of scope'. The section should state that the accounts give a true and fair view except for any adjustments that may have been necessary had the auditors been able to gain sufficient evidence about stock. It should also state that in respect of the limitation relating to stock, we did not obtain all the information and explanations that we considered necessary for the purpose of our audit and we were unable to determine whether proper accounting records had been kept.

(ii) *Debt*

It appears in this instance that there is no prospect of the debt being recovered. Best accounting practice would be to provide against that doubtful debt.

The audit opinion should therefore be qualified on the grounds of disagreement. The opinion section should be headed 'Qualified opinion arising from disagreement about provision for debtor'. It should state that the accounts give a true and fair view except for the disagreement about the debtor provision.

In a paragraph above the opinion paragraph, the auditors should give details of the disagreement.

(iii) *Cash flow statement*

As the client is a plc, its accounts should include a cash flow statement.

The audit opinion should therefore be qualified on the grounds of disagreement. This disagreement is not pervasive to the accounts, it is limited to the cash flow statement, so this would be an except for qualification.

The opinion section should be headed 'Qualified opinion arising from disagreement over the omission of the cash flow statement'. It should state that the accounts give a true and fair view and have been properly prepared in accordance with the Companies Act except for the omission of a cash flow statement.

The omission should be detailed in a paragraph above the opinion section, where the auditors should give details of the net cash flows and state that in our opinion, information about the cash flows is necessary for a proper understanding of the company's affairs.

(iv) *Legal claim*

The auditors need to determine whether the legal claim is a material matter and even whether it is pervasive to the accounts as a whole. For example, if the customer involved is a major customer, it could be that an adverse outcome could affect the going concern basis of the company.

It appears that the disclosure in the financial statements is adequate and there appears to be no basis on which to make a provision in the financial statements. Therefore there is no question that there is a disagreement in the audit.

However, the audit report will be affected by the fact that there is an uncertainty affecting the business. The auditors will have to decide whether the inherent uncertainty is material or fundamental. If material, it does not need to be mentioned in the audit report. However, if we decide that it is fundamental, the report should contain a paragraph giving the appropriate details. It should also state that the opinion is not qualified in relation to this matter.

Thereafter, no reference should be made to the legal claim in the opinion section of the report.

20 INTERNAL AUDIT REPORTING

Tutorial note. This is a useful question to work through as it covers issues relating to the objectives of internal audit as well as how internal audit will report on matters arising within the company. While there is no formal requirements for how internal audit reporting will be presented, it is important that the Board are familiar with the customs that will be set up so that they are best placed to interact with the internal audit department and to facilitate the department's suggestions.

MEMORANDUM

To: Board of Directors
From: Head of Internal Audit
Date: June 2003
Subject: Internal audit objectives and reporting

(a) **Objectives of internal and external audit**

The main functions of internal and external audit are very different, although some of the means of fulfilling their objectives are the same.

The external auditors are appointed by the shareholders to report on the stewardship of the directors. The role of the external auditors is defined by statute and the report produced by the auditors states whether the financial statements give a true and fair view and have been properly prepared.

In contrast, internal auditors are employed directly by the managers of the company. They are not independent of the management of the company, but work for it. Their work is likely to be more varied and wide-ranging than the external auditors, and they report to the Board or to the Audit Committee on the results of that work.

The internal auditors will be concerned with monitoring the effectiveness of all controls within a business and with the risk management policies of the business. The objectives of the internal audit team are controlled by management.

(b) **Design of a new accounting system**

The internal auditors should be involved in some degree at all stages of the design of a new accounting system.

There are three main stages of development:

- Feasibility studies
- System development
- System specification and construction

At each of these stages, the internal auditor is in an ideal position to ensure:

- All the proper controls that are required have been built in to the system design
- The system meets company standard along with the design process itself

In effect, the internal auditors will be putting their customary skill of internal control evaluation into practice even before the system is devised and is running. The internal auditors will look for key attributes in the planned system:

- Is the benefit worth the cost of the system?
- Is the planned system complete?
- Are the outputs (reports) relevant and will they be produced in a timely manner?
- Will the system be secure from internal and external tampering?
- Is staff training on the new system necessary and has it been planned?

During the feasibility stage, the auditors should ensure that all user departments have been consulted and had input as to the key risks which the system is trying to answer. The internal auditors should assess any assumptions which have been made as part of the planning, for example, estimates of future trading growth.

As the development stage commences, the internal auditors should ensure that the system development is properly documented. Once the system has been developed, the internal auditors will be required to test the new system. The tests should also be properly recorded.

(c) **Reporting**

As has been mentioned above, the internal audit department report to the Board of Directors and/or the Audit Committee. It is up to the directors to determine whether they would prefer that the internal audit department report routinely to the Audit Committee, with any pressing matters being passed on to the full Board. In either case, there may be occasions and some matters where it appropriate for issues to be reported directly to the audit committee, only. An example of such instances could include the suspicion of a senior management/director fraud.

In contrast to the external auditors, internal auditors are not required by law or other regulation to produce a particular format of report. Therefore, how the internal audit department report is also dependent to a degree on the requirements of the Board.

However, there are some basic elements of internal audit reporting that are likely to be included in most reports.

Internal audit will largely produce two types of report:

- Risk-based reports
- Performance enhancement reports

In the scenario looked at in (b) above, where the auditors were reporting on the design and operation of a new system, this would be a risk-based report. However, the new system might have been investigated because internal audit produced a performance enhancement report suggesting future action.

Both types of report will probably conform to the accepted business report which consists of an executive summary, followed by a detailed report and appendices. They are likely to include recommendations and action points, together with details of how such plans would be implemented, when, by whom, and at what cost.

Internal audit reports will usually come with a distribution list to enable each reader of the report to know who is also reading it. They will also come with a date and a reference number. The report should also state whether it is final or draft. Internal audit reports may be produced so that they may be modified when feedback is obtained. Modified reports should state clearly that they have been modified and indicate the feedback that led to the modification.

21 'TAP!'

Tutorial note. In part (a) you are asked to discuss the audit risks in the scenario. Remember that there will be some inherent risk in the audit from the fact that this client is a charity (such as additional regulatory requirements and unusual income) but there these are not exclusively the inherent risks. Don't put an imaginary 'charity hat' on to the exclusion of everything else. Breaking your answer down into the components of audit risk helps to structure your answer. If you are thinking in terms of the components of risk as you read through the scenario, it might help you see the various risks that are contained in the scenario. Don't be afraid to mark your question paper as well – scribble things down as they strike you.

Part (b) should be fairly straightforward. Remember, when suggesting audit procedures, be explicit about what you are going to do. Don't just 'check invoices'. Explain which invoices and why.

In part (c) you should be able to think of many more than 5 marks worth of controls which the charity could implement over cash, as you have not been told of any that they have. Remember to think in terms of control objectives – why is a control needed and what is it trying to achieve? Then you will be suggesting relevant controls. Try and be realistic as well. The Trustees want genuine business advice, not crazy schemes.

(a) **Audit risks**

This 'overall' risk comes before all the others

There is a higher audit risk associated with a charity as in the event of problems arising and litigation taking place, the audit firm could experience a significant amount of bad publicity.

Inherent risks

(i) **Cash**. The charity operates with a high number of cash and cheque transactions. A substantial part of their **income** comes from cash donations. Put another way, it is likely that very little of their income comes from direct bank transfers. Also, it is likely that many of the **expenses** which 'Tap!' incurs are also cash expenses. Cash is **risky for audit purposes** because it is **susceptible to loss, miscounting or misappropriation**.

(ii) **Charity**. The theatre company is a charity, and is therefore subject to a high degree of **regulation**. This raises the risk for our audit.

(iii) **Accounting specialist**. The charity employs an administrator, but there is no mention of an accountant. It is **unclear who is going to draft the charity accounts** (which must comply with specialist requirements) but it does not appear that a specialist exists to undertake this job. This increases the risk of errors existing in the accounts.

(iv) **Completeness of income**. As the charity appears to have **no control** over the primary collection of income from box office receipts, there is a significant **risk that income is understated** and that the theatres have not accounted properly to the theatre.

(v) **Disclosure of income**. The disclosure of income must be considered. It is unlikely to be appropriate to show the 'net income from theatres' figure. Rather, the gross income less commission should probably be disclosed.

(vi) **Expenditure**. The charity expenses may be well-recorded, or they may be **difficult to substantiate** – this is not clear. It may also be difficult to substantiate payments made to build wells in Africa. We currently have no knowledge about how that aspect of the charity operates. It will be important to check that expenditure is made in accordance with the trust deed. Some necessary administrative expense will not necessarily be conducive to the aims of the charity. We must ensure that it is all analysed correctly.

Control

Structuring your answer by components of risk makes it logical/easy to read

There currently appear to be **no controls over cash** in the charity.

Detection

This is a **first year audit**, so there is little knowledge of the business at present. It is also the **first ever audit** of the charity, so the comparatives are unaudited. We must make this clear in our report, and we will need to undertake more detailed work on the **opening balances**. As the charity is to a large degree **peripatetic**, we may find audit evidence difficult to obtain, if it has not be properly returned to the administrative offices.

Conclusion

This appears to be a high risk first year audit. It is likely to result in a qualified audit opinion.

(b) **Audit procedures**

Income from box office takings

Income from box office can be **verified to the statement from the theatre** and the **bank statements** to ensure that it is complete. The **commission** can be agreed by **recalculation**.

It might be necessary to **circularise a** number of the theatres and request **confirmation of the seats sold** for each performance to ensure that income is completely stated on the return from the theatre. [However, if theatres have been defrauding the charity, they are unlikely to confirm this to the auditors. This may have to be an area which is aided by stronger controls over income.]

Income from buckets (theatres and streets)

We must discover whether the charity fill out 'counting sheets' when the buckets of money are originally counted. If so, the **money in buckets can be verified from the original sheet to the banking documentation**.

Do not be afraid to conclude that there may be insufficient evidence

However, in the **absence of strong controls** over the counting, it will be **impossible to conclude that this income is complete**.

Income from other donations

Donations made over the phone should have been noted on documents then retained at the administrative offices. Donations made by post should have **original documents**. A sample of these should be **traced to banking documentation** and bank statements.

Again, in the **absence of originating documentation**, it will be **difficult to conclude that income is fairly stated**.

(c) **Controls over cash**

Tutorial note. Three good suggestions should be sufficient to gain you 6 marks. We have included others as there are a large number of suggestions that can be made.

Income from box office takings

It would be a good control over completeness of income to request a **schedule of seats sold** from the theatres for every night a performance is given. This is likely to be information that theatres can print off their systems with no trouble. This will lead to the theatre company having more assurance as to the completeness of income.

Income from buckets

As this income is highly susceptible to loss or misappropriation, strong controls should be put in place:

(i) **Number of people**. If possible, the charity should assign **two people** to each bucket during the collection phase and two people should count the money in the bucket at the end of the day. These people will act as a **check on each other** to ensure that cash is kept more secure.

(ii) **Security**. The security arrangements for buckets should be strong. The charity could invest in a **transportable safe** in which to store the money between collection and banking. It might also be wise to use **collecting tins** rather than buckets, as this simple measure would ensure that the cash was less open to the public. The cash should also be **banked frequently**. It should not be kept not banked for 24 hours after collection.

(iii) **Recording**. A record should be made of cash counts and it should be signed by both the people that undertook the count. These can provide an initial record of the cash takings.

Other income

The controls over other income will be restricted by the number of staff at the Leicester office. It appears that only the administrator may work there regularly. If this is the case, it is going to be difficult to introduce supervision into the cash operations.

All phone donations should be **recorded on pre-numbered documentation** so as to give evidence of completeness.

As the administrator largely works alone, it would be a good idea for the Board of Trustees to carry out a cyclical review of the work of the administrator. This would provide a useful protection from problems for both the charity and the administrator.

Make sure your suggestions are relevant and possible

Index

Note: Key Terms and their references are given in **bold**

REVIEW FORM & FREE PRIZE DRAW

All original review forms from the entire BPP range, completed with genuine comments, will be entered into a draw on 31 January 2005 and 31 July 2005. The names on the first four forms picked out will be sent a cheque for £50.

Name: ______________________ **Address:** ______________________

____

How have you used this Text?
(Tick one box only)

- ☐ Home study (book only)
- ☐ On a course: college ______________
- ☐ With 'correspondence' package
- ☐ Other ______________

Why did you decide to purchase this Text?
(Tick one box only)

- ☐ Have used complementary Kit
- ☐ Have used BPP Texts in the past
- ☐ Recommendation by friend/colleague
- ☐ Recommendation by a lecturer at college
- ☐ Saw advertising
- ☐ Other ______________

During the past six months do you recall seeing/receiving any of the following?
(Tick as many boxes as are relevant)

- ☐ Our advertisement in *ACCA Student Accountant*
- ☐ Our advertisement in *Pass*
- ☐ Our advertisement in *PQ*
- ☐ Our brochure with a letter through the post

Which (if any) aspects of our advertising do you find useful?
(Tick as many boxes as are relevant)

- ☐ Prices and publication dates of new editions
- ☐ Information on Text content
- ☐ Facility to order books off-the-page
- ☐ None of the above

Which BPP products have you used?

Text	☑	**Success CD**	☐	**i-Learn**	☐
Kit	☐	**Success Tape**	☐	**i-Pass**	☐
Passcard	☐	**Big Picture Poster**	☐	**Virtual Campus**	☐

Your ratings, comments and suggestions would be appreciated on the following areas of this Text.

	Very useful	*Useful*	*Not useful*
Introductory section (Key study steps, personal study)	☐	☐	☐
Chapter introductions	☐	☐	☐
Key terms	☐	☐	☐
Quality of explanations	☐	☐	☐
Case examples and other examples	☐	☐	☐
Questions and answers in each chapter	☐	☐	☐
Chapter roundups	☐	☐	☐
Quick quizzes	☐	☐	☐
Exam focus points	☐	☐	☐
Question bank	☐	☐	☐
Answer bank	☐	☐	☐
List of key terms and index	☐	☐	☐
Icons	☐	☐	☐

	Excellent	*Good*	*Adequate*	*Poor*
Overall opinion of this Text	☐	☐	☐	☐

Do you intend to continue using BPP Products? ☐ Yes ☐ No

Please note any further comments and suggestions/errors on the reverse of this page. The BPP author of this edition can be e-mailed at: catherinewatton@bpp.com

Please return to: Catherine Watton, ACCA Range Manager, BPP Professional Education, FREEPOST, London, W12 8BR

REVIEW FORM & FREE PRIZE DRAW (continued)

TELL US WHAT YOU THINK

Please note any comments and suggestions/errors below.

FREE PRIZE DRAW RULES

1 Closing date for 31 January 2005 draw is 31 December 2004. Closing date for 31 July 2005 draw is 30 June 2005.

2 No purchase necessary. Entry forms are available upon request from BPP Professional Education. No more than one entry per title, per person. Draw restricted to persons aged 16 and over.

3 Winners will be notified by post and receive their cheques not later than 6 weeks after the draw date.

4 The decision of the promoter in all matters is final and binding. No correspondence will be entered into.

See overleaf for information on other
BPP products and how to order

ACCA Order

To BPP Professional Education, Aldine Place, London W12 8AW
Tel: 020 8740 2211 Fax: 020 8740 1184
email: publishing@bpp.com website: www.bpp.com
Order online www.bpp.com

Mr/Mrs/Ms (Full name)
Daytime delivery address
Postcode
Daytime Tel Date of exam (month/year) Scots law variant Y / N

	6/04 Texts	1/04 Kits	1/04 Passcards	***Success CDs	Big Picture Posters	8/04 i-Learn	8/04 i-Pass	Virtual Campus
PART 1								
1.1 Preparing Financial Statements	£24.95	£10.95	£6.95	£14.95	£6.95	£34.95	£24.95	£90
1.2 Financial Information for Management	£24.95	£10.95	£6.95	£14.95	£6.95	£34.95	£24.95	£90
1.3 Managing People	£24.95	£10.95	£6.95	£14.95	£6.95	£34.95	£24.95	£90
PART 2								
2.1 Information Systems	£24.95	£10.95	£6.95	£14.95	£6.95	£34.95	£24.95	£90
2.2 Corporate and Business Law **	£24.95	£10.95	£6.95	£14.95	£6.95	£34.95	£24.95	£90
2.3 Business Taxation FA2003 (12/04 exams)	£20.95	£10.95	£6.95	£14.95	£6.95	£34.95	£24.95	£90
2.3 Business Taxation FA2004 (**8/04** for 6/05 exams)†	£24.95			£14.95	£6.95			£90
2.4 Financial Management and Control	£24.95	£10.95	£6.95	£14.95	£6.95	£34.95	£24.95	£90
2.5 Financial Reporting (7/04)	£24.95	£10.95	£6.95	£14.95	£6.95	£34.95	£24.95	£90
2.6 Audit and Internal Review (12/04 exams)	£24.95	£10.95	£6.95	£14.95	£6.95	£34.95	£24.95	£90
2.6 Audit and Internal Review (**9/04** for 6/05 exams)†	£24.95			£14.95	£6.95			£90
PART 3								
3.1 Audit and Assurance Services	£24.95	£10.95	£6.95	£14.95	£6.95		£24.95	
3.2 Advanced Taxation FA2003 (12/04 exams)	£20.95	£10.95	£6.95	£14.95	£6.95		£24.95	
3.2 Advanced Taxation FA2004 (**9/04** for 6/05 exams)†	£24.95			£14.95	£6.95			
3.3 Performance Management	£24.95	£10.95	£6.95	£14.95	£6.95		£24.95	
3.4 Business Information Management	£24.95	£10.95	£6.95	£14.95	£6.95		£24.95	
3.5 Strategic Business Planning and Development	£24.95	£10.95	£6.95	£14.95	£6.95		£24.95	
3.6 Advanced Corporate Reporting (7/04)	£24.95	£10.95	£6.95	£14.95	£6.95		£24.95	
3.7 Strategic Financial Management	£24.95	£10.95	£6.95	£14.95	£6.95		£24.95	
INTERNATIONAL STREAM								
1.1 Preparing Financial Statements	£24.95	£10.95	£6.95			£34.95	£24.95	
2.2 Corporate and Business Law	£24.95	£10.95	£6.95					
2.5 Financial Reporting	£24.95	£10.95	£6.95			£34.95	£24.95	
2.6 Audit and Internal Review	£24.95	£10.95	£6.95			£34.95	£24.95	
3.1 Audit and Assurance Services	£24.95	£10.95	£6.95					
3.6 Advanced Corporate Reporting	£24.95	£10.95	£6.95					
Success in Your Research and Analysis								
Project - Tutorial Text (10/04)	£24.95							
Learning to Learn (7/02)	£9.95							

SUBTOTAL £

Occasionally we may wish to email you relevant offers and information about courses and products.
Please tick to opt into this service.

POSTAGE & PACKING

Study Texts

	First	Each extra	Online	
UK	£5.00	£2.00	£2.00	£
Europe*	£6.00	£4.00	£4.00	£
Rest of world	£20.00	£10.00	£10.00	£

Kits

	First	Each extra	Online	
UK	£5.00	£2.00	£2.00	£
Europe*	£6.00	£4.00	£4.00	£
Rest of world	£20.00	£10.00	£10.00	£

Passcards/Success Tapes/CDs

	First	Each extra	Online	
UK	£2.00	£1.00	£1.00	£
Europe*	£3.00	£2.00	£2.00	£
Rest of world	£8.00	£8.00	£8.00	£

Grand Total (incl. Postage)
I enclose a cheque for £
(Cheques to *BPP Professional Education*)
Or charge to Visa/Mastercard/Switch
Card Number
Expiry date Start Date
Issue Number (Switch Only)
Signature

We aim to deliver to all UK addresses inside 5 working days; a signature will be required. Orders to all EU addresses should be delivered within 6 working days. All other orders to overseas addresses should be delivered within 8 working days. * Europe includes the Republic of Ireland and the Channel Islands.† **For 6/05 exam, New edition Kit, Passcard, i-Learn and i-Pass available 2005 .** ** For Scots law variant students, a free **Scots Law Supplement** is available with the 2.2 Text. Please indicate in the name and address section if this applies to you. ***Alternatively, Success Tapes are available for the same papers, all £12.95.